REMEMBERING AMERICA
A *Sampler of the WPA American Guide Series*

GENERAL STORE

110405

REMEMBERING AMERICA
A Sampler of the
WPA American Guide Series

Edited by Archie Hobson
With Introductions by Bill Stott

COLUMBIA UNIVERSITY PRESS
NEW YORK   1985

Library of Congress Cataloging in Publication Data
Main entry under title:

Remembering America.

Bibliography: p.
Includes index.
1. United States—Description and travel—1920–1940—
Guide-books. 2. Federal Writers' Project. I. Hobson,
Archie, 1946–   . II. Title: American guide series.
E169.R395   1985   917.3′04927   85-3763
ISBN 0-231-06050-5

Columbia University Press
New York   Guildford, Surrey
Copyright © 1985 Columbia University Press
All rights reserved

Printed in the United States of America

Clothbound editions of Columbia University Press books are
Smyth-sewn and printed on permanent and durable acid-free paper
c 10 9 8 7 6 5 4 3 2

Book design by Ken Venezio

Contents

ing / ironing / visit / candlewick bedspread / log rolling / company coming
signs / the meanest man in the world / coroner

THE PEOPLE

MOVING ABOUT

HIGHER CALLINGS

and trios / filibuster / drunkenness / shall I jump or slide? / jail / withdrawals / the Loomis Gang / Singleton's skin / squawkers / martial law

THE END

Editor's Preface

MY INTEREST in the American Guide Series has at least three sources. I think that these suggest ways in which the material in this collection will appeal to different readers.

First, I knew of the Guides, vaguely, before I got my hands on any of them. A child of the generation that produced them, I shared the general awareness of various New Deal "arts" undertakings, particularly the work of the Farm Security Administration photographers; but the Federal Writers' Project (FWP) remained somewhere just outside my experience. It was only after I began research for this anthology that I discovered family and friends had worked on the Project. Bill Stott, in his introduction to this volume, has described the huge membership and breadth of activity in the FWP; I am certain that many of you looking into this book sense, as I did, connections with the Federal Writers.

Before I learned what my connections were, however, I discovered the Guides themselves. To be precise, I discovered the Maine Guide in my town library and read through it cover to cover. Where they described familiar territory, I saw immediately a key to the Federal Writers' method: to seize on something, often a single fact or anecdote, and make it stand for a place. If the place in question was your place, you knew they "missed" a lot. On the other hand, they had only 441 pages, for instance, to describe the state of Maine. Part of the fun was seeing what they had chosen in your town; it was not likely to be the obvious "tourist attraction."

As for the other places, the ones you didn't know, what could be more enticing than this understated form of "coverage"? Learning of a township where early inhabitants—squatters—had dressed as Indians to scare off landowners, and that "when officers of the law arrived the little settlement would appear entirely deserted, except for a few loitering Indians who greeted the baffled visitors with stolid indifference," I was much readier to visit than had I been told the ages of all the churches and whether there was a lake to swim in. Considering that we will never visit every place we hear of, how much better to have some fuel for the imagination instead of "travel facts"! The Guides are a mine for anyone who likes to speculate, who likes some solid material to build with—particularly, it struck me, for writers. In fact, almost the minute I put the Maine Guide down, bits of it began to work themselves into my own writing.

The third source of the Guides' appeal for me is the obvious one: I love to travel. Not just the "object" but the process of travel fascinates me.

In particular, I have a fondness for one mode the Guides seem deeply sympathetic with, although they mention it rarely—hitchhiking. Cars make hitchhiking possible, of course, and the Guides are car books. To judge from my experience, though, even touring drivers find it hard to escape from their "destination," from the sense that the landscape is something to be gotten through. The hitchhiker has something over the driver—a kind of controlled submission to chance, an intentional randomness.

Some of the most intense travel experiences I have had came when a driver dropped me off somewhere I had no preconceptions of. The roadside becomes intimate very quickly. Later, driving over old hitching routes, I was able to identify spots I stood at; but they weren't the same places—in the car, I wasn't *there*. Put down abruptly on a new piece of the earth, your senses open wide to clues. Perhaps there is the almost-identifiable smell of some agricultural process nearby. Perhaps there is the sound of children singing a song you strain to understand. Perhaps the hints are much subtler. The place offers a challenge. Many ten-minute impressions remain with me after twenty years.

To me the Guides are even more attuned to this haphazardness than to the fully intended trip by car. I think it could be because the Writers, collecting information, stopped everywhere, and gathered impressions as well as facts. Look at the tour sections of the Guides, if you can find them. They have this stop-and-start-again feeling from one end of the country to the other. It is an enormous country; if you set out to walk it, so as to get the kind of closeness to detail I relish, the state of Maine alone would take a lifetime. And the effort—the athleticism—would dull the openness to chance; distance and destination would assert themselves.

The Guides, though, give us in a set of books "coverage" of all the states, coverage of the kind I have been describing. Reading them, I feel I am hitching through the country—being taken from town to town, crossroad to crossroad, by a constantly changing fleet of drivers. Each has something particular to show me; whatever it is, it will confound the grand conclusion I was forming in the last town. This journey has, to me, the feel of truth.

ARCHIE HOBSON

Acknowledgments

.

THIS BOOK began in the Reference Department of the Columbia University Press, one of the rare places that has a nearly complete set of the original state Guides of the American Guide Series. The Columbia University Libraries provided the missing volumes, as well as much secondary material on the history of the Federal Writers' Project and related matters. The Library of Congress provided information that was unavailable at Columbia. A list of the original Guides from which the selections were taken appears in the back of this book. Most of the original Guides are now in the public domain, but for those still under copyright, we would like to thank the holders of those copyrights who have kindly given us permission to reprint excerpts and illustrations from them: Pete Spivey, Press Secretary to the Governor, State of Alaska Office of the Governor, Juneau, for *A Guide to Alaska: Last American Frontier*; Ralph D. Turlington, Commissioner, State of Florida Department of Education, Tallahassee, for *Florida: A Guide to the Southernmost State*; James R. Thompson, Governor, State of Illinois, for *Illinois: A Descriptive and Historical Guide*; Dave Piker, Director, Communications Services, Indiana State University, Terre Haute, for *Indiana: A Guide to the Hoosier State*; the State Administrative Board of the State of Michigan, Lansing, for *Michigan: A Guide to the Wolverine State*; Sheldon Hackney, President, University of Pennsylvania, Philadelphia, for *Pennsylvania: A Guide to the Keystone State*; Donald Haynes, State Librarian, Virginia State Library, Richmond, for *Virginia: A Guide to the Old Dominion*; Willis H. Hertig, Jr., Director, State of West Virginia Department of Natural Resources, Charleston, for *West Virginia: A Guide to the Mountain State*; Oxford University Press, New York, for *Idaho: A Guide in Word and Picture* and *North Dakota: A Guide to the Northern Prairie State*.

I would like to thank my colleagues at the Press, particularly Judith Levey, Editor-in-Chief of Reference Books, for their support and for making it possible for me to compile this book while working at the Press. Of those who encouraged me from outside the Press, I want to single out Bill Stott, Director of the American Studies and American Civilization Programs at the University of Texas, Austin, whose enthusiasm for the project and insightful comments on it have been crucial. As Editorial Consultant, he also suggested organizing the book under the broad headings found here and wrote the general and chapter introductions.

Finally, although it seems presumptuous, I am grateful to the Federal Writers themselves, a few of whom I am fortunate to know or have known. I do not assume that they would agree entirely with the use this anthology makes of their work; but if it helps to make more people aware of their contribution to our literature, I, at least, will be satisfied.

A.H.

Illustrations

ILLUSTRATIONS were an integral part of the American Guide Series. Many of the state and city Guides contained reproductions of black and white drawings, photographs, etchings, woodcuts, and other kinds of graphics—done in the 1930s by members of the WPA's Art Project and representing a wide variety of styles and approaches. Assembled here is a selection of these original illustrations. Like much of the text of the book, they offer unique glimpses of America's folk culture.

The sources of the illustrations are listed below by chapter. The number in parentheses following the state or city name is the page in the original Guide from which the illustration came. A list of the original Guides can be found on page 381.

Frontispiece: South Dakota (390). *Introduction:* p. 1 Texas (375); p. 5 Utah (152); p. 9 Wisconsin (148).

THE LAND AND ITS IMPROVEMENTS. *Natural Conditions:* p. 15 Arizona (9); p. 19 Colorado (24); p. 23 Alabama (27). *Buildings:* p. 27 Alabama (8); p. 31 Colorado (463); p. 34 Texas (99). *In the Towns:* p. 36 South Dakota (95); p. 40 Georgia (517); p. 44 South Carolina (97). *Monuments and Remains:* p. 48 South Carolina (136); p. 52 Arizona (130); p. 55 Wyoming (205). *The Wilderness:* p. 57 Alaska (xlvii); p. 61 Arizona (281); p. 65 Texas (111). *The Urban Scene:* p. 68 New York City (182); p. 71 Louisiana (161); p. 75 New York City (3); p. 79 New York City (427).

WORK. *Working on the Land:* p. 83 South Dakota (218); p. 86 Louisiana (60); p. 91 Pennsylvania (168); p. 97 Colorado (167); p. 102 Virginia (105). *On the Water:* p. 105 Alaska (350); p. 109 Louisiana (78); p. 113 California (244). *Factory and Workshop:* p. 119 Utah (112); p. 124 Alabama (179); p. 126 New York (104). *In the Ground:* p. 131 Alaska (56); p. 136 Colorado (181); p. 140 California (65). *Trade:* p. 144 Alaska (41); p. 149 Minnesota (81); p. 155 Utah (267); p. 159 New York City (56).

EVERYDAY LIFE. *At Home:* p. 165 Alabama (129); p. 169 Texas (149);

REMEMBERING AMERICA
A Sampler of the WPA American Guide Series

Introduction

R EMEMBERING AMERICA is a book of selections from the American Guide Series. The series—sometimes called the WPA Guides, sometimes simply *the* Guides—was written in the 1930s by writers on relief who were paid by the federal government to write about the state, city, town, or locale where they lived.

This book collects about five hundred passages from the Guides. The passages are fascinating in themselves. They are also a fair sample of what was strongest and most original in the Guides.

The passages are arranged thematically in chapters, each of which has a short introduction that casts some light on the chapter's topic and its relation to American life in the thirties and, occasionally, before and after.

THE GUIDES were written by members of the Federal Writers' Project (FWP). The FWP, part of the New Deal's Works Progress Administration (WPA), started in 1935 and ended in 1943. In those nearly nine years it employed from 3,500 to 6,700 writers, editors, researchers, and clerical workers (about

2 percent of the WPA's workforce); spent a total of $27 million; and produced, including the Guides, more than 276 books, 701 pamphlets, and 340 "issuances" (articles, leaflets, radio scripts)—enough to fill seven 12-foot-long shelves.

The FWP's mission was the same as the WPA's: to create appropriate work for Americans who otherwise would have had none. The FWP was one of four WPA "arts" projects. The other three projects (Theatre, Music, and Art), which were better known at the time, produced plays, concerts, murals, paintings, graphics: things an audience could enjoy. FWP writers collected interviews, life histories, folklore, historical records: things intended to be of use to posterity. The work they did for an audience of their day was the production of the American Guide Series.

A Guide was done for each of the 48 states and Alaska (there was no Guide to Hawaii). In addition, Guides were published to most large cities (New York had *two* Guides) and many towns and places of local interest. The Guides followed a formula established by the FWP headquarters in Washington. Each state Guide had three parts. In the first, short essays covered the state's natural and political history, economy, social life, racial and ethnic groups, arts, and recreation. In the second, the state's most important cities or towns were described individually, with a map showing their points of interest. The third—and largest—section gave detailed road tours across the state on the principal highways, from east to west and north to south. The tours recounted mile by mile what a driver would see: every town, village, and conspicuous crossroads, and everything of note along the way.

There had never been anything like the Guides' portrait of America before, and there has been nothing since.

THE GUIDES were written to serve automobile tourism, which by the late thirties was big business. We now view the Depression as continuing until war production picked up steam in 1939 or, indeed, until Pearl Harbor. But to people living at the time, 1936 (say) felt very different from (say) 1932— and much better. Whereas in the early years of the Depression people stayed home because money was tight and they were fearful, by 1936 Franklin Roosevelt had worked a bit of his magic; the economy was recovering and people's confidence had begun to return. Car travel was easier than ever before, with the national highway system virtually complete and a new institution—motor hotels, newly named "motels"—catering to overnight trips.

Even wealthy Americans had good reason to see America first (a slogan of the time), considering how dismal circumstances were in Europe.

Of course, there already were travel books describing the U.S. and its parts, but not the way the Guides do. The Guides do not accept the notion that tourists want only a good time, with never a disturbing thought. A Guide reader encounters economic history as well as quaint amusements, social commentary as well as famous shrines. (Indeed, "quaint," "amusement," "famous," and "shrine" are words the Washington FWP tried to ban from the Guides as belonging to travel literature of the wrong sort.) The Guides seldom gush and boost; they describe, analyze, criticize.

The Guides were originally published in the late thirties and early forties. Many of the state Guides have been reprinted and republished in updated editions since then. The revised editions sometimes abridge the earlier Guides' historical analyses and omit or tone down their criticisms, thus bringing them more into line with the travel-book norm. Their America is a diminishment of the country the Federal Writers wanted to bring alive.

As THE writer and social critic Anita Brenner describes the mid-thirties:

"There were quite of lot of us riding around the country at about the same time, in search of the same information. We pulled in and out of industrial centers, spent many days in small towns, hung around CCC [Civilian Conservation Corps] camps and other federal projects, stared appalled at the shanty settlements and cabin villages of our pariahs—Negroes, Mexicans, poor whites . . . picked up all sorts of people constantly, and listened and listened and listened."[1]

For a variety of reasons, the experience of the Depression turned many Americans' attention inward, toward their country. Among their discoveries was the fact that the automobile had made the nation's cities quite different from the typical Old World cities that ended abruptly in open fields. The auto had spread the city out, dribbled it across the landscape. The auto, newspapers, movies, and the radio had brought metropolitan culture into the hinterland to a far greater degree than was true elsewhere.

The Guides both recorded this fact and tried to shout it down. They looked for what was special about every town and village in the country, what set each apart from the others. When Mabel Ulrich, the Director of the Minnesota Guide, ridiculed the notion that one town or state or region was "romantically different from any other in the country," the FWP Guide editors in Washington corrected her: "What we want," they repeated, "are the cus-

toms and characteristics that differ sharply from those of any other State.
. . . You say you have no folklore other than Indian and Paul Bunyan. We
advise that you interview prisoners in the penitentiary." Whether or not Ulrich followed this advice, she came to believe that the FWP's local bias called
forth much that was best in the Guides. To get the "color" and "vividness"
Washington demanded, the Guide makers had to dig; what they found and
put in words were the "minor differences among towns superficially much
alike." By recording these nuances, they revealed "an America that neither
the historians nor the imaginative writers of the past had discovered."[2]

THE AMERICA the Guide writers found and created is amply shown in this
book. It is a beautiful country: fun-loving, energetic, idiosyncratic, anec-
dotal, rural, populist. It is a country of excess: of *not only but also, you ain't
heard nothing yet, and then, and then, and then*—a country that can't be
known better, only *more.*

The American Guides' America in a sense never existed, except in the
minds of the American people. It could only be written about when, as had
happened by the 1930s, anthropological method was understood and felt to
be respectable alongside "real" history.

The "people's" America presented in the Guides was a good deal more
hopeful and resilient than many Americans then felt their nation to be. Some
critics criticized this and talked about the FWP's "romantic nationalism" and
"factitious Americanism." To those of us living half a century later, whether
the Guides were true or untrue to actuality may no longer matter much.
What we read here seems about as real (or as illusory) as our dreams.

So what if the Guides are more upbeat than circumstances justified? *That*
tells us something important about the time and our predecessors' uneasy
courage. Harlan Hatcher, the FWP Director in Ohio, predicted that the
Guides would finally be understood "as a heartening monument to the sta-
bility of America, long after the bitter years of the 1930s have been forgotten."[3]

From where we now stand, that prediction looks right on target.

THERE IS an important character in this anthology who is never mentioned
in the Guides. He is Adolf Hitler. Hitler, European Fascism, and the Second World War—which, from 1936 onward, most Americans knew was
coming—explain a good deal about the way the Guides sound and the attitude they take toward the United States.

As we suggested earlier, the Guides were not written in the Depression we know from textbooks, with their photographs of breadlines. Breadlines happened in the first half of the decade, and the Guides were written in the second half, the half where the schoolbooks turn their attention away from the U.S. This part of the thirties saw economic recovery at home—albeit a slow and unsteady recovery, marred by the "Roosevelt recession" of 1937–38, when the President, fearful of inflation, cut back the number of workers

employed by the WPA. Abroad, the whole decade, but particularly the second half, was marked by disaster: Japan's takeover of Manchuria; Hitler's rise to power; the Reichstag fire; the Nuremberg laws depriving German Jews of their citizenship; Italy's invasion and conquest of Ethiopia; the failure of the League of Nations; German reoccupation of the Rhineland; the Spanish Civil War; the Russian purge trials; Japan's invasion of China; Germany's invasion and takeover of Austria; appeasement at Munich; the dismemberment of Czechoslovakia; the start of German concentration camps for undesirables; the Russo-German Non-Aggression Pact; Germany's invasion of Poland; World War II.

The America that looked so bad in the early years of the decade looked fine in the later. Lots was wrong with it, but it was better than anywhere else. People could differ about things—even life-and-death things like politics, economics, religion, race relations—and not fear for their lives.

In part because of when they were written, then, the Guides became celebrations of what was felt to be uniquely American: our diversity and our tolerance of diversity. (The political word that characterizes this virtue is, of course, "democracy," a very popular word at the time.) All *this* is America, the Guides say, having pointed to the countryside, every city, most towns and villages, and to the amazingly various lives being lived there. And there. And there.

American culture in this period extolled the diversity of the land and its people in countless sentimental effusions, two of which still spring to our lips: the songs "God Bless America" (1938) and "This Land Is Your Land" (1940). Father Divine, Archbishop Spellman, Mayor LaGuardia, and the head of the American Legion marched in New York's May Day Parade. The Communist Party U.S.A., hoping (until the 1939 Soviet-German pact) to find allies against Hitler, recruited with the slogan "Communism Is Twentieth Century Americanism"; New Masses, the party magazine, had an "I Like America" subscription drive.

By 1941 the influential critic Malcolm Cowley was comparing America to the lost world of Atlantis, a blessed land where "very ancient animals continue to flourish". Communist and capitalist, conservative and liberal, Socialist and Social Darwinist, America Firster and interventionist.

These prehistoric monsters are not friendly to one another. . . . But all of them were produced by the same conditions and depend for their survival on the same biological environment. . . . All of them, however much they differ on other subjects, are determined to believe that their lost world will continue to exist.[4]

Eleanor Roosevelt, with typical straightforwardness, sounded the fundamental theme: in diversity there is strength.

America is composed of all the races, and Herr Goebbels has told the Germans that there our weakness lies. With so many racial types existing in the United States, the social tension, he prophesies, will tear us apart. And Hitler is sure that he can foist revolution on us because of our wide variety of religious beliefs and racial origins.

Herr Goebbels, Herr Hitler: you have pointed out not our weakness but our strength.[5]

For all their celebrations of America, the Guides do not get this sentimental or nostalgic, certainly not in the tour sections, from which most of this anthology is drawn. They manage the considerable feat of loving an endangered America without shedding tears.

WE KNOW little about the typical working day of an FWP employee. Maybe there was no such thing.

Only a minority of Project members were actually writers; the rest were educated, unemployed people: teachers, librarians, office workers. In some sparsely populated states, the Writers' Project had only three or four writers. Or even fewer: Vardis Fisher, Idaho's FWP director, could find no writer in the state to employ besides himself.

Although some FWP members and some outside critics argued that FWP writers should be treated like other WPA artists and allowed to do their own creative work on government time, only a few writers with the New York City Project enjoyed this privilege. For other writers the job requirements varied widely. Some had to spend 40 hours per week in the office; some, 30; some had to put in an appearance only once every week or two. Some had to produce a certain number of words: 750 a day was one standard, 1,200 to 2,000 a week was another. Some writers had almost nothing to do. Others, like Conrad Aiken on the Massachusetts Project, found themselves overworked because, as Aiken remembered, "Nobody else could write!"

It did not take a writer to gather the facts that went into the Guides, and this work was usually done by nonwriters following Washington's directives about the sort of information needed. Some of these nonwriters were young people working their way through college with the help of the National Youth Administration and lent to the Project to help with research. Once collected, information went to the state FWP headquarters, where it was written up according to the Guide formula drawn up in Washington. Many of the state Guides were essentially written by one person. Vardis Fisher wrote Idaho; Merle Colby, Massachusetts; Opal Shannon, Iowa; Louise Dubose, South Carolina; Alice Corbin, New Mexico; Rebecca Pitts, Indiana; and Grace Stone Coates, Montana (when the Montana Guide was published, Coates said she would not even buy a copy because she knew it by heart).

Once a State FWP had produced a draft of its Guide, a regional editor and then the Washington editors worked it over. The pattern for the whole FWP was that of "corporate journalism," the new way of gathering, checking, and writing information pioneered by the Luce publications, *Time*, *Fortune*, and *Life*, which were enjoying their greatest prestige. If, as sometimes happened, a State was unable to finish its Guide, a small team of writers and editors traveled from Washington to do the job.

The Guides, in short, not only arose from a unique historical circumstance; they were written in unusual ways. Some of their copy was written by people who had all the time in the world to say what they wanted to say about a subject (America) toward which circumstances made them feel especially fond. Some was written by ambitious young writers trying their wings in descriptive passages a bit longer than really was called for. Some of the copy was written by overworked pros struggling to make sense of chaotic fieldnotes amassed by unintelligible researchers. Some was pruned by regional editors disgusted with the excesses of young writers, or by fact checkers who found that what the state wanted to claim was contradicted in every obvious reference source. Some was jazzed up by Washington staffers hoping to bring a dead page to life.

And did this confusion of research, writing, checking, revising, double checking, and re-revising produce a masterpiece? No. Not by the commonly accepted standards. But it did produce something special. Even those who disparage the FWP have warm words for the Guides. Harold Rosenberg, a conspicuous FWP writer and later the New Yorker's art critic, loathed the Project ("badly conceived . . . directed by the wrong people . . . did little for American writers beyond supplying some with jobs . . . contributed nothing to American letters"), yet admitted: "The State Guides have received much and well-deserved praise; the enormous piles of American facts racked together in them have a fascination independent of structure and style."

The fascination is not only the result of the facts communicated. The many minds that worked over the words in a passage sometimes came up with a statement so clear, simple, and inevitable as to be elegant. Reading this book you will again and again find things that cannot be better said. Consider *Bayside* in "On the Water," *Red Bat* in "In the Towns," *Thendara* in "Famous and Unknown."

THE FWP writers often did not take much pride in their job. Like other WPA members, many were ashamed at having to accept relief work. For them, the goal, as Henry Lee Moon recalled in 1967, was to "stay on the Project as long as you had to, and get off as quickly as you could."[6] Former FWPers do not boast about the connection. Saul Bellow, for instance, worked for the Project, but his entry in *Who's Who in America* does not mention it.

Nonetheless, many good writers, editors, academics, and "communicators" worked for the FWP. Here is a list of some of them, with apologies to those omitted who deserve inclusion and to those included who would prefer omission: Lionel Abel, Conrad Aiken, Nelson Algren, Henry Alsberg (Director of the Project), Nathan Asch, James Aswell, Saul Bellow, Josef Berger, Ray Allen Billington, Helen Boardman, Maxwell Bodenheim, Arna Bontemps, B. A. Botkin, Harvey Breit, Sterling A. Brown, John Cheever, Merle Colby, Jack Conroy, Edward Dahlberg, Katherine Dunham, Loren Eiseley, Ralph Ellison, Kenneth Fearing, Vardis Fisher, Carl Foreman, Sol Funaroff, William Gibson, Lou Gilbert, H. R. Hays, Zora Neale Hurston, David Ignatow, Weldon Kees, Katherine Kellock, Clair Laning, Ulysses Lee, Meridel LeSueur, Saul Levitt, Ross Lockridge, Bert James Loewenberg, John Lomax, Willard Maas, Vincent McHugh, Claude McKay, Norman MacLeod, Jerre Mangione, Henry Lee Moon, Willard Motley, Max Nomad, Roi Ottley, Kenneth Patchen, Ted Poston, Samuel Putnam, Philip Rahv, Kenneth Rexroth, Harold Rosenberg, Isaac Rosenfeld, Harry Roskolenko, Sam Ross, Mari Sandoz, Ross Santee, Lyle Saxon, Eli Siegel, Studs Terkel, Parker Tyler, Dorothy Van Ghent, Margaret Walker, George Willison, Richard Wright, Anzia Yezierska, Frank Yerby.

Some of these people—Aiken, Algren, and Asch, for instance—were already published writers, but broke. Most were young writers starting out. As the list suggests, many of the FWP's notable writers were black. The writer who gained most from the Project was, perhaps, Richard Wright, who quit a post office job to join up; in 1938 won a special *Story* magazine contest limited to FWP members (the judges were novelist Sinclair Lewis, reviewer Lewis Gannett, and Book-of-the-Month Club president Harry Scherman); thanks to the *Story* award, got *Uncle Tom's Children* published by Harper and Brothers; was moved from Chicago to the New York City Project and allowed to do whatever writing he chose; used this time to write much of his masterpiece, *Native Son*, which was published by Harper and a Book-of-the-Month Club selection in 1940.

Some critics have disparaged the quality of the FWP writers, one critic saying that the writers of talent could be counted on one hand or, at most, two. Plainly untrue. An enterprise that meant to keep out-of-work writers alive and doing something useful and pertinent to their skills, and that, in fulfilling its mission, gave sustenance to a Nobel literature laureate (Bellow), our finest black novelists (Ralph Ellison, Richard Wright), and a host of writers, editors, and teachers remembered fifty years later needs no apology on the ground of quality.

To DATE there are two books on the FWP, from both of which a good many of the facts in this introduction are borrowed: Jerre Mangione's memoir-cum-history, *The Dream and the Deal* (Boston: Little, Brown, 1972), and Monty Noam Penkower's *The Federal Writers' Project: A Study of Government Patronage of the Arts* (Urbana: University of Illinois Press, 1977). Material is also borrowed from my *Documentary Expression and Thirties America* (New York: Oxford University Press, 1973), which discusses the Project and the Guides while examining the documentary motive at work in art, literature, and media during the period. Those who want to know more about the FWP and what it did are directed to these books and to books and articles they cite.

The best way to get acquainted with the Guides is—no surprise—to read them. Many state Guides, in updated versions, are in print. The original Guide to each state is in most libraries in that state. Big libraries will have Guides to neighboring states, perhaps even many states.

Two influential fans of the American Guides were John Gunther, whose *Inside U.S.A.* (1947) frequently cites them, and John Steinbeck. The book that did most to revive interest in the Guides was Steinbeck's *Travels with Charley: In Search of America*, in which the following paragraph appears:

If there had been room in Rocinante [Steinbeck's camper] I would have packed the W.P.A. Guides to the States, all forty-eight volumes of them. I have all of them, and some are very rare. If I remember correctly, North Dakota printed only eight hundred copies and South Dakota about five hundred. The complete set comprises the most comprehensive account of the United States ever got together, and nothing since has even approached it. It was compiled during the depression by the best writers in America, who were, if that is possible, more depressed than any other group while maintaining their inalienable instinct for eating. But these books were detested by Mr. Roosevelt's opposition. If W.P.A. workers leaned on their shovels, the writers leaned on their pens. The result was that in some states the plates were broken up after a few copies were printed, and that is a shame because they were reservoirs of organized, documented, and well-written information, geological, historical, and economic. If I had carried my guides along, for example, I would have looked up Detroit Lakes, Minnesota, where I stopped, and would have known why it is called Detroit Lakes, who named it, when, and why. I stopped near there late at night and so did Charley [Steinbeck's poodle], and I don't know any more about it than he does.[7]

In 1961 a complete set of the state Guides was appraised at $700; a couple of years later, thanks to Steinbeck, such a set was worth four or five times as much.

THE GUIDES have contributed to the making of hundreds of books. They will contribute to countless more. They offer the richest composite word portrait we have of our country—an astonishing gift from a period of hard times.

BILL STOTT

NOTES

1. Anita Brenner, "Rorty Reports America," *The Nation* (February 12, 1936), p. 194.

2. Mabel S. Ulrich, "Salvaging Culture for the WPA," *Harper's* (May 1939), p. 656; Katherine Kellock, "The WPA Writers: Portraitists of the United States," *The American Scholar* (Autumn 1940), p. 474.

3. Harlan Hatcher, *The Columbus Citizen* (November 16, 1941), quoted in Monty Noam Penkower, *The Federal Writers' Project: A Study of Government Patronage of the Arts* (Urbana: University of Illinois Press, 1977), p. 241.

4. Malcolm Cowley, "The Michael Golden Legend," in *Decision* (July, 1941), reprinted in *Think Back on Us . . . : A Contemporary Chronicle of the 1930s*, Henry Dan Piper, ed. (Carbondale: Southern Illinois University Press, 1967), pp. 195, 196.

5. Eleanor Roosevelt (text) and Frances Cooke Macgregor (photographs), *This Is America* (New York: Putnam, 1942), unpaginated.

6. From a Dec. 7, 1967 interview quoted in Penkower, p. 161.

7. John Steinbeck, *Travels with Charley: In Search of America* (New York: Viking, 1962), pp. 120–21.

The Land and
Its Improvements

Natural Conditions

"EVERYBODY TALKS about the weather, but nobody does anything about it."

This truism is less true in America than almost any place on earth. Many Americans actually do something about the weather. They move.

The moving has been going on for a good while, as is apparent in the story *eighteen hundred and froze to death*. That it was still going on in the 1930s we know from the great migration we now refer to by a novel and film, *The Grapes of Wrath*, and by the phrase *Dust Bowl*. But there is happier evidence: look at a *man of substance* at the far end of the journey.

Leaving aside migration, the responses to bad weather boil down to scientific tinkering *(rainmakers)*, hopeful faith *(praying for rain)*, and, toughest of all perhaps, acceptance *(rivergees)*.

Bad weather is not the only natural plague. Consider *grasshoppers*. Or the *optical delusion*. Or *summer fever* in the north.

HURRICANE-CONSCIOUS. From August to October, Floridians [along the southeast coast] are hurricane-conscious. One day the newspapers report on an inside page the gathering of a tropical storm, usually somewhere in the West Indies, the hurricane incubator of the hemisphere. If the storm is of dangerous intensity and proceeding toward Florida, it "makes" the front page the following day. As the storm approaches within a few hundred miles of the coast, the news is "boxed," accompanied with a diagram charting the storm's course. Radio programs are interrupted by announcements from the weather bureau. On the mainland the wind blows steadily toward the storm center, but the sun shines and people go quietly about their business. If the hurricane shows no signs of shifting its course or diminishing in volume, police and welfare agencies prepare for action. Trucks and busses are sent to evacuate people in outlying sections; they come with their bedding and cooking utensils to set up housekeeping in churches, auditoriums, and other build-ings. Merchants remove signs and board up shop windows. Home owners brace their weaker trees, trim off limbs that might fall on roofs. Chimneys are capped and window and door crevices plugged, for the torrential rain does more damage than the wind. Bathtubs and all available receptacles are filled with water for drinking purposes in case the town's pumping plant is disabled; oil lamps and stoves are brought out and filled; stores sell candles by the dozens.

Few outward signs of excitement appear along the streets; citizens move about calmly, listen to sidewalk radio reports, and consult barometers. As the storm strikes inland, the towns along its path, one by one, are cut off from communication with the world as wires go down. A heavy sky and scurrying dirty gray clouds block out the sun. A drizzle begins and turns to rain, followed by a deluge as the wind gradually increases to a lashing gale, accompanied occasionally by lightning and a continuous rumble of thunder scarcely discernible above the roar of wind and rain. All electric power is cut off to avoid danger from live wires. Palms bend to the ground under the howling blast, shaking free their "hula skirts" of dead fronds; pines are snapped or twisted off; sheds and flimsy roofs fly into space; streets become rivers; stalled cars are abandoned.

Some of the more reckless don bathing suits and venture out, but it is difficult to stand up against the wind. Guests in hotels gather in candle-lit lobbies and hold "hurricane parties," but most people remain at home to look after their property.

After a dozen hours at the most, the worst is over, but rain and unsettled weather may continue for several days. Householders and city trucks clean the debris from lawns and streets; fallen trees and poles are removed, and wires restrung. Roofing concerns do a rushing business, carpenters and painters work overtime, until reconstruction is completed. As a rule, the normal community routine is disrupted for several weeks.

Florida

EIGHTEEN HUNDRED AND FROZE TO DEATH. The year 1816, "the famine year," or "eighteen hundred and froze to death," brought the greatest physical hardships that the inhabitants of [Vermont] as a whole have ever known. On June 8 a foot of snow fell and blew into drifts two and three feet high. There was a little snow in July and August and a heavy frost on September 10. Almost no crops were harvested that fall. Much of the livestock in the State perished, the hay crop having failed. Nettles, wild turnips, hedgehogs, and other crude substitutes for ordinary fare kept all but a few of the human inhabitants from starvation, but the suffering was so intense that the year proved a vital factor in greatly increasing the emigration from Vermont to the lands of promise in the West, particularly Ohio—an exodus that was duplicated in all the New England States.

Vermont

PRAYING FOR RAIN. A favorite story is told of a great drouth that occurred [at Summerfield] years ago, and of the strange sequel to the people's prayers for rain. Crops were scorched and ruined, livestock suffered, and wells dried up. Assembling in the community church, the alarmed people called upon A. H. Mitchell, Methodist minister, and Dr. Drury Fair, local physician, to lead the prayers. Preacher Mitchell, a large man with a powerful voice, pleaded for a great downpour; but Dr. Fair, small and quiet-spoken, asked for soft showers. As he prayed, rain began falling. It fell in torrential sheets in the vicinity of the Mitchell home, where trees and chimneys were blown down, but at Dr. Fair's, there was only a gentle shower.

Alabama

RAINMAKERS. It was during the summer of 1893, after a period of relentless drought, that [the Upper James River] country was invaded by the "rainmakers," a small group of shrewd promoters who attempted to exploit the misfortunes of the farmers. Ridden by despair as they watched their green fields wither and brown under the blistering glare of the sun, farmers of the early 1890's were ready to welcome any scheme, no matter how impractical, that might bring precious moisture from cloudless skies. Descending like a welcome Moses upon a thirsty land, a Kansas man named Morris promised to bring water from the heavens instead of coaxing it from a rock, as the Israelitish leader did. He guaranteed to bring water to any community within five days, provided suitable remunerations were forthcoming from the inhabitants.

His first engagement was by the farmers on the eastern slope of the James River valley, where he guaranteed to produce a half-inch of rain over an area of 300 square miles within five days, or receive nothing; if successful, he was to be paid $500. Soon after he began operations, dark clouds hovered overhead, and the farmers were jubilant. But on the second day a brisk wind sprang up, sweeping the clouds eastward. That evening Watertown, 50 miles distant, received a drenching downpour. The rainmaker said this was his rain and that the wind had carried it away. Undismayed by his first defeat, Morris persisted in his efforts, and on the evening of the last day the promised area had received a full half-inch of rain, and the rainmaker his $500.

Flushed with victory, Morris was besieged with offers from all over the State. He next moved into Aberdeen but found entrenched there a rival named Capt. Hauser, who had begun operations in the top story of a business building, erecting on the roof a long pipe that emitted a stream of evil-smelling gases day and night. With both rainmakers working desperately, Brown County residents fully expected a cloudburst. But three days wore away and no rain fell. Capt. Hauser's time was up, but Morris still had two days left. On the last day Morris once more brought rain, dampening the Fourth of July picnics. The thirsty soil received more than .5 inches, and Morris again collected $500.

There were three general schools of rainmaking. One group used the artificial explosion method, such as artillery or dynamite. This was supposed to cause condensation and the falling of water. Many communities in North and South Dakota tried to bring rain through their own efforts, and instead of paying the rainmakers $500, bought dynamite and ammunition with which they bombarded the upper air.

Most reputed rainmakers favored the hydrogen method, which consisted of the emission of this light gas in large quantities. A combination of the two methods was used in the most desperate cases. Even a school for rainmakers was started, but history fails to reveal that the school had sufficient graduates to form an alumni association.

Later experiments of rainmakers were not so successful and they lost the confidence of the public. When drought struck the following year, the mayor of Aberdeen set aside a day of prayer for rain, and the rainmakers were forgotten.

South Dakota

RIVERGEES. The Mississippi flood of January-February 1937 imposed upon Memphis the huge task of providing for an estimated 50,000 to 60,000 refugees. Bewildered sharecroppers, fisherfolk, and river-town people from Mississippi, Arkansas, and Tennessee—most of them suffering from hunger and exposure—poured into Memphis by train, truck, rescue boat, and "footback." Through the efforts of every available civic and social agency, a rescue program met practically every human need from the moment of registration to the departure of the last refugee group.

At the Mid-South Fairgrounds, the largest refugee camp, barracks were erected, and the adjacent Fairview High School was converted into a major base hospital. The sick were cared for in the wards of John Gaston, Baptist, Methodist, St. Joseph's, U. S. Veterans, and Marine Hospitals. Eight hundred and six patients were listed as refugee emergency cases; 2,089 were immunized against typhoid fever and smallpox. In addition to the fairgrounds camp,

14 school buildings were converted to refugee service. Negro refugees were provided for in the north hall of Ellis Auditorium.

The "rivergees" sang:

> Down at the Fairgrounds on my knees,
> Prayin' to the Lord to give me ease—
> Lord, Lord I got them high-water blues!

Edward Hull Crump (Boss Ed), a notable figure in Tennessee politics, took a leading part during the flood. He donned a pair of high-topped boots and went out to the levee to encourage the workers. Negroes of the chain gang sang loudly when they saw him:

> Oh, the river's up and cotton's down,
> Mister Ed Crump, he runs this town.

"Do you think the levee will break?" a visitor asked one of the foremen. "Hell, naw!" was the reply. "Why are you so damn sure?" "Mister Crump say it won't."

To some of the Negroes and poor whites, the experience was a holiday. Many of them had never been more than a few miles from home. Social workers found hundreds who did not know their last names or the State and county from which they had come. Used to an unvarying diet of "sow bosom," sorghum, and corn mush, they devoured fruits and good beef with the wonder of children drinking their first pink circus lemonade. People warped and stupefied by pellagra responded quickly to balanced diet and left the refugee camp cured.

Tennessee

GRASSHOPPERS. Probably nothing in the natural history of the West has excited more interest than the grasshopper plagues in the seventies. As early as 1856 the Rocky Mountain grasshoppers, probably encouraged by continued dryness and warmth during the summer months, swarmed over present Nebraska and parts of the neighboring States. In the next 17 years there were six more invasions, less destructive to crops, but discouraging to the farmers. The locusts made their worst and most memorable attack in 1874. The Indians prepared a mash of the grasshoppers and ate it, faring better than the settler who depended for a living upon the crops the pests overlooked. Many pioneers sold or gave away their claims and returned East; at least one drove a wagon with the sign: "Eaten out by grasshoppers. Going back East to live with wife's folks." Others, determined to stick it out, took up the hunting life of the Indians, living on dried buffalo meat and trading the hides for other supplies. Still others retreated to the older communities where conditions were better and worked there as hired men.

Nebraska

INLAND SEA. Lake Superior, though but a remnant of its glacial predecessor, is still the largest body of fresh water in the world—383 miles long, 160 miles wide, and 1,290 feet deep—and has a tide which at maximum is about three inches.

This great inland sea has a profound effect on Duluth's climate. Its waters vary in temperature only a few degrees throughout the year. In those occasional winters when the lake remains open, lake winds tend to temper the cold, but more frequently there is ice for 20 or more miles from the shore. Despite Duluthians' claim that their city is the healthiest on earth and that their thermometers go no lower than the Minnesota average, they cannot deny their joy when the end of the long winter is heralded by the breaking up of the lake's ice. On that day all downtown seems atingle with a new excitement. The common salutation "Have you seen? The ice is going out!" is heard again and again. All who can, get into cars and drive along the North Shore to see for themselves the crumbling and shifting of the great gray sheets before the determined advance of blue water.

Minnesota

SUNSHINE CITY. Although many Florida resorts have featured their abundant sunlight, St. Petersburg alone has been shrewd enough to capitalize on "Old Sol" and to spend $1,000,000 advertising itself as the "Sunshine City." To make the name authentic, the publisher of the city's afternoon paper announced that he would give away his entire edition every day the sun failed to show its face up to 3 o'clock. In 26 years the paper was distributed free 123 times, an average of less than 5 editions a year. The record endurance contest was 546 days, ending on a Friday the 13th in 1935. Letters addressed "Sunshine City" are sent to St. Petersburg.

Having advertised its place in the sun, St. Petersburg provided its visitors with ample means of absorbing the ultra-violet and infra-red rays. More than 5,000 green benches, in recreation centers and flanking the sidewalks of the principal thoroughfares, have converted the city into a park. Their color, size, and design are standardized by municipal ordinance. These slatted divans serve as mediums of introduction, with the weather the opening and principal topic. Operations, symptoms, and remedies run a close second. The benches are the open-air offices of the promoter, the hunting grounds of the real-estate "bird dog," a haven for the lonely, and a matrimonial bureau for many. They have figured in fiction, swindles, and divorce courts.

Florida

WHISKY AND A GOOD SET OF TEETH. Among the tales of the early plainsmen and buffalo hunters is the story of the hunter on the Staked Plains, who, with a party killing buffalo, was overtaken by a "norther" (a plains blizzard) while far from camp. Having scant clothing, no shelter, and no matches, and being bewildered by the storm, he bethought himself to crawl inside a green buffalo hide, wrapping it tightly about him. When morning came he found that the hide had frozen stiff and that he was unable to move or extricate himself. Several days afterward he was found and released by his companions. Upon being questioned as to how he managed to survive the experience he explained that, had it not been for the possession of a quart of whisky and a good set of teeth, he "surely would of froze to death."

New Mexico

OPTICAL DELUSION. [From] the fire-tower on Green Mountain, once known as Seven Mountain, . . . there are wide views; the Presidential Range is impressive from this point. Portland and the Atlantic Ocean are visible on clear days. It is said that a carpenter building a summer hotel here in 1857—burned three years later—declared that one very clear day he picked out a ship coming into Portland Harbor and could distinctly see that its cargo was West Indian rum. A county historian avers that it was probably an optical delusion, the result of looking so often through a glass in common use in those days.

New Hampshire

BLIZZARD. South of Wall, in 1905, thousands of cattle and horses drifted over the wall of the Badlands and perished during the tragic May blizzard that left in its wake utter ruin for nearly every stockman in the western part of the State. The storm, starting as rain, gradually turned to snow which fell steadily and thickly. Riding in on a strong north wind, the blizzard howled across the open stretches with unleashed fury. What had been balmy May weather soon changed to the bitterest storm a severe winter could offer. Striking at a time when livestock had just shed winter coats, the blizzard forced the bewildered animals to drift with the wind until they floundered helplessly into snow-filled draws to die. Barbwire fences of homesteaders added to the toll, for large numbers of stock drifted against them and piled up. South Dakota is a country of extremes, evinced by the fact that a mild warm day, may, in a few hours, be changed into one of biting cold, and vice versa. People who have lived in the State long will recall how they have often retired at night with the thermometer hovering near zero, to be awakened in the morning by water dripping from the roof, the sudden change being due to a chinook wind from the Rocky Mountain area.

South Dakota

DUST BOWL. Great dust storms here are at once magnificent and terrifying. They move forward in sky-high walls, black and ominous, and plunge
the land into darkness. Sand sifts into houses and automobiles, even into
intricate working parts of fine machinery. Often these storms cover vast areas.
That which harried Colorado, Oklahoma, Kansas, New Mexico, and Texas
on May 12, 1934, carried dust eastward across the United States to fall on
ships far out at sea.

Scores of families were driven out by drought and wind. The dust piled
up in drifted ridges, buried fences and idle machinery, swirled high about
sun-warped buildings. But the wheat farmers of the ravaged Colorado plains
are a hardy stubborn breed; most of them stayed on, believing that droughts
occur in cycles. During the worst periods nothing could be grown; the air
was hardly to be breathed. Even travel was sometimes precarious, for when
the storms descended, cars were marooned on the highway, their drivers forced
to wait until visibility returned. The wind that scoured the land to the raw
subsoil drew from these men and women a grudging and bitter humor.

"Part of my farm blew off into Kansas yesterday, so I guess I'll have to pay
taxes there, too," said one. "The wind that blew south Wednesday passed
over my place came back yesterday and dropped some of the land it took
away," said another. They told stories of "black snow" storms so dark they
couldn't see to lace their shoes. A drop of water fell on a man, said one of
his neighbors, "and we had to throw two buckets of dust in his face to revive
him." A stranger driving through the region stopped at a farm house to remark at a cloud in the blazing sky. "Think it'll rain?" he inquired. "Hope
so," said the farmer, "not so much for my sake as the children's. I've seen
rain."

Colorado

HARD WINTER. In 1740–41 occurred the "hard winter." Dr. Mac-
Sparran, the Episcopal minister in Narragansett, stated that the cold was so
intense during this winter that "a man drove a horse and sleigh on the ice
from Hurlgate, near New York, to Cape Cod." It is certain that persons "passed
and repassed from Providence to Newport on the ice, and from the main
shore of Connecticut to Montauk Point." There were more than thirty
snowstorms, besides small flurries. On the 10th of March the snow was three

feet deep; in the middle of April it was still lying in drifts by the fences. The intense cold caused a great loss of cattle and sheep and was especially destructive to game.

Rhode Island

MAN OF SUBSTANCE. An expansive mood is one of the most familiar and sometimes costly first responses to a Florida winter sun. The person noted for taciturnity in his home community often becomes loquacious, determined that those about him shall know that he is a man of substance. This frequently makes him an easy prey to ancient confidence games; sometimes leads to unpremeditated matrimony; and almost inevitably results in the acquisition of superfluous building lots.

Florida

SUMMER FEVER. Perhaps nowhere else in the whole Territory of Alaska is the contrast between summer and winter so marked as in this bustling city, 120 miles south of the Arctic Circle. During the long summer days, when the temperature frequently rises to 90° in the shade and the nights are brief intervals of twilight between sunset and dawn, a kind of fever seizes the citizens of Fairbanks. With only one hundred days to wrest gold from placer or drift, to raise cabbages, potatoes, and hay in the fields, and tomatoes and green vegetables in the greenhouses, to make new strikes or to develop old ones, to supply the vast expanse of the Interior with transportation, household goods, mining equipment, and technical direction, everybody works most of the daylight hours. Stages, trucks, and private automobiles come and go south to the copper country and the coast region around Valdez, east to the gold districts from Cleary to Circle. Trains and motorcars arrive on the Alaska Railroad from Anchorage, Seward, and Matanuska Valley; silver Lockheed Electras arrive from Juneau to the southeast and depart for Nome to the northwest; small red or yellow freight or passenger Stinsons and Bellancas dip and soar on their way to or from Wiseman, north of the Arctic Circle, Goodnews, Bristol Bay, the Alaska Peninsula, and the Kuskokwim. The revolving oven of the North Pole bakery ships loaves of bread by train, plane and auto as far as Bethel on the lower Kuskokwim. In the lobby of the three-story, 120-room Nordale Hotel miners and prospectors from all over Alaska, the States, South America, Canada, and Russia sit on modernistic chromium chairs and swap experiences from the world around. The only residents of Fairbanks unaffected by the summer fever of activity are the guests from remote sections of the Interior languishing in the "skookum house"— the Fairbanks jail.

Alaska

Buildings

THE QUICKEST index to the human meaning of a place is its architecture. Because human meaning is what the Guides want, each spends a chapter on the architectural styles found within its state. Both grand and humble styles are discussed: Greek Revival and *grain elevators*. Indeed, the nameless style that so dominates the American landscape that we call it "vernacular" (a fancy word for commonplace) gets close attention. And judgments are rendered: the Federal Writers were not afraid to use words like "pretentious," "awkward," or "ugly."

Most of what the Guides say about buildings is not about style. Instead, they describe the uses to which buildings are put. The Guides look through a building to the life that happens within. Thus, in a Delaware *observatory* we learn a little economic and social history. A South Dakota *cupola* informs us about extreme Plains weather. An *arbor* built by its community shows the community's values; so does a *crematory*, which was built despite its community.

Some buildings in the Guides reach back to the Neolithic revolution when man turned farmer (the *adobes* of the Southwest), and beyond—to hunter-gatherer days (the *lodges* of the Dakota tribes).

DOG TROT. The simplest form of the log cabin was generally the same throughout early America. But the double cabin, known in Alabama as the "dog-trot" or "breezeway" house, was a distinctive innovation in the Mid-South. To enlarge his home the pioneer often followed the easy expedient of building a second cabin near the first and joining the two with a porch, either open or roofed. Often the family dogs retreated from the sun to the shade of the roofed space—hence the name. During the blasting heat of summer this space was used as a dining place and a spot for general gatherings, where breezes could sweep through unimpeded.

Alabama

GRAIN ELEVATORS. Indigenous to Minnesota, and almost completely ignored by its people, are the stark, unornamented, functional clusters of concrete—Minnesota's grain elevators. These may be said to express unconsciously all the principles of modernism, being built for use only, with little regard for the tenets of esthetic design. Everyone has seen the rhythmic repetition of these cylindrical forms accented by the shadows made by the hot summer sun, and the whole dignified mass set against the sky; yet it remained for European visitors to discover that while Minnesota sought for artistic expression in other directions, it had achieved in its grain elevators a signal triumph of functional design.

Minnesota

LODGE. As evening came on, within the dome-shaped lodges [of the Missouri Valley tribes] there was much feasting, especially if it was the time of the new corn. The doorway of a lodge was protected by a kind of porch and hung with a buffalo hide. From behind the windshield just inside the doorway shone the light of the fire, which was built in a stone-lined depression in the center of the lodge, with a hole in the roof to carry off the smoke. This opening also served as a skylight. To the right of the doorway, in a small corral or stall, were the favorite ponies, safely confined for the night. Boxlike beds for the master of the house, his wife or wives, and his children, were arranged along the wall on the other side. These were made by covering sturdy wooden frames with hides. In the rear stood an altar—a tall hide-covered structure somewhat resembling a canopied chair—in which were placed all the sacred objects and most prized possessions of the head of the house. Over the fire about which the family or families had gathered—usually two or three families and their relatives lived in one lodge—were kettles of food cooking for the evening meal. [George] Catlin says the Indians ate whenever hungry, or about twice a day. The pot was kept boiling, and each one helped himself. Anyone in the village who was hungry was free to go into any lodge and satisfy his hunger, although the lazy and improvident were scorned.

Overhead, the light from the fire flickered on the huge supporting uprights of the lodge, where hung articles of clothing, tools from the garden, and weapons for war and hunting. Months before, with infinite labor and no little ingenuity, and hampered by the imperfections of the crude tools and equipment at their command, these early Dakota farmers had cut great cottonwood logs from the Missouri bottomlands and dragged them to the top of the bluffs, to form the framework for this earthen home. The lodges varied from 30 to 90 feet in diameter. After a little sod had been removed from a space of the desired size, to form a smooth, firm floor, four heavy posts were fixed upright not far from the center, to support the great roof, while at some distance out from these a circle of smaller posts was set to hold up the sides. Rafters of moderate-sized timbers were placed over these supports, after which the whole was overlaid with willows, hay, and earth—a humble covering that guarded with all its passive, effective impenetrability against both the sweltering heat of summer and the intense cold of winter.

North Dakota

OBSERVATORY. [Cochran Grange, on Delaware's Levels,] has a portico of tall square columns with a fanlighted doorway, and a smaller two-story wing; both wings have the square boxlike lines characteristic of the period. The nearly flat roof of the main wing is surmounted by a glass-enclosed observatory—in this house and others like it, a symbol and expression of wealth. Nothing in Delaware agriculture before or since has quite matched the spectacle of well-groomed ladies and gentlemen taking their ease in the obseratories on top of their fine houses, watching their Negroes at work in the broad grain fields and peach orchards, or merely enjoying the view in the pride of possession.

Delaware

ROW HOUSES. Not so old nor so grand as the Victorian row houses are the row houses built near the turn of the century in a band around the older core and housing a considerable part of [Baltimore's] inhabitants. Their number is so great as to make them the most characteristic sight seen by the hurried visitor. Even in an era of standardized construction, the uniformity of these houses from block to block is amazing.

From one street to the next is a solid line of two-story houses of yellow brick; the next may be of red. Some rows are blank and severe, others are cluttered with fussy gables, but within each block there is no variation, so that even the owner must recognize his own door by the number. The most striking feature of these uniform houses is their uniform white steps, which are always just scrubbed or being scrubbed. In some blocks the steps are of white stone, in others they are of wood painted white. The people scrubbing them may be Negro servants—male or female—or they may be housewives, or schoolgirls wearing silk stockings, but the pattern is the same—gleaming white steps and kneeling scrubbers—for mile after mile around the city.

Maryland

ADOBE. In appearance like scattered stones carelessly thrown at the foot of the mountain backstop, the light-colored houses—square and hard as stones, but not made of stone—are fashioned of mud (adobe). The thick layer of creamish, tannish, or reddish mud filling all the cracks makes the houses as snug as birds' nests. Every year or two they must be replastered with mud mixed with sand and straw. More straw is used in Taos than in other places in the state, giving the houses a golden glint in the sunshine. Nevertheless, they have a gloomy look. They seem to be crouching close to the ground for protection from some unknown thing, and seem little taller than the hollyhocks screening their tawny walls.

New Mexico

SHEEP WAGON. Within a radius of 50 miles of [Buffalo] there are more sheep than in any similar area in the United States. Sheep wagons are seen on the top of many a hill, and bands of sheep graze along the roadside. A visit to one of these wagons will be of interest perhaps to anyone who has never seen one. But first locate the herder. He may object to strangers invading his home without permission. He will be somewhere close by with his sheep, and will gladly show how he, the last of the nomads, lives. But do not expect to find him different from anyone else who tends animals or works on a ranch. He wears no distinctive garb and talks no special "lingo."

The sheep wagon is reminiscent of the pioneer covered wagon, except that it is much shorter and the canvas is pulled taut, eliminating that ribbed appearance. Mounting a set of steps, or walking up the wagon tongue, to the doorway, the visitor sees before him a marvel of compact and convenient living quarters for one person. At the right, close to the door, is a small camp stove and above is a set of shelves for dishes and utensils. Along either side are benches, formed by extending the wagon bed over the wheels; in the center of each of these benches is a trapdoor that opens into a "grub box," extending down into the space between the front and back wheels. Here the herder keeps his bread, cereal, meat, and light groceries. The two benches terminate in a bed across the end of the wagon—a board bunk, which may or may not have a set of springs, but has a mattress and bedding such as is found in any bunkhouse. Under the bed is a recess which sometimes has a drop door in front. Here the herder keeps his potatoes and bulky articles; and here his dog sleeps at night—and retires to it in the daytime when the herder inadvertently steps on his foot. Over the bed is a small window, hinged at the top and manipulated by a rope attached to the bottom, so that the herder can open and hold it at any angle desired by simply tying the rope. This window, being at the opposite end of the wagon from the door, insures perfect ventilation and also permits the herder to look out over his sleeping flock at night without getting out of bed. For this reason the wagon is always placed with its door facing away from the bedground. The door is cut in two, crosswise in the middle, the upper and lower halves swinging independently on their own hinges, making it easier to keep the wagon at any temperature desired without a direct draft on the stove. There is no table in sight until the herder either swings it up from the front of the bed and props it with its one leg, or, more likely, pulls it out flat from beneath the bed, the exposed part being held firm by the part that remains beneath the bed.

Such is the herder's happy home, a model of compactness and convenience. His personal belongings are kept on a shelf above his bed. There is plenty of room in the wagon for one person, but two would crowd it. Perhaps that is the reason why there are so few married herders, or at least herders whose wives live with them in the wagon. There is distinctly no room for temperament, and the sheep wagon will probably continue to be in the future as it has been in the past, the refuge of the married man and the hiding-place of the bachelor.

South Dakota

ARBOR. Until the last decade, every Arkansan was familiar with the sight of the "brush arbors" that sheltered worshipers during summer revivals. The men in any neighborhood could build a brush arbor in a day or so by placing poles upright in the ground and making a roof of leafy boughs. These rustic structures had no walls, but around the four sides were scaffolds, where pine-knot torches burned at night to cast a fitful glow over the audience. Although summer religious sessions are still fairly common, they are now usually held in permanent camp buildings, in the open air, or in tents; brush arbors are seldom seen. The kerosene lanterns that eventually took the place of the pioneers' pine torches have now given way to electric lights dangling from a wire, or the headlamps of automobiles parked around the benches.

Arkansas

BOTTLE HOUSE. Though at the height of the boom two railroads entered [Rhyolite], the only evidence of them today is the ruins of one elaborate depot, now open at intervals as a casino to attract visitors from Death

Valley. Notable among the ruins is the Bottle House, whose walls were built of quart beer bottles, laid horizontally, and integrated with adobe. Victorian jigsaw frills hang from the eaves of the gabled roof, and a dried coyote from one gable end. Since 1939 this has been a free museum of desert relics whose owner depends on the sale of curios for support. Around the house is an amazing garden; among pieces of glass purpled by the strong sunshine, bits of unusual rock, old cart wheels, figures from toyshops, old mortars, and what-not are many kinds of cactus and small delicate desert flowers.

Nevada

SUNDAY HOUSE. Scattered throughout [Fredericksburg] are numerous small houses, closed and dark during the week, but bustling with activity on Saturdays and Sundays. These so-called "Sunday houses" are reminiscent of the not long distant past when roads were bad, transportation slow, and the frugal farm families from the adjacent valleys had to spend a night in town to shop Saturday and to attend church on Sunday. The "Sunday houses" are still maintained as a convenient and economical way of spending the weekend in town.

Texas

CREMATORY. The LeMoyne Crematory [at Washington is] a one-story brick building with a chimney at each end of its gabled roof, erected by Dr. LeMoyne in 1876 and said to be the first crematory in the United States. Local opposition forced construction men to work at night. The grave of Dr. LeMoyne, marked by a simple granite monument, is directly in front.

Pennsylvania

BEAN-VINER. Between Delaware Bay and the western Maryland-Delaware Line, State 18 runs across the flat, sandy plain of Sussex County marked by small farms and squared-off blocks of loblolly pine timber. Cornfields alternate with fields planted with tomatoes, peas, and other cannery crops. Along the road the occasional sheds covering heavy machinery are "bean-viners" to which lima bean vines are brought by the wagonload to be thrashed. The beans are packed in water-filled containers and rushed to the canneries. The strong sour smell around a bean-viner arises from the great heaps of fermenting vines that have been thrown out by the machine.

Delaware

CONTINUOUS ARCHITECTURE.Early Vermont farmhouses, invariably of wood, were built primarily to meet utilitarian requirements. The great body of this work consisted of simple buildings, adapted to rural purposes. . . . The earlier practice of connecting house, barns, and shed—a concession to the rigors of winter—was later abandoned in the interests of sanitation, but many examples of this "continuous architecture" remain.

Vermont

GIANT BUREAU. The Giant Bureau [of High Point], symbolizing the city's position as a furniture-manufacturing center, houses the office of the Chamber of Commerce. It was built in 1925 of wood painted white, is 32 feet high, 27 feet long, and 14 feet wide. A square screen on the top represents a mirror. The front of the building is designed to simulate a bureau with drawers and knobs.

North Carolina

CUPOLA. One of the features of early residences in South Dakota was the cupola perched on top of many houses. Because of the frequent snowstorms that often reach blizzard proportions, combined with the lack of landmarks on the flat prairie, the cupola, like the Old North Church, was used to hang lanterns in so that members of the family, neighbors and strangers could find their way on stormy nights. The extreme weather has had its effect on architecture. Windows and doors facing north are avoided, especially in the open country, where icy wintry blasts seem to penetrate even the sideboards. And protection in summer against the bright sun is acquired by means of wide porches and awnings.

South Dakota

HOGAN. The Navajo country in Arizona—the tribe occupies an equally large area in New Mexico—is characterized by elevations that range for the most part between 5,500 and 9,000 feet above sea level and by a broad plateau modified by mesas, buttes, volcanic necks, gorges, and washes. On the sculptured ledges of its canyons are the remains of cliff dwellings a thousand years old. Wind-blown brown sand covers the area in an uneven layer. Its sagebrush, greasewood, yucca and grasses are varies by pine forests and zones of pinon and juniper. . . .

The many Navajo hogans along this route are built of logs and covered with mud and sod; each has a doorway facing the east and a smoke hole in the center of the roof, but there the uniformity ends. In some the logs are laid horizontally, with six or eight sides and a dome-shaped roof; in others the logs are vertical and the hut has a roughly conical form. Generally there is a sheep corral and a summer arbor near by. Although the hogan is but a mud hut, its mythical prototype is thus described by the Navajo: "Built of poles of white shell, turquoise, obsidian, jet, and red sandstone" at the entrance is "a fourfold curtain of dawn, skyblue, evening twilight, and darkness."

Arizona

In the Towns

THE GUIDES, being travel guides, are place- rather than people-centered, and towns—crossroads, vacation camps, trading posts, hamlets, villages, tank towns, suburbs, county seats, upstart cities—are the Guides' main characters.

The tour sections were intended to depict every town (hamlet, village, etc.) with such insight that readers would see what made it different from any other.

Often the difference is a special economic role, as in *artists' colony* and *railroad village*. But it can be much less: a *band concert*, a *liars' bench*, a *courthouse*.

Usually the difference is tied up with history, real or imagined. A *tabernacle* sums up Pitman, New Jersey; the *Bark Shanty Times* captures the essence of its town, although the paper is defunct and the town has changed.

What made one town matter in state politics and a neighboring town not? In one rivalry, the outcome depends on *who's got the safe*; in another, it is balanced *on the head of a pin*.

ARTISTS' COLONY. The plaza sleeps undisturbed in the sun, the old well in the center and the bandstand ordinarily giving no sign of life. Life and interest in the town's activities are evident along the uneven sidewalks, fronting the stores where white-robed Indians lean against a sunny corner to watch the Anglos pass or to visit among themselves, Spanish-speaking residents from near-by ranches here to barter produce for manufactured necessities, and sightseeing tourists peering in curio windows. Artists laden with sketch-easel and paint box, or new canvases to hang in the gallery, thread their way among the others, or stop to arrange a posing date with one of the Indians.

New Mexico

BAND CONCERT. During July and August, Band Concert Night (Wednesday and Saturday) is a big event for farm families in northwestern Iowa. An atmosphere of excitement and hurry is felt all day. The children start doing the chores without urging; the farmer hastens to do the milking. The mother and daughters spend the afternoon pressing clothes. Supper is hurried through and dishes are washed; chickens are shooed into coops so they can be locked up before the family leaves. Just at dusk the family turns down the dusty country road toward the highway and town. If they are late there will be no parking places near the band—a minor tragedy, for with good luck the family can sit comfortably in the car, munching popcorn, listening to the band, and watching the crowds stroll past. There is real competition for parking places; townspeople, to the dismay of rural folk, often park their cars in the late afternoon, and walk home to supper and back again in the evening for the sake of an advantageous spot.

The band is often a heterogeneous group, made up of older people who have played in it for years, school teachers who have just come to town and are earnestly endeavoring to take an active part in the life of the community, high school students, and even grade school children. When the crowd approves of the music, all the cars set up a great honking of applause; sometimes every piece is followed by a chorus of raucous sirens.

Iowa

A MAN FOR BREAKFAST. The St. James Hotel [in Cimarrón], now operated as the Don Diego Tavern, was built in 1870–80 and run by Henry Lambert, who before coming to New Mexico had been chef for General Grant and Abraham Lincoln. This inn was frequented by outlaws and was the scene of 26 killings. Whenever a man was shot in the hotel, townspeople would say, "Lambert had a man for breakfast." The *Las Vegas Gazette* once reported: "Everything is quiet in Cimarrón. Nobody has been killed for three days."

New Mexico

COURTHOUSE. Flemington . . . is a quiet little village that was catapulted into the front pages of the world's newspapers in January, 1935, during the trial of Bruno Richard Hauptmann for the murder of Charles A. Lindbergh, Jr. Press stories at the time recounted the angry bewilderment of the local citizenry at the spate of strange people the trial brought into the community. A walk through the town brings the feeling home. Here in a setting of white, green-shuttered houses, business makes haste slowly. There is still a general store where the latest sheet music dangles invitingly over silk hose, and penny candy fills a counter carrying a copy of Pearson and Allen's *Nine Old Men*, a testament to the existence of open minds in this conservative stronghold. The cars parked near the county courthouse, Main St., seldom bestir themselves the day long, and shady side streets are all but deserted. The courthouse is the center of life in the community. Built in 1828, the great Grecian Revival building was the seat of the law in Hunterdon County a century before newspapers learned how to string telegraph wires from their offices to the scene of a murder trial. Just opposite, the four-story Union Hotel—a lumbering, Hudson-River-Bracketed structure of nondescript date, sparrow-grass architecture, tall double-decker porches, and the genial vapidity of the nineties—serves the barristers who amble back and forth across the street to the courthouse.

New Jersey

FREE LIBRARY. The Washington County Free Library [in Hagerstown] is a two-story concrete structure with limestone front and trim and an entrance loggia flanked by Ionic columns. The building houses an institution established in 1901 through the efforts of a clergyman, a banker, a papermaker, two lawyers, a farmer, and a storekeeper—public-spirited men who had already been impressed by the success of other county institutions. Its sound and progressive development was largely the work of the first librarian, Miss Mary L. Titcomb. One of the first county libraries in the United States, it began service in a section where bookstores were unknown, where there was only one small private high school, and where reading was looked upon as the privilege of the idle and the rich. But as soon as the doors were opened, everybody wanted to "join the Library." A countrywoman with her first book wrapped in her starched gingham apron remarked as she left the building, "It's a great day when poor folks like us can take home such handsome books." And a rural boy who had happened to draw one of Shakespeare's plays, returned it with the request: "Give me another by that same man; I think he's a right good writer."

Service to outlying districts was first initiated by placing cases of books in general stores, schools, and private homes. After a few years direct delivery to borrowers was begun; a two-horse wagon equipped with outside bookshelves began to make tours even in remote country districts. Eventually the plan was widely copied abroad as well as in America. The institution now possesses more than 37,000 volumes, employs three trucks in their distribution, and has several permanent branches. The work is supported by endowments and gifts, as well as by city and county funds.

Maryland

LIARS' BENCH. In the center of the village [of Nashville] is the two-story courthouse (1874) of scarred and faded red brick, heated with wood-burning stoves. On the courthouse lawn is the liars' bench, rendezvous of the accomplished dawdlers who gather here to prevaricate in pleasant and friendly rivalry. Famous over the county, the bench is armless at one end and has a seating capacity of six. Here disciples of Munchausen gather, bask in the sun, and exchange magnificent tales. When a bigger and better story is told by some person standing, the man seated at the armless end is pushed off to make room for the expert.

Indiana

THE PATTERN OF PESOTUM. The pattern of Pesotum . . . is as familiar and recurrent in this area as the John Deere tractor and the Harvester plow. Dominated by the grain elevator on the railroad, its life revolves around the storage and shipping of grain. The highway, paralleling the railway tracks, is the business street. Grocery, drygoods, and farm-machinery stores; a tavern, pool room, and barber shop; bank, post office, and at least two churches care for the needs of the town and its nearby farms. Away from the highway on the half-dozen streets are the residences, usually frame. There are no curbs; the paved streets merge in an irregular line with the narrow parkway. Lawns, flower beds, and vegetable gardens surround the houses. At the edges of the village are the larger homes, the cemetery, and then the abrupt beginning of farm and field.

Illinois

RED BAT. On Mitkoff Island, 111 miles northwest of Ketchikan and 108 miles southeast of Juneau, is Petersburg . . . , a modern fishing town and a center for fox and mink raising. This is glacier country: the sun is hot, the air clear, the wind pure and heady. The lawns are close-cropped and gay with flowers, and autos speed along the plank streets. On rafts in the harbor are floating houses painted with red lead, complete with window curtains. Lanky blond Northerners lean against the wall and watch tourists lift the cover of a box labeled, "Red Bat: Dangerous When Flying," that contains a brickbat.

Alaska

REFINERY. The establishment in 1917 of the Shell Refinery in the suburb of Roxana, southeast of the Standard Oil plant, gave . . . impetus to the growth of Wood River. In the past two decades the city has completely outgrown its jerry-built aspect, and its general appearance has been improved by the development of a large community park. . . . Frequently noticed by visitors, but imperceptible to residents, is the acrid odor of oil that pervades the town on summer days. More unforgettable is the piercing moan, as of some great beast in pain, that often comes at night when the stills are shut down for cleaning—the sound of whirling brushes sweeping through the vast network of pipes.

Illinois

COW BELLS. Brownsville's old homes stand beneath magnificent trees, and in almost every yard are beds of hollyhocks, larkspur, and asters. The town still lives along the grooves of the 1850's. Everybody hereabouts is a good story teller. Barn-raisings, quilting parties, bran-hullings, apple peelings, logrollings, and singing parties are a major part of its social life. Square dances are as common as the tales of "hants" in Edmonson County, which is rich in folklore. Brownsville is so quiet that the tinkle of the cow bells going to pasture in the morning and coming back to the barn in the evening is as significant to its residents as reveille and taps are to soldiers.

Kentucky

On January 14, 1889 an ordinance was passed [in Roseburg] to prevent the use of bells on cows and other domestic animals between the hours of 8 P. M. and 6 A. M. Previous to the ordinance one citizen frequently detached the bells from cows and threw them in the gutter when on his way home in the evening, thus hoping to get a good night's sleep.

Oregon

MINING TOWN. Belfry, . . . one of the coal-mining communities that are strung out along Pond Creek for approximately 15 miles, is typical of the numerous half-abandoned mining towns of the area. They are unincorporated and, with their unpaved streets and unpainted buildings, come into view like blighted spots on the land. They have all the inconveniences and few, if any, of the comforts of modern towns of equal size, and none of the advantages of the agricultural countryside. Small drab houses, most of them in need of repair, huddle close together along the deep valleys or stand uncertainly on the mountain sides. Most of them are of boom-time flimsiness, with one thickness of board in the walls that rest on slender, often tottering, posts, many are papered with newspapers and patched with cardboard to shut out draughts. Dark hills of coal tailings blotch the sides and bases of the larger hills. The numerous abandoned mines are marked by warped and dis-jointed frame tipples and entrances, weathered to a dull gray. Only the waters of Pond Creek, now littered with tin cans and other refuse, suggest the nat-ural beauty that was destroyed by industrial development when it penetrated the formerly inaccessible places.

Since the middle 1920's, the miners of the Pond Creek region, when not totally unemployed, have worked only part time. Some of the towns are slowly reviving on a new pattern. Mining, of necessity, is no longer the sole oc-cupation. Odd jobs in lumbering, agriculture, road building, government projects and construction, supplement the employment, mostly seasonal, that is still afforded by the mines. The groups of men clustered around a store or the local "joint" are part of the army of former miners. Life in the coal-mining towns is meager and hard. The customary diet of the miner and his family consists chiefly of beans—and more beans—corn bread made without milk, and "bulldog gravy," a mixture of flour, water, and a little grease. In the summer those fortunate enough to find a small patch may grow a few vegetables, but for the most part they grow pumpkins. There is little or no milk available even for the children. As a result diseases of malnutrition are common. Leisure is abundant and money scarce. Brawls and an occasional shooting, a bit of penny- and nickel-gambling, all of them usually enlivened with moonshine, are the recreation of the men.

Kentucky

ON THE HEAD OF A PIN. Stromsburg and Osceola were once bitter ri-vals in their desire to become the county seat of Polk County. An election was held in 1916 to decide the issue. Osceola won, largely because it had widely distributed small cardboard maps with pins stuck in at Osceola. As the map more or less balanced on the pin, this proved Osceola's claim that it was "the center of the county."

Nebraska

VINEGAR BEND. Vinegar Bend [is] a lumbering and turpentine center. A large sawmill once operated here on the Escatawpa (Choctaw: "Where the cane is cut.") River, with convicts under lease from the state. Bringing li-quor to the company's property was strictly forbidden, and smuggling "moonshine" into the lumber camps from the deep swamps became a profitable, though risky, business. Whenever a person was observed carrying a jug or can, its contents was immediately questioned by the guards. So frequently was the claim made that the container held vinegar, that the place became known as Vinegar Bend.

Alabama

RAILROAD VILLAGE. Mathiston . . . is a railroad village where life revolves about the comings and goings of the daily train. At train time natives gather about the low frame depot; when the train arrives the bulky mail bag is tossed off, milk cans are packed in the baggage car, a few passengers climb aboard, and the train pulls away. Activity is then transferred to the post office. Young and old gather to visit while the mail is being put up—one of the pleasantest of village customs.

Mississippi

BARK SHANTY TIMES. Port Sanilac . . . was called Bark Shanty Point by the first settlers in 1844, who found upon the site a shack that had been occupied four years earlier by a group of Detroit tanners who had come here to manufacture tanbark. During the middle nineteenth century, the community was known throughout the Thumb for the *Bark Shanty Times*, the only daily newspaper in Michigan without reporters or an editorial staff, printers, presses, deadlines, or wire services. Despite these handicaps, the *Times* came out daily with all the news of the locality, reaching its greatest popularity in 1856. The manner of publication was original: the editor, who was postmaster and storekeeper, placed on his counter large sheets of newsprint paper and a supply of lead pencils. Customers and visitors were urged to write any news they had, or to contribute stories and editorials. There were no editorial taboos; contributors wrote what they pleased. When one day's edition had been thoroughly read, the sheets were bound in volumes and filed. Many local citizens and traveling salesmen were regular contributors. During the presidential campaign of Douglas and Buchanan, one "editorial" questioned: "Who ever heard of such a place as Kansus! They say the Damakrats has split and one Buckannon has carried part of 'em off, clean up salt river; and Mr. Duglis has got together part of 'em and is goin' to make squatters of 'um." Another local scribe rose in defense of Bark Shanty as a name: "Quis [a visitor] says our place has a lop-eared name; the first part, he thinks has affinity with the canine race, or close affinity to the rine of a certain tree. The latter, he thinks, is significant and analagous to the place. But," he continued, "I don't respect his judgment altho the muse has said good name is a good thing, which we admit we think ours is a good one." A descendant of the editor today owns the cancellation stamp of old Bark Shanty post office and, each year, stamps about a hundred envelopes at the request of visitors.

Michigan

SAFE. Marvin . . . was originally known as Grade Siding, owing to its situation on the railroad; but in 1882 a post office was to be established and a more dignified name was needed. There was a Marvin safe in the railroad office and a local punster suggested that Marvin was a "good, safe name."

South Dakota

MUNICIPAL BONDS. Carlinville [is] widely known throughout the state for its million-dollar Macoupin County Courthouse . . . , which local wags have nicknamed "The White Elephant." In February 1867 the county commissioners ordered a $50,000 bond issue to erect new quarters for the county offices. The bonds bore 10 per cent interest and were to be repaid within 10 years, but this sum scarcely laid the foundation. More and more bonds were issued, and taxes rose higher and higher, until a "courthouse tax" of 50¢ on each $100 valuation in real, personal, and mixed property was levied. This the taxpayers bitterly fought, but without success. In January 1870 the building was completed at a total cost of $1,380,500, but not until July 1910 was the last bond retired. Citizens of the county then staged a two-day celebration, which was attended by Governor Charles Deneen. Natural gas, recently discovered in the vicinity, was piped to the courthouse square, and as a climax to the celebration, the last bond was burned by the Governor. As the scrap of paper crumbled to ashes, 20,000 people shouted themselves hoarse, and the whistle of every factory and mine in the county was blown for ten minutes.

Illinois

FOOTBRIDGE. At Curry, . . . the halfway point between the coast and the Interior, passengers spend the night in the Curry Hotel, operated by the Alaska Railroad. The hotel has excellent modern accommodations for 150 guests. After a day of traveling on the Alaska Railroad, most people after nodding over dinner are glad to hurry upstairs to bed and fall instantly asleep to the murmur of the Susitna River. There is nothing else to do, anyway, as there is neither bar nor library—not even a newsstand. The wildest extreme in excitement offered is a walk across the suspension footbridge spanning the Susitna up a trail on the opposite bank through a series of berry patches.

Alaska

JUG. Templeton [was] known from coast to coast during prohibition days for its bootleg rye whiskey. Many giant stills were operated in the vicinity. During the period when Templeton basked in illegal glory, a small brown jug was suspended across the main street.

Iowa

TABERNACLE. Pitman['s] . . . population is almost tripled in summer by religious vacationists. One-story cottages for the visitors contrast with the solidly built homes of the residents of this prosperous town. Alcyon Park, on the southern edge of Pitman, offers occasional horseracing, auto racing, and night baseball. Alcyon Lake is popular for fishing, swimming, and rowing.

The Gloucester County fair is held in Pitman every fall. Within a circular area of several acres enclosed by a paved road, known as Pitman Grove, is the Tabernacle . . . , in which the two-week meeting of the Pitman Grove Camp Meeting Association is held each summer beginning about August 1. Pitman Grove is a survivor of the camps established during the religious upheaval after the Civil War. From the tabernacle 12 streets radiate like the spokes of a wheel, following the plan of the holy city in the Book of Revelations. This summer path of earlier Methodists was carpeted with rustling leaves that blew into the tabernacle and were seized by the preacher as the likeness to fallen man, dead in sin.

New Jersey

FIRE FIGHTERS. The Independent Fire Company, . . . one of two independent fire companies in Charles Town, occupies a three-story, gray-painted brick structure, erected in 1895, with square towers at the front corners. A garland of black crepe often hangs over the entrance, for the fire company honors the memory of deceased members by hanging crepe for 60 days. The company was organized in 1884 under Captain Julius C. Holmes. Upon organization of the group there was a heated contest between Holmes and J. W. Russell for captaincy of the company, and when Holmes won, Russell seceded with his supporters and formed the Citizens Fire Company. For a number of years the two companies were bitter rivals and when both answered a fire alarm the members spent as much time fighting each other for the honor of putting out the fire as they did in fighting the fire. The company that succeeded in attaching its hose first had to patrol the line to prevent members of the other group from cutting it. The rivalry gradually died out, but the town still has two companies.

West Virginia

WHO'S GOT THE SAFE? Warren . . . , seat of Marshall County, almost lost that distinction when in 1881 the county commissioners from Argyle and Stephen, constituting a majority, resolved that "the county seat of Marshall County is hereby located in the townsite of Argyle." They moved and seconded that the county safe and its content of legal papers be placed in the sheriff's charge and conveyed to Argyle. Then for almost 10 years it became, to quote the Argyle *Sheaf*, a game of "Who's got the safe?" Loyal citizens of each town delighted in gathering together and with sleigh or wagon removing the safe and all other office equipment from one town to the other. County government of a sort would be temporarily set up in the town having possession of the safe until the citizens of the rival town could gather sufficient strength to repossess it. At times only the counsel of a few calm heads averted the swinging of fists or the brandishing of firearms. After the battle had been carried on in private arguments and heated newspaper editorials over a period of years, it was decided to take the issue to the voters, and the matter was finally settled on election day, when in a violent snowstorm almost every voter turned out. Warren received a majority of 303 votes.

Minnesota

PREACHING LIME. An outstanding institution of early Kemmerer was the saloon of "Preaching Lime" Huggins, who claimed that he never served a drink to a man already "under the influence." Over the mirror behind the bar hung mottoes: "Don't buy a drink before seeing that your baby has shoes"; "Whatever you are, be a good one"; "Fill the mouths of the children first." One patron remarked that he liked Preaching Lime's place because he could repent while sinning and "get the whole thing over at once."

Wyoming

Monuments and Remains

ONUMENTS ARE what the past wanted to be remembered by. Which is no reason to ignore them. They are propaganda (a dirty word in America in the 1930s; still a disparaging word), but then so are most things done in public.

Remains are . . . remains. Often the past didn't mean to keep them, but there they are—what's left over when thieves are done *biting the bullet.*

Social historians, who were fashionable in the thirties and who are even more so today, prefer remains to monuments. They think remains—birth, marriage, and death statistics, census tables, deeds and estate records, literacy counts—are less contaminated with self-interest.

The Guide writers liked remains, but they liked monuments too. In answer to the charge that the past uses monuments to mislead to future, the writers might have said something like this:

"If you can learn what the past wanted you to learn, while at the same time *realizing* that this is what you have done and knowing *why* the past wanted to be understood thus, you have done something worthwhile. You have gotten into another's mind and seen the way someone else wanted the world to look."

———

FOREST LAWN. Forest Lawn Memorial Park, [at] Forest and Glendale Avenues [Glendale], described by Bruce Barton as "above the level of this world, a first step toward Heaven," is a 200-acre graveyard—one of the most elaborate in the world and one of the most important commercially. Those who own burial plots here must be content with flat inconspicuous markers for their dead, though they may erect costly memorials of a type that the management approves for the embellishment of the park. The park's statuary ranges from reproductions of the works of Michelangelo—Forest Lawn is "the only place in the world where all Michelangelo's great works are gathered in one place"—to the Duck Baby, the Spirit of Forest Lawn. There are two churches in the park: the older one, the Little Church of the Flowers, which has a Bride's Room, a carved oak contribution box, a framed tribute from Barton, and alcoves where, according to the management, "songbirds trill the melody of love," became so popular for weddings that a second church had to be constructed to avoid embarrassing traffic tangles. The Wee Kirk o' the Heather is a copy of the church where Annie Laurie worshipped; near it is the Annie Laurie Wishing Chair, constructed with stones obtained from the old church in Scotland; tradition, says the advertising literature, has it that the fairies have blessed these stones and that fortune will forever smile on the bridal pair that sits in this seat on the wedding day.

California

ATHEIST. On a knoll in Oak Ridge Cemetery [in Buchanan], an unusual monument marks the grave of Joseph Coveney (1805–97), atheist. A native of Ireland, Coveney settled here in 1836. His monument, elaborately carved with weathered atheistic inscriptions, was made in England, because no local stonecutters would work on the lettering.

Michigan

BOOT HILL. About 1872 two cowboys, camped on this [Dodge City] hill-site, had a gunfight. One was killed and the murderer fled. The dead man, friendless and unknown, was wrapped in his blankets and buried where he fell—with his boots on. So was Boot Hill dedicated.

Deaths in Dodge City during the first five years were frequent—and usually sudden. Often the victims were known only by a first name or an alias. Public concern with the last rites was brief. Some had rude pine coffins; others, wrapped in their blankets were buried as they fell—with boots on, or under their heads for a pillow.

Merritt Beeson, local historian, and son of Chalk Beeson, widely known Dodge City pioneer, says the burial of Alice Chambers, dance hall girl, on May 5, 1878, was the last on Boot Hill.

In 1879, when a schoolhouse was built on the site, the bodies were moved to Prairie Grove Cemetery; and with one exception were buried side by side, in four rows. Alice Chambers lies a short distance away, alone.

In 1927 the city bought Boot Hill as a site for the City Hall, built in 1929 and 1930. It is a two-story structure built of yellow brick and concrete, with a tile roof, and houses the offices of city officials, and the fire and police departments. A. R. Mann of Hutchinson was the architect. Near the main entrance is the Cowboy Statue, a well-proportioned figure modeled in con-crete, representing the western cowboy in the act of drawing his gun. To the left of the entrance is the Longhorn Statue—the heads and yoke of an ox team molded in concrete on a concrete base. These monuments recalling the Dodge City of the 1870's and 1880's were modeled by the late Dr. O. H. Simpson, a local dentist.

Near the hall is a clever but rather macabre hoax, also modeled by Dr. Simpson, and "planted" as a bit of atmosphere for a Rotarian convention held in Dodge City in 1930. This is an imitation graveyard with markers at several "graves" bearing the fictitious titles of early-day tough characters— "Shoot-em-up Ike," "One-Eyed Jake," "Toothless Nell." Partially exposed and weathered concrete skulls and boot toes give the expected thrill.

The local Rotarians, infected by the spirit of Dr. Simpson's hoax, "planted" an old cottonwood tree on the hillside and passed it off to visitors as the historic gallows tree from Horse Thief Canyon. It still stands—a rope, dan-gling suggestively from a high crotch, draped around the dead trunk.

A veteran Dodge City peace officer, attired in cowboy regalia, is stationed in a small tent south of Boot Hill graveyard site. Tourists who visit the Hill are entertained with anecdotes of early day Dodge City and are requested to sign their names in the Boot Hill guest book.

Kansas

BITTERWEED. In the Confederate Cemetery on the outskirts of [Okolona] are buried 1,000 soldiers killed in the Federal raids. The older inhabitants have forgiven and forgotten the fighting and burning, but they still say that it was the Commissary Department of the Federals that first brought the bitterweed into the prairie. If eaten by cows, the weed gives a bitter taste to their milk, and because the prairie is a dairying section this often bitter-tasting milk is a constant reminder that Federal troops once fought their way across the flat landscape.

Mississippi

LITTLE JAKE. The statue of "Little Jake" Seligman, surmounting a four-faced clock atop the Tower Building in a triangle formed by Genesee, Lapeer, and Jefferson Avenues, is a self-erected memorial to Saginaw's best-known clothing merchant. Little Jake's incredible merchandising exploits made him a legendary figure of the lumber era, and his activities as a banker, real-estate dealer, and operator of a horse-drawn street railway added much to the luster of his name. Seligman purchased the Tower Building in 1890, apparently for the sole purpose of erecting the clock and statue, administrative rights to which he retained, when he sold the building a short time later. The life-sized copper figure of Little Jake, who was only four feet, four inches tall, is attired in a long coat and high hat. When the figure was unveiled, many residents assumed that it was a likeness of some Civil War general, a misidentification that infuriated Little Jake and led him to affect garments and attitudes increasing the similarity between the statue and himself.

Although it is the most enduring of his advertising stunts, the clock-statue inspiration was no more spectacular than others employed by this Barnum of merchants. To attract crowds, Seligman often scattered coins into the street from an upper story of his store, and hired bands to march through the city. When lumberjacks surged into Saginaw at the end of the spring drive, Little Jake threw vests to the throng, promising free coats and trousers to the men who captured them in the ensuing free-for-all. Jake kept his word by presenting the victors with coats and pants, but the vests were usually torn to shreds in the battle, and Seligman was happy to replace them—for $10 or $12 apiece.

Little Jake moved to Detroit in 1892, but before leaving he offered to sell the clock and statue to the city for $1,200. The council demurred, replying it felt sure that such a "public spirited" citizen would donate the memorial to Saginaw. In this, the city fathers underestimated Little Jake's genius for salesmanship. After prolonged dickering, the city paid Little Jake's sister-in-law $600 for the statue and clock and appropriated $150 a year to keep the latter in running order.

Michigan

THE SUNSHINE LADY. In Oakdale Cemetery [Hendersonville] is the tomb of the Sunshine Lady, Mrs. Charles B. Hansell of Atlanta, Georgia. Mrs. Hansell came to Hendersonville about 1900 suffering with tuberculosis. Before her death she requested that she be buried so that the sun would always shine upon her body. In the top of her concrete tomb are numerous lenses through which the skeleton was visible until the tomb was covered in 1939.

North Carolina

BITING THE BULLET. [At Jockey Hollow, Morristown] a large amount of work has been done by the Civilian Conservation Corps in re-creating typical log huts and other units of the Continentals' camp grounds of 1779–80 and 1780–81. From old maps and war records the locations of trails and roadways have been charted. Signs guide visitors to sites occupied by various brigades, to a reconstructed hospital hut and to other points of interest. Lead bullets flattened by human teeth have been found on the camp site. Soldiers who had been caught stealing food from nearby farms customarily chewed on a bullet as the lash was laid on their bare backs as many as 100 times or more.

New Jersey

BIG THUNDER. Belvidere was of early significance as a principal stop on the Chicago-Galena stage route. Among those who lent color to the young community was Big Thunder, a Potawatomi chief. So popular was he that after his death his body lay in state in a small stockade near the site of the present courthouse. Soon the chief's knife, tobacco, and most of his clothing disappeared. In course of time even his bones were filched by souvenir hunters, who, passing through the town by stagecoach, visited the stockade while the horses were being changed. But the young men of the village, wishing to keep the stockade attractive to tipping travelers, obtained a supply of sheep and hog bones and solemnly distributed them to curio collectors as part of the remains of Big Thunder.

Illinois

AMERICAN JURISPRUDENCE. On the highway near the Butler County Poor Farm . . . are two statues carved by A. Burris, an inmate of the farm. The larger figure, *American Jurisprudence*, is that of a woman holding aloft a bottle in one hand and the scales of Justice in the other. The second statue, *Crime Against Civilization*, also the figure of a woman, is a protest against the tendency of courts to give the custody of children to women who are unfit to care for them.

Kansas

LAST MAN'S CLUB. Included in [Stillwater's] educational facilities, which are used by a large portion of the population, is the Carnegie Public Library. On exhibit in the library is a bottle of wine over 50 years old, and the minutes of the annual meetings of a veterans' organization, the Last Man's Club of Company B, First Minnesota Volunteer Infantry, formed here on July 1, 1884, by 34 veterans of the Civil War. At that time they set aside the bottle of wine, to be drunk by the last surviving member of the club. This proved

to be Charles Lockwood, but he never drank the wine, because of its sentimental associations with his dead comrades. Lockwood died in 1935.

Minnesota

ON ACCOUNT. At Hayes' General Store, west of the [East Hartland]
cemetery, hangs an old army rifle, used by a discouraged Civil War veteran
to end his earthly troubles. The grocer took the rifle as payment "on account."

Connecticut

WAR OF WORDS. Massaponax Church . . . , a rectangular brick structure, built in 1859 and owned by a Baptist congregation, witnessed at least
one battle during the War between the States—a long battle of words inscribed by soldiers on the rear wall of the gallery. "How many traitors have
you killed and where are you now?" wrote one Yankee. "I don't know," was
the scribbled answer, followed by, "In the hospital, I hope," signed Rebel.
"John G. Hamilton, from Richmond. Homeward bound," stands out among
lines of vitriolic verse, scathing denunciations of leaders on both sides, crudely
drawn cartoons—all tied together with faintly penciled signatures.

Virginia

CONSCRIPTION. Five blocks north of the [Comfort] post office, on the
main street, is a monument in honor of a group of German settlers who,
rather than serve forced enlistments in the Confederate Army, fled toward
Mexico. Overtaken by a Confederate force at a crossing on the upper Nueces
River, they were attacked and most of them killed. After the Civil War the
survivors and friends of the slain gathered the remains and returned them to
Comfort, where they lie beneath the monument.

Texas

REPEAL STATUE. The Repeal Statue, near the tulip beds [in Druid Hill
Park, Baltimore], is believed to be the only monument in the country commemorating the repeal of the eighteenth amendment. It is a rough stone in
which has been carved cherubs operating a distillery with corn and grapes

in the background. The stone was carved by John Monroe, English sculptor, and was placed in the old post office in 1894. William H. Parker, who had helped erect the post office, bought it when the building was razed in 1932 and presented it to the Park Board with the understanding that it be erected when the "country went wet again." It was brought here in 1933.

Maryland

CONTRACTORS. West Portal . . . is called "Little Switzerland" by its neighbors, because of its mountainous setting. A bold swindle was perpetrated here 40 years ago by two supposed contractors from New York, who arrived to construct a big "Government project." They imported 1,500 Italians from New York, charging each one $5 for his job, and hired local farmers to aid in building a large stone wall in the form of a square. At the end of the month, before anyone had been paid, the contractors disappeared. The owner of Van's Swimming Pool (admission 25¢) used part of the stone for construction of his home.

New Jersey

OPERATOR. The decline of Folsom as a shipping center began in 1908 when a flood swept away most of the buildings and drowned seventeen persons. Near the north end of the town is the foundation of an old telephone exchange, marking the site of the home of Sarah J. Rooke of whose heroism the townspeople still speak. On a night in August, 1908, Sarah, a telephone operator, heard the buzz on her switchboard and answering it, was told: "The river has broken loose! Run for your life!" She did not run. Realizing that many persons were unaware of the impending disaster she called them, one by one, till the flood swept her cottage away; her body was found in the wreckage eight miles below the town. In the Folsom cemetery a granite monument to Sarah Rooke was paid for by over 4,000 contributors.

New Mexico

SCYTHE TREE. In 1861 James Wyburn Johson, a farm boy [in Waterloo, New York], hearing of the firing on Fort Sumter, made up his mind to carry on the tradition of John Brown. Hanging his scythe on a six-inch sapling, now the Scythe Tree . . . , a large Balm of Gilead poplar, he said, "Let it hang there till I get back," and enlisted. He was killed in battle in 1864. The tree has grown around the scythe, so that today only six inches of the blade sticks from the trunk; the handle has rotted away long ago. On Memorial Day ceremonies are held at the tree, and an American flag flies over it at all times.

New York

POPLAR TREE MONUMENT. [In a cemetery near Gnaw Bone, Indiana] is a Poplar Tree Monument . . . to John Allcorn, who was crushed to death by a poplar tree he had felled. There were no sawmills in the vicinity and consequently no lumber available for a rough box. A neighbor sawed off seven feet of the trunk of the tree that had killed Allcorn and hollowed it out for a coffin. Some time later a poplar shoot appeared at the head of the burial mound and became the tree that is John Allcorn's memorial.

Indiana

WHISKY BOTTLE TOMBSTONE. [At the Clayton cemetery] over the grave of Amos Mullins, is the Whisky Bottle Tombstone. Mullins was a heavy drinker and his wife an ardent teetotaler. In her efforts to lead him away from his bad habit she tried everything—cajolery, nagging, threats. Finally she lost all patience and told him to go ahead and drink himself to death. She threatened to put a whisky bottle tombstone at his grave, and she did. The monument is a replica of a bottle, standing several feet high. A counterpart, even to the stone cork, stands at the foot of the grave.

Alabama

F. LoPinto

The Wilderness

BEFORE, SAY, 1750 nobody with any sense liked wilderness. The place to be a human was among others of your kind, in town. The Massachusetts Bay Puritans were typical; they came to America not to make frugal clearings in the woods but to build—in the famous phrase of their leader John Winthrop—"a city on a hill."

What they found was an awful shock, one that resonates throughout the writing of our immigrants. "This town was settled . . . by Germans who immigrated to this place with the promise and expectation of finding a prosperous city," says an old grave marker recorded in the Maine Guide, "instead of which they found nothing but a wilderness."

Although wilderness is nature without man, this chapter suggests that most of us understand it best in human terms. As we see in *hollers*, a few people can make themselves at home in wilderness; *cat fanciers* bring along their pets. Most of us feel more comfortable, though, when we tame wilderness with a story: a tall tale like Jim Bridger's *petrified air*, or a romantic legend like the *daughters of the sun.*

The wilderness in the Guides seems pretty orderly, and that fact is significant. New Dealers, much as they respected nature, wanted to control it. We see this in *The River*, the celebrated 1936 government film about the Tennessee Valley Authority, or in any of the cement-and-steel playgrounds the WPA built for children to skin their knees on.

Or we see it in the heroic figures the decade imagined at work in nature: Paul Bunyan and Johnny Appleseed, who were prominent in poems, songs, and radio shows of the time; the Green Giant, who came out of the Depression with a smile, a jumpsuit of leaves, and the nickname "Jolly"; Superman, conceived in Manhattan in 1938; and such later arrivals as Chiquita Banana and Smokey the Bear, who first appeared in 1944.

BIG BEND COUNTRY. The Big Bend Country [in central Washington], a rugged plateau cut by deep coulees and scarred with patches of scab rock, is treeless except for a few willows, quaking aspens, and cottonwoods, which grow beside the shallow lakes and streams. It is a desolate-looking country in midsummer, when heat waves shimmer over the roads and scorching dry winds blow across the sage lands; and is even more desolate in winter, when storms sweep down from the Canadian plains and drive the snow into smudgy, hard-packed drifts, across the roads. The main highway, a ribbon of gray asphalt bordered by barbed-wire fences, against which winds have piled the skeletons of last year's tumbleweeds, Russian thistles, and Jim Hill mustard, winds toward the horizon. Telephone poles, their green insulators catching the sunlight, race dizzily toward the speeding motorist; by him flashes the endless procession of signboards advertising shaving marvels, chewing tobacco, and patent medicines.

Yet, desolate as the region is, it has moments of distinctive beauty. Spring transforms the barrenness for a brief season: wild flowers and grass almost overnight cover the hillsides; serviceberry bushes, rooted precariously in rocky promontories, become swaying towers of white blossoms; lupine and sunflowers make a tapestry of blue and gold. Even the dun-colored sage takes on a livelier hue. In summer, purple shadows of late afternoon lie on the bare brown hills; seas of ripening grain are rippled by vagrant breezes; and the multi-colored walls of rocky canyons glow in sharp contrast to the green water of the river below. Autumn brings goldenrod by the wayside, flocks of whistling blackbirds in stubble fields dotted with pyramids of yellow straw, and wild geese, flying wedges in the cloudless evening sky, honking their way southward. Even in winter there is magnificence in the seemingly limitless expanse of snow-covered hills, and in the flaming sunrises that transform the sky with rippling colors.

Washington

HOLLERS. Good roads, automobiles, and the radio have brought "civilization" to much of the mountain country; but in the isolated *hollers* change comes slowly and through the young people. Many highlanders live in cabins built a hundred years ago. They plant crops, make soap, and cure ills by the same methods their ancestors used. The mountaineer kills his hogs and splits his rails when the moon is "right," and he plants some potatoes on Good Friday, even if he must dig in the mud to do so. Housewives trudge miles to the nearest crossroads store to trade butter, eggs, and chickens for salt, sugar, coffee, and snuff.

The older generation may have little formal education, but they have a great store of learning handed down by word of mouth. Through them are preserved many old English and Scotch ballads and dances. Even their language, quaint to lowlanders, is an Anglo-Saxon survival. Like Chaucer, the mountaineer often says *hit* for it. Like Shakespeare he calls a bag a *poke* and green garden stuff *sallet*.

North Carolina

CAT FANCIERS. Idaho was once a refuge where birds were numbered in millions, but cat fanciers, tiring of too many pets, now take the beasts on fishing trips and turn them loose. The United States Biological Survey says the common cat, gone wild, is one of the three most destructive animals in Idaho. A domestic cat goes wild in a few weeks, and many parts of the State, once ringing with birdsong, are now in the possession of English sparrows and cats. But the State is still so rich in bird life that a few years ago the Cleveland Museum of Natural History sent an expedition here to discover how many varieties there were. Authorities estimate that there are fifty million cats in the United States that kill hundreds of millions of birds annually, but parts of Idaho, such as the Primitive Area, are still huge bird sanctuaries.

Idaho

DUNES. The dunes rise so abruptly and so surprisingly in . . . the San Luis Valley that they seem to have been scooped up by a giant's hand. One explanation of their presence is that the sands once constituted the bed of a great inland sea and were blown by the prevailing winds against the western wall of the Sangre de Cristos, where they piled higher and higher through the ages. Others ascribe them to the wear and tear on the sandstone of the so-called Santa Fe formation in this region, augmented by sand blown in from the valley.

The sand of the dunes, for the most part, is of extremely fine grain. Under a magnifying glass the particles appear white, red, pink, green, gray, and of mixed hues, which accounts for the dunes' remarkable coloring. To a hiker on the smooth slopes, the sand masses are tawny, but from a distance—they are visible for 70 miles—the colors change constantly with the light; in the glare of the sun they are creamy white, but shadows bring out chocolate and purple tones, and the setting sun paints them a brilliant red. By moonlight, the shadowed and whispering ridges present a cold, eerie, and forbidding appearance; on such nights the legends of the dunes are told anew, in appropriate setting. The only vegetation on the dunes are long coarse grasses and sunflowers that grow in the shallows between hillocks. . . .

The best view of the dunes is obtained by walking across a half mile of sandy waste and climbing upward along the slopes; it is not advisable, however, to penetrate far into them alone, or without water, as there is danger of becoming lost. The dunes are never static; a constant breeze stirs the surface, and the hiker may be walking through an ankle-deep sandstorm while his head is in clear air. When the wind is blowing strong, or sliding occurs on the steep lee sides of the dunes, weird moaning sounds are heard. When persons slide down the long slopes between the hummocks, a deep rumbling sound sometimes reverberates through the sand and is audible a quarter of a mile away. Informal skiing tournaments are held on the slopes; sweeping down from one of the higher crests provides a thrill said to be unsurpassed by the snow sport. During electrical storms the air above the dunes becomes so charged that a man's hair "stands on end."

Colorado

PETRIFIED AIR. Jim Bridger (1804–81), who came West with General William H. Ashley's men in 1822, followed the trails for about 50 years; the whole central and northern Rocky Mountain area was his range. Men who

came to the frontier convinced of their own superiority often had to be led through the wilderness like children by Bridger. To compensate himself for any annoyance, Jim poked elaborate fun at their ignorance and credulity. The "flora and fauna of Jim Bridger's country" became legendary lore. One of his favorite yarns involved a petrified forest, in which he tried to jump across a gorge and found it too wide; had not his weight been supported by petrified air, he would have been killed.

Wyoming

EFFIE, THE HILLBILLY STRIPTEASE DANCER. As hard-surface roads reach inward to the hollows and settlements, bringing or following radios, gas stations, movies, and dine-and-dance halls, the old customs undergo a gradual change. Some compromise with urban ways of living is necessary when the last frontier may be only a few hundred yards from an express highway, sandwiched between a billboard and a mountain. On fence lines, telephone poles, and barn sides, from mining towns in southwestern Virginia to farm lanes in the Shenandoah Valley, posters proclaim the union of hinterland and city and advertise the virtues of "Effie, the Hillbilly Strip-tease Dancer." This type of artist, born of crossroad and urban music hall, appears at local theaters with a noisy hoedown band that probably had its origin in the woods of Manhattan and borrowed its folk-songs from Tin Pan Alley. But it is by such blending that a people will find themselves and cre-ate a native art and culture—a culture that ranges from symphonic compo-sitions of the city to Negro spirituals of the lowlands and from story-ballads of the hills to trade rhymes of heavy industries. It is Virginia and America.

Virginia

STILL HUNT. It was the Indian squirrel-shooter . . . who established the vogue of the "still hunt," still popular in the Kiamichis. With the idea of obtaining game with the least amount of effort, the still hunter goes out at daybreak, when no breeze is blowing to ruffle the leaves of the trees. Finding a likely spot, he halts and stands immobile watching the tree-tops, where any movement of a squirrel will attract the eye. Then the shot, which must be quick and accurate.

Oklahoma

CRAZY MAN'S COULEE. [Outside of Williston is] Crazy Man's Coulee. . . . One day in the early 1880's Robert Matthews . . . , the first settler in the region, was seated on the steps of his ranch house just west of the ravine when he saw a man, dressed in skins and with hair falling to his shoulders, come out of the thickets in the coulee. Matthews knew that no one lived in' the country for miles around, and was interested in learning his identity. When the man saw the ranch buildings, however, he started away, broke into a run, and disappeared into the brush along the creek running through the ravine. About a year later a man similarly dressed, perhaps the same person, came out of the brush and repeated the performance of the previous year. Matthews remarked to his wife. "That is surely Crazy Man's Coulee over there. That's the second wild man who has come out of it."

North Dakota

BIG THICKET. Kountze is adjacent to the Big Thicket, a well-named forest area that covers approximately two million acres, and in places is so thick with undergrowth as to form an almost impenetrable jungle. The paths of Indian hunters and wild beasts were long the only roads through this wilderness, and even the Indians avoided straying far from these beaten trails. The first white man to come here found scattered droves of wild cattle and goats that are presumed to have strayed from the mission herds of the Spaniards. The thicket was said in early times to have been 113 miles long, and in some places, 42 miles wide. Unlike similar areas in other parts of the country, it is neither swamp nor marshland, but dry and rich of soil, except in a few places where widening bayous have formed small muskegs.

Nearly every variety of hardwood and of pine native to this latitude is found here. Of late, lumber and oil companies have greatly depleted the timber growth, but large areas remain in a natural state. Vines, creepers, and shrubs abound, their blossoms running the scale of the spectrum. There are rare ferns, some six feet tall, and botanists have discovered seven varieties of orchids. The streams, lakes, and pot holes are bordered with wild flags and iris, white and red lilies, hyacinths, and cat-tails. Some of the palmettos grow to the height of eight to ten feet before the fronds begin, the more common variety forming a kneehigh mass of tossing green.

Nearly every stream, lake, and pond in the thicket offers excellent fishing. Bears and panthers—once numerous—are still found, chiefly in the more inaccessible parts. Deer bound unexpectedly from cover, and small game is plentiful. The eastern part of the thicket has a Lost Creek, which drops suddenly into a hole at the foot of a large tree between Bragg and Honey Island, to reappear just as suddenly from under a bank of ferns northeast of Saratoga, more than five miles to the south.

The Big Thicket encroaches rapidly on cut-over lands. At one place it is said to have extended 60 miles in the past 40 years. Modern roads now traverse the thicket, and here and there small lumber or oil towns have sprung up. Also scattered within its tangle are the cleared places of settlers, who wage a constant fight against the rapid growth.

During the Civil War the area became a refuge for service-dodging Texans, and gangs of bushwhackers, as they were called, hid in its fastnesses. Conscript details of the Confederate Army hunted the fugitives and occasional skirmishes resulted. Down through the years have come many tales of lost travelers, of sudden disappearances, of murder, and other crimes committed here.

There still are parts of the thicket of which little is known. Hunters rarely venture far into it and then only with a guide familiar with the region.

Texas

BADLANDS. Half a mile away is a skyline with a broken and serrated edge as sharply etched against the sky as if just struck off by the sculptor's chisel. The broken edges of this skyline assume every conceivable shape and form, with here a minaret and there a castle, here a pyramid and there a tower, and here a projection that started out to be a peak and became a glistening candelabrum; this fantastic skyline stretches in either direction as far as the eye can see, with infinite variation.

Likewise, there is no sameness in the mighty wall below. At one point the clay has been whipped by wind or water into a series of fluted columns supporting a giant table. At another, a sheer wall rises to a peak in a gigantic pyramid of dazzling whiteness. Here and there are subtle bands of color, harmonizing with one another, and yet distinct; while at intervals is a band of red. And sometimes upon the benches there is a touch of green where grass or shrub is striving for a foothold, or where the stunted cedars raise their wizened heads against the white wall behind them.

The region is particularly fantastic by moonlight, with no clearcut edges, but ghostly shapes and shadowy walls; it is a city dead, untenanted; a thousand monuments, their faces blank, their feet in shadow. And over all there rests a deep silence, except when some late car roars through a pass, leaving a stillness deeper than before.

South Dakota

DAUGHTERS OF THE SUN. There is a legend that some Indian hunters, lost in the [Okefenokee] swamp, found an enchanted island. Suddenly, a group of beautiful women appeared and placed before them delicious fruits, marsh eggs, and corn pones and, warning them that their husbands would kill all intruders, pointed out a path by which the lost Indians could return safely home. No sooner did the hunters set foot on the path than the women vanished, and in spite of many efforts the Indians were never able to rediscover the island or find these "Daughters of the Sun."

Georgia

READERS OF THE *BOSTON TRANSCRIPT*. The Indian name of [Middleton] island, Achakoo or Atchaka, means "without a harbor," as there is no safe anchorage along its coast for boats of any kind. The island is off the course of ships, and for months at a time no smoke or sail is seen. Since 1890 Middleton has been leased by the government to various private concerns as a breeding farm for blue foxes, and several voluntary Crusoes have lived there. One such, a Bostonian who emigrated to the Yukon during the gold rush, lived for some time with his wife on the island. Once a year he brought from Cordova a year's file of the *Boston Transcript*, and each morning after breakfast he and his wife eagerly read the paper—exactly one year after publication.

Alaska

STRANGE. Strange Creek . . . has its center across the Elk River at the mouth of a stream of the same name. Originally called Turkey Run, the creek was named for William Strange, who wandered from a surveying party near the headwaters of the Elk in 1795; his companions searched for him in vain. Years later, on the bank of Turkey Run, 40 miles from the spot where he was last seen, his bones were found beneath a great beech tree, against which leaned his rifle, the shot pouch dangling from the ramrod. Carved in the bark was this couplet:

> Strange is my name and I'm on strange ground,
> And strange it is I can't be found.

West Virginia

DEER JACKING. [Eastern Maine] is one of the many hunting regions where the illegal practice of "deer jacking," less frequent today, was popular. The bright light of a hooded lantern or of a flashlight fascinates the fleet-footed animal, making him a target for the huntsman's bullet. When shot, the deer seldom drops immediately, but runs sometimes for hours, the hunter in hot pursuit. This phase, known as "deer running," develops fleet runners, particularly in deer-jacking expeditions when the law is pursuing the hunters as swiftly as the hunters are pursuing the deer.

A story is told of a Washington County stripling who, left unwarned on sentry duty at Cedar Creek, Virginia, when a retreat was ordered, found himself alone facing the advancing enemy. He made his solitary retreat from Cedar Creek with the speed he had acquired in deer running in the Meddybemps region. He is said to have reported at Harpers Ferry, West Virginia, 19 miles from his post, in advance of the dispatch bearer, who was on horseback.

Maine

LODESTONE. US 2 passes through a gap in the Penokee-Gogebic Iron Range, enters a dense forest of second-growth popple and birch, with occasional farms in the clearings, then crosses the Montreal River. . . . Somewhere in this wooded region, according to Indian legend, there was a mysterious lodestone so highly magnetized that it drew to itself all metal objects. A malignant spirit fallen from the sky or cast down by the Thunderbirds was believed to inhabit the stone. It was said that once a Dakota war party armed with metal weapons passed by and all but one man disappeared. Lumber cruisers used to complain that their compasses would not work in this region; lumberjacks occasionally claimed that axes, saws, and peavies mysteriously disappeared from the woods.

Wisconsin

IN THE BACK COUNTRY. In the back country around MacClenny and near-by towns the widely scattered families are frequently interrelated, forming a rather clannish group, and are apt to look on outsiders with suspicion. Among themselves, however, there is little restraint. Their social affairs are strenuous, not to say violent. Their dances bring together old and young from miles around; on the appointed night merrymakers arrive in battered flivvers, in wagons, on mules and horses, or on foot, at the country dance hall, usually of frame, hidden among the pines along a meandering sand road. Gasoline lanterns throw a dazzling bluish light on the dancers as the frail hall shakes under the thud of feet in a vigorous square dance to the accompaniment of fiddles, guitar, and piano.

Men leave the dance hall frequently to refresh themselves from bottles or jugs. There is often as much fighting as dancing. A muttered word—a curse— a flashing blow—and chaos! All dash from the hall, for propriety demands that a man must extend his enemy an invitation to "step outside" to settle their differences. Now and again a gun or a knife is used, and another blood feud is started. Rarely are such proceedings reported to the authorities; retribution for anything less than murder is a personal matter, affording no cause for "the law to mess in."

Florida

"AIN'T YOU GLAD YOU'RE OUT OF THE WILDERNESS?" Certain solemn authorities have asserted rather dogmatically that Colorado enjoyed no music until 1861 when Bishop Machebeuf came from Santa Fe to Denver with a wheezy little melodeon. The fact is, however, that for two years every better gambling saloon in the Territory had boasted of an orchestra and had resounded day and night to the combined strains of a banjo, fiddle, and jangling piano, with a cornet or piccolo on occasion. In a spirited but usually vain endeavor to drown the clamor from the bar and gaming tables, musicians lustily played and sang "Lily Dale," "Oh, Susanna," "Sweet Betsy from Pike," and other favorite songs of the day. At the Denver House, a hastily erected log structure roofed and partitioned with canvas, described by Horace Greeley in 1859 as "The Astor House of the Gold Fields," orchestra leader Jones and his spirited men were interrupted by sporadic but not unforeseen bursts of gunfire that sent them diving for shelter behind a low iron-plated enclosure. Before the smoke had fairly cleared away, they were up again desperately playing and singing:

> Ha, boys, ho!
> Ain't you glad you're out of the wilderness,
> Ain't you glad you're out of the wilderness?
> Ha, boys, ho!

Colorado

The Urban Scene

Much of the New Deal's political strength was centered in the cities, and its populistic ideology extolled cultural diversity of the kind found in a large city. For both these reasons the Guides meant to capture urban life in its raucous variety—as, say, Reginald Marsh did in his energetic paintings.

To our eyes now, though, the cities in the Guides seem quite like the small towns of the countryside. Life is slow, almost bucolic; the finding of *no skeletons* creates the same sort of interest it would in a village. The scale is wrong: it is steadily human; we read about individuals, not hordes. And the minority group members portrayed are not, by our standards, "ethnic" enough; they belong to the homogenized middle class.

Many Americans in the 1930s were uneasy about extreme cultural differences and about extreme individualism. Both things seemed to threaten the general welfare.

Also, the New Deal was actually more concerned with rural and small town America than with the city. This country bias runs deep in our character, certainly back to Jefferson. There were, of course, excellent reasons for Franklin Roosevelt's administration to be more concerned about rural America than urban America. Bad as things were in the cities, they were much worse on the farms—in the Dust Bowl, for example, and in the South ("The South presents right now the nation's No. 1 economic problem," Roosevelt announced in 1938).

But both the city and state Guides do offer us some glimpses of the extraordinary variety found in American urban life. We note the contrasts of *U Street* and *Central Avenue*, or the extremes of *Hollywood Boulevard* and *Union Square*. We see people at work, displaying *union buttons*, or *on the beach*, waiting. And, finally, we wonder about city life in the *metropolis of isms* and *hobohemia*.

———

METROPOLIS OF ISMS. Socially . . . , Los Angeles is a medley of many philosophies and ways of life. To the newcomer southern California is a curiously exciting combination of massive mountains, blue sea, Spanish romance, and Hollywood glamor, offering many of them a welcome change from the stereotyped patterns of the old home town. Here is a spirit of live and let live that encourages the transplanted Iowan or Bostonian to experiment with the unconventional in dress, houses, ideas, and religions. Countless movements flourish in Los Angeles, from the crusades of such religious sects as the Rosicrucians, the "Mighty I Am Presence," and Aimee Semple McPherson's Church of the Four-square Gospel, to groups organized to promote a score of economic and political doctrines. If Los Angeles has been called "the capitol of crackpots" and "the metropolis of isms," the native Angeleno can not fairly attribute all of the city's idiosyncrasies to the newcomer—at least not so long as he consults the crystal ball for guidance in his business dealings and his wife goes shopping downtown in beach pajamas. His, too, are many of the notions given form in grotesque architectural effects, and he is frequently of the crowd that rushes movie stars on their appearance in theater lobbies for gala premieres. Yet it is true that most people in Los Angeles, like American city dwellers everywhere, live in the usual apartments and suburban houses, work in stores, offices, and factories by day, and spend their evenings quietly at home listening to the radio, playing bridge, or reading the popular magazines.

California

HOBOHEMIA. Bughouse Square, Walton Street between Dearborn and Clark Streets [Chicago], separates Newberry Library from Washington Square, the oldest park in the city. This is the outdoor forum of garrulous hobohemia. On summer nights local and visiting intellectual hoboes and hobophiles expound unorthodoxy, sociopolitical and sexual. Tourists in the many sightseeing buses that tarry in the square frequently find themselves the target of a verbal barrage.

Illinois

ALLEY SYSTEM. [Freed blacks in the thousands migrated to the District of Columbia at the end of the Civil War.] As the flood swept in, McClellan's Barracks housed them, and then numerous barracks were built in Washington and Alexandria. Two hundred tenements were fitted up at Campbell Hospital. Many Negroes settled in the neighborhoods of the old forts. The Fort Reno settlement in Tenleytown is one of the last of these to succumb to fine suburban developments. In the main, however, philanthropic efforts did not prove equal to the housing shortage. Real-estate agents floated a project that resulted in Washington's notorious "alley system." The deep back yards, and even the front yards provided by L'Enfant's plan, were found to promise more alluring rewards than lovely gardens. Lots were divided and the rear portions sold separately. The first of the ill-fated alleys, as the present-day Washington knows them, were laid out in 1867. In 1897 there were 333 alleys, inhabited by approximately 19,000 people, more than three-fourths of them Negroes. Shacks costing as little as $10 proved highly profitable investments. Here, in these disease-infested sties, ex-slaves got their first taste of freedom. And it is here that, in too large numbers, their children's children still drag out their lives.

District of Columbia

CENTRAL AVENUE. Central Avenue, [St. Petersburg's] "White Way," extends rulerlike for 7 miles across the peninsula, a 100-foot boulevard linking Tampa Bay with Boca Ciega Bay, and the dividing line for north and south streets. Along its lower reaches are faded brick and frame structures that make up the town's original business area of the late 1890's. Westward from the waterfront Central Avenue presents an abrupt mounting skyline; closely grouped hotels and business blocks of light brick and stucco emerge above the trees to give the city a profile. The brick-paved streets and bench-lined sidewalks are unusually wide, and although curbs are low, ramps are provided at nearly all downtown street intersections.

Here, in a compact area, open-air shops, often in ancient frame houses, false-fronted for business, elbow lofty hotels and office buildings—a contrast in style, size, and material rather than age, for the city is so young that its pioneers still take part in community life. Fruit stands and fruit-juice dispensaries abound; curio shops blossom with the tourist influx, offering, among other novelties, live alligators, miniature turtles, and doll-size green benches.

Branches of Fifth Avenue shops lift haughty eyebrows at less exclusive bazaars; health-food restaurants challenge glittering cafeterias, but do not provide the latter's bargain breakfasts, music, and lucky number drawings, nor do their menus include the ever-popular bowl of mush. In busy arcades one's blood pressure is taken for a dime; one can invest in an orange or tung-nut grove, dine at numerous nickel lunch counters, and have the future foretold by a pseudo gypsy.

Florida

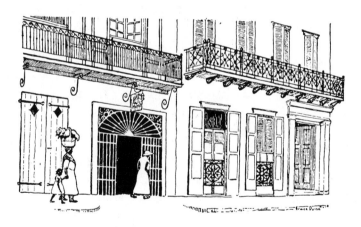

NO SKELETONS. Big Eleven Lake, 11th Street from Washington Boulevard to State Avenue, [in Kansas City,] was, according to local legend, the haunt by night of sinister characters and the scene of many diabolical murders, the bodies supposedly committed to its muggy waters. In 1934 it was drained, the bottom sanded, and the banks sodded and decorated with a scalloped rock design. After being refilled by the springs that feed it, it was stocked with fish from the State Hatchery. The draining took place before a large and curious audience, but when it was emptied, no human skeletons were found, only a gold watch, an automobile tire, an assortment of tin cans, and some fish.

Kansas

ON THE BEACH. Some of the streets near the [Baltimore] water front have a teeming life quite different from that of other parts of the city. The section of town centering around South Broadway is the haunt of the thousands of seamen—ashore between trips or "on the beach" [unemployed]—who man the ships constantly moving between Baltimore and the remotest parts of the world.

This has been the haunt of seamen since Baltimore became a port. Along the shore of this point were the yards in which the Baltimore clippers were built. Having escaped improvement as well as the fires so common in most districts where the inhabitants have little responsibility of ownership, South Broadway remains early Baltimore. Narrow streets, many of them still cobblestoned, are lined with brick houses, close together, whose age is clear in their shuttered windows, dormered roofs, and paneled doors.

Seamen seldom go far from the foot of Broadway. Here and on the narrow intersecting streets—Shakespeare, Aliceanna, Thames—are the stores, saloons, restaurants, and dine-and-dance taverns they patronize. Here also are the Seamen's Mission and the Anchorage (a branch of the Y.M.C.A.). At the union hall, Fleet Street and Broadway, the seamen stand by for assignments, and on summer days when the Broadway market is not used for sales they gather in the lower section to swap yarns.

Greeks, Italians, Scandinavians, South Americans are here—representatives of virtually every maritime nation on the globe. Workers on Bay and river boats are also here, though the blue-water men feel quite superior to the green-water men. There is trouble at times, but at worst these visitors settle their arguments with fists, or with a leather glove holding ball bearings or other metallic bits. Many of them see nothing wrong in smuggling and get past the customs officers when they can, with dope, perfume, surgical instruments, foreign-made pistols, and other articles. As a whole, however, they give the police little trouble; in fact they are more often victims than criminals, being preyed upon by all manner of land sharks and "con" men.

Maryland

WHISTLEPUNKS AND SHOVEL STIFFS. Courage and vision and water, mighty as they were, could not alone build a State or a city. For that, manpower was needed. Men came from northern Europe, thousands upon thousands of them, and for thirty years poured into [Bridge Square, Minneapolis] to sit shoulder to shoulder on the curbs all day, by night to sleep shoulder to shoulder in the dreary flophouses that topped the employment offices, while they waited to be sent to the timber, to the wheat fields, to the railroad camps, or to the mines. The square became the greatest labor center in the Northwest. Most of the jobs offered were seasonal, and back again came "whistlepunks," "shovel stiffs," and harvest hands by the hundreds to spend their pay in ways often highly disturbing to the more respectable citizenry. Bridge Square was a sore spot then, as it is now, but much of the time it could be ignored by a proud city growing steadily away from it, and after all, those high-booted, checked-shirted lumberjacks, and those solid, blond Norse harvest hands brought good money to the merchant's coffers. In those heydays of expansion there was a job for every man, and Bridge Square, while admittedly ugly and perhaps not very fragrant, was generally regarded as an inevitable symptom of the city's youth and vigor.

Minnesota

THE PEOPLE. A visitor may spend weeks in Detroit without receiving the impression that he is in a city of more than 1,500,000 inhabitants. The streets bear a heavy load of traffic, but there is no subway, no elevated, or any visible proof that they would pay their way if constructed. There are crowds of pedestrians downtown, as in any big city, but these crowds soon thin out. Where, then, are all the people? A vantage point near one of the large factories at the end of a working shift will provide the answer. Here is the most exciting spectacle in all Detroit. The exodus of the crowd from a big football game is as nothing compared with it. Shrieking whistles signal the end of the work period, and the factory disgorges a veritable flood that fills the streets almost from curb to curb. It is a flood, not of men solely, but of automobiles, and on the steering wheel of each are the calloused hands of a workingman.

Here are the people of Detroit.

Michigan

UNION SQUARE. Union Square district belongs to the working people of New York. It is an amusement center, but its ornate moving-picture theaters, glittering marquees, and gaily lighted buffets are fewer in number and less persuasive than those of Times Square. It is a shopping mart, but few of its stores have the fine goods and appointments of the Fifth Avenue fashion center: instead, their bare floors may be filled with racks holding scores of garments, many models of a kind, and their show windows, in many cases, are packed with cheap merchandise. The movie houses, likewise, offer the most for the money—double features and "screeno"; the dining places are cafeterias and lunchrooms, where large portions of plain food are dispensed for nickels, dimes, and quarters.

Before these cheap stores, cheap movies, cheap restaurants passes a ceaselessly moving crowd of men, women, and many children, of all nationalities. Hawkers and pitchmen find this street easy pickings among customers who can afford the little luxuries of Union Square—pretzels, sliced coconut, gloves, scarves, neckties, and popular song sheets. They buy magic "roots" which sprout fullblown artificial gladiolas, peonies, or regal lilies; prophecies from a turbaned seer; risqué cartoons; or a dozen low-quality socks for fifty cents. Many beggars—legless beggars on rollerskate platforms, footless, handless, or blind beggars; playing the saxophone, the guitar, singing—move slower-paced through the crowd. The poor, they know, give to the poor. Passers-by stop at the busy newsstands for political literature, and along the curb newsboys hawk the *Daily Worker* and other radical newspapers of every shade. Youths and girls rattle collection boxes for the benefit of many causes— the Chinese people, Jewish refugees, political prisoners, or workers on strike.

New York City

BANANAS. Bananas are unloaded at the Thalia Street wharf, which is used by the United Fruit Company. The wharf has two sheds, one for bananas and another for passengers. The greatest activity on the waterfront will be found where the larger steamship companies make their landings, and there is always a lively scene when a passenger boat docks. Half a dozen railroad spurs run into the banana shed at right angles and extend out to the riverside platform. Here are located the banana conveyors, constructed so that they can be lowered into the hatchways. Workmen in the hold of the ship place the bunches of bananas in the conveyor pockets which lift them to the wharf, where they are taken by carriers who tote them on their shoulders to railroad cars after being sorted, at sight, by men skilled in the profession. There is an element of danger in the work as tarantula spiders and large, green snakes (tree snakes and small boa constrictors) often hide in the bunches. The overripe and broken bunches are sold to peddlers, who resell them in trucks and wagons in the city streets.

New Orleans

D. spiegel

HOLLYWOOD BOULEVARD. Hollywood Boulevard, running due east and west, is the main thoroughfare. Known simply as "the Boulevard," it is a clue to Hollywood's character: a contrast in sophisticated luxury and small-town naivete. Shops, office buildings, movie houses, and skyscrapers make it the central business and amusement district; yet it is also a promenade where people saunter along to look at one another and at window displays. Costumes worn on the Boulevard, as elsewhere in Hollywood, are informal and colorful. There are men in polo shirts and sports jackets; women in a variety of costumes, slacks and dark glasses predominating. White is popular from spring to fall. At night thousands of names and slogans are outlined in neon, and searchlight beams often pierce the sky, perhaps announcing a motion picture premiere, perhaps the opening of a new hamburger stand.

California

JUNK BAGS. Viewed from the piers near the Battery end of South Street [Manhattan], the East River bridges—Brooklyn, Manhattan, and Williamsburg—form a superimposed pattern of steel and stone, like a photograph from a camera that was jarred during exposure. Across the river, on a bluff overlooking the plebeian harbor activities, are the staid residences of Brooklyn Heights, for more than a century the center of wealthy conservative society.

The rumble of speeding trucks, the blasts from nearby steam shovels, and the intermittent whistles from passing river traffic join in crescendos of dissonance. Sailors in pea jackets and dungarees, workmen in overalls, neat office clerks and shabby drifters throng the highway. On mild sunny days the drifters sit along the docks with their "junk bags," share cigarette butts, and stare endlessly into the water. In winter they cluster in little groups about small bonfires; many sleep at night in doorways with newspapers for covering. Others join the homeless men who sleep in the Municipal Lodging House, Annex No. 2, in the old ferry shed at the foot of Whitehall Street, which can accommodate about 1,200 nightly.

New York City

PANORAMA. [The Calumet's] industrial panorama is striking by day and beautiful by night. Broken only by three small parks, the 16-mile crescent of the lake shore, from the Illinois Line on the west to the eastern edge of Gary, is a continuous array of manufacturing plants. In sections of Hammond and East Chicago, factories hug the water front and sprawl southward into these cities. Over the entire district are the smoke of the steel mill, the smell of the oil refinery, and the glow of the blast furnace. Always there is the clang of forge, the roar of wheels, and the thunder of dumping slag.

Column after column of stacks pour forth steamy white or heavy black smoke. Giant steel towers supporting high-tension cables stride over the region. Great gas reservoirs move imperceptibly up and down in huge steel frameworks. Cranes, oil distilleries, collieries, and giant factories stand silhouetted against the sky. Hundreds of oil tanks, silver gray or oyster gray, dot the area like mammoth mushrooms.

Barrack-like buildings of gray corrugated iron blend into the monochrome. Freight engines weave in and out with long strings of cars. Great banks of coal lie waiting for blazing furnaces. Bridges lift over the ship canal so that steamers and ore boats may pass. Everywhere in the composite of movement and noise thousands of workers hurry in and out. The only variations in the whole smoky, busy picture are occasional administrative, laboratory, or hospital buildings of brick, surrounded by small landscaped plots.

At night, myriads of lights outline shafts, tanks, and framework. Flames from open-hearth furnaces light the sky for miles. Black smoke gathers into clouds.

Indiana

U STREET. Of the chain theaters owned by the Lichtmans, three are located on U Street, the thoroughfare of Negro businesses and pleasure-seekers. The Howard Theater, something of a theatrical institution, affording both movies and fast-stepping, high-hearted shows, attracts an audience of both races. Poolrooms, short-lived cabarets, beer gardens, and eating places, from fried-fish "joints," barbecue and hamburger stands, to better-class restaurants, do an apparently thriving business. And yet, when the outsider stands upon U Street in the early hours of the evening and watches the crowds go by, togged out in finery, with jests upon their lips—this one rushing to the poolroom, this one seeking escape with Hoot Gibson, another to lose herself in Hollywood glamor, another in one of the many dance halls—he is likely to be unaware, as these people momentarily are, of aspects of life in Washington of graver import to the darker one-fourth. This vivacity, this gaiety, may mask for a while, but the more drastic realities are omnipresent. Around the corner there may be a squalid slum with people jobless and desperate; the alert youngster, capable and well trained, may find on the morrow all employment closed to him. The Negro of Washington has no voice in government, is economically proscribed, and segregated nearly as rigidly as in the southern cities he contemns. He may blind himself with pleasure seeking, with a specious self-sufficiency, he may point with pride to the record of achievement over grave odds. But just as the past was not without its honor, so the present is not without bitterness.

District of Columbia

BELLEVUE. Bellevue, like all large municipal hospitals, is still to some extent the object of fear and rumor, for in handling vast numbers of humanity's underprivileged it naturally has a high death rate. Almost vanished, however, are such once popular superstitions among the poor as that of the "Black Bottle," used to do away with troublesome patients. In the past, charges of unsanitary conditions, a depleted commissary, political graft, and inadequate care by nurses and orderlies had considerable basis in fact. Scandalous conditions at the hospital—lack of supplies and often food, vicious surroundings, and untrained female prisoners acting as nurses—contributed to a frightful mortality during the cholera plague of 1832, when more than thirty-five hundred New Yorkers died of the disease and a very few who entered Bellevue recovered. Again, the Civil War all but demoralized the work of the hospital. The school for nurses was established after an investigation by public-spirited women disclosed that the nurses "were nearly without exception to the last degree incompetent. . . ."

The pesthouse and prison atmosphere of Bellevue's past has been obliterated. Through the years the hospital has steadily improved, and today it ranks as one of the best medical centers in the world. To the average New Yorker, Bellevue Hospital is a reassuring symbol of man's humanity to man. To the poor of the East Side, admission to the hospital often represents a dividing line between illness and good health, life and death.

New York City

SAND BAR. Minnesota Point, a narrow strip of land, is basically nothing more than a sand bar. In places scarcely a block wide, but extending nearly six miles from the Duluth Canal to the [Lake] Superior entry, it is one of Duluth's most distinctive features. Before the days of the automobile, the more prosperous of the city's residents established a summer colony here where they had a boat and yachting club and a swimming beach. But modern transportation put an end to the seclusion and the Point began to decline in popularity. Recently it has become popular again, for hay fever sufferers have found that its air is almost always free from irritating pollen. For about half of its length it is well built-up with homes, stores, a modern school, and fire department—a village apart. A bus line connects it with the Duluth street railway system. The back yard of a Point resident is a sand beach; if he lives on the bay side of the avenue, often scant; but if on the lake side, wide, white and gently sloping. Often the sand forms small dunes, constantly moving about, burying vegetation; most yards have high board fences or snow fences to keep it back. After a big blow from the lake, a stroll along the Point may prove a pure adventure of discovery. Anything is likely to turn up: logs, trees, boxes, dead gulls, perhaps a beaver or a porcupine, wreckage from ships, light bulbs, and always an assortment of flasks.

Minnesota

UNION BUTTONS. In union-minded San Francisco, more than 120,000 of whose inhabitants belong to labor unions, the principle of collective bargaining has come to be accepted as a matter of fact. In the neighborhood of the port, where the outward signs of the labor movement's flourishing condition are most apparent, longshoremen swing along the streets with union buttons conspicuously displayed on their white (union-made) caps. Big Irish teamsters driving their trucks down to the docks wear union buttons; so do the Italian fishermen, the taxi drivers, streetcar conductors and motormen, newsboys and bootblacks. Almost every restaurant, bar, barber shop, drug store, and laundry displays a union sign. The A. F. of L. unions are strong among teamsters, streetcar employees, and workers in the building trades and service industries, including retail store clerks, hotel employees, and others; the C. I. O. unions, among longshoremen, warehousemen, newspapermen, and smelter and tunnel workers. In recognition of labor's strength, employers have organized in distributors', waterfront employers', hotel owners', and other associations covering all the major industries.

California

TREE OF HOPE. On the sidewalk in front of the Lafayette [Theater] stands the stump of the original Tree of Hope, a Harlem landmark for many years. Out-of-work Negro actors and actresses used to stand around the tree and exchange information about jobs. When one of them got work he ascribed his good luck to the tree and would kiss it in gratitude. From this custom the tree acquired its name. When it had to be cut down because of age it was replaced by another that stands a few feet away. The new one was dedicated by Bill "Bojangles" Robinson, famed dancer and Harlem's leading stage luminary. One of the community's wealthiest and most active citizens, Robinson is also the locality mayor of Harlem. (A locality mayoralty is an unofficial position that is given to a popular citizen by other members of the community.)

New York City

OH YEAH? In the case of the universal *oh yeah?* we have an expression wherein the logical content is no less powerful for being somewhat subtle. It reflects an attitude toward the city's life-processes—the good-humored cynical reproach, the brief signal of frank disbelief, the useful beats of *stalling* in the rhythm of a situation, the projection of the speaker's hope, disgust, anger, love, philosophy, politics or unqualified withdrawal. In his routine chatter, the New Yorker cannot get along without his *oh yeah?* It is his most valuable buffer, knout, pacifier, and bubble-pipe, a necessary protective lubricant in the daily wear and tear.

New York Panorama

Work

Working on the Land

ALL PEOPLE who work with their hands are partly invisible," George Orwell wrote in 1939, after observing the lives of Moroccan peasants. "And the more important the work they do, the less visible they are."
In one sense, though, people working the land are the most visible of workers—certainly to a traveler in a car. And not just visible: comprehensi-

ble. Industrial sites are closed to casual view; we pass a series of blank buildings in which something (but what?) is being produced (but how?). Farmers, ranchers, land movers, loggers—these we understand.

Perhaps, as Orwell suggests, we understand them so well that we close our minds to them. For us, their reality is part of the world's furniture; we move around it easily without ever quite seeing it.

As always when handling the theme of work, the Guides mean to make us see.

Here are glimpses of life on a *trail crew*, of the lot of a *bronc rider*, of work in *celery* and *asparagus* fields. Off the road, but visible to us, are a South Carolina *skidder crew* and a Minnesota *wild rice* gatherer. Bygone trades, like that of *bone hunters*, are not yet lost to view.

The troubles of American agriculture at the time were widely known and discussed. There is a brief appearance by the two groups at the center of liberal concern in the thirties: western *migratory workers* and southerners engaged in *tenant farming*.

BRONC RIDER. Most cow outfits of any size have a special rider whose string is made up of broncs (young horses he is breaking) and old outlaws that the average cowboy either can't or won't ride. Pride is his chief incentive, for he receives only about ten dollars extra a month to ride these wild devils and do the work of a regular hand besides.

Pebbles, a bucking horse at the Cross-S outfit, spent his whole life in the rough string. Unlike others of his kind, he would often go for a month without as much as a hump in his back; but the instant he felt his rider off balance he would begin bucking violently and seldom failed to throw his man.

One autumn in the early twenties when Robinson and Young owned the outfit, Pebbles was in the rough string ridden by a kid from Texas. For two weeks Pebbles behaved and the kid grew careless. He was trying to head a steer on a steep hillside when it happened. None of the punchers saw the ride but all of them heard it. Some of the horse's jumps were thirty feet, straight off the hill, and each time he hit the ground it started a small avalanche. One of the punchers roped Pebbles as he came in sight of the holdup. He had bucked off both saddle and bridle. At the foot of the hill they found the kid, unconscious and up-side-down but still in the saddle with both feet planted firmly in the stirrups. In a little while he came to and was able to ride a gentle horse to camp where the wrangler held him while the cook painted his face, hands, and arms with iodine. For three days the cook fed him soup from a spoon. By the fourth morning when the outfit was preparing to move, one of the kid's eyes had opened a little and he was able to use one hand. Every man offered to lend him a gentle horse but the kid declined. "I can't lace up a tree," he said, "but if you boys will saddle him for me I'll try Pebbles again." And it was Pebbles he rode.

Bronc riders have always been a breed unto themselves. An old Cross-S cowpuncher once remarked: "A bronc rider may be long and thin and then again he may be short but no matter how he's built, one thing is certain. He's made of whalebone and rawhide."

Arizona

CALIFORNIA BOUND. *California Bound*—1939: On the highways leading into California there appeared in the late 1930's, among the long lines of streamlined automobiles, more antiquated vehicles. Like the covered wagons of earlier days they carried all their owners' worldly goods: those elemental necessities that change but little in 80 years—pots, pans, bedding, basins, washtubs. These latter-day prairie schooners, like their predecessors, stopped for the night at wayside camps, where the informality of hardships loosened tongues. Once again campfires burned along western trails—but the stories told around them resembled not at all the stories of the earlier pioneers. "The dust was drifted high as the window sills." "The cattle died a-lookin' at you." "Wouldn't a blade of grass grow anywhere in the valley."

Over the spirits of the starving migrants the desolation they had seen lay heavy—until they remembered that they were going to California. That horizon was a bright one, for they were sure that in a State which supplies nearly half the Nation's fresh fruit and a third of its truck crops there would be a place for them among the pickers. What few of them had learned was that earlier immigrants—Japanese, Mexicans, Filipinos—had swarmed so thickly over the fertile acres that wages never rose above the standard accepted by coolie and peon labor. Or that they would have to make their homes in districts like the one where in 1934 the National Labor Relations Board found "filth, squalor, an entire absence of sanitation, and a crowding of human beings into totally inadequate tents or crude structures built of boards, weeds, and anything that was found at hand to give a pitiful semblance of a home at its worst." For these workers the workmen's compensation law failed to operate, the State's minimum wage law for women and minors was ignored, medical aid was denied unless death was imminent, and labor contractors took an exorbitant percentage of wages—wages which averaged, in 1935, but $289 per family, including the income of all its members. Such were the conditions that awaited 97,642 Dust Bowl migrants in 1936 and 104,976 in the following year. In 1938 they were arriving at the rate of 10,000 a month. Their coming served to bring to people's consciousness the long unsolved problem of how to feed, clothe, and shelter the hundreds of thousands of homeless farm workers who follow the crops over the State.

California

BLACK PATCH. South of the Kentucky Line, US 41E runs through the Black Patch, an area noted for the production of darkfired tobacco. Throughout the year tobacco dominates the scene as it dominates the economic life of the section.

In February or March smouldering fires dot the hills as the plant beds are burned to kill vegetation, seeds, and roots. After the ground is pulverized and the dust-like seed sown, the plant bed is framed and covered with white canvas to protect the plants from cold, insects and wind-blown seeds.

In May or June the plants are set out in a carefully prepared field. The richest farmers use a horse-drawn mechanical setter which makes a furrow, waters the plants as they are dropped and then packs them down with dirt.

But most of the transplanting is still done by hand and must be postponed until rain has moistened the ground.

During the summer months the tobacco requires almost constant care. It must be hoed and sprayed with Paris Green or arsenate of lead. The farmer watches anxiously for rust or wildfire and the ever-present tobacco worm, a singularly unattractive pest with a long green body and a horned head that continues its cycle from moth to chrysalis to worm, defying all methods of eradication except removal by hand. The tobacco must be "topped" to give it breadth of leaf rather than height, and the suckers—small leaves that grow on the plant and sap its vitality—must be cut away.

When in late summer the leaves are dark green and crinkled, the crop is ready for harvest. It is hung on sticks four feet long and taken to barns. There for a traditional forty days and forty nights it hangs above a carefully tended fire. The finest barns have ventilators and a thermometer and hydrometer to insure the proper degree of heat and moisture during the long vigil. But the average farmer uses patience, experience, and "horse sense," knowing that his long summer's work may be ruined in an hour if too much dry heat "kills" the tobacco by destroying the oils that give it pliability and flavor. When the curing has been completed the tobacco is stripped from the stalks and tied into "hands"—convenient bundles containing five or six of the big leaves—to wait transportation to the market.

Tennessee

HOP-HARVEST DANCES. West of Middleburg State 30 crosses Schoharie Creek into the region of the valley's most prosperous farms. At the turn of the present century these were the richest hop fields in the world. Serried rows of uprights studding an occasional field are reminders of the time when Schoharie hops brought wealth to the valley farmers. Villagers today tell wistfully of hop-harvest dances that progressed up the valley night after night until dawn. There was little time for sleeping; with huge beefsteaks and apple pie for breakfast, the laborers returned to the fields to work, and then to the barns to dance again at night.

Decline of hop-growing began in the nineties when the blue mold, blamed on an excess of lime in the soil, blighted the fields. With no effective means to attack the scourge, farmers continued to grow hops for what they could get out of them, until prohibition forced them into dairying and the growing of wheat, oats, and buckwheat; some experimented with a blue potato or sought to solve the mystery of the sweet plum tree that, they contend, refuses to bear fruit if planted more than one mile from Tim Murphy's grave.

Small hop yards have reappeared in recent years, and the natives take heart when they hear again the cheery voices of the hop-pickers in the late summer; the growers still search the vines for the bright-colored larvae called "hop-merchants," which they examine for the gold or silver spots by which they prognosticate the price they will get for the crop.

Summer mornings and evenings the road is alive with large stake-body trucks packed with Italian women and children being transported between Utica and the pea and bean fields in this region; they harvest the crops at so much a bushel, large families working cooperatively and building up a credit of several hundred dollars, which they receive in a lump sum at the end of the season. Some families prefer to accept the meager accommodations that the farmers provide in the low, one-story connected cells that straggle on the roadside and which the temporary inhabitants humorously christen "Blue Heaven," "Never Rest," and "Bean Manor."

New York

KING COTTON. The people in [the Mississippi bottoms] talk about cotton, they dream about it, they wear it, and like millions of Americans they eat foods made from cottonseed oil. In the off-season they are, like other Southerners, slow of both movement and speech, but when cotton is in their devotion to the crop alters them completely. Hours before daybreak they are up fighting its enemies, and their days are spent coddling and pampering it. Even when "the river comes to see them" they do not measure the flood in terms of personal inconvenience so much as by the damage inflicted upon the cotton.

For eight miles south of Wilson stretch cotton plantations owned by the Wilson Company, marked by green-painted and red-roofed tenant houses. Cotton here, as elsewhere in the county, is usually planted during the latter part of March or the first part of April, in carefully prepared soil. A series of gears in the bottom of a mechanical planter causes the seed to drop at regular intervals. About four weeks after planting, side plows tuck the earth around the young plants, leaving them on ridges so that crews of Negro men, women, and children can thin the cotton and hoe out the grass and weeds. The successive warm days and nights and the endless weaving of cultivators and shovel plows to pulverize the soil promote a rapidity of growth which is almost tropical, and in early June the blossoms appear. The blossom is white in the first stage, pink in the second, and at the end of the third stage falls off, being replaced by a rudimentary boll, or square. . . .

During the summer the cotton choppers clean grass and weeds from the rows, grunting with each stroke of their hoes. In mid-July cultivation ceases. There is then little or no work for the tenants to do, so entire families spend long, lazy days on the nearby bayous and sloughs fishing for catfish, a prized delicacy. The first bolls of cotton open early in August, and now every able-bodied worker in the entire countryside crawls with bent back from daylight till dark to pick his 200 or 300 pounds of cotton, dragging a long bag behind him as an ant drags a crumb of bread.

Arkansas

The activity of cotton is in two fever-pitch stages, the first, when the planter is preparing his spring planting, the second, when the crop is picked and ready for market. From December until March, Greenwood is absorbed in handling the planter's crop production loan. For whether the planter owns 200 or 2,000 acres, he has a ritual to follow before he may actually put the seeds into his ground. He must get a waiver on his mortgage and record it in the chancery clerk's office. He must make out a budget, work and rework it until it is approved by the lien holder (factor), the mortgagees, and all parties concerned. His certificates must be signed by the county agent, his abstracts must be made by reputable authorities. Repeated inspection is made of his plantation by land examiners of the various mortgages. All this activity naturally involves endless waiting on street corners and in outer offices, yet the planter takes it good-naturedly. A majority of the men with whom he does business are his friends, and conferences usually end as social occasions. When, at last, after having signed away practically every earthly possession including radio and automobile, and after specifying the exact number of acres to be planted in cotton, the amount of seed and the kind of fertilizer to be used, the number of bales of hay the mules will eat, the gallons of gas the tractor will consume, and how many pairs of shoes the children will need, the annual ordeal of the crop production loan is over. The planter will receive the money in monthly installments, duly witnessed and countersigned.

The marketing season, usually from the latter part of August through

Christmas, keeps Greenwood tensely holding its breath until the price of cotton is somewhat stabilized. For with the price, the whole economic and social life of the town is inextricably bound. Everyone from the tenant Negro to the land-owning planter feels the repercussion of a "good" or "bad" year.

Mississippi

Near the river, [in Selma] Negro laborers, their naked backs glistening in the sun, work among the cotton bales. A laborer pauses a moment, lifts his head and sings:

> King Cotton makes my bread an' meat,
> so why worry 'bout de sun an' heat

And his comrades join in the refrain:

> Pile King Cotton high—
> 'Till he tech de sky!

Alabama

WILD RICE. Wildrice grows profusely in Nett Lake. To gather it Indians paddle into the swamp, two men in each canoe; while one rows the other threshes the rice heads into the boat with two sticks. On shore the rice is heated in large kettles over open fires to loosen the hulls and enhance the flavor. Then it is poured into wide, bark baskets and is tossed and shaken until hulls, stalks, and foreign substances have blown away. The rice is then placed in a cement or wooden vat, and a man or boy with moccasins on his feet "jigs" it, with a peculiar tramping step, to loosen all shells from the grain. Again the rice is tossed, then bagged and marketed.

During the rice-gathering season occur many of the ceremonial dances. Early in the evening natives carrying packs and bundles begin to file into the "coliseum" to the roll of the tom-tom. An occasional jingle of bells and the moving crowd direct visitors to the building in front of which serious-faced men are skillfully drying and stretching the drums over the fire. Within the dimly lighted octagonal dance hall, the drummers on a raised center platform begin a measured beat, and the chorus of voices swells into a musical story of wars, victories, love, and hate. Out of the darkness colorfully dressed girls dance into the circle, using a halt step to the rhythm of the tom-toms. Bending the right knee at each inflected beat, they shuffle to the left and continue the circling, swaying motion. Suddenly youths, dressed in brilliant, bead-trimmed suits with feather and fur ornaments, rush into the room keeping time with the rhythmic sounds. Each youth wears a headdress which partially covers his face. He steps lightly on his toes but thumps his heels on the floor twice with each beat of the music. His body twists and turns, almost touching the floor, and the dance is concluded with extraordinary skill and agility. . . .

Minnesota

SKIDDER CREW. South of Latta lie some of the State's best timberlands. Narrow dirt roads, deeply rutted, head into the thick woods, where tangled vines barely give room for the logging trucks to pass. Farther in the swamp the roads are raised on double wooden runways, which end at a planked island known as the loading yard. To the top of a tall straight "rig" tree, stripped of its branches, are attached guy wires and a cable, like streamers from a Maypole; the puffing steam engine, or "skidder," furnishes power for the cable, which hauls great logs from the depth of the swamp to the loading yard. The scraping rhythm of a crosscut saw is followed by a warning yell. The tree crashes to the ground—gum, pine, oak, or sycamore—perhaps 75 feet tall and from 50 to 200 years old. After being measured with an 8-foot rod and shorn of its top, the log is fastened to tongs at the end of the cable.

The crew calls out that all is ready; the operator of the engine, about 1,000 feet away, answers with a toot of his whistle; the cable stretches taut, and the log creeps to the loading pile near the rig-tree. Here it is sawed into sections, placed on a heavy truck, chained down with others, and started on its journey to the lumber mill. A Negro picks up the cable tongs, hooks them to the traces of his mule, and rides back into the swamp for another log.

About two dozen men, usually Negroes, compose a skidder crew and pull about 3,500 feet of logs a day. At noon the men sit in the hot sun to eat their lunch of corn bread, string beans, and fat back, washed down with buttermilk. Toward night they pile into a truck for the lumber camp a few miles out of the swamp. Whites and Negroes live in separate camps—Negroes in portable shacks with two narrow rooms and a tiny porch, whites in slightly more permanent structures. After a 5-day week of hard work, Saturday and Sunday are apt to bring demoralization. Arguments that pass off quietly on work days may burst into fatal stabbings or pistol fights after the men have visited liquor shops in town. Lumber camps are temporary affairs, remaining in one place for a few months to several years.

South Carolina

SHEARING. At shearing time—late May and early June—the big sheds on sheep ranches are busy places. In preparation for the shearing, the rancher builds jugs (pens) of boards wired together, and arranges a runway through which a few sheep at a time are passed on their way to and from the pens. Large ranches use power-driven clippers, which shear the sheep more closely and rapidly than do hand shears. On the average small ranch, however, hand shears continue in favor.

Professional shearers travel in crews from ranch to ranch. Many start out early in the year and follow the season from Mexico to Montana.

Shearing weather is usually hot, and the wool is oily and heavy. Wranglers shove, tug, and whoop as they drive five or six sheep at a time down the runway to each pen. Sometimes the frightened creatures resist so stoutly that they have to be dragged or half carried; sometimes wranglers "fox" them by leading a trained wether before them down the runway.

As the sheep enter the jug, each shearer catches a ewe by a hindleg and hauls her to a sitting position. He begins shearing at the head, going down the throat or between the ears. If the ewe is a yearling, she is apt to struggle and to be nicked by the shears. If old, she sits quietly, knowing what a great relief it is to be sheared. Rams always fight, and shearers receive extra pay for working on them. Only the most expert shearer can take fleece after fleece without nicking a sheep. A man in a hurry occasionally kills one that plunges. The sheared sheep are cleared out and the pen refilled while the shearer has his last ewe on the floor. At times almost all the pens are empty at once; shearers call for more woolies while they briefly hone their shears; wranglers sweat and whoop and curse.

As the dirty gray fleece folds off, leaving the sheep a clean white or whitish yellow the shearer bunches the wool with his feet and hands, ties it with a string, drops it over the side of his jug, with almost a single motion. At the end of the day he knows how many sheep he has sheared and how much he has earned by the number of strings remaining in his belt. A shearer who can clip 200 sheep a day with the power shears, or 100 with the hand shears, is the object of considerable admiration to neighbors, buyers, idle herders, and other spectators.

While the shearer straightens his back and smokes a cigarette, his helper sweeps the tags out of the pen. The tags—fragments of wool matted with dirt and manure—follow the fleeces into an 8-foot wool sack suspended from a 12-foot platform, and packed solidly—but not too solidly—by a "stomper" who emerges from the sack as it fills. His is very hard work, for the wool, full of dirt and ticks, rolls in on him; his spot is the hottest and grimiest place in the shed. When the sack is full, he sews the mouth with twine; it is then loaded on a truck or placed in a warehouse to await the buyer's inspection.

In the heat the odors of men and sheep blend into one master stench compounded of sweat, oily wool, sheep manure, and tobacco.

The denuded sheep are lank and awkward, many of them bloody; a glance at them explains why "homelier'n a sheared sheep" has become an everyday westernism. They are run through a tank of creosote solution for disinfection, then marked with the owner's symbol in red, green or black paint, and taken to the summer range.

Montana

CELERY. South of San Diego US 101 runs through a dismal stretch of factories, ancient frame buildings and tide flats, and passes among orange and lemon groves and fields of celery. The celery farms in southern California, ranging from 1 to 80 acres, are operated almost exclusively by Japanese. Seed, fertilizer, and water are expensive and the inherent thrift and industry of the Japanese farmer is an absolute necessity for successful celery cultivation. Japanese orderliness is clearly evidenced in the clean look of the farms. Celery seed is usually planted in greenhouses but when started outside, cheesecloth must occasionally be used to protect the young plants from the cold. In either case, from five to seven weeks growth is necessary before it is transplanted. Some areas along the coast harvest throughout the year, with the principal harvest between December and April.

California

HUSKING CONTEST. Brandon [is] a little village in the center of a community where "earmarks" of the old-time husking bee have been partially retained in a new and exciting sport—the corn husking contest. A national contest is scheduled at Brandon in 1938. Whereas the husking bee was a social gathering for the small farmers whose "heap" of corn was counted by scores instead of thousands of bushels, the husking contest is primarily a competitive game, the number of bushels husked being important only in determining the winner. The husking bee in homestead days was a major social event, for that was long before automobiles, movies, or night clubs. Neighbors helped one another and, while husking was only incidental to the social end of the gathering, every man kept at his task, lured by the prospects of finding a coveted red ear which entitled him to kiss the lady of his choice.

But the husking contest is a game of skill, speed, and endurance. The growth of the sport in South Dakota is evinced by the fact that 14 counties entered the State contest in 1935. An outgrowth of an idea of Henry Wallace, Secretary of Agriculture, who believed something should be done to develop a sport from the subjects farmers talk about, the husking contest was slowly evolved to settle the perennial arguments of braggarts as to who was the best husker in the community. Despite the progress of husking machinery, many young farmers today are pointing their efforts toward competition in the annual meet.

Strict rules have been devised to make these contests genuine proofs of skill and endurance. These rules must be obeyed to the letter. With two rows assigned to each man, the contestants line up at one end of the field. The equipment of each consists of a team and wagon, selected by lot among the entrants. The wagon has a high bang-board on one side to deflect the corn into the wagon-box. Behind each man is a gleaner, a sort of umpire who picks up the nubbins left to determine the thoroughness of the contestant. The husker is required to take loose corn lying either in the two rows, or between them. If he does not take it, the gleaner will pick up what he missed and this will be counted against him. Coaching is prohibited, but hundreds of spectators follow the huskers.

The contest lasts 80 minutes and is started by two shots, a minute apart. The first shot is a warning to get ready; the second a signal to begin husking. With the second shot the excitement begins, simultaneously the huskers swing into action. The golden ears beat a rapid tattoo against the bang-boards, and blend with the cheers of the spectators who throng the field behind the wagons, each trying to stimulate his favorite contestant to greater speed. A single shot stops the contest, and the winner is determined by subtracting deductions for gleanings and husks from the total weight of corn brought in from the field.

Taking root first in the southeastern part of the State, the husking contest idea is slowly spreading to other sections. In 1934 Richard Anderson of Brandon won the South Dakota championship and was runner-up in the national contest.

South Dakota

KNEE FARMING. West of Brimfield there are no towns on the highway for a distance of 32 miles. This stretch passes through the Indiana lake region and, although there are few lakes in the immediate vicinity of the highway, dozens of small resorts lie to the north and south of the route. The highway traverses the muck-farm area, where the black, wet mucky soil produces great quantities of onions, mint, and truck produce. This raising of garden vegetables on a large scale is referred to as "knee farming" and, while it requires a great deal of work, is highly profitable.

Indiana

COWBOY BALLAD. During the cattle drives, Texas cowboy music came into national significance. Its practical purpose is well known—it was used primarily to keep the herds quiet at night, for often a ballad sung loudly and continuously enough might prevent a stampede. However, the cowboy also sang because he liked to sing, and he was a spontaneous composer, creating ballads as he rode, often about some incident of the day's work. In this music of the range and trail is "the grayness of the prairies, the mournful minor note of a Texas norther, and a rhythm that fits the gait of the cowboy's pony." Of those early ballads there is no authorship record, and there are few of them that probably were not amended and added to by many singers. The men who devised them did not think of themselves as composers, and in addition they were modest. As one cowboy song puts it, "My name is nothing extry, so that I will not tell."

Texas

ASPARAGUS. From the Sacramento delta region comes nearly one-half of the United States asparagus crop and about 90 percent of the world's canned asparagus. In the level, far stretching fields Filipino field hands, decked in veils to keep the region's swarming gnats out of their eyes, cut the white and tender asparagus stalks as soon as they appear above ground. They thrust their long-handled knives into the earth to slice off the plants underground. The work starts at the break of dawn. The asparagus stalks are left in neat little piles along the furrows by the hands working with feverish haste lest the tender stalks wilt in the sun. In the old days, the piles of asparagus were picked up by small wagons drawn by horses shod with wide plates like snowshoes; now tractors are used, outfitted with tires wide enough to keep them from sinking into the soft earth. The asparagus is rushed to nearby canneries, where it is cleaned, canned, cooked, and sealed—all within a few hours from the time it is cut.

California

BONE HUNTERS. After the great herds were ruthlessly reduced to a few scattered remnants, hunters and homesteaders were forced to descend to the comparatively dull business of gathering up and selling the bones of the thousands of slaughtered buffalo. They were piled in huge ricks along the railroad and shipped East for fertilizer. By 1881 it was estimated that Kansas had received more than two million dollars for bones alone. During this period it was a popular saying that in Dodge City buffalo bones were legal tender.

When Rexford was founded, in the early 1880's, the vast flat prairie here was a mat of buffalo grass so thickly strewn with bleaching buffalo bones that it seemed a field of white lilies stretching to the horizon. Many early settlers eked out a livelihood by gathering these bones and hauling them to market, whence they were shipped to fertilizer factories. They composed a pathetic ballad, "The Bone Hunters," and sang it at their dreary task.

Kansas

SKY-LINE. [Northwest Washington is] a heavily forested region of large cedars and firs. Supplemented by "gyppo" outfits (small crews of men subcontracting certain portions of the job), the work of cutting this great timber goes forward under the direction of the contractor. Logging with a "sky-line" outfit entails expensive preparations, warranted only in large tracts of timber. First, two "spar trees" are selected, one at the pole deck (point of loading), and the other near the far side of the tract. A "high-rigger" climbs to the top of the tree to be felled, by looping his belt around the trunk and driving his spurs into the heavy bark, and then descends, stripping the tall, straight trunk of its branches as he goes.

At a point 120 to 150 feet from the ground, he chops or saws away until the top slowly leans over, falls away, and tumbles to the ground, leaving the bare pole swaying. The rigger clings to it as it whips about. Great care must be exercised in the use of the ax as a miss would sever the safety belt. The great cable is then suspended between the two spar trees, near the tops. Upon this aerial, or highline, is a huge block that acts as a trolley for the several cables suspended from it and the logs, or trees, being hauled to the pole deck. When the donkey engine begins to wind up the main line, the log is raised until it is suspended in mid-air, then drawn on to the pole deck.

Washington

TENANT FARMING. These 225,617 Mississippi tenant families, both white and Negro, are divided into three classes: first, renters, who hire land for a fixed amount to be paid either in crop values or in cash; second, share-tenants, who furnish their own equipment and work animals, and agree to pay a fixed percent of the cash crop (cotton) as rental; and, third, sharecroppers, who pay a larger percent of the crop, and in turn are furnished the land, implements, animals, fertilizer, house, fuel, and food. The first group, few in number, are removed from the cast of subservient tenancy by their relative independence. The second and third groups are the dependent workers. The share-tenants, supplying much of their equipment, pay the landowner one-fourth or one-third of the crop. The share-croppers, supplying almost nothing but their labor, usually pay one-half of the crop. Both groups, however, must pay out of their own share for all that is supplied them in the way of seed, fertilizer, and food. Of these two groups, approximately 60 percent were croppers, or specifically, 135,293 of the 225,617 tenant families, in 1930, were in the lowest category of dependence.

From the beginning of the development of cotton, labor costs have been more subject to control than the costs of land, equipment, seed, taxes, and interest. That this traditional cheap labor is now provided by the tenants is proved by their standards of living. Submerged by practically every other force in the economy of cotton, they are reduced to the level of bare existence. The size of the tenant family bears no relevancy to the shelter provided; it is up to them to crowd somehow into the traditional three- or four-room house on the tenancy. And though land is both productive and abundant, their diet is probably the meagerest and least balanced among any large group in America. Food crops mature during the same season as cotton, making it virtually impossible under the one cash-crop system to raise subsistence crops. Indeed, the growing of household produce is not encouraged by landlords, whose viewpoint must reflect the wishes of financial backers. The final decision in the matter, as on the question of acreage to be planted or the amount of fertilizer to be used (theoretically the prerogative of the landowner), also rests with the men who advance money for the crop. Obviously, the diet of the tenants is largely limited to dried and canned goods from commissaries and local stores. This food and other necessities, obtained on credit during the crop season, is called "furnishings." It must be paid for out of the tenant's share of the crop at harvest time.

Mississippi

HOG DRIVERS. Between 1848 and 1872, Alexandria almost rivaled St. Louis and Chicago as a pork-packing center. In the peak year of the industry (1869–70), 42,557 hogs were slaughtered and packed, and droves reaching 1,000 were driven in from as far away as 100 miles. Like the cowboys, who quiet their cattle with low-sung lullabies, the hog drivers developed sing-song chants. One ran something like this:

> Hog up. Hog up.
> Forty cents a day and no dinner.
> Straw bed and no cover.
> Corn bread and no butter.
> Hog up. Hog up.
>
> *Missouri*

DAIRY RANCHERS. Tillamook . . . , seat of Tillamook County, is the prosperous trade center of the dairying region. Early in the morning the dairy ranchers—never called farmers—begin to arrive at the factory weighing-in platforms, where an attendant checks the quantity of milk delivered and takes samples for the butter-fat test that determines the rate of payment. After the ranchers have delivered their milk they drive to the whey tank to load empty milk cans with the liquid that is left after removal of the milk curd. This whey is valuable as hog feed.

By eight in the morning, after all the milk has been received, the cheese-makers empty the fresh milk into huge stainless steel vats and add rennet, salt, and coloring matter to it before turning steam into the jackets around the vats. As soon as coagulation starts long rakes of wire begin a steady movement through the curd to cut and break it. When the curd has been completely separated from the liquid it is pressed into molds of various shapes that have been lined with cloth. Finally, the containers of the new cheeses are stamped with the trade name and coated with paraffine. The round disks are placed in long rows in curing rooms where cool air of constant temperature is circulated.

Butter-making is now being carried on in connection with cheese-making in various places, the cheese being made from the skim milk.

Most cheese-masters are quite willing to permit visitors to sample the pleasant-tasting fresh curd. Even visitors who do not care for its taste usually

like to eat a small amount because of the peculiar squeaks produced when
it is chewed. Here are cooperative cheese factories that are well worth a visit.
Oregon

TRAIL CREW. Founded in 1880, Vernon was luridly colorful during the
first years of its existence, because of its position on the then active Western
Trail. Its stores carried huge stocks of supplies, for here the majority of trail
masters outfitted for the crossing of the wide stretch of uninhabited country
between the Red River and Camp Supply, on the Canadian. Under normal
conditions it took from 16 to 18 days to cover that distance with an average
herd, and everything needed by the crew of 15 or more cowboys had to be
purchased and loaded here. Then, too, this was the last chance for the hands
to "wet their whistles" in the rip-roaring fashion of the day, and they made
the most of it.

The herds were bedded down on the flats outside of town and held by the
unfortunates who had drawn herd guard positions. The rest of the crew rode
to town, tied their horses to the long hitching racks that lined both sides of
the main street, and clattered into the saloons, most of which had gambling
and dance halls.

So intent were these riders of the long trail on having their last fling that
they sometimes got out of hand and a trail boss, ready to move on, found
himself unable to collect enough sober hands to push the herd across the
river. Often the inebriated ones were "corralled" by force, taken into camp,
and placed on their horses. Sometimes a ducking in the muddy waters of
the river proved sufficient, but many a bleary-eyed cowpuncher rode away
from Vernon in the dust of the herd with a dark brown taste in his mouth
and a head that throbbed with every step of his horse. Those were wild days
and wilder nights, as the town welcomed and said *adios* to passing herds.
Texas

WHEAT. Characteristic of [the] region [around Kent] are the alternate
stretches of growing wheat and fallow land which in early summer resembles
a vast checkerboard of tawny grain and dark, harrowed earth. To conserve
the scanty moisture wheat is planted in alternate years, and where the soil
is not being cropped it is harrowed repeatedly until the surface is a fine mulch
that rises in slow-moving pillars of dust enveloping tractor-drawn harrows as

they crawl across the long undulations of the land. From any eminence on the highway a far-flung panorama of gold and umber gives a sense of space, distance. The wind blows much of the time, and to escape it ranch houses are built in depressions, a circumstance that makes the rolling country seem uninhabited save for ranch crews and their machines, diminished by distance to the size of insects, at work in some immense, unfenced field. At harvest time the whole countryside is suddenly alive with the business of getting in the grain. Tractor-combines, with their crews of itinerant laborers, set out across the golden slopes where a single swath may take a half day or a day to cut. The wheat towns, quiescent during the rest of the year, spring to life as wheat-laden trucks swing toward the elevators. On Saturday nights harvest hands congregate in the nearest towns where cafes, small movie houses, and general stores keep open late. The atmosphere is predominantly male, for harvest hands, unlike the fruit pickers, do not bring women folks with them. At this time, in the small towns, waitresses and female clerks attract more than customary attention.

Oregon

TANNERS AND HOOPERS. Soon after the War of 1812, the hush of Catskill forests was shattered by the ring of axes, the rumble of wagons, and the work songs of men. Shiploads of raw hides from South America hove up the Hudson and were trucked up over mountain peaks to tanneries blooming on the edge of every hemlock forest. Tanning required one cord of bark to every ten hides; since the largest wagon could carry only enough bark for five hides, tanners found it economical to bring the raw hides to the bark.

The hides were "sweated" in liming vats for removal of hair, then passed to the first of a long row of tanning vats containing various solutions of tanbark, sumac acids, and water—the vats close together so that a husky man with a fork could lift a hide from vat to vat without waste of time. The hide finally emerged, tanned and ready for drying and shipping. The process, like a modern assembly line, was endless.

Tanbark peeling attracted many muscular migratory workers who worked for a few weeks in early summer while the sap was high and bark was loose. The work was hard, from sunup to sundown. A good bark peeler could pile two cords a day, for which he was paid as much as $2.75, bountiful wages for the times. Life was one continuous camping out, ever on the march for the retreating hemlock. The men lived in hemlock shanties slapped together in a few hours. The bark peeled off, millions of feet of potential lumber were left to rot and burn on the mountain sides. The dried, brittle logs were tinder for forest fires, and what man had failed to waste, fire did.

Following the bark-peelers, the hoop-making industry developed, prospered on a lesser scale, and died about 1890. In winter, sapling poles, eight feet long for barrels and five for kegs, were hauled to the hoop-makers' huts. The shaver split the sapling in the center, working on a bench similar to the old cobbler's stool. Leaning forward he placed his drawknife at the head of the pole and, with an oarsman's stroke of the body, pulled it toward him.

The hoop-shaving art was largely practiced by men of great solitude who lived in huts "constructed almost as simply as those of the woodrats, made of sticks laid across each other without compass or square." They had long and tangled hair; arms and backs bent by constant moving of the shaver's knife; "dress that was a ludicrous mixture of two-years'-old store garments and the pelts of animals; tongues glued to taciturnity from endless weeks of silence. . . ."

New York

MIGRATORY WORKER. US 99 runs through the heart of the great Central Valley, a desert of almost unbelievable fertility under irrigation. But irrigation demands unremitting toil; the omission of a single quarterly watering throughout might kill every tree and cultivated plant on the vast valley floor. Farming here is not farming as Easterners know it; most of the ranches are food factories, with superintendents and foremen, administrative headquarters and machine sheds. Even the owners of small ranches usually concentrate on a single crop; and they must send to the store if they want as much as one egg. In addition to the permanent employees the valley uses a great deal of seasonal labor that forms a constant problem. The migratory worker, constantly on the move to catch the harvest seasons of one crop after the other—peaches, walnuts, apricots, grapes, celery—never stays long enough in any area to establish himself as a citizen. He lives apart from other residents, occasionally in barracks behind the fields and orchards, more often in crude shelters of his own devising along the river bottoms. Because there are too many who want work, the migrant cannot command an adequate return for his labor. The inhabitants of the towns do not know him and his family and local governments feel no responsibility for him. No one knows how to help him with his problems and no one knows how to get along without his help.

California

CHISHOLM TRAIL. [Most famous of the great cattle trails, from Texas north through Oklahoma to Kansas railheads; its great period was the 1870s.] The cattle were driven along the trail in herds of 2,500 to 3,000, usually under the command of a drover who had contracted with one or more ranchers to move their cattle to the railhead. An average-sized herd taxed to the utmost the skill, patience, and endurance of a trail crew composed of the drover, ten or twelve experienced cowhands, and a horse wrangler or two. Another member of the crew was the cook, known to the others as "the old woman," although his colorful and forceful speech was scarcely in character, especially when trying to persuade dead-tired cowboys to get up for breakfast at daybreak.

After breakfast the wranglers rounded up and brought in the "cavvie yard" or "remuda," as the herd of cow ponies was called. The cavvie yard consisted of 50 to 100 horses, for each cowboy had from five to eight mounts. He used his best pony—one that was gentle, sure-footed, and not easily excited—for night herding. He rotated the others in his "string," changing mounts twice a day.

The order of march was almost military; every man had his appointed station. The two most experienced cowhands rode at the front, one on each side, and pointed the herd. Other punchers rode behind them at regular intervals. The rear was brought up by green hands who were given the disagreeable and exhausting job of prodding along the "drags"—animals that could not keep pace because they were weak, footsore, or lame. A herd on the march would usually string out along the trail for a mile or two. A drive of 12 to 15 miles was a good day's work.

Late in the afternoon the drover or trail boss rode ahead, with the chuck wagon and cavvie yard behind him, to find a suitable camping ground for the night. As soon as one had been found, the cook, who had to know how to skin mules as well as flip a flapjack, unhitched his team, hobbled them and began preparations for supper. As half the crew ate, the other half tended the cattle. At dusk all helped to bed the herd, driving it into as small a space as possible by riding around and around it. Two cowboys were always on duty throughout the night, being relieved at appointed intervals. Those on guard circled the lowing cattle in opposite directions, occasionally soothing the restless or frightened animals by singing to them.

Before lying down on the prairie for the night, and wrapping himself up in blankets, every cowhand saddled and bridled his night horse, and either picketed him close by or went to sleep with the reins in his hand, so that he might be up and in his saddle instantly in case of a stampede. Stampedes were frequent, especially on stormy nights with heavy thunder and lightning. With the roar of a Niagara the herd would be off across the prairie, with all hands trying to reach the leaders and turn them until they came around in a large circle. Gradually the cattle were forced to mill in a smaller circle, and when the herd had at last been calmed it was carefully guarded on the spot for the remainder of the night. Next morning there was always a wide search for "strays," which sometimes were found as far as 40 miles off. Some drovers and trail bosses kept logs of their journeys, like the masters of whaling ships, and these prairie logs contain many passages such as this:

June 1   Stampede last night among 6 droves & a general mix up and loss of Beeves. Hunt Cattle again. Men all tired and want to leave. . . . Spent the day in separating Beeves & Hunting—Two men and Bunch Beeves lost— Many Men in trouble. Horses all give out & Men refused to do anything.

2nd. Hard rain & wind Storm   Beeves ran & had to be on Horse back all night. Awful night. wet all night   clear bright morning. Men still lost quit the Beeves & go to Hunting Men is the word—4 P.M. Found our men with Indian guide & 195 Beeves 14 miles from camp. Allmost starved not having a bite to eat for 60 hours   got to the camp about 12 M *Tired.*

Kansas

On the Water

BEFORE THE railroads, water was America's most important highway. For a long time, the main-traveled road was the *Erie Canal*; we remember the songs of the *chanteyman*. We learn, by indirection, of the wealth of coastal shipping, beset by *mooncussers*.

Much of the chapter we are on the waterfront, with glimpses of the working *bayside*, of the lives of those who seek the *key log* on a Wisconsin river and of *sponge divers* in the Gulf of Mexico. The arcana of trades like *clam tapping* and *smelt* fishing are revealed. All is not work, however; *Coney Island* is also by the sea.

There are water communities: the Mississippi's enterprising *batture dwellers* and the Ohio's easy-going *shanty-boaters*. Water being a mystical substance, there are legends, like that of *Ebo Landing*.

As always in the Guides, center stage belongs to the common workingman, here a Florida *fisherman and guide*, gravely (a word dear to writers of the time) going on with life.

OHIO VALLEY. [US 30] runs the length of the Northern Panhandle of West Virginia, a narrow and highly industrialized strip between the Pennsylvania Line and the Ohio River. Beyond this smoky region of mines and mills the highway winds along the wooded banks of the broad and shining river through many old towns, settled more than a century ago when the Ohio was the main artery of travel to the newly opened West. Water-borne traffic declined with the building of the railroads, but many of the river ports survived to become prosperous trading centers when oil and gas fields were later discovered in the vicinity. . . .

Eastern manufactures were floated down the Ohio on flatboats to the western and southern settlements, where they were exchanged for the frontiersmen's flax, ginseng, beeswax, and hides. Today the same route is followed by Diesel-powered towboats, each pushing a dozen or more 2,000-ton barges, laden with iron, steel, metal products, coal, oil, ore, gasoline, naphtha, or other goods, through a channel maintained at a uniform depth by Government dams. The red flames of the giant mills, under pillars of acrid black smoke, illuminate the soot-covered hills once lighted only by campfire. Here are dank odors of mine pits and the blue haze of potteries and glass plants. The clank of the oil derrick, the chug of the compressor, the roar and grind of metal fabrication processes, the thunder and crunch of foundry machinery, the rattle of mechanized farming equipment, the swish and rumble of highway transportation, the assorted wails and shrieks of factory whistles—all have drowned out the last echoes of the frontier along the narrow valley of the stream known to the first French explorers as La Belle Rivière.

West Virginia

EBO LANDING. Ebo Landing . . . , on Dunbar Creek, [is a] point where cargoes of slaves were landed. On one occasion a group from the Ebo tribe refused to submit to slavery; trusting that the waters which had brought them to this country would carry them back to their native land, they were led by their chief into the water and, singing tribal songs, disappeared under the waves. Even yet Negroes will not fish in these waters, for they imagine they hear in the murmur of the river the songs of the Eboes.

Georgia

ERIE CANAL. The south side of the [Mohawk] river has its share of old Dutch houses, sites of Indian castles and Colonial forts, shrines to Jesuit missionaries, factories and railroads, Palatine settlements, Revolutionary battlefields, old taverns, and monuments to native sons who made good; but greater than these, though so unobtrusive as to be easily missed altogether, is a wide cattail-choked ditch paralleled by a bank wide enough for a set of automobile tracks—the old Erie Canal bed and towpath. Here and there the bed is filled in; stretches of it are marked by huge steel towers carrying high tension wires; the road runs along it for many miles, crossing and recrossing it from side to side, with the river stretching away to the right. . . .

On hot summer days neighborhood boys use the lock as a swimming hole; a hundred years ago 20,000 boats passed through it in one season, an average of one for every 17 minutes night and day. The canal was choked with barges pulled across the State by mules and horses, carrying settlers' supplies to the West and farm products to the markets of the East. Forty thousand emigrants rode the packets in one year. Packets had priority over freighters; if a freighter neglected to drop its tow rope to let a packet pass by, a sickle-like knife protruding from the packet's bow cut the rope.

By 1845 the canal had become the State's biggest employer with 25,000 men, women, and boys working on 4,000 boats and barges and at the canal basins; wages were about $20 a month for steermen, $12 for adult drivers, $10 for boys, and $8 for deckhands. Child labor thrived: an estimated 5,000 boys, "specimens of depravity" who gravitated to the canal from city and country, drove the mules along the towpath; at the end of the season they would "haul up at either end and git what you can."

The "canawler," half sailor and half landlubber, swore, drank, and fought hard. The boys fought for their turn through the locks and were often joined by captains and crews in knock-down, drag-out brawls. Whisky sold for 6½¢ a pint, applejack 25¢ a gallon. The story is told of a captain who sent a boy ashore for rum and bread; when the boy returned with two loaves of bread and one jug of rum he was thrashed for buying too much bread. At each lock and basin, the latter with coal, grain, and supply warehouses, there was a tavern where boat crews laying by overnight would gather, and "the squawk fiddle and the wail of the accor-deen would mingle on the evening air with the rasp of rugged voices raised in song;" they created their own balladry, reflecting their hard, careless, peregrinating life:

> 'Tis haul in your bowlines,
> Stand by that old sorr' mule;
> The cook she's on a racket,
> She acts just like a fool.
> For the Erie she's a-risin'

An' our gin 'tis gett'n' low:
An' I hardly think
We'll strike a drink,
Till we reach old Buffalo.

New York

KEY LOG. The biggest log jam in Wisconsin history occurred at Grand-father Falls on the Wisconsin River a few miles above Merrill. Here 80,000,000 feet of timber piled up in a great mass, damming the river for miles; heavy logs were stacked like jackstraws to heights of 20 feet or more. Searching for the single key log, lumberjacks and river hogs dragged out sticks until a cave was formed in the head of the jam. Each log was removed at great peril, for with the removal of the unidentifiable key log the whole mass would come crashing downstream, crushing anyone caught within the cave. Blasting finally broke the jam without loss of life.

Wisconsin

CHANTEYMAN. The first chanteys used by the lake sailors were undoubt-edly brought here from the oceans, but, as more and more sailors came from lake ports, some of these songs attained a local flavor. The chantey differs from other songs in that the rhythm is of much more importance than the words. They were used to assist a group of men to work in unison on a cap-stan, windlass, or a line where united effort was necessary. Usually some individual known as a chanteyman would "line out" with a verse—that is, he would sing half of a couplet—and then the whole group would join in on the chorus, usually of two pronounced beats that would provide for two good pulls or whatever type of effort was required. The chanteyman would continue with the second half of the couplet while the men rested, and they in turn would follow with another chorus accompanied by two more pulls. This procedure would be continued until the work at hand was completed. A good pronounced rhythm was all-important; the words might be about anything—the ship's officers, the cook, the food, incidents on the trip, or events ashore. A good chanteyman could make up verses as long as the work at hand required.

Old lakesmen tell of a custom that was not unusual, of sailors using the chanteys while in waterfront saloons, where the heaving was done on glasses instead of on lines.

Old residents of the waterfront along Port Huron still tell of hearing the sailors aboard tows of schooners approaching Lake Huron chanteying lustily during the daytime or night, as they made sail preparatory to dropping the tug as they entered Lake Huron. Similar accounts come from Mackinac Island. The crews of schooners windbound under the lee of the island would at times awaken the villagers in the dead of night with their chanteys, as they heaved in their anchors or made sail before continuing their trip. Still other accounts come from a number of the dune-locked harbors along the west Michigan shore, where vessels frequently put in to wait out severe storms.

Chanteying practically disappeared from the lakes in the late eighties with the advent of the donkey engine, which did most of the heaving formerly done by men, and it ended completely in the last years of the schooner era, when the largest of these vessels were converted into barges and towed behind steamboats.

Michigan

MOODS OF THE RIVERS. For more than 150 years [Point Pleasant] has depended on the moods of the rivers for bread and butter, for conversation, for periodic excitement. The day of the sidewheel packet is gone, but the Ohio is still the life force of the town, which profits from its drydocks and the manufacture of steel-hulled watercraft. Although an early traveler described the village as "above the danger of overflowing," the rivers invade the lower levels of the town every spring, an occurrence which townspeople accept with equanimity. When word flies about that "she's risin'," throngs crowd the river banks to exchange reminiscences of past floods and speculations on the size of the imminent one. The flood finds the town in holiday humor; every garage gives birth to a johnboat, and the average householder, having stowed his goods safely on the second floor, spends his time rowing about the streets in conventional flood attire—heavy jacket, hip boots, and derby hat.

West Virginia

BAYSIDE. The industrial life of [Everett] centers in the area along the bayside and the river front. Here, fringing the city, are factories and mills with their stacks and burners, smoking volcanoes by day and glowing infernos by night. Except when a holiday or curtailed production brings a temporary lull, the air reverberates with the whine of saws, the strident blasts of whistles, the hiss of steam, and the clank of wheels as engines shunt cars of freight on the sidings.

Moored along the docks are freighters, their strong booms swinging incoming cargo to the docks and outgoing cargo, mostly lumber and lumber products, to the decks and into the holds. Quickly the gangs of longshoremen load and unload the slings, expertly using their claw-like hooks, and alert to the hazards of snapping cables and shifting cargo. Trucks rumble over the docks, which vibrate on supporting pilings. Dotting the bay are numerous pleasure craft, trawlers, sturdy tugs with rafts of logs in tow, and rowboats, in which fishermen drift for hours with the tide or row, race forward, with the peculiar skill and ease acquired only through years of practice.

The prevailing westerly winds are usually brisk and occasionally become gales that whip the slate-gray waters of the bay into whitecaps. Sometimes a pall of fog settles over the area, and then foghorns moan their warnings to shipping. The salt air is charged with the pungent odor of seaweed from the brine-soaked tidelands, the resinous tang of newly cut lumber and of smoke from the burning slabs and sawdust, the clean odor of tar from nets and creosoted pilings, and the musty smell of rotting logs, heavy with barnacles. At night the low, musical throb of Diesel engines and the impatient chugging of gasoline motors float across the water, or the whistle of a train, clear and resonant, echoes through the moisture-laden air.

Washington

CONEY ISLAND. Summer crowds are the essence of Coney Island. From early morning when the first throngs pour from the Stillwell Avenue subway terminal, humanity flows over Coney seeking relief from the heat of the city. Italians, Jews, Greeks, Poles, Germans, Negroes, Irish, people of every nationality; boys and girls, feeble ancients, mothers with squirming children, fathers with bundles, push and collide as they rush, laughing, scolding, sweating, for a spot on the sand.

The mass spreads southward in the direction of the beach and boardwalk and the numerous bathhouses. The bathhouses range from large establishments with sports facilities, swimming pools, and restaurants to minute backyard dressing rooms. One of the largest is the Municipal Baths, Surf Avenue and West Fifth Street, where lockers rent for ten and twenty-five cents each. From the boardwalk the whole beach may be viewed: bathers splash and shout in the turgid waters close to the shore; on the sand, children dig, young men engage in gymnastics and roughhouse each other, or toss balls over the backs of couples lying amorously intertwined. Luncheon combines the difficulties of a picnic with those of a subway rush hour; families sit in wriggling circles consuming food and drinking from thermos bottles brought in suitcases together with bathing suits, spare clothing, and water wings.

A moving throng covers the boardwalk from the outer rail to the food and amusement booths. The air is heavy with mixed odors of frying frankfurters, popcorn, ice cream, cotton candy, corn-on-the-cob, and *knishes* (Jewish potato cakes). Skee ball, ping pong, beano and other amusements and games of chance are played and watched by hundreds.

After sunset the Island becomes the playground of a mixed crowd of sightseers and strollers. On the Bowery, wedged between Surf Avenue and the boardwalk from Feltman's to Steeplechase, the shouts of competing barkers become more strident, the crowd more compact. Enormous paintings in primitive colors advertise the freak shows, shooting galleries, and waxworks "Chamber of Horrors." Riders are whirled, jolted, battered, tossed upside down by the Cyclone, the Thunderbolt, the Mile Sky Chaser, the Loop-o-Plane, the Whip, the Flying Turns, the Dodgem Speedway, the Chute-the-Chutes, and the Comet. Above the cacophony of spielers, cries, and the shrieks and laughter, carrousel organs pound out last year's tunes, and roller coasters slam down their terrific inclines. In dance halls and honky-tonks, dancers romp and shuffle to the endless blare of jazz bands.

About midnight, the weary crowds begin to depart, leaving a litter of cigarette butts, torn newspapers, orange and banana peel, old shoes and hats, pop bottles and solid cardboard boxes, and an occasional corset. A few couples remain behind, with here and there a solitary drunk, or a sleepless old man pacing the boardwalk. The last concessionaire counts his receipts and puts up his shutters, and only the amiable roar of the forgotten sea is heard.

New York City

BURNING ICE. Pepin . . . , first settled in 1846, has quiet streets, sloping lazily toward the river. Along the water front are sleepy hotels where fishermen gather about the stove and spend the long winter hours swapping yarns. Their speech draws many images from the great river. Seeing a drunken man staggering up the street in early spring, an idler remarks, "He's sure goin' up the river," and his crony replies, "Yep, he's gonna burn all the ice out of Lake Pepin."

Much in Pepin is reminiscent of the time when the river brought a steady flow of commerce and strangers; many of the people here remember the life Mark Twain wrote about, when boats shallow enough to "flat on a heavy dew" moved slowly among the bars and bottoms of the river.

Wisconsin

FISHERMAN AND GUIDE. Florida fishermen are of two types: the net fishermen and the sportsman's guide. The former are always vitally interested in whether mullet, Florida's staple fish, will bring 3¢ or 4¢ a pound on a particular day. In every fishing village stand great racks on which nets hang drying in the sun. While the menfolk concern themselves with the catching, icing, and marketing of fish, the women keep the nets in repair, constantly mending and reweaving gaps torn by sharp fins. Long before daylight, fishermen and their families are up preparing for the day's toil. Dawn finds their small string of boats, the majority provided with "kickers" (small engines), heading for the tidal lagoons and the narrow channels between the reefs. Just before the tide changes, nets are set in wide semi-circles to catch the fish as they come down with the tide. When the fish strike the net, their gills become enmeshed. Hauled in, the fish are dumped into bins partially filled with cracked ice for delivery at the market before sundown.

The sportsman's guide, usually a lone wolf, owns a sturdy motor launch, kept spotlessly clean, in which he carries from two to a half dozen anglers into the Gulf for deep-sea fishing. He knows the best fishing grounds and the hours that bring the grouper, mackerel, king fish, snapper, or tarpon to the banks and passes. On board are flies, plugs, hand lines, spoons, rods, reels, gaffs, sinkers, leaders, and bait: shrimp, shiners, crabs, and cut bait. The guide is less interested in the quantity of the catch than in the sport afforded his patrons. A number of good strikes and a few big fish landed make a successful day for him. Chartered boats for deep-sea fishing are available at a number of Carrabelle piers.

Florida

MOONCUSSERS. [One section of Marblehead] is Barnegat, long ago named for the town on the New Jersey coast where "mooncussers" lured vessels to destruction by false lights from shore, with the purpose of plundering their cargoes. (A mooncusser is one who curses the moon for its hindrance to his nefarious designs.)

Massachusetts

ALE-WIVES. [At Fairport] are factories of the menhaden industry, large brick and frame buildings with towering smokestacks. Here oil is extracted from menhaden, and fertilizer is manufactured from the residue. The fish— called also "ale-wives"—of a variety not commonly used as food, are related to both shad and herring and resemble shad in form and color. They are caught in the Atlantic off the coast of Virginia and Maryland, from steamers equipped with "purse nets" from 1,080 to 1,200 feet long. These nets are hauled between two row (purse) boats. When a school of fish is sighted by the lookout, the small boats are rowed parallel to each other until they reach "striking distance." Then the boats describe a circle in their course, each paying out its part of the net. When the boats meet, completing the circle, the ends of the net are fastened together, and a "tom" (a ball of lead) is thrown overboard to form a fulcrum by which to "purse" the net at the bottom. This is accomplished by means of a line attached to a ring in the tom and by other ropes passed through rings attached to the net at bottom and sides. The bottom of the net thus is brought together, forming a bag and enclosing the fish.

The steamer conveys its catch to the factory where the fish are boiled in large vats to extract the oil. Some steamers are equipped to "cook" aboard during the fishing. The average catch is about 350,000 fish. The yield of oil is from five to six gallons per 1,000 fish. The product is marketed as whale oil, olive oil, and cod-liver oil, in diminutive bottles, the labels of which proclaim it as cure for many ills.

Virginia

CLAM TAPPING. [Damariscotta] clammers, who live in shacks near the salt water during the summer, tap along the beaches at low tide, causing the clams, disturbed by the vibrations, to spout out tiny streams of water that betray their hiding places in the mud.

Maine

SPONGE DIVERS. With the perfection of deep-sea diving equipment in 1905, a colony of Greek sponge fishermen abandoned the waters of Key West and the method of "hooking" sponges with long poles in shallow water, and came [to Tarpon Springs] to fish far out to sea, using divers to gather the sponges. Because of their willingness to remain at sea for long periods, their courage in overcoming the hazards of their craft, and their sound marketing methods, they have made Tarpon Springs one of the largest sponge markets in the world. As in other fishing communities, the life of the Greek colony centers around the docks, on the Anclote River, to which the 70 or more boats in the fleet bring their catches. . . .

When the fleet departs, a bearded priest of the Greek Orthodox Church blesses each boat, and the air is filled with the calls and farewells of friends and families of the fishermen. While it is away, the houses clustered around the docks look like a discarded stage set. The only stir is in the stores, restaurants, and a few curio shops. But four times a year, barring storms, the fleet turns homeward with its cargo of sponges—always for Epiphany services, always at Easter, and then the whole community assembles to greet it. The gaily-painted boats come slowly up the Anclote channel, their decks heaped high with sponges; soft rubber diving suits dangle grotesquely from the stays. Blue and white pennants fly at the mastheads, and the Stars and Stripes at the sternposts, and lettered high on the bows are such names as *Venus*, *Apollo*, *Venizelos*, or *Bozzaris*, the last for the doughty Greek patriot who "slew a thousand Turks before breakfast." As the boats are warped in and tied up, the docks and narrow lanes about them ring with music, laughter, and the rhythm of folk dances.

The olive-skinned spongers debark immediately to celebrate in churches and in other places less sacred, leaving their haul behind to be sold at the Cooperative Warehouse, a rambling jail-like structure with iron-grilled storage cells that segregate the catches. In an open court sponges are sold at auction each Tuesday and Friday. Members have the right to reject bids which they do not consider high enough. Annual sales approximate $1,000,000.

Many who come to visit Tarpon Springs wonder at the size of the fishery, not realizing the innumerable uses of sponge. In addition to its conventional bathroom uses, sponge is in demand by surgeons and by manufacturers of linoleum and soundproofing materials, and is utilized for padding clothes, for fertilizers, and for cleaning garments. In glass factories it is indispensable, since it is fireproof and can be used for wiping off hot glass.

In the course of their operations the sponge fishermen occasionally make rare and valuable finds on the ocean floor. In 1938 a local deep-sea diver, Sozon Vatikiosis, brought in two seashells of hitherto unknown varieties, described by the Smithsonian Institution at Washington, to which they were sent, as "tea-rose blossoms turned to stone in the full flush of their blooming." In honor of the diver, one was named *Conus sozoni B.*, and the other was named for his wife, *Fusinus helenae B.*; in accordance with scientific practice, the "B." is for Dr. Paul Bartsch, Curator of Mollusks at the Smithsonian, to show that he named them. The value of these shells, the only ones of their kind yet discovered, can be judged from the fact that collectors pay from $600 to $800 for a specimen of another beautiful variety, of which there are 22 known examples.

Florida

BATTURE DWELLERS. Batture dwellers, who build their houses of driftwood salvaged from the Mississippi, inhabit a ramshackle shanty town sometimes called "Depression Colony," located between Carrollton Avenue and the protection levee at the Jefferson Parish line. It is composed of a wide variety of shacks, neat little cottages, and houseboats. The houses are built on stilts and are safe from all but the highest flood stages. During low water the batture is laid out in little gardens with chicken coops and pig pens. When the water rises, the livestock is taken up on the little galleries that run at least part way around each house and the occupants remain at home until "Ole Man River" becomes too dangerous. Driftwood in the river supplies ample fuel; the river, plenty of fish; and the nearby willows, material out of which wicker furniture can be made and sold from house to house in the city. There is no rent to pay, as the batture is part of the river and the property of the United States, and consequently beyond the reach of local ownership or taxation. The varied occupations of the dwellers include fishing, wood-gathering, and automobile repair work; many work on Federal relief projects. Drinking water is procured from the neighborhood merchants.

New Orleans

SHANTY-BOATERS. Below Eureka the Ohio winds in a series of broad sweeping curves, with the sharp rubble banks of the upper valley giving way to swampy spongy shores on both sides. As fishing is good here, the stretch is a frequent port of call for shanty-boaters. These boats, generally flat bottomed, but often built to resemble an ark, cruise the thousand miles between Pittsburgh and Cairo each year. The shanty-boater lives in the small cabin on his craft; the river and its banks provide his food; driftwood for heating and cooking is to be had for the taking, while a little backdoor begging at farmhouses usually provides him with castoff clothing. More energetic shanty-boaters work a few days each week ashore; they are invariably jacks-of-all-trades, their footloose life developing in them both an amazing versatility in handicrafts and an earnest desire to practice these crafts as seldom as possible.

Not all houseboat dwellers are shanty-boaters, this term being applied mainly to those whose wanderlust keeps them from settling in one spot for any great length of time. Cheerful, hospitable with what little he has, shiftless and slovenly, the typical shanty-boater leads a fairly carefree existence. His whims and moods are dictated by the vagaries of the river, which gives him sustenance and transportation. When left high and dry, he shores up his boat and waits for high water to put him afloat again—a few months of waiting mean nothing in his life of leisure. He is generally law-abiding, but his neighbors include a few elements who impart a bad reputation to all shanty-boaters by distilling and selling cheap whisky, and by hiding criminals until all trace of them is lost in the vague peregrinations and trackless wanderings of the boats. Yet his fellow boatmen include a number of Gospel preach-ers—elderly men, as a rule, who have grown weary of worldliness and ded-icated themselves to the regeneration of the water gypsies. These preachers travel continuously, and their boats are welcome wherever shanty-boatmen congregate.

West Virginia

PEARL BUTTONS. Today [Andalusia's] sole industry is the manufacture of pearl buttons from clam shells found in the shallow sloughs and lagoons of the Mississippi. The clams are gathered in flatboats that drag behind them chains with dozens of four-pronged hooks. Open mussels close their shells instantly upon the hooks and are hauled into the boat; in shallow water the clams are gathered with rakes and forks. Button-making is a slow and tedious hand operation; each button is shaped singly by a rapidly revolving, water-cooled, cylindrical cutter, against which the shell is held. The size of the buttons is determined by the shape and thickness of the shell, which vary widely in different kinds of mussels.

Illinois

SMELT. The summer homes and cottages of Boyne City . . . extend more than four miles on both sides of Lake Charlevoix and up the Boyne River from its mouth. In contrast, the business section is small and compact. Still standing are the ruins of a sawmill, a charcoal foundry, and other plants utilizing forest products. A sole leather factory employs approximately 300 men the year round, but the tourist trade is the principal source of revenue. The smelt runs in the river in late March or April (the fish do not move until water temperature reaches 36°) start the recreational season. Some 4,000 visitors attend the three-day Smelt Festival, ceremonies of which include the crowning of a Smelt Queen, and a banquet. When a run starts, usually at midnight or later, an official turns on lights over the river and fires his gun.

At this signal, thousands of people with nets and waders rush into the water. For 30 minutes the fishermen stumble about and dip frantically, putting their catch into barrels, baskets, and sacks, or piling the fish in heaps along the shore. Then the lights go off and the dippers are ordered out of the water. About three hours later, a second period begins, and, if fish are still plentiful, a third dipping is permitted just before daylight. The netting goes on until the spring run is ended, the catch usually exceeding 25 tons of marketable fish. In winter, hooking the smelt through the ice of Lake Charlevoix is a popular sport. About 400 fishing huts are hauled onto the ice to make the shanty community, Smeltania, which has a mayor, city manager, and a police force to direct traffic. For the season's largest catch, usually exceeding 8,000 smelts taken by hook and line, a prize is awarded.

Michigan

Factory and Workshop

IN OTHER chapters of this book, the Guides depict work on land and water. Here the focus is indoors and, generally, industrial.

American writers of the thirties saw factory work as the unexplored frontier of their craft, much as writers of the 1960s saw sex. They wanted to find a language adequate to describe what takes place on an *assembly line*, making *paper* or *plate glass*, in a *steel mill* or *mill village*. As you will note, the language they came up with borrows, of necessity, from the jargon of specific trades.

The way the writers treat these special "trade" words, often putting them in quotation marks so they will not be buffeted by the ordinary words in a sentence, suggests the respect that most intellectuals then felt for physical labor and the people who do it. The critic Henry Hart wrote in 1935 that "the day in a life of a man who spends nine hours in front of a punch press or on a ship has more reality, more beauty and more harmony than you will find in all of Park Avenue." The patient thoroughness with which industrial work is described here means to tell us readers that, as the woman says in *Death of a Salesman*, attention must be paid.

MILL VILLAGE. At 5:30 in the morning the mill whistle rouses the sleeping village. Women hastily cook breakfast—grits, coffee, fatback, puffy biscuits, and sometimes eggs. Overalled men sit down to the table with their womenfolk, who wear cotton dresses and rayon stockings, and have permanent waves. A few minutes later, at three warning blasts of the whistle, hundreds of men and women from 16 to 50—but most of them from 20 to 35—hurry to their places in the mill. The buzzing of spindles and clattering of looms, so deafening to the visitor, do not disturb the accustomed ear; nor do workers seem to mind the heavy close air. Some mill hands develop an affection for their machines. "I shore love it," said one man of his loom. "This same one has belonged to me for 25 years or more. But I'm scared of it just the same—it'll bite me if I don't watch out."

Bales of cotton are brought from the warehouse to the bale-breaker, which splits open the 500-pound bundle of lint. The cotton is sucked through a vacuum tube to the picker-room, where trash that escaped the gin is removed. Then it goes through the lapper and slubber, which form it into bands, first broad, then narrow. These are seized by the carder with its hundreds of little teeth that shape the lint into loose rolls, ready to be twisted by the spindles into tight, strong thread. Some of the thread is wound on bobbins for the woof, or cross-thread of the cloth. Young workers grab the full bobbins from the machines, and replace them with empty ones. In the slasher room the warp, or lengthwise thread, is dipped in starch and wound on drums. After the warp dries, the drums are attached to looms in the weaving room. The bobbins dart back and forth between the alternating threads of the warp, and the cloth is woven. The whole process is merely an intricate mechanization of the age-old craft of spinning and weaving. Negroes are employed about the warehouses, power plants, and grounds, but seldom operate machines. Women generally work the spindles and men the looms. The finished cloth is inspected by girls, and sent to the baling machines, where it is wrapped for sale. It is usually bleached and printed at another mill.

There are many pauses in the eight-hour shift, during which workers go out for a cold drink or a cigarette, some of the older women dip snuff and gossip, the young folks make dates, and the men discuss lodge affairs, politics, or "the union." When the noon whistle blows, everybody swarms home to dinner—fried meat, bread, coffee, fresh or canned vegetables—eaten to the blaring of a radio. The workers are in the mill again from 1 to 4 o'clock; the second shift then takes charge if business is good. Farm and factory are closely related in South Carolina, and the spirit of independence traditional on the farm is often retained in the mill village. But a vague boundary line has grown up. The mill worker, obedient to whistles and machines and economic authority, feels himself different. Once begun, the mill life is hard to escape. Marriages are early and large families the rule. A man needs children to support him when his eyes are too dim and his hands too stiff to tend the machines.

South Carolina

ASSEMBLY LINE. On entering the interior of the automobile factory, the visitor is momentarily stunned by the deafening noise and the feverish motion of men and machinery, under the light of overhead arc lamps. Machinery is everywhere; presses, drills, grinders, punches, and cranes swing and gyrate and throb. Loaded conveyors pass overhead, following an intricate pattern. Electric trucks move slowly through the aisles. Amid the apparent confusion, men labor intently. Groups of workers hover around a huge press, timing their movements to the mechanical monster; here and there goggles, masks, or hoods cover faces bent over sputtering welding machines. In the aisles, in the recesses between lathes, workers carry tools, run errands, deliver messages, consult charts and schedules.

The impression of chaos soon changes, and the seemingly unrelated activities are recognized as parts of a whole that functions with clock-like coordination. "Progressive assembly" brooks no interference or deviations. The naked frame is placed on the "line," which runs the entire length of the factory. Moving slowly, the chassis is "dressed," as other parts are attached to it by mechanics who stand in a row on each side, each worker performing a single operation as the unit reaches him. Axles and wheels are attached as the frame proceeds; motor and radiator are installed. At the final assembly, the body, which has been traveling along a different conveyor, is lowered to the frame. Instruments and lights are installed and connected, and, after a final inspection, the car leaves the line under its own power.

Michigan

MEN. Detroit needed men. Not skilled men. Just ordinary, healthy, fast-moving men, preferably young and only intelligent enough to do as they were told and determined enough to keep doing it.

Well, men were available. The boys of those unfortunates who had bought the submarginal acres up in the pine belt were ready to go out on their own. And there wasn't much need of them at home. A man could work his back sore and his heart sick even on pretty good land, those times, and not get anywhere.

So into Detroit went the sons of farmers. And the sons of small-town merchants who were having a struggle because the farms weren't doing so well. And the sons of lumber jacks, who had figured on going to the woods themselves, even if the woods were only remnants of what they had been when their fathers were young. And the sons of miners who were spending more days sitting around the house than they were in the shafts. Township after township was drained of its youth. Older men went, because in those days your fortieth birthday had not become a point of terror. County after county was tapped for labor, and still it was not enough. Up from the Appalachians came another army. From the Deep South arrived the Negro by thousands. The World War ended. Old nations, revived nations, nations never heard of before Versailles, poured their legions into Detroit, to become parts of Michigan, and how is a State type to evolve under conditions such as those?

Michigan

FURNITURE. The manufacture of furniture begins in the lumber yard, where various kinds of lumber are piled on trucks and transported to dry kilns to be seasoned and dried. The material is then removed to the culling room, where it is cut into suitable lengths. Thence it is sent to the machine room to be fashioned into various sizes and shapes, according to style and design. In the upholstering department, women cut and sew materials, while the men specialize in "springing up"—arranging and tying the springs. Skilled workers perform the upholstering proper. A greater division of labor, resembling the assembly line of an automobile factory, has recently been introduced in the trade. No one man finishes an entire job. Some upholster only the arms, others the backs, while still others produce only cushions. In the finishing room, workmen apply coats of filler, stain, and varnish. Before the last coat, the first and second applications are rubbed, to produce a smooth surface and prepare the wood for the final finish.

The hand-carving room is the aristocratic department of a furniture factory. Here expert craftsmen produce expensive furniture on machines that carve as many as 18 pieces at one time. The operator guides his master tool over the model or master-piece, which has been carved by hand. The finishing touches to the machine product are applied by skilled hand carvers. Knobs, handles, and other trimmings are attached in the turning room. The piece is next sent to the packing room, thence to a warehouse or a shipping room.

Michigan

MILL HOUSING. Boarding Blocks . . . , Canal St. [Lewiston], opposite the Bates Mill, are reminders of an earlier industrial period. These three-story, brick structures were built by the company for its employees, following a practice common among industrial establishments in the last century. Country girls, eager to get work in the mills though it meant working long hours for small pay, came to the city and created a demand for suitable lodging facilities. Mill owners erected these "boarding blocks," dividing them into tenements for groups of 15 or 20 girls, and let them to "boarding mistresses." Girls paid $2 a week for board and room and, under the maternal eye of the boarding mistresses, the blocks were conducted as strictly as a girls' school. The blocks, occupied by millworkers' families, are the property of the mill.

Maine

STEEL MILL. The Wheeling Steel Corporation Plant . . . consists of long, slender, A-type structures of brick and corrugated iron, covering the larger part of a 1,160-acre tract of land surrounded by a bristling steel fence. These smoke-streaked red buildings house seven mechanized hot mills, with an annual capacity of 72,000 tons of sheet steel; the mills add a rumbling threnody to the song of industry which rises high above the whistling winds that sweep down the valley. Bars of metal brought from the furnaces at Benwood and Steubenville are here heated and rolled by "roughers" and "catchers," who feed the bars through roughing mills until the sheets reach the proper thickness for finishing. A "charger" then guides them to the furnace conveyor, where the sheets are reheated and again rolled until they reach four or five feet in length. A "matcher" then shapes the sheets for final rolling, and a "doubler" folds the sheets into four thicknesses called a "pack." Again reheated and passed between the rolls of the mill until they reach the desired size and thickness, the sheets are stacked by a "piler," and each pack is shaped to size by "shearmen" operating great electrically powered knives capable of slicing four thicknesses ^f steel in a split-second; after the sheets have been separated, they are pickled, annealed, cold rolled, or terne-coated, depending upon the specifications of the order. Each mill is under the supervision of a "roller," who, with two helpers, is responsible for the proper operation of the mill.

West Virginia

THREE-WAY WELD. For many years "Dunk" Dunkelberger was a blacksmith at Yachats for several gyppo logging outfits. One day a hobo entered the shop and asked for a job. Business was slack and Dunk wanted to get rid of the "bo" as quickly as possible, so he told him that the job was his if he could make a three-way weld, a task that was considered impossible. Then Dunk went out to lunch chuckling to himself and expecting the tramp to be gone when he got back. The hobo was gone when he returned, but he left behind Dunk's duckbilled tongs neatly welded together about the horn of the anvil in a perfect three-way weld. It took Dunk almost two days to saw and file the tongs from the anvil and retemper its horn.

Oregon

SUGAR BEETS. The beets are carried into the factory through flumes filled with warm water, which is agitated by a washer equipped with rotating paddles. They fall upon hopper scales, are weighed, and then drop into a slicer that cuts them into long thin strips, called "cossettes," but known as "chips" to the workers. These are carried along high-speed belts into a battery of cylindrical tanks where hot circulating water extracts the juices. What remains is diverted either to the wet-pulp silo and stored, or is passed through heated drums where the pulp is dried. Part of the dried pulp is pressed into blocks known as "bull biscuits." The men handling the pulp, which has an unpleasant odor, as well as the trucks transporting it, are called "high smellers."

The juice is put through several chemical processes, repeatedly filtered, and run into evaporators, to emerge as "evaporator thick juice." Treated with sulphur gas and carefully filtered, the clear sparkling liquor, known as "blowup thick juice," passes into vacuum pans and is boiled until the sugar begins to crystallize. High speed centrifugal machines separate sugar crystals from the syrup. The wet sugar passes into granulators, where it is dried and screened; the dry sugar is sent to the warehouse for packing in barrels, sacks, and small packages. Workers engaged in the latter process say they are "making pups."

Colorado

SHRIMP PICKING. The canning and packing plants [in Biloxi] are built out over the water to facilitate the unloading of boats and the disposal of refuse. The plants employ men, women, and children to pick the shrimp, which have been packed in ice for several days to make them brittle enough to handle. The picking tables are long troughs down which the shrimp baskets are rolled. The pickers, standing on each side of the table, remove the head and scales from the shrimp with a single dexterous twist. Buckets of alum water into which the pickers dip their hands neutralize the shrimp secretions. Payment for picking is made by weight, the wage running not quite one cent a pound. The average skilled picker earns $1.50 a day, with a few making as high as $2.50. Whistles let the pickers know when a day's supply of shrimp has been brought in, and the pickers work as long as they care to, or until the supply is exhausted. The average picking room is the scene of much conversation and occasionally a hair-pulling combat, when someone tries to edge another out of the weighing line. While the picking of shrimp is a fairly easy process requiring no tools, oyster shucking is a skillful operation, and the proficiency attained by some of the workers is amazing. Frequent shucking contests are held, with rivalry running high between contestants.

Mississippi

WALL PAPER. The Joliet Wall Paper Mills . . . is one of the six Joliet mills, which produce one-third of the country's wall paper. The visitor is first taken to the damp, warm boiler room, where dynamos generate electricity for the entire factory; from there to the raw material warehouses, which are piled high with chalky Georgia clay and huge bales of white paper already cut to wall paper width. Next visited is the color room, stacked with barrels of pigment and equipped with large grinding and mixing machines in which the colors are prepared in dry form.

In the actual printing room the air is pungent with the ammonia used to treat the soy bean color oils. Here are the printing machines, extending in vertical rows, a city block in length. The paper, fed from rolls in slow-moving festoons, is given a ground coating of the desired tint, picked up in loops by wooden fingers resembling broom handles, and slowly carried along drying units in a current of warm, dry air. Fed back into the machines, it is imprinted with as many as 12 different designs and colors. Carried back in dense scallops over the heaters, through a washing fluid, and into a long drying room, it is caught up by reels and wound into regulation rolls.

Illinois

GARMENT CENTER. Sixth, Seventh, and Eighth Avenues, main routes for heavy-duty traffic, are packed with trucks and buses. The curbs of side streets are lined with trucks unloading bolts of materials and loading finished garments while other trucks wait for an opening. Through narrow traffic holes along the curbs, "push boys" guide handtrucks with garments swaying from racks made of metal pipes. Into these crowded streets at noon, thousands of workers, East and South European by origin, Italians and Jews mostly, descend for food, fresh air, and sun. (Few women workers appear in the noonday crowd, for most of them bring food from home and eat in the workrooms.) They pour from the buildings, congregate in groups, jam into lunchrooms and cafeterias, and gather around pitchmen. A few minutes before one they take a final puff at the cigarette, look fondly once more at the warming sun, throw away the butt, and crowd the doors to the buildings.

The average shop has two main sections: showroom and workroom. The former is generally long and ornately decorated, with one side partitioned into booths. In these, buyers for stores sit and appraise the latest fashions displayed by mannequins.

Refinements of the showroom are totally lacking in the workroom. Walls and ceilings are whitewashed; floors are bare, Placed close to the many windows are long cutting tables where a motor-driven blade can cut through as many as four hundred thicknesses of some materials in a single operation; and rows of electric sewing machines can needle fabrics at the rate of three thousand stitches a minute. The workers are Negro and white, native and foreign-born; women outnumber men three to one.

The great number of independent shops in the garment center is illustrative of the industry's peculiar make-up. The process of centralization and monopoly that shaped other large industries has not operated to any great extent in the garment trade, largely because the style factor makes it an extremely speculative business. Instead of the assembly-belt system that obtains, for example, in the automobile industry, garment production is relatively dependent on the skill of the operator, who in most cases sews the entire garment. The so-called manufacturer, or jobber, may do only a portion of the actual manufacturing. Contractors assume the responsibility for the sewing and finishing or whatever "cut work" the various manufacturers send to them. This subdivision of the industry has increased competition all along the line, among manufacturers, contractors, and workers. The result has been a chaotic system of production, reflected each year in the amazing rate of bankruptcy that has been as high as 20 percent among "inside" manufacturers, and 33⅓ percent among contractors.

New York City

PAPER. In the paper mill [at International Falls] the pulpwood is first sent through "slashers," which cut the 8-foot pieces into shorter lengths; then through huge "barking drums" where all bark is removed from the blocks; and next to "chip" machines in which each "stick" is cut into thousands of small pieces. The chips are conveyed to the sulphite house, dumped into large cookers, and steamed in an acid that disintegrates the wood. Huge stones reduce the wood to a fine fiber. This pulp is mixed with an equal amount of sulphite pulp, which then undergoes a series of treatments until it is spread out in a semiliquid state on a fine wire screen to drain; then pressed through a series of heavy rollers. The web of damp paper travels over and under a series of great steam-heated drying rolls and emerges completely dry, to be wound on spindles. The pulp, which is 90 percent water when it leaves the headbox, emerges as dry paper in less than a minute. The factory works night and day and produces 1,100 feet of paper a minute.

Minnesota

CIGAR MAKERS. The tobacco is brought from bonded warehouses and kept in air-conditioned rooms. A bale consists of 80 *manojos* or 320 *gavillas*, the latter known in English as "hands," each containing up to 50 leaves. Stems are removed from leaves by "strippers" and the tobacco delivered to "grabbers" or *boncheros* who make up the inside of the cigar known as the "bunch," filler, or *tripa*. The wrappers or choice leaves are picked by "selectors" and passed on to the cigar makers, men and women, who make the finished product.

Cigar makers, or *tabaqueros*, work at long tables in double rows. These are grouped in units, each known as a *vapor*, the Spanish word for ship. Each worker is permitted to take out, free, three cigars a day, provided they are carried in plain sight, and allowed to smoke as many as he pleases on the job. The finished cigars are tied in bundles of 100, known as a *rueda* or "wheel," and graded by experts, *resagadors*, according to color that ranges from *claro claro*, very light, to *colorado*, red, and *maduro*, dark. The embossed bands and cellophane wrappers are applied by machines, and the cigars are packed into labeled boxes by hand. The tobacco left over from the making of cigars, called *mogolla*, is ground into small pieces for scrap or filler. All those who prepare the tobacco are known as clerks or *dependientes*. Readers, or *lectors*, who formerly read to the workers were abolished in 1933 because of the introduction of radical literature, but in many factories radios have replaced them.

A cigar that does not taper is called a "straight," and a tapering one is known as a "shape." The end of the cigar placed in the mouth is the *cabeza*, or head, the lighted end is the "tuck," the flare, or the *campana*, meaning bell. In making tapered cigars, a cutting process where the worker employs a special knife, a *chabeta*, is referred to as an "operation." Cigars are made in various shapes and sizes, the more popular known as "blunts," "panetelas," and "perfectos."

Florida

PLATE GLASS. The main plant of the Pittsburgh Plate Glass Company . . . extends for a mile along 3rd Avenue [Ford City] in a series of long squat units of red brick. Said to be the largest plant of its kind in the world, it is composed of two sections, one of which turns out plate glass and mirrors; the other produces optical glass and "Carrara glass," a facing material sometimes used as a substitute for tile. Approximately 2,000 workers are employed.

The first American glass furnace, built near Jamestown, Virginia, soon after its settlement in 1607, operated but briefly. The industry was more substantially established late in the eighteenth century in Boston, New Hampshire, and Pittsburgh, where plate glass was first made in 1853. The district around Pittsburgh is a center of the glass industry because fuel—coal and natural gas—and necessary raw materials, chiefly sand, soda ash, potash, and lime, are found here in abundance. Glass sands contain a large proportion of silica, an important ingredient. The potash and soda ash absorb the impurities in the melted silica. Lead is added to increase the brilliancy of the glass and render it heat-resistant.

The batch (raw ingredients) is melted in a tank furnace or in clay pots of a ton-and-a-half capacity. A temperature of about 2,600°F. is necessary to complete the melting process. The method of handling molten glass depends upon the object to be produced. Hollow vessels are blown, with compressed air machines replacing human blowers. For plate glass, the molten mass is poured evenly on a casting table covered with a steel slab, and rolled to a thickness of approximately half an inch. To prevent sudden cooling and consequent shattering, the plate is then rushed to the lehr, or annealing oven, a tunnel-like structure approximately 800 feet long, where it passes through gradually diminishing temperatures until it emerges, after five hours, at room temperature. The plate is polished by huge revolving disks of iron, with progressively finer grades of sand and emery, until irregularities and imperfections have been removed. Then rouge, red oxide of iron, the finest abrasive known, is applied with felt buffing disks until the surface is brilliant and flawless.

Pennsylvania

In the Ground

THE AMERICAN myth begins with riches in the ground. Columbus's journals show that even during his desperate first voyage the idea of gold—"the yellow metal that drives white men crazy," as an Indian later called it—never let go of him. In the 19th century, the gold rushes called forth much of the nation's westward expansion—in effect, out of the ground. In the 1930s, as today, the romance of *prospecting* lingered on.

Location is everything, or almost. Your backyard may have a *mastodon* or a marketable *great hole*. Failing to find a treasure, you can try to pilfer or counterfeit one: see *high-grading*, see the *stone giant*.

The ground workers at the center of the thirities' imagination were the coal miners. Here are accounts of the *colliery* and *Harlan County*, Kentucky, the focus of bloody unionizing.

PROSPECTING Not all the pay dirt in Montana has yet been found; there remain many gulches that have been but lightly prospected. Most prospectors get only 50¢ to $2 out of a day's work, but the possibility that the gold panner who finds a little in a creek may find more in a lode nearby is alluring.

Prospecting requires only a long-handled shovel and a pan. For actual placer mining a ditch is dug, and a few boards and nails made into a sluice box about 6 feet long, a foot wide, and a few inches deep. A strip of carpet is laid on the bottom; over it are placed several pieces of wire screen for riffles. The box is set at a slight angle to allow coarse material to run out; water from the stream is led into it. The gold caught in the riffles settles in the carpet, which is washed at the end of the day to recover the embedded metal. The foot of gravel next to bedrock is richest.

Monarch is an old, partly deserted mining town at the junction of two gulches whose creeks join the Belt. From this point prospectors, with some grub and an extra pair of socks in their packs, go into the hills to look for pay dirt. A mine that yields a profit, or at least gives a fair return in gold is known as "good ground." Placer gold is of four grades: nuggets, coarse gold, fine gold, and flour. Nuggets range from a dollar up in value. Coarse and fine gold can be caught in ordinary sluice boxes with little loss, but flour is so light that it washes out of the sluices with the water. When a considerable quantity of flour gold is found, miners use quicksilver in the riffles of their sluices and allow the mixture to settle in woolen blankets; they burn the blankets (if they are old) or wash them, to recover the amalgam, which is then heated to drive off the quicksilver. Several machines for recovering flour gold by combining gravitational separation with the amalgamation process, have been patented.

Montana

HIGH-GRADING. Throughout the boom years "high-grading"—the stealing of high-grade ores—flourished. Ore in excess of $2,000,000 was stolen in a decade, it has been estimated, the thefts ranging from what could be carried away in lunch pails to carload lots. Stolen ore was disposed of through a "fence," usually an assayer or a miner who owned a producing shaft. One notorious gang bribed the teamsters of a rich mine, unloaded the ore at a convenient spot and replaced it with bags of low-grade stuff. So general did high-grading become that for a time mine owners provided rooms where workers were compelled to change their clothes and have their lunch pails examined before going off shift. Even so, several men were discovered trying to smuggle out small amounts of gold concealed in their beards.

Colorado

DEEP MINES. In the deep Butte mines air-driven drills stutter like machine guns as they bore into the rock half a mile or more below surface. The men who operate the drills, set the explosive charges, and muck (shovel) the ore into chutes, work strenuously and often under trying conditions. Engineering specifications provide for a system of compressors that force fresh air through pipe lines into the mines, and of exhaust fans that remove foul air. Because of oxidation in the ore, and because of the heat of the water that seeps into the mines, temperatures sometimes reach 125°F. Large sums of money are spent by employers and union authorities in helping the men learn safe working methods and to acquaint them with first aid practices. Much progress has been made in improving working conditions. Many methods and devices for the protection of life and health among the 7,000 miners have been introduced. Improvements in practice include wet drilling, wetting of "muck piles" before shoveling, and underground spraying. Masks have also been tried. Blasting fills the workings with fumes that remain for hours; therefore, most of the blasting is done between shifts. Electric signal systems are used in all the deep mines.

Montana

PANNING. The simplest method of recovering placer gold is by panning. The gold pan is a circular dish of sheet iron with sloping sides, varying from ten to eighteen inches in diameter, and having a depth of from 2½ to 3 inches. The pan should be light and strong, with smooth inner surfaces kept free from grease and rust. Sometimes gold pans are made of copper, so that the bottom may be coated with mercury to catch the fine gold often otherwise lost.

The pan is filled about two-thirds full with the material to be tested. It is then placed under water, and any clay pieces or hard lumps are broken up with the hands. The pan is now raised until it is just below the surface of the water and is shaken vigorously from side to side with a slightly circular motion to keep the lighter material in suspension and work it out of the pan, which is slightly tilted away from the operator. The motion keeps the material in agitation, allowing the heavier part to settle while the lighter is washed over the lip of the pan. This is brought about by alternately raising and lowering the lip above and below the surface of the water. The pan should occasionally be lifted from the water and shaken vigorously with the same circular motion, to hasten the concentration without the chance of some of the gold being washed out. The procedure is continued until only the gold and the heaviest material remain. About this stage of the operation it is well to transfer the panning to a tub of water, so that any of the gold that may be washed out can be recovered by panning the contents of the tub.

The final residue is dried, and the magnetite, which always accompanies placer gold, is drawn away with a magnet wrapped in a thin sheet of paper. In this way the magnet may be easily cleaned by drawing it out of the paper. The coarse gold can now be picked out, and the fine gold recovered by the amalgamation process, or by blowing the sand away with a straw. An experienced panner can mine about one-half to three-quarters of a cubic yard of gravel a day.

Alaska

LOCATION. To locate a lode mining claim or group of claims the claimant must place a location or discovery monument at the point of discovery—the point where evidence has been found of one of the numerous minerals, precious, semi-precious, or common, used in the trades and industries. The discovery monument may be a wooden stake supported by loose stones or earth, or it may be of stone or earth without the stake. A notice of location is placed with the monument, generally protected by stones, in a small can to prevent its blowing away. The notice follows a prescribed form. The claim cannot be for more than 1,500 feet along the vein or lode, or have a width of more than 600 feet—300 feet each way from the vein. The notice must give the position of the discovery in relation to some permanent feature of the landscape, name of the claim, the date of location, and the name of the locator. Names of witnesses may also be inscribed.

The law allows twenty days for establishing boundaries, which is done by placing stakes or monuments at each corner and at each side center of the rectangular bit of land. Ninety days are allowed to dig a location or discovery shaft, four by six by ten feet, or an equivalent, such as an open cut or trench, and to record a certificate of location.

Nevada

HARLAN COUNTY. Natural advantages favoring cheap coal production in Harlan were seized upon in 1910 by local enterprise. Capital was secured, a railroad was built, and in 1911 the first coal was shipped. Men flocked in from the surrounding hills to work at the mines, and the population of the county increased at an extraordinary rate. Mountaineers, drawn from their hill farms by the high wages, or what seemed so to them, came to the mines to work, to live in company shacks, to trade in company stores, and to be policed by company guards.

Limitations imposed on workers became irksome, but it was not practicable to resist the rulers of the county, who were mainly intent on protecting their income and on blocking all organization that might threaten it. Labor unions were told peremptorily to keep out, and the Harlan County Coal Operators' Association showed that on this point it meant business. In the course of five years of operator rule Harlan County became known as "Bloody Harlan," and labor conditions there became popularly identified with those in Kentucky as a whole.

The real boom came with the World War. The demand for fuel by the steel mills and other plants manufacturing munitions drove coal prices high enough to make operation highly profitable even in this field, which had to ship in competition with northern fields having much more favorable freight rates. Competition for labor raised the wages of miners to abnormal heights. Men flocked down from the hills, where many of them had never seen $100 in cash in the course of a year, to earn much more than $100 in the course of a month. The companies hastily built shacks and barracks to house them and opened stores to get their trade. The new industrial workers were a bit like sailors on shore leave; cash for something to spend and there seemed no limit to the flow. Many, unaccustomed to paying rent and buying foodstuffs, spent the whole of their wages the day they received them and had to go in debt to provide themselves with room and board until the next pay day. In no time their ignorance of money values had put them into the hands of those willing to profit by it.

The end of the boom came when the war was over and the demand for huge quantities of coal fell off. The first to suffer in the deflation of production and prices toward peacetime levels was the miner. Men were laid off and wages cut. The uprooted hill people either had no land to return to or could not face return to the isolated cabins; miners who had poured in from other fields found no other fields that wanted their labor. Bitterness flared in every coal district. The absentee owners who demanded profits were often represented locally by natives of the district or by the kind of men who always flock to boom towns, and the old feud spirit flared up with a bitterness equal to that of the most spirited days of the Hatfield–McCoy war. Strike-breakers were sent in from outside to guard closed mines or to keep mines open during strikes, and people on both sides of the struggle used guns, as they had long been accustomed to do in times of stress.

Well-meant attempts to mediate by "furriners" were notably unsuccessful, in part, because of unfamiliarity with the local people and customs, and in larger part because of the complicated economic problems involved. The post-war flare-up gradually became less violent, though the struggle continued; the economic collapse that came on after 1929 brought it to white heat again.

Kentucky

QUARRY. Harris Quarry . . . , in Lincoln township, now appears . . . as a ragged limestone wall rising above a pond made by the flooding of the old pit. The first shelf of the quarry is said to be some 35 feet below the water level, and the bottom much more. The quarry was first worked by Thomas Harris, a contemporary of Roger Williams, and one of the first settlers within the present township. The quarry has not been used for a long time, except as a convenient place in which to drop automobiles on which the owners would like to collect insurance.

Rhode Island

MINE FIRE. New Straitsville [was] laid out in 1870 by a mining company, . . . at one time numbering 2,500 residents. It is the center of the New Straitsville Mine Fire Area which has received wide publicity. Since 1884 a subterranean coal fire has been raging here which experts say may continue to burn for 100—or even 1,000—years unless abatement plans are successful.

The fire was started when a handful of desperate miners, in one of the most bitter strikes in Ohio history, seized a number of loaded coal cars, doused them with oil, and pushed them blazing down five different shafts. Twelve square miles have become slowly toasting earth where cisterns steam and dry up, where potatoes are dug precooked, where an $80,000 school building is overheated when the furnace is turned off. During half a century 12,000,000 tons of coal have burned beneath the surface; damage has been estimated at $50,000,000. Today the landscape is a weird sight. Paved roads are sunk as much as five feet; miniature volcanoes erupt eerily overnight; streams of hot water run through the woods where trees have been scorched or felled; flowers bloom without regard to the season; and over all is a sulphurous stench, faint but persistent.

Several attempts to limit the fire's spread have been made. Cement walls were sunk but they cracked; a creek diverted into the openings emerged as steam. In 1937 the WPA allocated $360,000 and hired 400 local coal miners in a major effort to save this valuable coal field. Three noninflammable barricades, mud-packed tunnels, one a mile and a quarter long, are being sunk in key positions in the belief that the fire can be trapped and will ultimately burn itself out. Employees on the project, which will require several years for completion, feel the heat of the flames less than 50 feet from where they work. One completed barricade has saved a 5,000,000-ton field, and the other two will confine the fire to an area of 30 square miles.

Ohio

LIGNITE. Southwest of Sidney are miles of weirdly eroded buttes. Below the river breaks . . . lignite coal workings, large or small, are occasionally seen. Some, little more than holes in the hillsides, have been made by industrious farmers, who have dug their winter's supply of fuel out of veins 4 feet or less in thickness. Such mines do not justify the expense or trouble of installing equipment, and they are usually worked with the simplest tools. An auger and a tamping bar are used to place charges of blasting powder; in some places a single small home-made rail-car or wheel-barrow rolls out the coal. The miner must accustom himself to working in a cramped and, at first, uncomfortable position. He must also learn to recognize certain danger signs, for cave-ins are not unknown.

The larger mines are sometimes of the strip type. Several farmers bring horses or tractors, plows, and fresno scrapers, and remove the overburden. This may take days or weeks. They then blast the exposed coal into pieces small enough to be loaded on wagons and trucks, and haul it to some sheltered storage place, such as a cellar; coal of this type disintegrates rapidly when exposed to sunlight and air.

Montana

COLLIERY. Coal mining methods vary with geological structure. Where coal lies close to the surface it is recovered by a method known as strip mining. . . . In most cases, however, the veins are far underground and are reached by a shaft driven into the earth. The shaft, invariably vertical and sometimes reaching a depth of 3,000 feet, provides a passage for the hoist, an open elevator that carries miners up and down and lifts coal to the surface. As each vein is reached, a gangway or tunnel is run off at an angle. Along these gangways are breasts, or working faces, which miners attack with dynamite, drill, and pick. Huge lumps of coal are loaded into small dump cars drawn along a narrow gauge track by an electric "mule."

In spite of innumerable safety precautions, the miner's work is hazardous. Gangways are narrow and often slippery; dynamite sometimes goes off prematurely; supporting timbers occasionally give way, releasing an avalanche of rock, coal, and dirt; a cave-in may block the flow of air; deadly and explosive gases are ever present in pockets and recesses.

The loaded cars are hoisted to the surface and shunted to the breaker. Mammoth breakers handle the output of several mines, in some cases 12,500 tons per day. A belt conveyor or electric hoist carries the coal to the top of the breaker. In modern plants huge electric magnets suspended above the conveyor belt extract "tramp" iron, an incombustible impurity. A stream of water washes away silt and loosened impurities. The coal is then directed into primary cones, which contain a mushy mixture of sand and water constantly agitated. The mixture floats coal while the heavier impurities—rocks, "bone," and slate—sink to the bottom and are drained off through a trap. Some breakers use the "jig" method—a vertical pulsation of water and sand

Fifteen tons of water are pumped for every ton of coal mined. The coal is then crushed into domestic sizes by revolving steel-toothed rolls. A secondary cone eliminates newly released impurities, and the coal undergoes another laundering as it passes over screens for final sizing just before it is poured into railroad cars. In the most efficient breakers it takes less than 13 minutes for newly mined coal to be turned into a salable commodity.

Pennsylvania

THE STUFF THAT BUSTED PARLIAMENT. The Durango *Idea* reported in 1885 that a group of local men, organized in military formation with a major, captain, and several lieutenants, had left to explore recently discovered ruins near La Boca, New Mexico, where they were to "dig up Aztecs." A caravan of 30 horses and 15 burros was required to transport the "explorers" and "the following necessities to military life: 5 cases of chewing tobacco, 3 cases of beer, 10 gallons of heavy liquids, 4 burro-loads of the stuff that busted Parliament, 7 reels of fuse, a box of soap, 2 boxes of cigars, a fish line, 20 pairs of rubber boots, 200 loaves of bread, a can of lard, and one pound of bacon." In a footnote the editor added: "Ranchmen, beware! These folks are bad after chickens and other ranch truck."

Colorado

BLASTING. The town of Bingham Canyon . . . slouches up a narrow V-shaped gulch, sprawls over the steep sidehills, and finally collapses near the enormous open-pit mine of the Utah Copper Company. The single street meanders up the canyon, framed by wooden houses and business buildings. Dwellings rise abruptly from the street, and second-story balconies lean precariously over the sidewalks. Unpainted lumber shacks are strewn carelessly over the canyonside, and here and there is a handkerchief-sized plot of grass. There is little or no class distinction in Bingham, where portly matrons chat amiably with girls from the "houses." Twice a day an ear-splitting whistle blows, warning of a coming blast at the pit. Housewives grab anything that might be jarred loose, including their children, for when the blast comes, the whole town bucks like a bronco. The night blasting can be heard in Salt Lake City—a deep rumble coming weirdly at three in the morning.

Utah

STONE GIANT. In October 1869, . . . the "Cardiff Giant" was unearthed by workmen digging a well on the farm of William Newell. The giant figure, over 10 feet tall and proportionately broad, frightened Onondaga Indians, who immediately recalled their legend of the stone giant of the Cardiff hills who made forays into Indian villages each morning and chose a warrior for breakfast. As curious crowds gathered, Newell erected a tent over the hole and charged admission. Doctors and archeologists examined the figure and proclaimed it a petrified human being, even pointing out the stony pores. A group of businessmen from Syracuse and neighboring communities purchased the "corpse" and placed it on exhibition. It was sold and re-sold, its value ever increasing until a one-eighth share was worth $25,000.

The hoax was revealed when physicians discovered that the giant was solid gypsum and had no petrified heart, lungs, or other internal organs. Investigation diclosed that George Hull of Binghamton, Newell's brother-in-law, had contracted to have the figure cut from a two-ton block of Iowa gypsum by stoneworkers in Chicago. A wet sponge filled with sand was used to erase chisel marks; the "pores" were made with needles and a hammer. The figure was boxed, shipped by rail to Union, near Binghamton, then hauled overland at night in a large wagon and buried, late in 1868, at the future "well" site. Despite the exposure, dozens of Cardiff Giants toured American medicine shows and fairs. P. T. Barnum, unable to purchase the original, had a duplicate made. In 1934 the giant was taken from a warehouse in Iowa, exhibited at the State Fair in Syracuse, then shipped back to Iowa to become a permanent exhibit in a private museum.

New York

GREAT HOLE. [A] great hole in the side of a mountain . . . is visible from the road [near Henry]. To reach the hole it is necessary to cross a meadow afoot. According to an old-timer, it was in the night of the second day of November, 1917, that he was awakened by a terrific sound that brought him out of bed with his hair standing on end. He went outside, expecting to see the sky falling or the earth splitting open; and on the next day discovered that a hunk had dropped out of the mountainside not far away. This hole is about 150 feet across and about 75 feet in depth on its upper side. In the bottom of it is water of unknown depth that formerly was lucid but is now covered with a brown or green scum that looks like heavy wallpaper. A part of the sheer walls are of earth, a part of stone; and the strange thing about it is the fact that this enormous piece of mountain dropped and disappeared from sight into a body of water, the depth of which nobody has been able to learn.

Idaho

THE LOST DUTCHMAN. There is a saying in the Southwest that "the mines men find are never so rich as those they lost." To prove it, Arizona's folklore is filled with stories of fabulous deposits of precious metals found, and then lost, and searched for diligently through two or three generations. Every section of the state has its share of lost mines, but probably the most famous one is the Lost Dutchman Mine in the Superstition Mountains about thirty-five miles east of Phoenix. The long series of very interesting legends dealing with this rich gold mine begins with a young Mexican lover fleeing the wrath of his sweetheart's father and seeking refuge far north in the forbidding Superstitions. He is supposed to have found the great gold deposit when its location was still a part of Old Mexico, but the Gadsden Purchase was about to take place, so the young man's entire Mexican community formed a great expedition and made the long march into the Superstitions. There they mined as much of the gold as they could carry and set out jubilantly for home. But the Apaches ambushed them, and killed the entire party—four hundred men—except two young boys concealed under a bush. These two children found their way back home, and grew up with the knowledge that they alone knew the location of the mine. When they were old enough they took a third partner and went to the Superstitions, finding the mine without difficulty. They had hardly begun to dig, when the Dutchman came along.

The Dutchman was a prospector with a long white beard, and his name was Jacob Wolz, or Walz. He had been prospecting in the Superstitions, and a band of Apaches had driven him into a part of the mountains he had never seen before. He stumbled into the camp of the Mexican boys and became friendly with them and they told him about their mine. Wolz killed the three Mexicans and from about 1870 until his death the mine was his.

As stories of the Dutchman's gold ore spread around Phoenix and Florence, many prospectors tried to trail him into the mountains but he outwitted them, or killed them. Wolz is said to have admitted killing eight men because of the mine, including his own nephew. He died in Phoenix about 1884, with a shoe box of the beautiful ore under his bed. Almost with his last breath he gave a friendly neighbor directions to the mine, saying they must be followed exactly as the mine entrance was concealed under ironwood logs covered with rock. Unfortunately the most important landmark in Wolz's directions, a palo verde tree with a peculiar pointing branch, could not be located then or later.

Arizona

SIREN. On February 5, 1922, underground water flooded the [Milford] mine and 42 men were drowned. Although the mine was pumped out, not a body was found for months; a year elapsed before the last victim was recovered. Out of this tragedy a ghost story has developed around the figure of Harley Harris, hero of the disaster. When the water burst into the mine, Harris, who was within the mine, twice sounded the siren warning and then tied a rope around his waist so that the weight of his body would keep the siren shrieking. He died in his efforts to save his companions. Later, when work was resumed, many of the men left because they believed they could hear the siren and could see Harris with the rope tied around him. The day following the disaster, a woman whose husband had been trapped hurled herself into the dark waters; the miners thought they heard her voice, too, shrieking and moaning in the dark.

Minnesota

E. CLAMPUS VITUS An imposing structure [in Sierra City] is the Busch Building (1871), which has two stories of brick and a balcony and third story of wood. Over one of the doorways are the initials "E.C.V.," standing for

"E. Clampus Vitus," the hilarious "Incomparable Confraternity" that swept through the mining country. It was organized in Pennsylvania in 1847 and transplanted to California before 1853. The organization was one of the biggest hoaxes of a country where hoaxes were the order of the day. The initiations were masterpieces of ingenious and humorous torture, and only those who survived them understood what E.C.V. stood for. So powerful was the sway of the mysterious brotherhood as developed by the miners that newcomers found they could not conduct business in mining towns until they had joined it. When Lord Sholto Douglas brought his theatrical group to Marysville, he found the first night audience too small to pay for the rent of the theater. Enlightened by a friendly miner, he applied for membership, and thereafter the miners flocked to his company's presentations.

California

$35 AN OUNCE The latest chapter in the history of the search for gold [in Washington] began in 1933, when the price of gold rose from $20 to $35 an ounce. The new price made possible the resumption of operations in many long-abandoned properties, and also gave great impetus to prospecting. Thousands of men, many of them unemployed, took to the mountains to search for new deposits, or combed over the mining districts for gold that might have been overlooked. In many cases, owing to lack of experience or some other factor, these latter-day prospectors were unsuccessful, but a few of the more skilled or more fortunate came upon important new sources or rediscovered old ones.

Washington

MASTODON. Johnstown . . . is like a hundred other villages in the Middle West, with two-story brick buildings facing the village green, prim frame houses, and an air of contentment. In August 1926, a farmer digging in his garden at the eastern end of the village was astonished to uncover the skeleton of a mastodon 8 feet high and 15 feet long. The Cleveland Museum of Natural History purchased it.

Ohio

NORTHERN ALASKA TRADING COMPANY

IDEAL ROOMS
DAY · WEEK · MON

F.LOPINTO

Trade

I F I had to go back and start life over again I would not only give serious
thought but probably would give first thought to making advertising instead of the law my career," said Franklin Roosevelt in 1931 while
Governor of New York. His praise of advertising was in fact a bit of huck-
sterism: he was addressing a convention of advertisers and wanted to get them
to sell the idea of government planning the way they sold cars and deodor-
ant.

But just because he wanted to win friends to his cause doesn't mean he
wasn't sincere. No doubt he did consider advertising the crucial art for any
public official (during the 1920s the advertising profession had sold nothing
so well as itself). His cousin Theodore Roosevelt had seen the Presidency as
a "bully pulpit"; Franklin, in a time no longer dominated by the church,
saw it as a broadcasting medium with the highest ratings and best sponsor.

In this chapter on business we see advertising, publicity, salesmanship,
call it what you will, to be of long date in America. Trade ranges from the
primitiveness of *street criers* to that commercial establishment, the *country
store*, to the sophistication of the *blue book*. It succeeds by meeting a felt

need—legal (the *five and ten cent store*) or not (a *knife and gift; rumrunning*).

Contrary to prejudice, some advertising can be almost too truthful, as in the promotion of the *Naked Truth Saloon* and *not clover seed*.

———

COUNTRY STORE. Strasburg . . . is notable chiefly as the location of the Garver Brothers Store, N. Wooster Avenue, where it is possible to buy a needle or a reaping machine, a pair of overalls or a fur coat. This extraordinary small-town department store occupies 90,000 square feet of floor space and grossed more than $500,000 annually during the leanest years of the early 1930's; the *American Magazine* has called it "the largest country store in America."

Founded in 1866 by Phillip A. Garver, the store operated along conventional lines for 20 years; then his sons, Rudolph and Albert, took over its management, circularized the entire countryside with handbills and announcements, established friendly and accommodating relationship with their customers, and increased the business tremendously. After 1907, when Albert Garver became sole manager, the company instituted a card-index record of every man, woman, and child living within 18 miles of Strasburg. Garver anticipated the needs of everyone in the area. He kept himself informed about the births, deaths, new arrivals, departures, car purchases, house remodelings, fires, and weddings of the countryside. He inaugurated stunts, sales, dollar days, anniversaries, parties; he sent his own help to plow or harvest for sick farmers; and he advertised and continued to mail circulars to his ever-growing clientele. He gave a poultry party once, releasing 100 chickens, ducks, and turkeys with the understanding that whoever caught a bird owned it. The party attracted 6,000 people and $5,500 in business. On another occasion he inquired about the merchandising needs of two Amish farmers who had stopped in the store to warm themselves; from this chance meeting sprang the Amish department of the Garver store, which does a large mail order business with members of the sect throughout the United States and Canada.

Ohio

FIVE AND TEN CENT STORE. The five and ten cent store originated [at Watertown] during county fair week in 1878. Frank W. Woolworth (1852–1910), a clerk in Moore & Smith's general store, piled leftover odds and ends on a table and put up a sign: "Any Article 5¢." The entire stock was sold out in a few hours. Inspired by this success, Woolworth opened his first store in Utica the following year.

New York

FUNERAL SCALP. It was an Osage custom to bury with a tribesman the scalps he had taken; and to send a warrior to the next world without at least one scalp was considered a tragedy. However, as intertribal warfare waned, the problem of getting a scalp to bury with a dead man became more and more acute and the custom arose of sending out secretly what were called mourning parties to bring in a scalp. To waylay and kill a Pawnee or other Indian might lead to war; and so scalps of isolated white men were in demand.

Pond Creek [is] a small tributary of the Caney; local legend has it that one of the last funeral parties sent out by the Osages in search of a scalp to bury with a dead warrior came upon two loggers in camp here, Jack Wimberly and Al Gifford. The Osages were not interested in Wimberly's red hair but craved a bit of Gifford's scalp, and offered him twenty ponies for a narrow strip just above the forehead. Gifford, of course, refused to deal with them, whereupon they took the strip by force—and next morning the twenty ponies were duly delivered.

Oklahoma

KOREMLU. A dramatic idea of the [Food and Drug Administration's] enforcement work can be obtained from a visit to room 2816, South Building, the "chamber of horrors" of food and drugs. Of the many types of fraud exhibited in this room, some involve products harmless in themselves but without curative value; others which are veritable agents of death, though sold to deluded victims as the last word in medical science. The exhibit reveals the weakness of the drug laws, as in many cases the administration can do no more than publicize the facts. For example, one product exhibited is "Koremlu," advertised as a depilatory and sold at $5 a jar, until damage suits forced the Koremlu concern into bankruptcy. Koremlu failed to remove superfluous hair on legs and arms as promised, but got into the blood stream, removed scalp hair, and paralyzed victims. There is no law which could prevent the old company from reorganizing or some new one from marketing the same product again.

District of Columbia

NAKED TRUTH SALOON. Somewhere on Main between Eighth and Ninth [in Boise] a saloon operated a half century ago. Managed by James Lawrence and known as the Naked Truth Saloon, it advertised itself in most astonishing fashion.

Friends and Neighbors:
Having just opened a commodious shop for the sale of liquid fire, I embrace this opportunity of informing you that I have commenced the business of making:
Drunkards, paupers and beggars for the sober, industrious and respectable portion of the community to support. I shall deal in family spirits, which will incite men to deeds of riot, robbery, and blood, and by so doing, diminish the comfort, augment the expenses and endanger the welfare of the community.
I will undertake on short notice, for a small sum and with great expectations, to prepare victims for the asylum, poor farm, prison and gallows.
I will furnish an article which will increase fatal accidents, multiply the number of distressing diseases and render those which are harmless incurable. I will deal in drugs which will deprive some of life, many of reason, most of prosperity, and all of peace: which will cause fathers to become fiends, and wives widows, children orphans and a nuisance to the nation.

Idaho

REAL ESTATE. Hollywood's history is typical of that of many towns founded during the real-estate boom of the 1920's. Some have become ghost towns in the flatwoods; some of the more fortunate, like Hollywood, withstood the violent strain of deflation and have survived.

During early days of development here, 1,500 trucks and tractors were engaged in clearing land and grading streets; two blocks of pavement were laid each day. Hollywood Boulevard, the first to be cleared, was in its time the widest paved thoroughfare in Florida. A cement broadwalk two miles long was built along the waterfront; two yacht basins, designed by General George Washington Goethals, chief engineer in the construction of the Panama Canal, were dredged and connected with the Intracoastal Waterway. A large power plant was installed, and when the city lights went on for the first time, ships at sea reported that Miami was on fire, and their radio alarms and the red glow in the sky brought people to the rescue from miles around.

Hollywood had a fleet of 21 buses constantly on the road, traveling 1,000 miles and more to bring in prospective purchasers of lots, who were given free hotel accommodations, refreshments, and entertainment, "with no obligation to buy." They were driven about the city-to-be on trails blazed through palmetto thickets; so desolate and forlorn were some stretches that many women became hysterical, it is said, and a few fainted. A large tent served both as office and auditorium, in which guests received lectures twice a day. Society leaders and titled personages of Europe were given choice sites to induce others to purchase lots nearby. Golf, swimming, and tennis champions were brought in to demonstrate their prowess and act as instructors at new courses, pools, and courts. Men prominent in business, politics, and the arts were hired to stimulate sales, either by pep talks or personal contacts. Some became so enthusiastic, perhaps influenced by their own oratory, that they organized "cities" of their own. Every salesman had his "bird dogs," who met trains and buses, talked to passing motorists at filling stations, restaurants, and hot-dog stands, or roamed at large, rounding up prospects.

Auctions were popular, both for the Grand Opening, and whenever sales lagged. Patrons were attracted by blaring bands, free banquets, vaudeville shows, and the drawing of lottery tickets. Doctors, dentists, merchants, barbers, and motormen abandoned professions, trades, and prosperous businesses to become real-estate salesmen. Anyone could obtain a license, either to set up on his own or to join a large sales organization. Today, as a result of past experience, applicants for a license must have been a resident of the State for 6 months, must furnish character references and credentials detailing their activities for the preceding 10 years, and must pass a rigid examination on real-estate law and finance.

At the beginning raw land could be bought at $100 to $1,000 an acre; the cost of grubbing ranged from $30 to $100; the surfacing of streets and the laying of sidewalks added $500 to $1,000 to the cost of an acre, which was usually divided into five 50-foot lots. Landscaping costs ran as high as the promoter's imagination and purse allowed him to go. Whole developments were planted with 2-foot Australian pines at 10¢ each; others, with 20-foot royal palms at $100 to $200 each. Spectacular publicity campaigns were launched locally and on a national scale. One promoter with a lavish development in south Florida spent $3,000,000 on advertising in less than a year.

Florida

GARGLING OIL. The businessman who put Lockport on the map in the 1870's was John Hodge, proprietor and manufacturer of Merchant's Gargling Oil, a remedy advertised to our grandparents as "good for man or beast"; one of Hodge's stunts was to send a steamer bedecked with banners over the Niagara cataract.

New York

BLUE BOOK. In Arlington Annex one could obtain for twenty-five cents a copy of the *Blue Book*, official directory and guide to Storyville. The *Blue Book* listed in alphabetical order and in separate sections respectively the names and addresses of all the prostitutes in the place. It also contained many advertisements from local and national distillers and cigarmakers, as well as a few from neighboring drugstores and taxi companies. Most enticing of all *Blue Book* contents, however, were the puffs and occasional photographs, which extolled the graces and qualifications of Storyville's most prominent sirens.

"Why visit the playhouse to see the famous Parisian models," urged one of these, "when one can see the French damsels, Norma and Diana? Their names have been known on both continents, because everything goes as it will, and those that cannot be satisfied with these must surely be of a queer nature." Another assures the reader that he "can travel from one end of this continent to the other, but to find another good fellow as game as Gipsy (Shaffer), who is always ready to receive and entertain, will be almost an impossibility." A third proclaims that Miss May Spencer has the distinction of conducting one of the best establishments in the Tenderloin District, "where swell men can be socially entertained by an array of swell ladies." "If you have the blues," says a fourth, "the Countess (Willie Piazza) and her girls can cure them." And so they went on and on, each mistress attempting to outdo her rivals in luring the wealthy "sport" to her palace of joy.

New Orleans

ILLEGAL TENDER. Free coinage of aluminum was tried in Elkton three years before the Presidential campaign of 1896, when William Jennings Bryan stumped the country for free coinage of silver. Suffering from a lack of anything to use as a medium of exchange, mainly because of hard times, Elkton businessmen concocted a plan to employ aluminum money in lieu of a more precious metal. Accordingly, they hired a St. Paul firm to "make money" for them. Thin strips of aluminum were cut to imitate the respective denominations of coins and the name of a firm was printed on one side.

The plan worked remarkably well for a time. When purchases were made with legal coin the substitute would be given out in exchange. Mr. Jones would take his change from the grocer and buy meat with it. The butcher would spend it in other stores or buy a calf or a hog from a farmer. But retribution was not far distant. A United States inspector dropped in one day and notified the businessmen that they must cease the practice. Furthermore, he told them that they were subject to a fine of $100 in real money for every aluminum coin dispensed. From Elkton the inspector went to St. Paul where he closed the money-making plant. Satisfied that the Elkton men had no fraudulent intent, he gave them time to call in the illegal coins. Eventually all the bogus money was redeemed, and Elkton returned to the gold standard.

South Dakota

PINCH TRADE. In 1847 [the Talladega] region was the gold-mining center of eastern Alabama. Prospectors scoured the hills, and boom towns sprang up overnight when strikes were made. Trails were widened into roads for

supply wagons, bringing merchandise to the new Eldorado. Miners spent
their dust freely and trade was conducted on the "pinch" basis. A drink of
whisky cost the amount of dust the bartender could pick up and hold between thumb and finger, roughly reckoned as a dollar—bartenders and store
clerks with broad fingers were in great demand.

Alabama

AUCTIONEER. [Springfield's] busiest period is from January through June
and July, during which tobacco auctions are held daily. The crop begins to
come to town around Christmas time. Powerful trucks and two-horse wagons covered with bed quilts crowd every highway and form long lines up to
the warehouse receiving platforms. Foreign buyers arrive to join the local
experts who represent many foreign as well as domestic interests. The spicy
smell of tobacco permeates the town. Negroes sing as they handle the leaf,
the wordless, improvised music slipping from corner to corner of the big
warehouses and echoing among the rafters.

Graders from the Bureau of Agricultural Economics arrive with their intricate system of classifying the leaf. Grade A is the choice wrapper leaf, B
fillers and snuff tobacco, C the thin light leaf and cheap cigar wrappers, X
the worm-eaten or rusted leaves known as lug. These groupings are modified
by many other symbols designating color, weight and length of leaf.

When he brings in his crop the farmer receives his "advance" from the
Association. This "advance" is the most important word in his vocabulary,
and perhaps to set it apart from common words he pronounces it with a
strong accent on the first syllable. Though it is literally an advance, it accurately predicts year after year what will be paid for each crop, and thus it
represents his annual income.

About the first of the year, when the season opens, the slow tempo of life
in the fields and the firing barn give way to activity that moves faster than
ticker tape. It revolves about the auctioneer with his rapid sing-song that is
understood by no one but the ten or twelve buyers who follow him about
the warehouse floor. Even the oldest resident, whose ears have rung with
this sound every year of his life, cannot tell you what the auctioneer says.
The farmer who raised the tobacco, though he watches anxiously from the
background, cannot understand this jargon. He only knows that his whole
year's crop can be sold in the time it takes him to cut a piece of chewing
tobacco from the plug in his pocket. He knows that repetition is the basis of
it, and sometimes he can catch a phrase like "a quarter" or "a half."

The auctioneer is admired by small boys, and occasionally one of them displays ability to imitate him, achieving the effect perfectly long before he knows the sense of a word he is saying. If he is also quick at figures and spends most of his adolescence in the tobacco warehouse, he will probably grow up to be an auctioneer himself, a profession—like the church—to which a young man is apparently "called."

Tennessee

SANTA CLAUS. Santa Claus [is] a tiny, quiet community with two general stores on its one street. The village was platted in 1846, and the suggested name of Sante Fe for the post office was ruled out because there was another Sante Fe in Indiana. Santa Claus was jocularly suggested as an alternative, since it was the Christmas season, and the name stuck.

Santa Claus becomes a beehive of activity with the approach of Christmas. From all over the world parcels pour in to be re-mailed in order to bear the Santa Claus postmark. In 1937 more than 600,000 pieces of mail passed through the little post office. Santa Claus's outstanding citizen was "Jim" Martin, postmaster for 38 years until his death in 1935, and Santa Claus to the Nation's children.

Santa Claus Park, on the highest hill of the village, has at its center a towering smiling granite Statue of Santa Claus, standing on a brightly silvered five-pointed star. The park and the statue, dedicated to the "children of the world," were sponsored by Carl A. Barrett of Chicago as a memorial to his family. In the park there is also a bell, rung in celebration at Wilkes-Barre, Pennsylvania, when the Declaration of Independence was signed; an Indian totem pole, donated by the Hudson's Bay Company; and a wishing well, locally built and donated, at which children can whisper their secret Yuletide desires.

A crater hole is being excavated in the park by the National Geographic Society and a rustic castle is under construction (1941). The cabins of the Hoosier Memorial Village will be outfitted with pioneer furnishings, including the toys and dolls of previous generations. Plans for the project include a nine-acre lake for swimming, boating, fishing, and skating. The roadway from the entrance to the center of the park is to be bordered by fir trees and will be called Christmas Tree Lane.

In the Enchanted Forest . . . a woods that might have sprung from a Walt Disney fantasy, is a miniature village of brick and stone castles built of materials ingeniously arranged to resemble candy and ice cream. Each gaudily decorated room is stocked with shiny new toys of all sorts from the daintiest of dolls to the most deadly looking air rifles. Within the Enchanted Forest is conducted a Santa Claus College . . . , a unique institution moved here by its operator, Charles W. Howard, from Albion, New York. Howard hopes to supplant the usual bored and unconvincing department-store Santas with efficient, cheerful child psychologists. The untrained Santa Claus with a meager knowledge of his role will be replaced by craftsmen who know toys and how to make them and who can give a practical demonstration for the children. After practical store work successful graduates receive degrees of BSC (Bachelor of Santa Clausing).

Indiana

WHITE ONLY. Legally, there is no racial discrimination in New York. Negroes were not excluded from or segregated in vaudeville and legitimate theaters until the early 1920's. Some New York theaters practice discrimination by refusing to sell tickets to Negroes or by maintaining that all seats are sold; others admit Negroes only to certain sections of the house. Except for some of the "little cinemas," there has never been discrimination on the part of motion picture houses.

Twenty years ago only Negroes of unusual distinction would dare to ask for accommodations in downtown hotels. Gradually, however, the larger hotels have become much more liberal in this respect. But discrimination in restaurants is still common. Of late, law suits have compelled many restaurants to alter their policy, and today a Negro can eat in many downtown restaurants without being asked to sit behind a screen or without finding that a cup of salt has been stirred into his soup. In some sections of Harlem itself there are bars and cafes that discriminate against Negroes; and the windows of many rooming-houses carry the familiar southern sign: "For White Only."

New York Panorama

BOOK OF SORROW. In the Corner Store, near the [Alexander] village center, hangs a large sign reading: "After 40 years of credit business, we have closed our book of Sorrow." This combination store, post office, information bureau, bank, and general gathering place is typical of the New England general store of the past. Here shelves of modern canned goods vie with bunches of fragrant pickling spices, dill-pickles in a barrel, beans in five- and ten-pound bags, penny candy, overalls, rubber boots, embroidery material and silks, and the heterogeneous mixture of merchandise required by village housewives and male "bargainers." In the evenings, the men gather around the pot-bellied stove set in its sawdust-filled square box—the latter for the convenience of tobacco "chawers"—to settle problems ranging in importance from international affairs to fence disputes.

Maine

SHIPOWNER'S INVESTMENT. No matter how successful a whaling voyage might be, the "fo'mast" hand rarely came off with anything to bank. His "lay" in the voyage was generally on the books, his profits were book profits. Against these were charged all his purchases, during a voyage of from three to five years, from the slop-chest aboard ship—clothes, tobacco, boots, etc.—at prices several times the value attaching to these goods elsewhere. If he had any surplus when he came ashore, the "sailors' boarding-houses" and the "land sharks" soon took care of that. The only thing that was dispensed free to the old New Bedford whalemen was a Bible. A well-known owner of one of that city's whaling fleets once described the Bible as the best cheap investment a shipowner could make.

Massachusetts

HIGH HAT. The high hat industry, a craft practiced in early Colonial days and lingering in remote spots until the War between the States, once flourished [at Brevard]. The town hatter made by hand wool hats, muskrat hats, and fine beaver hats. In this section any high hat is called a "beaver," or, in derision, a "bee gum." Owners of high hats once paid an annual State revenue tax of $4. A similar levy was made on those who carried gold-headed canes.

North Carolina

RUMRUNNERS. During prohibition, Ecorse became notorious as a rumrunners' paradise, for this section of the river was outside the jurisdiction of Detroit Police, and river islands afforded a measure of protection against the long arm of the Federal law. In this locality, where rumrunning reached its

greatest height, the traffic passed through three important phases during the
12 years the Eighteenth Amendment remained in force. At the outset, strong-
armed sailors, capable of rowing the river in an hour and forty minutes, made
trips between Canada and the United States, bringing in at each crossing
two or three cases of whiskey, valued normally at about $25 each, which
found a ready sale at $100 a case. As the traffic increased, this class of run-
ners was supplanted by young men with light outboard motorboats, which
not only cut the crossing time to about ten minutes, but carried so much
more liquor that the industry rapidly assumed big-business proportions. The
underworld stepped in, and gangsters with speedboats, armed and ready to
kill, took over the traffic. Ecorse became the Nation's Number One port of
entry for illicit Canadian liquors, and fabulous fortunes were made in the
business. The waterfront was shut off by a high board fence, and huge boat-
wells with bullet-proof doors were erected; at irregular intervals, powerful
speedboats, far swifter than the Government craft, whipped in from the
channel and disappeared in the wells. Minutes after a landing had been made,
fast motorcars were speeding with the heavy cargo toward clubs, roadhouses,
and private homes in Michigan, Ohio, and other States. The development
of Rumrunner's Row had been slow, but its fall was sudden and its demise
complete. After repeal, village authorities widened West Jefferson Avenue,
removed the shore-line fence, and established a municipal park and play-

ground along the waterfront. Soon every mark of the rumrunning era was effaced. Although the most spectacular business in Ecorse was gone, its passing did not affect legitimate commerce in the city.

Michigan

ELASTICITY. Hunterdon County residents have recently benefited by the elasticity of New Jersey's tax laws. Since 1937 when the official headquarters of the Standard Oil Company of New Jersey were removed to Flemington, bringing in new tax revenue, Hunterdon County residents have paid 50 cents less per $100 valuation. When the company moved from Linden to Flemington, its taxes were reduced from $1,400,000 to $270,000. Standard Oil had previously saved $587,366 by moving from Newark to Linden.

The headquarters of this, one of the wealthiest corporations in the world, consist of a sign upon a lawyer's office at 117 Main Street and a safe that contains those records required by law to be kept here.

New Jersey

MARRYING PARSONS. Elkton, . . . seat of Cecil County, [was the] Gretna Green of the East until 1938. A number of clergymen, aided by taxicab drivers and court clerks, formerly did a flourishing business marrying couples who had eloped. Until the 48-hour marriage law stopped this lucrative practice, Main Street was lined with signs advertising these "marrying parsons." An occasional manse still displays a weatherbeaten sign, but most of the preachers now devote their efforts to the gospel. The town now depends on the manufacture of pulp and paper, flour, fertilizer, and shirts.

Maryland

MUSICAL SAW. Besides being an important shipping and trading point for the regional dairy farmers, Fort Atkinson also has a cannery and plants that manufacture barn equipment and poultry supplies, "little pig" sausages, dairy equipment, hose, and saws, both ordinary and musical. The musical saws ground here are subjected to more rigid specifications than carpentry saws. Manufactured as alto, tenor, baritone, and bass blades, they are made straight-backed to permit a consecutive scale, and of smooth, homogeneous steel so that notes may run all through. For purity and clarity of tone they are the same thickness from tooth-edge to back, not tapered for clearance as are utility saws. Most ornate of the company's musical saws is a gold-plated model, its mahogany handles studded thickly with jewels. The local company not only offers a correspondence course in saw playing, but also publishes an annual called *Sawing News of the World*.

Wisconsin

SOFT DRINK. Hurley was a rendezvous for booze runners, gunmen, and criminals. In 1924, during prohibition days, there were 51 "soft drink" parlors; in 1938, 80 of its 115 business establishments were taverns, which so solidly lined six blocks of Silver Street that it was difficult to buy a meal. In gambling dens, where silver dollars serve as chips, suave operators often sit behind 30 or 40 stacks of "cartwheels" piled a foot high. Local bosses run the city but their names are seldom mentioned, for it is safer not to talk or snoop in Hurley. Late one night during prohibition days, three men encountered another with a suitcase and asked what he had in it. The man replied by drawing his revolver and shooting his questioner dead. At the preliminary hearing it was ruled that he had shot in self-defense.

Wisconsin

ICHTHYOL. Near Rozel, north of Great Salt Lake, are deposits of natural asphaltum that seep up from the bed of Great Salt Lake. A market is assured when production can be stepped up to a commercial level, for the asphaltum contains an exactly requisite amount of sulphides for production of rubber tires. This brown material also contains "ichthyol," a medicinal preparation used externally, in Webster's clarifying phrase, "as an alteratent and discutient." The Indians first discovered the medicinal properties of the asphaltum, but they have steadfastly refused to disclose its location despite a $50,000 reward.

Utah

IRISH NOMADS. By an underpass of the Nashville, Chattanooga & St. Louis Railway [outside Nashville] is . . . the camp site of the Irish Nomads. In the last week of April this roving clan of horse traders gathers in Nashville to attend the annual burial services of members who have died during the year. Between two and three thousands of them pitch their tents and park their trailers in the open field. Though they are often mistaken for Gypsies, these people are of pure Irish stock, devout Roman Catholics, and bear such names as Costello, Sherlock, and Gorman.

The clan stems from four families of horse traders who came to the United States in 1875. They have always confined their trading to the South. Today they travel about the rural sections in cars and trucks, stopping frequently to buy horses and mules. The buying is not restricted to fine work animals. Farmers know that the Nomads will take a sick mule or an overworked horse, if it is not too old. Skilled for generations in doctoring ailing horses, they are remarkably successful in salvaging such animals. At New Orleans and Atlanta the clan maintains depots on a communal basis, in which the animals are collected and sold at auction. A large part of the trade is with foreign markets. Much of the mountain artillery of the Italian Army was carried into the hills of Ethiopia on the backs of mules bought for the Italian Government by the Irish Nomads.

Tennessee

McCOY. A crossroads [between Sussex and Ross Corner] is marked by black and white directional signs, below which is a smaller sign reading, "This is McCoy's Corner." Most of the farm population for miles around needs no guidance to the white farmhouse . . . behind tall evergreens where William (Bill) Sharpe McCoy has lived for 50 years. During the last 40 years McCoy has been a horse dealer; he sells about 700 animals a year, not counting trades. He is a short, friendly man, with thin gray hair and a mustache; the trousers of his gray business suit are tucked into black puttees, and he wears overshoes around his stable and office behind the house. McCoy is his own banker in dealing with the farmers, keeping their notes and his other accounts in a green tin box that he carries out to his stable office every morning. If he needs cash, he can take a note on a horse to the Sussex bank and get it discounted. "But they wouldn't discount a note on an automobile," he says, "because there's too much depreciation." The best money he ever made was during the years that he ran a fertilizer factory. A relative, a veterinarian, kept him posted on mortally ill animals over a wide area. McCoy's follow-up system was successful, for he seldom hauled away a dead horse without selling a live one to the bereaved farmer. For six years McCoy was pianist for the Masons, and his violin has furnished many tunes for country dances. The violin bears a printed Stradivarius label along with the words, "Made in Germany"; a New York dealer once offered him $2,000 for it, but McCoy wouldn't sell.

New Jersey

KNIFE AND GIFT. The Get Service Station, 207 South Street, facing Madeleine Square [in Abbeville] houses the Gooch Collection. The collection consists of relics of Mexico's Revolutionary War; swords and guns of the Civil War period; arrowheads, spear points, stone knives, and flint drills collected in Louisiana, Mississippi, Texas, and Arkansas; and Indian bows and arrows, grinding stones, tomahawks, and other stone implements used by Indians in this part of the country. There is also a display showing the evolution of knives, and a collection of gypsy, Filipino, and African knives. The African knives were brought to Louisiana by slave traders in an attempt to evade the Federal law prohibiting importation of slaves; instead of selling slaves, a knife was sold and a slave added as a gift.

Louisiana

NOT CLOVER SEED. During the Revolutionary War, 16-year-old [Bailey] Rawson played the fife for a Massachusetts company. Before settling [in Rawsonville] and building a sawmill, he was a traveling farrier, riding horseback from town to town to follow his trade. On one occasion Rawson gathered several bags of sorrel seed, which he sold to innocent down-countrymen as "not clover seed." Some of the people who used the seed in expectance of raising a special variety of clover, became irate and carried the matter to court. When confronted by the law, the bland Rawson replied: "I sold the stuff for 'not clover seed.' If you can prove that they *are* clover seed, I will pay the damage."

Vermont

SLIDING SCALE. Stamford . . . , with its 33 hotels, large and small, including the Hotel Habana, which caters exclusively to wealthy Cubans and South Americans who spend their summers here, is the largest and most pretentious resort in the Catskills. Excellent facilities for golf, tennis, swimming, riding, mountain-climbing, and fishing provide rural recreation without sacrifice of urbanlike hotel conveniences. Exclusive, a rich man's paradise in many ways, the village has reversed the economic rule: many of the so-called public recreation facilities, which are privately owned, have a sliding scale of prices; fees bound skyward for the "undesirables" and decrease for those who are rich enough to be accounted desirable.

New York

STREET CRIERS. In the early morning Charlestonians are awakened by the rhythmic, melodious calling of Negro vendors hawking their wares. Shrimp tastes a little different, a little better, when bought from a dusky peddler who calls, as he passes the doorway—

> Ro-ro swimp
> Ro-ro swimp
> Roro-ro-ro-ro-swimp
> Come and git yo ro-ro swimp.

From the previous night's fishing of the "mosquito fleet," owned by Negroes, the vendors hawk their catch through the streets, singing an old song—

> Porgy walk
> Porgy talk
> Porgy eat wid knife and fawk;
> Porgie-e-e-e.

(Porgy is a small fish.)
The vegetable peddlers and the flower sellers also call, in Gullah cadence, from early morning until sundown. Negro children offer boiled peanuts for

sale, or vary their proffered wares with insistent offers to dance "the Susy-Q, the Charleston, the Black Bottom," or to sing a "church song," all for a "pinny."

The street-criers' contest is a feature of the nine-day Azalea Festival in spring, Charleston's biggest annual event. This opens with a gorgeous parade of floats, some carrying the queens who represent every county in the State. On the closing night, prior to the grand ball, the festival queen is selected from the galaxy of beauties and crowned by the mayor for a year's reign over the old city, which even after nearly 300 years is South Carolina's social capital.

South Carolina

Everyday Life

At Home

MOST INTELLECTUALS of the 1930s were feminists, their consciousnesses having been raised by the women's rights movement of the preceding generation. A large number of the Guide writers, editors, and administrators were women, as indeed an unprecedented number of the New Deal's executives were (about two FWP workers in five were women). A good many of these women were Lucy Stoners (there had been a vogue in educated circles in the 1920s) and, if they married, kept their maiden names.

The Guides give daily life and "woman's" work the same patient attention they give industrial labor. We learn of traditional cleaning methods like the *ash hopper* and *battlin' sticks*. We learn country customs like *company coming signs*, the *courting lamp*, *bug day*, and the making of *sorghum*. We see that housework too has its folklore and humble *ironing* once had an international resonance.

We are reminded that marriage does not always bring out the best in people (the *meanest man in the world*) and that, even before divorce was common, unhappy wives could find solace in an estranging *visit*.

SLEIGH. Sometimes, with the coming of dusk on winter evenings, bobsleighs slide away from darkened country homes, filled with all the members of the family, from grandparents down to babies. Often the sleigh will pick up additional passengers at a nearby homestead, and sometimes it becomes so crowded that there is scarcely room for the boxes of sandwiches, carefully wrapped cakes, and jars of pickles among the shuffling feet and heated rocks and bricks in the bottom of the sleigh. The singing creak of the sleigh runners accompanies songs that boom out on the night air. Presently a number of sleighs reach an appointed home, but they do not pause long. Across the fields the light of a farmhouse window offers a prelude to their welcome. They become studiously quiet until they reach the door, then burst in with shouts of "Surprise!" There follows a confusion of greetings and commands:
"Get a lantern."
"Put your horses in the east stall. John, show Henry where to put his horses, and—hey, John, turn Jip and Molly out to make room for Millers' team."
"Bring in them sandwiches I brought, Helen."
"Oh, heavens, you knew all about it—you're all dressed up and ready for us. With the country line it ain't possible to surprise anyone."
(Even where there is no country telephone line, it is considered something of a feat to catch the unsuspecting host or hostess napping. Yet all North Dakotans like surprise parties, and have them on birthdays, wedding anniversaries, and every other plausible occasion.)
The farmhouse is converted into a dual-purpose hall. The accordion is placed near the stove to "thaw out," wraps are deposited in corners, on chairs, and on beds, except the one reserved for the babies. Tables, the drophead sewing machine, and everything else that will serve the purpose are arranged for card playing. One room is cleared for dancing. After the first spurt of conversation lags, the musician takes his instrument on his knee, the floor is sprinkled with corn meal or grated paraffin, and soon the house is shaking from studding to rafter. Someone suggests a quadrille, or square dance, and the room resounds with the calls:

"First two gents cross over
And leave your lady stand,
Side two gents cross over,
And take her by the hand.
Salute your corner lady,
Salute your partners all,
Swing the corner lady,
And promenade round the hall."

"First couple to the right,
Birdie in the center and three hands round,
Birdie fly out and hunter step in.
Three hands round."

At midnight, after three or four hours of dancing and card playing, "the ladies" serve lunch. The hat is passed for contributions to the musician, but he does not take the money until he is through playing, which is usually about 3 o'clock in the morning. Then, after a general bedlam of looking for mislaid coats, the babies are carefully wrapped, the younger children are wakened and rub their eyes sleepily as they climb into the sleighs, the empty cake plates and pickle jars are collected, farewells are called, and horses, anxious to return to their own stalls, speed the drowsy parties home through the cold night.

North Dakota

BUG DAY. Among some farm people, if the cow is sick she has doubtless lost her cud and another must be made of an old greasy dishcloth and given her to chew; or if she suffers from hollow horn, her horn must be bored and salt inserted. If the crop is being planted it must be in the right time of the moon, for there are such things as good and bad luck. And then there are "bug days." "Pa was a-plantin' his potatoes when Alex come along and says, 'Mr. Jones, stop right where you are. Them 'taters won't git a chanct to make. The bugs'll git 'em. This here is bug day.' " Naturally Pa stops and waits till bug day has passed.

North Carolina

BARN DANCE. Residents of [the Colchester] district often participate in barn dances, especially just before haying or after the fall harvest. Dimly lit by kerosene lanterns, the great barn floor, smoothed through the years by the thousands of shuffling feet, is alive with merry dancers doing the old-fashioned square dances. Prompters are enthroned in the loft or stand atop an old fanning mill. Music is furnished by violins, banjos, and harmonicas, and the musicians often crowd into a feed or harness room just off the main floor. The Lancers, the Quadrille, Paul Jones, Captain Jiggs, Turkey in the Straw, Pop Goes the Weasel, and many other dances, offer entertainment and pleasure for the customers as well as exercise for the leather-lunged prompter who shouts: "Get your partners for a quadrille! Four more couples! Two more couples!" until the sets are filled. Typical calls through a number are: "Right and left six! Salute your partners: first couple lead up to the right, swing four hands halfway around, and right, and left six with your opposite couple! Lead to the next, ladies change, up to the last couple and swing four hands halfway around, and right and left six with your opposite couple! Balance your partners and swing your corners and promenade all!" Commands are given with all the authority of a drillmaster. The prompter taps the floor with his foot and counts the beat of the music. Hayseed and very dusty cobwebs fall from the ceiling onto the perspiring couples, fair faces are flushed, slick hair becomes dark with moisture, and the males rush for the cider jug the moment the last wailing note of the fiddle dies away.

Connecticut

ASH HOPPER. The ash hopper, a lowly and useful contrivance of pioneer days, no longer used in the lowlands, is still found in the back yard of every cabin up the hollows. It is made by cutting a V-shaped trough in a log, one end of which is elevated a few inches. Four posts are set up to support a frame upon which is placed the hopper, a pyramidal box with the apex resting in the inclined trough. Wood ashes are dumped into the hopper, which is kept covered until soap-making time, when water is poured into it, and the strong lye begins to drip from the trough. When a sufficient quantity has been collected, it is boiled in a large iron kettle with scraps of fat meat. After this boiling has gone on as long as some old experienced grandmother decides it should, the fire is drawn and the contents are allowed to cool. The product is usually a semi-solid, tan substance that lathers well and is a good dirt remover; its makers prefer it to "store" soap because it has a bite that assures them of its strength. Large families often make a barrel of this soap, and at intervals the soap gourd is filled from the barrel.

Tennessee

BATTLIN' STICKS. Between Geneva and Columbus, Negroes can often be seen washing their clothes near a flowing spring or small creek and beating them with "battlin' sticks." Their equipment consists of a large iron pot for boiling the clothes and a wooden block over which the boiled garments are battered vigorously with wooden paddles. This method of washing clothes is common throughout the rural sections of the state.

Georgia

BARN RAISING. Many of the barns in [the Dyer Brook] area were erected by barn raisings. Accumulating all materials, the proprietor would set a date, and farmers from the township and nearby territory would come and set to with a will, raising and boarding the frame work amidst much friendly laughter and shouting. At sundown the men and their families gathered nearby for a hearty meal laid on rough board tables beneath large shade trees; it was customary for the young folks to dance after supper in the new barn to the fiddling of square dances, jigs, and reels.

Maine

CRACKER. The cracker, a pioneer backwoods settler of Georgia and Florida, has come to be known as a gaunt, shiftless person, but originally the term meant simply a native, regardless of his circumstances. Belief that the name may have been shortened from "corn cracker" is given credence in Georgia, but in Florida it derives from the cracking of a whip. It is a name honorably earned by those who made bold talk with their lengthy, rawhide bullwhips in the days when timber and turpentine were the State's chief industries. Those enterprises involved heavy-haul jobs, with oxen the motive power, bullwhips to keep them moving, and the pistol-shot crack of these whips to signal the wearisome progress of the haul through the woods. Cracking the whip became, in fact, an art and a means of communication—an art of making a noise without permitting the whip to touch the animals, and a signal system by which conversations were held across miles of timber barrens. Today the whip crack echoes through the pines only when cowboys are rounding up their herds, and at rodeos and barbecues when the crackers demonstrate their skill.

The cracker's wants are simple—his garden plot, pigpen, chicken coop, and the surrounding woods and near-by streams supply him and his family with nearly all the living necessities. Fish is an important item of diet, and when the cracker is satiated with it he has been heard to say: "I done et so free o' fish, my stommick rises and falls with the tide." Any small income from his place is spent at the general store, and Saturday is the day to go to town and stock up with "bought vittles." His one luxury is tobacco. Snuff-dipping is still prevalent among the older womenfolk, though they scorn cigarettes as immoral.

Teas and brews from native plants and herbs supply remedies for most of the cracker's ills, although few households are complete without a drugstore malaria medicine, usually a volatile draught of cathartic and quinine to cure "break-bone" fever. Panther oil, when it can be obtained, is prized for easing stiff joints and rheumatism.

Superstition rules the life of the cracker; hunting or fishing or planting—almost everything he undertakes—is done according to accepted formula. He would no more set fence posts in the light of the moon than he would plant potatoes or other crops that mature underground.

Any windfall, or a considerable profit from crops, goes for an automobile, preferably a Ford, since the old Model T proved to be the most trustworthy on woods trails. His economic status therefore is known by his transportation, which falls into four categories: mule, Model T, Model A, and V-8; but the garage is the same, an open shed or lean-to.

Experience taught the cracker to resent intrusion and be suspicious of unfamiliar things and persons, particularly strangers who do not speak his idiom. Anyone approaching with a "How do you do?" is likely to be answered by an eloquent and disdainful expectoration. Generations of contact with hardship and poverty have made him undemonstrative, and he seldom displays any but the strongest emotions. He has appropriated the defensive guile of the Negro and turned it to good account in his dealings. Consequently he drives a hard bargain with soft words. The Yankee is his special prey and to best a Yankee by any device is legitimate. "In the winter," the cracker boasts, "we live on the Yankee, and in the summer on fish." Yet with all his bargaining craft, he is often cheated.

Florida

COURTING LAMP. The Samuel Whitman House . . . now the Farmington Museum, . . . is a carefully restored 17th-century dwelling. . . . A collection of lamps contains a "courting lamp," which timed the length of a suitor's visit.

Connecticut

IS THE MILL RUNNING? With the exception of farmers, it is said that there were more millers . . . and millwrights in . . . early years than all other tradesmen combined. It was common for travelers to be hailed with the question, "Is the mill a-runnin'?" Quite often the response was, "Crick too high," "Crick too low," or "Froze up." A variation of three feet in the water might clog the mill wheel or leave it dry; and since it was usually a long trip to the mill, it meant much to the farmer to know before he set out whether the mill was operating or not.

Iowa

SORGHUM. Camden . . . , seat of Benton County, is in a peanut- and sorghum-raising area. In September and October sorghum mills are busy along the roadsides. Smoke curls from wood clearings, and the lights from furnaces and lanterns glow far into the fall nights. The old-time horse-powered mills are still used, though steam mills are replacing them. The old mills can make from 75 to 125 gallons during a day and night cooking. After the cane has been brought to the mill, each man's crop is stacked in separate piles to await his "time to make." His team is hitched to the long pole (or tongue) of the mill and is driven in a circle to turn the wheels that crush the juice from the cane. This juice, looking like dirty green water, is caught in barrels and transferred to big flat pans over a brick or rock furnace. Some of the pans have gates; as the syrup reaches a certain stage ("thickens up"), the gate is opened to let it flow into the next pan. Foam rises as the liquid boils, and is skimmed off and thrown into a "skimming hole," dug at one side of the furnace. The "cooker" is kept very busy dipping the syrup from one pan to the other, or turning it through the gates, to keep it from scorching. The process requires great care; if the sorghum is not cooked exactly to the proper point, it will turn to sugar, become scorched, or have a raw taste.

Entire communities gather around the mills for "the cooking." From time to time the syrup is tasted with wooden paddles whittled out for that purpose. After the "making" is over, there is a big "get-together" and a candy pulling.

"They" (sorghum is never referred to as "it") are "larrupin good truck" for the table. "Lashings" or "slathers" (liberal quantities) of sorghum served with yellow butter on brown biscuits, batter cakes, or flapjacks is the "best eatin' ever intended to man." The bottom of a plate is covered with the thick "surrup," and butter mixed in thickly. The "mixtry" is eaten with a knife or sopped up with a biscuit. Sorghum seed, as well as molasses, is a source of income to the grower, and the cane itself is excellent stock feed.

Tennessee

CEMETERY CLEANING. Rutted sand trails lead into little country graveyards almost concealed by vines and underbrush among pines and blackjack oaks; few are fenced. Some markers are of concrete, one or two perhaps are of marble, but the majority are merely headboards, leaning at crazy angles, their inscriptions obliterated. On newer graves, weeded and swept clean of pine needles, appear flower offerings in mason jars and tin cans.

The annual "cemetery cleaning" is a popular holiday in many parts of rural Florida. On a specified day, usually in the fall, residents gather to clean graves, plant flowers, and enjoy an all-day picnic; food is brought by all families attending. Chicken, fried, baked, and stewed; salads of endless variety; biscuits; sweet milk, coffee, and tea; watermelon and orange preserves; pies; chocolate, banana, and pineapple cakes—all are spread out on long tables under the trees. To eat from one's own basket would show lack of appreciation for a neighbor's cooking. The picnickers wander along the tables, sampling the dishes, and praising the contributions of friends. After all are well stuffed, work in the cemetery proceeds in a somewhat desultory manner. One first cleans one's own family lot, then helps those with larger plots, and finally works on the graves of those who have no surviving relatives.

Florida

IRONING. The Old Devereaux House [in North Castine] . . . is a low-posted white house with central chimney, built in the 1780's. The dormers were a later addition. During the War of 1812, the Americans hid powder in a closet of the house. One day while Mrs. Devereaux was ironing, a party of British came to search the house. They failed to discover the powder for Mrs. Devereaux covered the closet with her freshly ironed clothes.

Maine

VISIT. As was customary among all pioneer American groups, [country] girls usually marry early, and frequently have large families. Divorce is rare, although, occasionally, a wife goes on an extended "visit" to her parents.

Missouri

CANDLEWICK BEDSPREAD. Dalton is the center of the candlewick-bedspread industry, which brings to northwestern Georgia an annual income of several million dollars. The unbleached domestic is stamped with a design before it is distributed to housewives, who draw and cut the threads and wash the finished bedspread. Along the highway between Dalton and Marietta tufted spreads, pillow cases, bath mats, and rugs are hung on display from clotheslines and fences in front of the farmhouses. The first impetus was given to the tufting industry in 1919 by Mrs. M. G. Cannon, Jr., of Dalton, who succeeded in arousing the interest of New York department stores in this handicraft. Many farmers have left the fields to help their wives with tufting, and entire families sit at work in yards and doorways. Spreads are also made in the Dalton factories, both by hand and machinery, for sale to outside markets.

Georgia

LOG ROLLING. In pioneer days, when the thick forests were being cleared, [the] region [around Elrod] was noted for its big log rollings. After the wasteful fashion of the frontier, the timber was completely destroyed; trees and underbrush were cut and burned, though sometimes the largest timber was girdled and left to rot and fall. When an area was to be made into "new ground" the men and women of the neighborhood gathered for the log rolling at the home of the settler whose land was to be cleared. Using smooth, strong sticks called hand spikes, the men in groups of from four to eight, dragged the logs together for a huge bonfire. The host supplied whisky for the occasion and the womenfolk held a quilting party, taking time, however, to prepare a substantial dinner for their men. A square dance, with a fiddler or two furnishing the music, closed the festivities.

Alabama

COMPANY COMING SIGNS. [T]he stranger [in the Louisiana countryside] is sure to be offered *café noir* (black coffee). In the true Acadian home the coffeepot never goes dry or becomes cold by day. Because of the flair of the Acadian for hospitality, many of his superstitions are connected with "company coming" signs. When a rooster crows before the home, the housewife anxiously watches the direction in which his head points, for from that direction a guest will come; a cat will also give this pertinent information by the line of its wagging tail.

Louisiana

THE MEANEST MAN IN THE WORLD. According to tradition, an early resident of Noble County was "the meanest man in the world." No names and dates are available, but the story has remained in circulation through several generations. A man grew tired of his wife and divorced her. She was unable to earn a living and was sent to the county poor asylum; in the meantime, her former husband remarried. At intervals throughout the year the poor asylum held a public paupers' sale when inmates of the institution were sold to the highest bidder and farmed out to work for the people who bought them. They were virtually slaves, receiving nothing but a meager living. This woman was put up for sale at a paupers' auction and her former husband, in the market for a woman to do the heavy housework that his new wife refused to do, purchased her.

Indiana

CORONER. One of Madison's pioneer physicians and its first coroner answered to the name of John Quincy Adams Harvey. He became "Doctor" because he had read a few medical books and did some emergency practice. Called on one occasion to a homestead cabin whose occupant had been found frozen to death, Coroner Harvey opened the door, glanced in, and instantly pronounced his verdict, "Deader 'n hell!"

Nebraska

Food and Drink

ECAUSE THE food we eat tells so much about us, some Guides include favorite local recipes. For the most part, though, when the Guides talk about food they are really talking folklore. Consider, for instance, the account of the origin of *Brunswick stew*.

Food making and eating are social activities in the Guides (see *supper* and *rag's out!*), though there is one instance of shameless joy at an appetite satisfied when no one else is looking.

As for strong drink, the Guides are, like American history, awash in it (see *moonshine, Our Girls, T-totalers*). Anecdotes about drink and drunkenness may be so abundant because the nation had just come through Prohibition (b. 1919–d. 1933), and both the Wets and the Dries had their stories, whether cheery or grim, fresh in mind.

Along with food and drink we find, appropriately, entries that might be categorized under the headings "packaging" (as in *crock*) and "table manners."

———

SUPPERS. Box suppers and pie suppers are given at various churches or school houses. Only pies, golden brown, fruity, and appetizing, are brought to the pie suppers, but for the box suppers the girls prepare elaborate boxed lunches, each trying to outdo the others in ornate trimming and sumptuous content. At suppertime, usually at the conclusion of a program or an amateur play, the pies or boxes are auctioned off to the highest bidder, the man who buys one eating supper with the girl who prepared it. Although none is supposed to know to whom the boxes or pies belong, a girl and her beau are seldom separated, but the man may have to pay an outrageous price if rivals or practical jokers suspect the owner and bid against him. There is always pride in the price, however, since it is an index of the girl's popularity, and the money goes to some worthy fund.

Pie suppers are particularly frequent during political campaigns, when the candidates are expected to attend—and to bid. Less financially exacting, but of more importance politically and socially, are the rallies and "speakings" accompanying political campaigns in rural districts. In many counties, notably in Howard, the candidates organize a joint speaking circuit. The ladies of the local church seldom overlook the financial possibilities of an ice cream supper, and, "given fair weather and a good crowd," the evenings are often more social than political.

Missouri

BURGOO. The old-fashioned barbecue was attended by people from the entire countryside, who gathered to hear fiery political speeches and consume quantities of burgoo. This delectable concoction is still regarded as a requisite to every large gathering in Kentucky; no political campaign can be launched or thoroughbred sale conducted without this as the main dish. Burgoo is a rich, thick soup or broth made with beef, chicken, and vegetables. Huge caldrons containing the highly seasoned mixture are fitted snugly over ditches in which wood fires have been built. Burgoo must be stirred continuously, and the process of making it requires 24 hours.

There is a tradition that Gus Jaubert, a French member of Gen. John Morgan's cavalry, originated burgoo at a time when food was so scarce that all men but the officers had to eat blackbirds. He prepared a mixture with blackbirds as the main ingredient, and the story is that the officers, upon sampling the dish, liked it so much that very little was left for the troopers.

Kentucky

BRUNSWICK STEW. Native to [Brunswick] county is Brunswick stew, a flavorous brew first concocted by a group of hunters. One of the party, who had been detailed to stay in camp as cook, lazily threw all the supplies into a pot, it is said, and cooked the mixture over a slow fire. When his companions returned, cold and exhausted, they found the concoction a most appetizing dish. The time-honored directions for making this luscious meal are: boil about 9 pounds of game—squirrels are preferred—in 2 gallons of water until tender; add to the rich stock 6 pounds of tomatoes, 1 pound of butter-beans, 6 slices of bacon, 1 red pepper; salt to taste; cook 6 hours and add 6 ears of corn cut from the cob; boil for 8 minutes.

Virginia

PONE. Good cooking is a Snow Hill tradition, whether the food is terrapin in chafing dishes, steamed oysters opened in the back room of a soda fountain, or the noted Sunday-pone of Worcester County. The latter is a damp but digestible form of corn bread (also called sweat-pone) that is cooked slowly all night in large iron pots. Nowadays the pone pot and its mixture of meal and molasses is put in the stove oven, but in old times it was set in the fireplace, covered with embers, and left until morning. The pots were also used to heat the family's Saturday-night bath water.

Maryland

GOD'S WELL. On Main Street [Westminster] is God's Well, now covered, which earned its named in 1806 when this section of the State suffered under a severe and protracted drought. The few fortunate owners of wells that had not gone dry locked their pumps and refused water to travelers as well as to their neighbors. Only the Misses Lydia and Betsy Winchester, aged daughters of the town's founder, threw open their gate and placed a sign on their well, "Free Admittance to All. Water Belongs to God." Travelers pushing westward paused to drink, as did many of the town's residents. Eventually, the story is, all wells in town except "God's Well" went dry. The old-fashioned, moss-covered bucket was never empty, the story relates, until the drought ended.

Maryland

CROCK. Worthington . . . , seat of Nobles County, when established in 1871, was a prohibition colony called Okabena (Indian, *the nesting place of herons*). Original deeds to downtown property forbade the sale of liquor on the premises, and even today local ordinances prohibit the sale of drinks stronger than 3.2 percent beer.

It is not true that Worthington citizens were completely weaned away from spirituous liquors, although a local pioneer story so relates. In 1871 a Worthington storekeeper smuggled in a crock of whisky and surreptitiously dispensed it as a side line to his regular business. Two of his patrons, knowing that there were only 5 gallons to begin with, decided to check up on the amount left for their future enjoyment. Throughout the winter they recorded their intake. When a compilation showed that they had already consumed more than 40 gallons, they indignantly confronted the storekeeper, and in fairness to him (fearing that their sense of taste might have been dulled by regular libation), they asked a friend to sample the strong drink. He testified that it bore no trace of whisky whatsoever, although the cork from the jug did smell faintly of it. The storekeeper then admitted that he had made a practice of replacing each drink sold with a like amount of rainwater. In this manner his customers had been "educated to get a kick out of water."

Minnesota

MOUNTAIN SQUIRREL. The highway [near Earl] traverses a vast sagebrush and mesquite plain, frequented by desert horned larks and sage hens, dotted with prairie dog "towns." These colonies, honeycombing large areas, are identified by hundreds of mounds of earth dug from the burrows. The favorite pose of the furry little animal is to sit erect on the edge of a mound, tiny forepaws uplifted. When alarmed, he shakes his bushy tail and, with a ludicrous flirt of hind legs, dives from sight. Although called a dog, probably from its shrill bark, the animal is a rodent of the marmot family. During the early 1890's enterprising ranchers killed, dressed, and shipped prairie dogs to eastern markets as "mountain squirrel." For several years they appeared on hotel menus in New York and Philadelphia; not until a buyer came west to contract for larger shipments was the hoax discovered.

Colorado

NUTTING. Much of the hilly area around Guthrie Center is cut-over timberland. Thick undergrowth and second and third growth timber splash the hillsides with color in autumn. Hazelnut bushes once grew in abundance here, and are still found in uncultivated sections of the region. The nuts grow in clusters, and have rough prickly shells that are thin, brittle, and easily broken.

Black walnut trees grow throughout this area. Every fall, following the first frost, nutting parties range the hillsides gathering the nuts. The trees are just beginning to flame with autumn color; the sky is a brilliant blue—a deeper color than in spring when it often seems washed with pale reflections of the last snow. With sticks and a noisy shaking of branches, the heavy green-hulled nuts are knocked to the ground and gathered into baskets or gunny sacks. Sometimes the nuts are pounded loose from the hulls before they are carried home. Otherwise the nuts are taken home and run through a hand cornsheller to loosen the hulls; they are then spread out to dry.

Iowa

CRACKED WHEAT DERBY. The MacFadden-Dansville Health Resort . . . is a large Victorian hotel established as a sanitarium in 1858 by Dr. Caleb A. Jackson and reopened in 1929 by Bernarr Macfadden, publisher and physical culturist, as a health resort.

The hotel has won wide publicity as the terminus of the Bunion, or Cracked Wheat, Derby, as the newspapers call it, an annual hike by Bernarr Mac-fadden and enthusiastic disciples, who during the two-week trek live on cracked wheat, raisins, brown sugar, and honey.

In the first derby in May 1935, of the 100 crusaders who left New York City only 38 arrived in Dansville, 325 miles away, sunburnt, blistered, and weary. The fourth derby, in 1938, started from Cleveland, Ohio; of the 110 starters, 100 were in at the finish, the good showing probably due to the addition of grapefruit and raw vegetables to the diet. Through cities the hike becomes a triumphal procession with police escort, band serenaders, welcoming speeches, and appearances in local theaters; in Dansville the survivors are rewarded with a sumptuous banquet and a weekend at Macfadden's health resort, topped off by hikes into the countryside.

New York

OUR GIRLS. The most exciting period in Hillsboro's history was the three days before Christmas 1873. On December 22, Dr. Dio Lewis, nationally known temperance lecturer, talked to the women of Hillsboro on "Our Girls." The next day he again spoke to the women, this time of his mother, of her courageous efforts to keep saloon keepers from selling liquor to her weakling husband, and of the evil that lurked in spirituous liquors. The women were deeply touched. Many of them had husbands who drank too much, and before they went home they had formed an organization called the Women's Temperance Crusade. Mrs. Eliza Jane Thompson, daughter of a former Ohio governor, Allen Trimble, was made their leader.

Tremulous at what they were about to do, the women, more than 70 strong, met early on December 24 at the local Presbyterian church, and were addressed by each of Hillsboro's pastors on the righteousness of their purpose. Discreetly the pastors withdrew to let the women pray for guidance. Guidance came, and out of the church and down the street filed a double column of women. They turned when they reached the first saloon, conquered a feeling they found "over-whelming to their finer sensibilities and shocking to their modesty," and entered. In that place of malty smells, shining spittoons, and sawdust floors, they sang a hymn, then knelt in prayer. The spokesman described their purpose to the barkeeper, promising him they would be back the next day; then silently they departed. The barkeeper must have been astounded; they had asked him to close his establishment!

For hours the strange spectacle continued until all of Hillsboro's 13 saloons, its drugstore dispensaries, and its hotel bars had been visited, prayed over, and apprised of the way things were to be. That night the women met at the church to cast up accounts and to make further plans. As they went home, their historian reports, "a last-quarter moon gave benediction through the still, white streets." They had done a good day's work, work that was to be repeated in the following days. In the end the harassed saloon keepers and liquor dispensers closed their bars, and sought worthier occupations or left town. Unsusceptible to these beneficent works, Dunn, a druggist, stubbornly insisted that he would continue to sell liquor by prescription. The crusaders erected a canvas and frame tabernacle in front of his store, sang and prayed with fervor, and sent Mr. Dunn into a high dudgeon. He sued them for trespassing and constituting a public nuisance. The case dragged on for some time until a high court awarded the plaintiff $5 damages. This slightly dampened the spirits of the women, and for some years the drugstore was the only oasis in Hillsboro's desert of prohibition. When repeal came in 1934, an Ohio State liquor store was placed in the former quarters of Mr. Dunn.

Ohio

RAG'S OUT! During the first six years of university [of North Dakota] history there were only two buildings on the [Grand Fork] campus. The main building, later known as Merrifield Hall, contained classrooms, book store, post office, and men's dormitory. The other building, later named Davis Hall for Hannah E. Davis, one of its early matrons, housed the girls' dormitory, and, in the basement, the university dining hall. Alumni of those days relate that the dining hall was a very popular place. When meals were ready to be served a napkin was hung out the basement window, and the first student in the main building who spied the sign, regardless of whether he happened to be in a class or not, yelled, "Rag's out!" The shout was taken up and a stampede to the dining room followed. This custom prevailed for several years. One day President Merrifield was showing some of his Eastern friends through the institution when suddenly "Rag's out" reverberated through the halls. The visitors wondered if there was a riot, and the mortified president realized for the first time how the dinner call sounded to outsiders. He suppressed it with difficulty, after many student debates on the sacredness of college traditions.

North Dakota

PEANUT CONSCIOUS. Suffolk has reason to be peanut conscious. Though 22 concerns, producing a variety of other products, employ about 2,500 workers here, the peanut easily dominates the commercial picture. Peanut farms of lower Tidewater Virginia and North Carolina send more than 50,000 tons of nuts yearly to Suffolk processing plants and the town's 9 large warehouses. All day long during the harvesting season trucks, piled high with nut-filled sacks, rumble through the streets; and in any season, when the wind blows from the factory quarter, the air is heavy with the oily-sweet odor that means local prosperity.

Of several varieties of *arachis hypogaea*—the peanut or "ground pea" that flourishes in the sandy soil of the region—three are favorites: Virginia Bunch, Virginia Runner, and Jumbo. The crop, planted in April, blooms in July and is harvested in October. After pollination, the blossom fades, the stem lengthens and thrusts its head into the earth, where the pod matures. Most crop operations—planting, cultivating, and harvesting—are done by machines, some of which work as many as four field rows at one time. Digging of the nuts is done with a complicated machine, which also strips off loose dirt; it is followed by a hand job of shocking the vines in the field, pods innermost, and by three weeks of curing. Next comes the whirring thresher, which, amid clouds of dust, strips the pods from the vines and feeds them into burlap bags. The nuts are then whisked away to storage warehouses, where a constant temperature of 40° F. prevents the growth of the saw-toothed weevil larvae. The vines make stock forage.

Processing plants are the principal peanut buyers. In the plants high-powered fans blow out stems and trash. Then the nuts to be sold raw for roasting are culled and graded; those to be used for confections, salting, and oil go first to shelling machines, where lightly crushed shells are blown away and nuts drop through grading slots in a jiggling, inclined table. These operations separate large, plump nuts from the inferior grades that will be crushed, to extract oil for cooking and butter substitutes. The residue from this process is sold as stock feed. Candy- and salting-nuts are lightly roasted to loosen the red skins and then blanched in rotary suction machines that also carry off the skins. After this, they pass an electric eye, sensitized to color, which selects the whitest nuts, and then are further culled by hand. Nuts for salting are conveyed to a huge machine, where they are cooked in oil, salted, and subjected to a final check by fluoroscope. Those for candy go straight to dipping machines for chocolate coating, or to mixing machines for a syrup bath before being pressed and scored into bars.

Virginia

BEEF TRUST. Every house in Loa, and in several other Wayne County towns, is a corner house; the remainder of each block is reserved for garden space. Wayne County people, like those of several other southern Utah areas, have their own "beef trust," taking turns at killing a beef to satisfy the local demand. Visitors cannot buy beef in the county; there are no butcher shops.

Utah

T-TOTALERS. A temperance society was formed [at Hector, on Seneca Lake] in 1818; the founders aimed at total abstinence as the cure for the evils of drink, but they omitted wine and beer from the pledge lest they defeat their purpose. In the 1820's other New York State societies incorporated the ideal of total abstinence in their constitutions. In 1826 the Hector society voted to offer its members the choice of two pledges, one for abstinence from distilled spirits and the other for total abstinence; in recording the choices the secretary placed a "T" before the names of those who had signed the total pledge, and they were called "T-Totalers." Teetotalism spelled the temporary decline of the local temperance organizations; many who would have subscribed to abstinence from hard liquor would not relinquish a glass of wine or a scuttle of suds. But Hector remained a desert for many years.

New York

SPRINGHOUSE. Almost hidden among cedars between two hills [South of Batesville] is a springhouse . . . , constructed in 1850, a structure of rough stone blocks tapering to a gable. The roof is of rafter and beam construction, covered by shingles. Many such shelters appear in the Ozarks, although most of them are neither so old nor so solidly built. Springhouses serve to protect the water in which milk, butter, and eggs are chilled. Mountain boys, after a hot day in the fields or an arduous squirrel hunt, sometimes steal into the nearest springhouse and refresh themselves with cold buttermilk taken from a crock set deep in the gravelly spring bottom.

Arkansas

MOONSHINE. [Chester County] was a moonshine center of West Tennessee. In the ravines of Dinney Hollows, in the wooded hills around Montezuma, and in the climbing pine country near Silerton, corn "likker" was illegally distilled. Along creeks hidden by salmon-brown sedgegrass, the moonshiners regulated their fires and tamped shortdough (a mixture of bran meal and water) around the thump-kegs (kegs or barrels through which the distillation coil passes) to keep them from leaking. Under the leaves in the hollows they stashed (cached) away the fresh corn in ten-gallon kegs and let it charter (char) for months. When aged, the deep red liquor was clear of verdigris (fusel oil) and held a bead the size of number five shot. There were no "rabbit eyes on it to pop off" (big bubbles that foam and burst as soon as the bottle is shaken). Certain brands were known as "creeping likker," because they kicked "slow and powerful." The coming of legal whisky in neighboring states has decreased the market for the best corn.

Tennessee

BIG THURSDAY. "Big Thursday" (2nd in August) at Bowers Beach has been a Delaware institution since the memorable day in 1852 when the new oyster ban was lifted. A law had been put into effect that year to prohibit the taking of oysters between May 1 and August 10. The people of the county, accustomed to eating their oysters throughout the year, winter and summer alike, impatiently waited until the opening day arrived. Falling that year on Thursday the day was a gala festival of tonging oysters and eating them raw or roasted, of fiddling and dancing, of talking and drinking and sleeping. When at last the covered wagons or hayracks departed they were loaded not only with oyster-stuffed men, women, and children but also with baskets of oysters in the shell carefully packed in wet marsh hay for storage in cool cellars for future use.

Ever since then Big Thursday has continued to be a celebration for the rural population of Kent County. Even the subsequent postponing of the oyster season until Sept. 1 has made little difference in the size of the crowds that stick to their day in August year after year. Now, instead of wagons, automobiles and trucks bring farm families from nearby necks along the bay or from piney-woods regions near the Maryland Line. Farm work is slack: corn is too big for cultivating, and tomatoes and other crops have not reached their peak. It is a good time to take a breathing spell from hot fields and hotter kitchens.

In election years Big Thursday crowds make an irresistible appeal to candidates for office. In a State where a farmer in overalls naturally addresses a United States Senator by his nickname, and the Senator just as naturally calls the farmer by his, gatherings like this are not to be neglected. The Delaware farmer feels that he should get some oratory, at least, in exchange for his vote, and he enjoys good old-fashioned campaign speeches. His stomach is full, his shoes are loosened or off, and he settles back comfortably to listen.

Delaware

STEAK. Cinnamon bears are common in all the high mountain ranges, and since they are classed as predatory, may be hunted at any time, though the pelts are best in the late fall, before hibernation. The meat is edible, but old-timers, at the prospect of a bear steak, quote the frontier recipe: "Take two pounds of meat from the rump, boil three days in a deep kettle with the head of an axe, and, then, throw away the meat and eat the axe."

Utah

Pastimes

I N THIS category we include both sports and entertainment, although some of the things we see happen here are more "sporting" than others.

The Guides meant to provide a cross section of the pastimes of the various classes in America. *Tournament* and *grabbling*, for example, take place in the upper South; presumably different people practiced each. Different regions, too, have different amusements.

Most of the pastimes are for groups, but not all. *Reading* is done alone because its devotee so chooses; *yodeling* is solitary by everyone else's choice. Fishing is a one-person sport, but the *pike* story suggests that its final enjoyment takes place before a crowd of listeners.

There is even attention paid to high culture: see *Chautauqua* and the *piano* of Vevay, Indiana.

RANCH DANCE. Before the fall round-up it was customary for one of the large ranches to "throw" a dance. Cattlemen and their households arrived by chuck wagon, buckboard, and on horseback, with bedrolls and personal articles for a two-day stay. The womenfolk brought home-cooked delicacies; the ranchman furnished meats, vegetables, and other staples, including several cases of whisky in pint bottles. Each man took his bottle, cached it in some safe place, and resorted to it whenever he was thirsty—which was often. When the pint was emptied, he called for another. No man touched another's bottle. After a big dinner at sundown, festivities began in the ranch-house living room, which was usually large enough to accommodate two dance sets of four couples each, with space for all fancy side steps and "pigeon wings." The orchestra usually consisted of a guitar, banjo, harmonica, and a violin or two.

With boot heels hooked over rungs of chairs tilted back against the wall, with a sand box spittoon within easy range, the musicians swung into such popular ditties as "Sandy Land," "Turkey in the Straw," "Money Musk," and "Good Old Turnip Greens." The "caller" stamped his feet, screeched a wild "ye-ow" to loosen up his vocal chords, and the dance was on. The cadenced thud of heeled boots, the clapping of hands, and the periodic yelps of the dancers continued until morning.

After breakfast the guests slept until noon, when horseshoe pitching, horse and foot races, pistol and roping contests were held. Around the campfire that evening, men and women joined in singing "The Lily of the West," "Clementina," "Sucking Cider through a Straw," and

> Old Aunt Sukey, a fine old squaw,
> Finest ever stepped along the Arkan-saw . . .
>
> *Colorado*

CALLER. The "caller" at the square dance is as important as the fiddler or his second. He tells the dancers what to do, but his directions are so enhanced by his poetical fervor, his humor, and his vocalizing that a visitor, unfamiliar with square-dance calls, can hardly understand the words, let alone translate them into commands. The caller is necessarily well acquainted with his audience and is apt to incorporate in his chants well-known bits of family history. He may also make observations upon love-smitten couples, the perils of store teeth at taffy pullings, or hint gently that his own art is a thirsty business.

Dance calls are fairly uniform throughout the state, but each caller puts his own stamp upon them. The result is a rich body of rustic rhymes. The following verses are typical:

> Break trail home
>   In Indian style;
> Swing the gal behind you
>   Once in a while
> Now grab your partner
>   And go hog-wild!

> Two little sisters
>   Form a ring,
> Now you're born
>   Now you swing!
> (A play on the expression "born to be hung.")

> Panthers scream
>   Bobcats squall
> House cat jumps
>   Through a hole in the wall.

> Eat ice cream,
>   Drink soda water;
> Some old man
>   Gonna lose his daughter.

> Ladies lead off
>   In the cowboy style;
> Stop and rope one
>   Every little while.

> Same ol' boys
>   An' the same ol' trail;
> An' watch the same ol' 'possum
>   Walk the same ol' rail.

> Walk the Huckleberry shuffle
>   And Chinese cling;
> Elbow twist and
>   The grapevine swing!

Swing your partners one and all,
Swing that lady in the checkered shawl,
Gents, hands in your pockets, back to the wall,
Take a chaw of terbacker and balance all.
Quit that hugging, ain't you a-shamed,
Promenade, Oh Promenade!

Oklahoma

TOURNAMENT. Possibly the oldest, and certainly the most picturesque, custom in West Virginia is the South Branch Valley sport of riding "tournament". . . . For more than a century and a half, succeeding generations of young men of this area, one of the first settled in the State, have kept alive this pastime, which is a direct lineal descendant of the feudal tournament or joust. A similar sport is practiced by the Lancers of the British army, but whereas the Britons tilt at a 6-inch board, the Knights of the South Branch tilt with needle-pointed lances, 7 to 9 feet long, at suspended rings, a half inch in diameter. Some of the lances are 60 to 100 years old. The tournament course consists of 3 arches, 60 feet apart, beneath which the horseman rides at a dead run. A ring is suspended in each arch, and the object is to get all three rings on the tip of the lance.

The tournament is attended by great ceremony and a fixed ritual that has never changed. The "Knights," who usually acquire their titles early in life, receive the "Address" delivered in the presence of the assembled audience, after which the conduct of the tournament is turned over to the "Grand Marshal," who calls the knights to post.

The Marshal calls the first rider: "Knight of Silver Bend—Ride!" and "Knight of Hampshire, get ready!"

The Knight of Silver Bend mounts his horse and with lance at rest rides slowly through the arches and in each arch suspends a ring. When the third ring has been hung, the Marshal calls in measured tones, as the contestant rides slowly to the extremity of the course: "Knight of Silver Bend————
—Sir Kni—i—ight!" Then, timed to a nicety, at the moment the rider reaches the end of the course: "CHARGE!"

At the command, the horseman wheels like a flash and, as he rides at full gallop, rises in the stirrups, sets his lance, and in a split second of time impales the tiny circlets on its point. Jabbing hard with a pencil at a one-inch curtain ring may give some idea of the keen eye, the steady nerve, and the perfect horsemanship this exacting sport demands.

The first three courses are run at 1½-inch rings. All 9-ring men, or the leading five, qualify for the course at ¾-inch rings. The final course is run at rings ½-inch in diameter (about the size of a little-finger ring). To the winner goes the privilege of naming the queen of the tournament; and to the next four, the right to select her maids in waiting.

West Virginia

PIANO. In the historical room of the Carnegie Library, one block east of the courthouse on Ferry Street, [in Vevay], is a Muzio Clementi piano, brought from England to this country in 1817. Made in the style of the clavichord with five and a half octaves, it was recognized as a fine instrument, a great improvement over the pianos of that period. Clementi (1752–1832), the Italian composer and pianist who created it, is known as the father of modern piano-building technique. The piano belonged to Mary Wright, daughter of an aristocratic but impoverished English family that came to this country in 1817 and settled on a land grant near Vevay. Deserted by her English fiancé, she lived bewildered and heart-broken in this wild, rough country. An accomplished musician, she found outlet for her grief and loneliness in weekly concerts which she gave for the pioneer folk of the community. On each occasion she descended the ladder from the second floor of her father's rough log cabin attired in court dress and jewels, and with a gracious bow seated herself at the piano and played her entire repertoire. Then without a word she would retire to her second-story room, and the guests would quietly depart. These concerts continued for 40 years without the piano ever being tuned, or the introduction of a new composition. The court dress grew faded and the jewels tarnished, but the same dignified procedure endured year after year. The only time Mary Wright ever left the house was to wander alone in the moonlight. She was found dead in her room in 1874, at the age of 82.

Indiana

CLUB. The most characteristic Nevada institution is the "club"—even the smallest community has one or two. But the gilded hot spots of the Reno and Las Vegas area are not typical. Basic equipment of the true Nevada club, which is usually in a former store, consists of a bar, a few slot machines, and one or more big round poker tables with low-hanging, green-shaded lamps over their centers. In addition there may be other gaming facilities and a dining counter. Primarily, the club is neither a gambling hall nor a saloon; rather, it is a social center similar in some ways to the continental cafe or beerhall. While a few habitues take at least one drink daily, or drop a coin into the slot machines—in lieu of club dues—they often wander in and out several times a day without spending money. As a rule windows are uncurtained and passersby need not even enter to discover whether friends are inside. While the majority of those frequenting the clubs are men, the presence of women draws neither comment nor notice.

Nevada

BATSHOOTING. After the War between the States [Kentwood] became popular with New Orleans excursionists. Picnics and barbecues were held, and the vacationists indulged in various sports, the most popular being trapshooting. Unlike the modern trapshooters who bang away at clay pigeons, these early excursionists substituted live bats which they brought with them in boxes.

Louisiana

DRAG HUNTING. Hitchcock Woods, [at the southwest] border of [Aiken], an area of nearly 20 square miles, where no automobile may enter save in case of fire, is the site of picturesque drag hunts. The drag hunt has been known in Aiken for many years, but it was not until 1916 that this sport became truly "smart." Hounds were brought from the North and club uniforms of green coat with yellow collar were adopted.

Drag hunting is a sport that has everything pertaining to a fox hunt, except the fox. It may include the presence of internationally famed huntsmen, thoroughbred horses, pedigreed dogs, and even a tea room in the woods—but no fox. A bag of anise seed is dragged over a laidout course, and the hounds, just as excited as in a true fox hunt, follow this scent. The drag lines consist of lanes cut through the woods, with rail fences providing barriers to horse and rider. These barriers in some cases are very high and spills are not infrequent. The racing idea is uppermost at all times and some of the drags are ridden at a terrific speed. A rider must keep with the hunt for the honor of the drag and his own stable.

Gentler events are the children's drags each Saturday, when the incipient sportsmen and sportswomen of the two boarding schools turn out. Older riders who prefer an easier pace join these drags.

South Carolina

DANCE COMMITTEE. Mexicans [in the Laredo area] cling to customs of their homeland across the river. One- and two-room *jacales* made of willow branches, daubed with mud or thatch, make homes for the humbler folk; milk goats, dogs and cats, chickens and children swarm over these *casitas*. The more prosperous enjoy formal dances; printed invitations are usually sent, but lacking these, a committee calls upon those to be invited— telephones are not used. Sometimes whole families attend; the girls are chaperoned. Often, between sets, talented guests are asked to entertain, and if a young woman is invited she is escorted to the center of the room by a committee, which rigidly stands guard beside her until she has finished playing, singing or reciting.

Texas

FIDDLER. The square dance fiddler's first concern is to carry a tune, but he must carry it loud enough to be heard over the noise of stamping feet, the cries of the "caller," and the shouts of the dancers. When he fiddles, he "fiddles all over"; feet, hands, knees, head, and eyes are all busy. He is usually supported by a "second," whose performance on the piano, guitar, banjo, organ, or another fiddle, gives the music additional resonance and depth.

The peculiar technique of the fiddler is foreign to the schooled violinist, for many of the effects are produced by tricks not included in the formal study of the violin. One trick, frequently employed to produce a distinctive twangy vibration, is to tune the G string a whole tone higher and then use only the other three; others are the accenting of the last of tied notes, and the playing of a double note on the same pitch. Such idioms are impossible to reproduce on any other than stringed instruments and, as the fiddler maintains, almost impossible for the conventionally trained violinist to play effectively. Deviations from the violinist's technique include supporting the weight of the instrument in the left hand rather than with the chin; playing entirely in the first position, usually holding the bow nearer the middle than the end; and bowing in quick, sawing motions. These methods of playing allow conveniences the trained violinist is denied—the fiddler's head is left free for nodding and emphasizing the music, and for smoking, chewing, and expectoration. It is said that the fiddler needs only his battered instrument, a chunk of rosin, a chair with a rawhide seat, and a dash of Old Nick to produce a concert.

Oklahoma

PIKE. Sizable pike are still taken in the Elk, but none compares with the giant hooked by "Squirrely" Carpenter in the 1880's. It was "the biggest durn pike I ever seed," said Squirrely, and there is reason to believe that it was the most elastic too. On one occasion when escorting a party of fishermen who had taken shelter from a torrential rain in the lea of Grove's Mill, he began on his favorite theme and, as he warmed to his story, became more and more excited as he described his titanic struggle. "And, gentlemen, I hope to die where I stand if that thar fish warn't 69 inches long!" he said, and as he stretched out his arms in a vain effort to demonstrate the length of the monster, his foot slipped on the mossy boards, and Squirrely tumbled backward into the forebay of the mill pond, then running four feet of swift water. Fished out before he struck the mill wheel, he was set dripping and spluttering on his feet. "Shelt," his son, who had not stirred from a comfortable seat against the wall, spat out a mouthful of wheat straw and observed: "Pap! If that durned pike'd been one inch longer, damned if I don't think hit'd drowned ye!"

West Virginia

GRABBLING. [Back country] men like to "grabble" for fish in sloughs, or holes of the river bank, a process that calls for wading naked into the water and running the hands under logs, or driftwood, and into holes for catfish. If they are bitten by snakes, they take a "slug of corn likker," but even the hardiest sometimes die. A tale is told of one man who was struck by a cottonmouth moccasin, a snake with a deep pit between eyes and nostrils, and squarish black blotches on its body. He swelled up "twicet his size at natural, and spots purple as pokeberries come out all over his hide."

Tennessee

GANDER PULL. The section of [Bloomfield] lying on the western side of the dividing creek was known as Gandertown because in early days the young men in this region indulged in gander pulling. A post set in the ground had a revolving crossbar from which a gander with a soaped neck was suspended by the feet. The men, mounted on horseback, rode at full speed past the post, attempting to seize the gander's neck as they went by. The prize was awarded to the contestant who succeeded in jerking off the head.

Kentucky

POKER. In 1902 a gambler known as the White Swede died in Hartville, and local legend relates that three gambler companions agreed to conduct the wake. Tired of staring at one another and at the corpse, they started a poker game; after sampling a bottle of whisky, they were moved to cut the corpse in. By dawn, the dead man had won enough to pay for his burial.

Wyoming

BOX-RUSTLERS. Washington's first theater, the Theater Comique in Seattle, was opened as a variety house in the basement of a saloon on Washington Street in 1876. It was of the "box" type: that is, it had a small stage and auditorium and, most important, a row of boxes around the sides, connected with a bar in the rear. The women did their song and dance on the stage and then, in costumes that for that period were considered the extreme of indecency, mingled with the customers in the boxes, encouraging the sale of liquors. The women became known as box-rustlers, and box-rustling theaters sprang up all over the West. In the 80's, under the stress of competition, managers began to improve their shows.

Washington

BOLITA. Although lucky pieces, powders, and potents are made in Tampa to expedite matters of love, finance, and health, many articles of this nature are imported by salesmen who solicit from door to door. Widely popular is a cone of incense which, when burned, reveals in the ash at its base a number supposed to foretell the current bolita winner. Bolita, introduced to Tampa by the Cubans in the 1880's means "little ball." A hundred balls, consecutively numbered, are tied in a bag and tossed from one person to another. One ball is clutched through the cloth and this bears the winning number. Played by Negroes and whites alike in Jacksonville, Key West, Miami, Tampa, and surrounding towns, bolita has sponsored a great variety of superstitions. Some of these, traceable to the Chinese, who brought the game to Cuba, include Oriental interpretations of dreams. As a result the sale of all dream books as well as publications on astrology and numerology has boomed. For thousands of Tampa folk bolita has invested nearly all the commonplace occurrences of life with the symbolism of figures. House addresses, auto licenses, theater stubs, steps, telephone poles, or anything that can be counted, added, subtracted, or divided, are grist for bolita. Equipped with the additional resources of voodooism, the Cuban Negro can begin with virtually any incident and arrive at a bolita number. He is equally adroit at explaining his miscalculations.

Florida

SNOW-SAILING. [The] land [around Montevideo] is so level that before the erection of modern wire fences snow-sailing was a popular and very exciting sport. Sail-sleighs, resembling ice boats and with room for supplies, shot across the snow with amazing speed, covering distances as great as 100 miles in a single day. Snow-sailing is still popular in some localities, but the long trips of former days are no longer possible.

Minnesota

DANCE. Shootings [in Sidney] were daily events that drew little attention. Someone was shot at a dance one night and instead of stopping the dance the incident only served to heighten the entertainment. The corpse was propped up in a corner and the dancing continued. During a later blast of gunfire, another man was killed. His body was set up beside that of the first victim. It was not until a third corpse was added to the group that the party came to an end.

Nebraska

NIGHT BASEBALL. Fort Wayne claims to be the birthplace of night baseball. On Saturday night, June 2, 1883, at the old League Park, which was then on the "flats" at what is now the foot of Calhoun Street, a team of professionals from Quincy, Illinois, played a team made up of students of the Fort Wayne Methodist Episcopal College under the "rays of electric light." The game was witnessed by some 2,000 persons, who saw the professionals defeat the students by a score of 11 to 10. The arc-lighting system was installed by the Fort Wayne Jenney Electric Light Company, predecessor of the present General Electric Company. The park was lighted by 17 arc lights of the Jenney low-tension type, using half-inch carbons, which furnished illumination equal to 4,857 gas burners. In brilliancy the spectacle was a great success, but as a specimen of ball playing it was poor indeed.

Indiana

SQUARE DANCE. [At the Pine Ridge Pavilion] on a Saturday night the traditional country square-dance is kept alive by a crowd of millworkers from Newton and city dwellers from points as remote as Newark and New York. While the factory hand and his girl are shouting, "He's down, he's up!" the local farmer and his sons and daughters take their several ways to the street corners and movies of Newton.

New Jersey

READING. The early 1900's ushered in a mild epidemic of killings. In 1902 William Dryburn and Barney Dunne were getting quietly drunk in their tent, and they disputed as to who was the best shot. Dryburn dared Dunne to shoot his hat off. Dunne raised his rifle and shot. Both men lost—Dryburn, his head, and Dunne, his wager, because he missed the hat and hit Dryburn square in the forehead. In 1904 E. H. Weeds of Fish Springs drove into Eureka looking for the sheriff. He had the blanket-wrapped body of his partner, A. F. White, on the floor of his buckboard. He explained that White insisted upon singing while he was trying to read. He served ten months in the county jail, reading his books in peace and quiet.

Utah

STURGEON. At [a] bridge [on the] Snake River [near Mountain Home], sturgeon fishing is a popular and most exciting sport. The equipment needed is several hundred feet of stout quarter-inch rope, a few feet of wire cable for a leader, and several strong iron hooks, baited often with raw beef. One end of the rope is tied to a tree on the bank and the other is anchored with a stone out in the river. When a sturgeon is hooked the fun begins. An old-timer here who captures sturgeon for a living usually hitches a team to the rope and after a long while of maneuvering drags the river-beast to the shore. Those who prefer fun that is more hazardous use a boat, manned, if the sturgeon is a large one, by several persons. The largest one ever taken from the river weighed nearly a thousand pounds but most of them are much smaller, and only those weighing less than two hundred pounds are of excellent flavor. Men fishing here perhaps ought to be warned of one danger; often a sturgeon when hooked will lead almost to the bank so gently that the one towing the line in will imagine he has no catch. But when one of these big fellows comes close enough to the bank to see his enemy, he turns with sudden and overwhelming power and speed, and many a man has had the flesh burned from his palms by a sizzling rope.

Idaho

COCK FIGHTING. On Deer Island . . . , a misnomered promontory jutting into Lake San Susan, is the Deer Island Pit, a barnlike structure with a seating capacity of more than 1,000, the scene of great activity and excitement during the cock-fighting season. The season extends from Thanksgiving to the Fourth of July, and reaches its climax here in January during the annual International Tournament, sponsored by the Orlando Game Club, one of the largest of its kind in the country. Held regularly since 1920, the tournament has become in its field what the Kentucky Derby is to followers of the turf.

For the occasion gamecocks are brought from Canada, Cuba, Mexico, Central and South America, and all parts of the United States. Some arrive by plane, others in private railroad cars. The fee for entering a string of birds is $500; they fight for a top purse of $4,000; during the boom fees ran as high as $2,000, and purses occasionally reached $25,000. Known as "mains," "hacks," or "meetings," the fights are not advertised by press or radio, but for several months before the tournament trade papers carry half-page announcements of the event, together with records of past performances of the contestants, and the advertisements of gamecock breeders and others connected with the sport.

The jargon of the cockers is apt to mystify the uninitiated. The metal spurs with which the cocks fight are known as gaffs, or "heels," which are fitted over the bird's spur (after it has been cut down) and held in place by a soft leather strap secured to the leg by waxed thread. Made of tool steel and costing $7.50 a pair, heels are limited in length to two and a half inches and must be conical in form; no sharp-bladed "slasher" types are allowed. To heel a bird properly is an art demanding knowledge and experience; the build of the bird, its stance, its fighting technique, the curve of its natural spur, must all be taken into consideration.

Birds are matched by weight. The minimum is 4.12 pounds; those weighing more than 6.02 pounds are known as "shakes" and fall into the heavyweight class, in which there are no limitations on poundage, as in prizefighting. A "blinker" is a bird blinded in one eye and is usually given a four-

ounce handicap. Rookies yet to pass their first moult are called "stags," and any mongrel is a "dunghill." Among blooded birds are many celebrated fighting strains, but the champions are usually Shufflers, Warhorses, Roundheads, or Mugwumps.

All battlers are put through a strenuous training period. For road work, they are "walked" on an open range to harden their muscles. They are tossed and "flirted" to develop wing power, balance, style, and punch. Miniature boxing gloves, or "muffs," are used in sparring matches. At times a stuffed cock on the end of a stick is the sparring partner.

The regulation pit is circular in form, 16 feet in diameter. As in the squared ring, fights are divided into rounds and usually last from 20 to 30 minutes. Prolonged bouts are transferred to a "drag" pit, where the birds battle to a finish under another referee.

To the International Tournament here admission is $5, but the matinee and night contests attract capacity crowds. Roars of applause greet the referee as he steps into the pit, raises his arm, and announces: "First fight . . . this afternoon . . . between Blue Falcon . . . weight, four-ten . . . and Irish Gray . . . weight, four-eleven and a half!"

The feathered warriors, their eyes gleaming wickedly, their curved gaffs shining, are brought in by their "pitters," or "setters," who are their seconds during the fight. Placed on measured lines at opposite sides of the pit, they are released at the referee's shout of "Fight!" Advancing warily, necks outstretched, feathers ruffled, the birds crouch, shuffle, feint, like boxers sparring for an opening. Suddenly, they leap into the air in a confused tangle of beaks, wings, and gaffs. They drop and rise to attack again with fury. Blue Falcon strikes quickly and both fall, locked together. "Handle!" calls the referee, noting that Blue Falcon has sunk his steel deep into Irish Gray.

The setters expertly separate the birds, stroke them, flex and rub their legs and thighs. At the end of 10 seconds the fight is resumed. As Blue Falcon rushes in, Irish Gray rises awkwardly on his spiked wing. They fly at each other and go down in a bounding ball. They pull apart; their long necks move in and out, and weave from side to side, like a rattlesnake's; powerful beaks tear wattles and combs. In a fierce encounter Irish Gray falls; Blue Falcon strikes at his prostrate foe, struts, and flaps his burnished wings. Watch in hand, the referee counts twenty. Irish Gray is still on the floor, bleeding in several places. Up goes the referee's hand as he shouts "Fight won . . . by Blue Falcon!" The crowd roars, and as much as $1,000 is won in a single side bet.

Florida

BADGER GAME. The history of no old Nevada mining town is complete without an account of a badger game. This was the standard method of hazing the tenderfoot and is still occasionally practiced. In the presence of the newcomer two men would argue as to whether so-and-so's badger could lick such-and-such a dog. The argument would wax hot and stop just short of blows, but end in a respectable bet on the outcome. Posters would then be placed notifying the town of the coming event and the boys would continue loud arguments over every detail. On the appointed day a large box containing the "Badger" would be hauled to the scene, chained and roped. One man would be selected to hold the dog and another to pull the badger from the box by a chain. Just before the fight was to begin someone would point out that the man who was to handle the badger had money on the fight and was disqualified. Arguments would start again and at last someone would suggest that the newcomer was the only person present without a stake on the fight. Pieces of stove pipe or tin would be wrapped around his legs, several pairs of gloves would be put on his hands, and he would be told to grab the chain, pull hard, and run. At the signal the "badger" box would be opened and the newcomer would rush off as fast as he could go in his armor—dragging a "badger" down the street.

Nevada

YODELING. Eagle Rock was used by Washington as one of a chain of observation posts that extended from Paterson to Summit. From here the countryside below was scanned for Tory raiders. A frequenter of Eagle Rock today (1939) is Carl J. Kress, the 32-year-old Orange bookbinder who holds a permit from the Essex County Park Commission to yodel in the reservation every morning between 8 and 8:45. Kress obtained the permit in 1936 after a policeman attempted to put an end to his Alpine habits on the ground that the park commission's rules prohibited singing or playing musical instruments on the reservation. At that, his unique grant allows him only "to yodel . . . subject to the rules and regulations of the park commission."

New Jersey

CHAUTAUQUA. Chautauqua . . . , with accommodations for 15,000 visitors . . . offers a varied program during July and August, including a summer school conducted by New York University, a public lecture series, and outstanding musical concerts. The movement was the child of the revival-camp meeting and of the lyceum, offspring of the American passion for painless self-improvement, and the mother of the radio program and the university extension course. Despite variations and mutations, the basic characteristics of the family persist. The exhorters and lecturers of the revival and lyceum days were the backbone of the Chautauqua; many of its graduates, including Edgar Bergen, are radio stars.

In 1872 John Heyl Vincent (1832–1920), a clergyman, was corresponding secretary of the Methodist Sunday School Association and editor of its publications; distressed by the lack of interest and education among Sunday school teachers, he attempted to inaugurate a new kind of teaching at Camptown, New Jersey. His first innovation was to make a large outdoor map of Palestine and to have his adult pupils follow him over it, telling the stories of Biblical events at appropriate places. The experiment was so successful that, with the aid of Lewis Miller, a businessman, he planned to hold a short term of school for Sunday school teachers at the campmeeting grounds at Chautauqua. Those who attended the first session, in 1874, went home filled with enthusiasm. In a very few years the attendance had become Nation-wide and "Chautauquas" had been organized in many other States. Before long the programs, always advertised as providing "pure, wholesome entertainment," were broadened, and by 1890 practically every type of entertainer now heard on the radio program was appearing before Chautauqua audiences—politicians, explorers, Swiss bellringers, banjoists, xylophonists, glee clubs, rabbis, priests. The exception was the "actor." The stage was still anathema to the church members of rural America and such actors as appeared—in carefully denatured versions of plays that were called "readings"—were disguised as "elocutionists" or "readers."

The all-time star of the Chautauquas was William Jennings Bryan, last of the line of American orators; audiences came year after year to hear him repeat the speech he made at the Democratic National Convention of 1896 in opposition to the gold standard, and swayed raptly as he concluded. "You shall not press down upon the brow of labor this crown of thorns, you shall not crucify mankind upon a cross of gold."

Chautauqua assemblies are still held, but in steadily decreasing numbers; the motion picture, the radio, and the motor car supply more entertainment than they can give and supply them the year round.

New York

Animals

THE DARLINGS of folklore and local history, animals figure large in the Guides—where it is tempting to say they are killed and eaten, put to work, or chased away, and let it go at that.

Animals indigenous to America get special attention: the bison miscalled buffalo, for example; the passenger pigeon, whose migrations made the day dark less than a century before human greed and carelessness exterminated the species, the last representative of which died on September 1, 1914, in the Cincinnati zoo; and the indestructible boll weevil.

Our fellow creatures here are treated with unaccustomed tolerance *(mine rats)* and unreasoning fear (the *miceless house*). They are the objects of civic amusement *(in defense of a bedbug)* and mistaken identity *(Old Bet)*. Man's best friend makes an expected appearance, as does that manlike beast, the bear.

IN DEFENSE OF A BEDBUG. The Old Oak Tree Inn [at Raymond], now burned, was famous as the meeting place of ministers, doctors, lawyers, and scholars of Mississippi. From it Andrew Jackson made an address during his visit to the town, and so great was his ovation that linen sheets were taken from the beds and spread upon the board walks for him to tread upon. From a bed in this hotel Seargent S. Prentiss arose in the middle of the night and made a speech in defense of a bedbug that had bitten him. It was heard by a mock jury and judge, and the bedbug was formally acquitted.

Mississippi

IN PROFOUND APPRECIATION OF THE BOLL WEEVIL. Founded in 1884 near an old settlement called Drake Eye, . . . Enterprise was based upon cotton. But when the boll weevil all but destroyed cotton in 1910, the worried planters, seeking another money crop, turned to peanuts. The result was so gratifying that they erected a Monument to the boll weevil in the public square. Its inscription reads, "In profound appreciation of the boll weevil, and what it has done to herald prosperity, this monument is erected by the citizens of Coffee County and Enterprise ." Three peanut processing plants at Enterprise handle approximately half of the county's yield. One of the largest peanut butter plants in the United States, located here, ships almost a carload of peanut butter daily.

Alabama

ELK. To the east [of Ouray] is a great natural amphitheater, part of the Ouray State Game Refuge. Densely wooded, but with many small parks, it is easily accessible on foot. Years ago the area was stocked with elk. Many are now so tame that they often wander along the streets of the town and through back yards, occasionally getting their antlers entangled in the family wash.

Colorado

COON DOG. Coon dogs are standard household equipment. The dogs are bright yellow, snuff-brown, or black-and-tan, long-eared, and sad-eyed. During the day they loll under the floor of the cabins and lazily scratch at colonies of fleas. At command they will rush into gardens or cornfields to chase out chickens or to lead pigs by their ears to the pens. These dogs, with short names like Drum, Ring, Gum, Rip, Biff, and the like, are the pride of their owners, who think the coon dog should replace the American eagle.

Raccoon and opossum hunts take place at night in the fall and winter. When the dogs are called for the hunt, they become very alert, and lead the hunters deep into the woods, calling mournfully as they pick up a trail. Having treed a 'possum or 'coon, they roar and leap around the tree trunk until the hunters arrive. . . .

Many times the 'coon escapes and takes to water, if a stream is near; it is an expert swimmer and will rest on driftwood and logs. When a dog swims near, the 'coon reaches out one paw or hand, and pushes the dog's head under water. These duckings will continue until the dog stays under, unless rescued by its master.

Tennessee

BATTLE OF THE FROGS. The Frog Pond . . . was the scene, in 1758, of Windham's famous Battle of the Frogs. A tablet marks the site of the incident, which has served as the theme of many ballads and stories. According to one version, the inhabitants of Windham were aroused one night in the summer of 1758, during the French and Indian Wars, by a terrific din. Believing that the town was about to be attacked by an army of French and Indians, the men hastily armed themselves and rushed from their homes to defend the settlement. The weird clamor, which seemed to be coming from the eastern hill, steadily increased. Above the shouts and blood-curdling warwhoops, the terrified settlers heard one persistent cry which they finally interpreted as repeated demands for the surrender of their two prominent lawyers—"Colonel Dyer and Elderkin, too." All night they stood armed, waiting for the attack. In the morning, scouts discovered thousands of dead frogs in a small pond nearby. A drought had reduced the pond to a narrow rill, and the frogs had engaged in a terrific battle in their efforts to reach the last remaining drops of water.

Connecticut

MICELESS HOUSE. [At Fenton] is the 12-room Miceless House, at Shiawassee and Adelaide Streets, built in 1890 by a man who had a great aversion to field mice. Its solid walls are so constructed as to eliminate completely any spaces in which mice might scamper.

Michigan

BURRO. The burro is a stubborn, lazy, contrary little animal; at the same time he is particularly well fitted by nature to serve the needs of the prospector. He is tough and sure-footed on the trail; he can do with less food, less water, and less rest than the horse, mule, or ox; he can subsist equally well on succulent green grasses or dry bark and weeds. . . .

Prospectors claim that without the burro the discovery of important mines and the development of the southwest might have been delayed for many years. Some aver that occasionally the burro has assumed the role of prospector; at times, in his independent search for food the burro has discovered mineral deposits for which men had searched for years.

Henry Wickenberg's burro is said to have been directly responsible for the greatest gold discovery in Arizona. The burro wandered from camp, and when Wickenburg sought him in surrounding hills, the animal, with proverbial contrariness, attempted to elude his master. Wickenburg, becoming angry, threw stones at the stubborn little burro. The stones were heavy and fell short of their mark, for they contained gold; the famous Vulture Mine at Wickenburg was thus discovered. . . .

Some prospectors believe that the burro is a sacred animal—that Jesus placed a cross upon the beast's shoulders as a reward for its service. In proof they will show a more or less distinct cross on every burro. They also claim that a burro never dies of natural causes. "Did you ever see a dead burro?" they challenge the skeptical, and the answer is usually, "No."

Arizona

MINE RATS. Mine rats are liked rather than otherwise by miners, as the men believe the rats will give warning of impending cave-ins and bad gas. Miners do not regard this as a superstition, as they say that the rats notice the slightest movement of the surrounding rock and scamper to places of safety. It is bad luck to kill a mine rat and a miner who does is in the same category as a man who, above ground, mistreats a dog. The underground rats live from the scraps tossed them from the miners' dinner buckets, and they become very accurate timekeepers, appearing at the exact moment the lunch hour begins, even before the miners sit down and open their pails. Miners who work for a long time in the same mine get to know the rats as individuals and naturally give them names such as "Old Gramp" or "Mike."

Arizona

CUSTER WOLF. Over an area 40 miles wide and 65 miles long, the white Custer Wolf ranged for nine years, killing $25,000 worth of livestock. In March 1920, the U.S. Biological Survey sent H. P. Williams into the district with instructions to "stay after the wolf." When Williams first saw it on April 1, two coyotes were acting as its bodyguards. The wolf seemed to tolerate them, because they warned him of danger, but never allowed them to come within 100 yards of him, or to feed from his kills until he had had his fill. Williams killed the coyotes, but spent weeks and months with traps and gun before he got the wolf. On the day the animal was killed, the telephone lines at Custer were busier than on the day the Armistice was signed at the end of the World War.

Wyoming

HODAG. Rhinelander's nickname, "the Hodag City," comes down from the days of Paul Bunyan when a fabulous beast called the hodag roamed the forests. Although it was supposedly extinct, one man in Rhinelander, Eugene S. (Gene) Shepard, stubbornly maintained that some hodags still lived in the remoter swamps. Everybody scoffed at him until the day a strange carcass was found in the wild swampland and brought to the city. Shepard confidently identified it as a hodag, and it became a seven-day wonder. From all over the north visitors came to marvel at this weird beast with bulging eyes, huge horns, great hooked claws, and huge gaping mouth filled with dagger-like teeth. Its hide was tough and brown, and a row of pointed spikes ran down the ridge of its leathery back to the end of its tail. By the time Shepard confessed that he had made the hodag himself, Rhinelander had received its nickname. Today the hodag has become a symbol of the north's old traditions, and Rhinelander high school athletes wear a hodag emblem on their jerseys.

Wisconsin

PACK RATS. In the desert surrounding Gila Bend are many pack rats, sometimes called trade rats from their habit of carrying off articles which they replace with a stick, a rock, or a piece of cactus. Pack rats have probably been responsible for many unsolved mysteries in Arizona. Three prospectors all but dissolved partnership because of strangely missing articles; the success of a surveying project was threatened when a pack rat absconded with the surveyor's only ruler; and a miner just missed landing on six purloined sticks of his own dynamite when he jumped a stream near his claim. Pack rats are indefatigable collectors. Slipping into camp they will take scissors, combs, socks, can openers, or any other articles that they are able to carry. These the rats invariably pay for in their own coin, and seem to think a pine cone for a razor is a fair exchange. They also hide things they do not take, putting thumb tacks in shoes, and socks in coat pockets. For their nests they work out individual architectural schemes, often developing formidable affairs. When cholla joints are plentiful, they fortify their nests with these spiney pieces of cactus till they are impregnable. In northern Arizona the Navajo rob the nests of the pack rats, use their store of nuts or sell them to the traders, and then eat the rats.

Arizona

SCRATCHING POST. Difficulties encountered by the telegraph line crews have a place in Wyoming folklore. Indolent buffalo still roamed the treeless prairie between Omaha and the Laramie Mountains in great herds. They regarded the newly set poles as scratching posts, and several bison could rub a pole out of the ground in a few hours. The line boss decided to spike the poles, points out, to discourage them. This, from the buffalo's point of view, added greatly to their value. Within a few hours, according to the legend, a waiting line of 30 buffalo had formed at every telegraph pole between Cheyenne and Omaha. And when a lone bison lumbered east from Cheyenne, oldsters allowed he had heard of a vacant pole "somewhere this side of Omaha."

Wyoming

MOTHER. Concord has enjoyed an uneventful and fairly prosperous history. The early settlers were bothered by bears. One of the animals, caught in a large trap, was being exhibited to the curious from miles around when he managed to shake himself loose and make for his tormentors. Unfortunately for him, he selected as his prey the child of one Rebecca Morse. Mrs. Morse promptly seized the trap and dispatched the bear with one blow on the head. Bears are still not infrequently slain in this section of Vermont, but by more modern means.

Vermont

HOTEL SNAKES. South Glastonbury is the home of the much publicized Rattlesnake Hunt Club, whose expeditions in Meshomasic State Forest and annual capture of numerous rattlers have attracted wide attention. The return of one member with a bag of seven rattlers to a New York hotel, the story of their escape, and the huntsman's subsequent single-handed recapture of the reptiles, has become a local legend.

Connecticut

OLD BET. Somers is "the birthplace of the American circus." In the center of the hamlet is the wooden Statue of Old Bet, the first traveling elephant, standing on a granite shaft. In 1815, Hachaliah Bailey purchased the animal from a ship captain, who had brought her over from England. Bailey named her "Old Bet" and began to exhibit her about the country. He added monkeys and a bear or two, traveling from place to place at night to minimize the "free show" possibilities.

Then "Uncle Nate" Howes, of South East, now Sodom, Putnam County, leased Old Bet from Bailey and introduced the first canvas-roofed "round top" to the circus industry. But Old Bet was neither old nor docile, and since little or nothing was known about the handling of elephants, it was not surprising that her behavior often excited apprehension among the villagers. Finally a group of fanatics in Connecticut who detected in her a resemblance to the Behemoth of Scripture shot her down. . . .

Opposite the elephant monument is the Elephant Hotel, a three-story brick structure, now the village hall of Somers. It was built by Bailey as a resort for the circus fraternity and for the entertainment of drovers, who were frequent guests.

New York

S.P.C.A. A bull and bear fight, typical of the entertainment of pioneers the world over, was staged in a pit at Custer City in 1879. Agents of the Pennsylvania S.P.C.A. ordered the fight halted, but spectators drove them from town after they had declined the promoter's invitation to "go ahead and stop it yourselves!" Meanwhile, the bear clambered out of the pit and ran amuck, inflicting slight wounds on a number of spectators. After considerable excitement he was roped and thrown into the arena, but refused to resume the fight.

Pennsylvania

PIGEONS. Genoa . . . is peopled by Italian fishermen and farmers whose ancestors came up the [Mississippi] river in 1848 from lead mines at Galena, Illinois. In Genoa they began work as fishermen; a few English, New England and German families moved in later, but the community remained distinctively Italian. In early days tremendous flocks of wild pigeons flew close to the cliffs behind the village, and men standing on the bluffs knocked them down with long willow branches. One year, when nesting pigeons covered the islands for 7 miles up and downstream, people went out with nets and brought back as many as two barrels of pigeons each.

Wisconsin

BLACK ROBE. During the summer of 1868, immediately after the close of the war over the Bozeman Road, Father Pierre Jean De Smet preached the first Catholic sermon in the vicinity of Sheridan, before a large gathering of the Crow Nation. A legend of a miracle the "Black Robe" (as Father De Smet was called by the Indians) performed to illustrate the potency of the white man's God is still repeated in the valley. Because white men had brought war and pestilence with them into the West, the Indians regarded their God with suspicion and mistrust. When De Smet arrived in the Crow camp, a chieftain pointed out an aged buffalo bull near by and commanded the priest to approach him and place his hand on the head of the enraged animal. De Smet, the legend says, approached the bison warily, expecting to be gored. But the sun glistened on the silver crucifix that hung from the Black Robe's throat, and the bull was hypnotized by the reflection; he stood very quiet while the priest reached out and scratched his head. Then De Smet returned to accept the homage of the tribesmen.

Wyoming

TURKEY TROT. Cuero is nationally famous for its Turkey Trot, usually held every second year in November. This festival features the unusual spectacle of thousands of turkeys marching down the main street, headed by a trumpet corps and a band, and followed by the gaily decorated floats of the "Sultana" of the festival and her attendants. It is the turkeys' big day, and for most of them their last, as the majority of the birds are taken immediately to the pens of the large packing plants to be killed, dressed, and shipped to all parts of the country. Newspaper and newsreel men are among the 20,000 visitors who usually attend Cuero's Turkey Trot, and the event receives nation-wide publicity.

Texas

TEDDY BEAR. Roosevelt . . . owes its existence to Theodore Roosevelt's penchant for bear hunting. In October 1907 Roosevelt and several noted Louisiana hunters stopped at a hunting lodge which had been set up on Tensas Bayou near the present village. A bearded hunter, Ben Lilley, came out of the swamps to help search for bears and, according to one account, chased a bear into a hollow tree trunk, where he held the animal by lying on his back and thrusting his feet against the bear's posterior. The rest of the party soon came up and Roosevelt got his bear. During the hunt other more dignified kills were made by the President, who does not record Lilley's feat in his account of the expedition *(In the Louisiana Canebrakes)*. This expedition is said to have inspired the manufacture of the subsequently popular toy, the "teddy bear."

Louisiana

A LADY—AND A MOTHER. Theophilus Haecker, ... although popularly known as the "father of Minnesota's dairy cooperatives," is best known among professional men for his early research on feeding standards for dairy cows. Mr. Haecker's early schooling was interrupted by the Civil War, in which he served, and was resumed at the University of Wisconsin, where, after several interruptions, he was employed as dairy specialist. He came to the University of Minnesota as an instructor in 1891 and was placed in charge of the Dairy School two years later. He authored a saying, oft repeated among dairymen, "Treat the cow kindly, boys; remember she's a lady—and a mother."

Minnesota

PET CEMETERY. Left from Ontarioville, on the main graveled road running due south, is the Illinois Pet Cemetery. . . . . Here are buried canaries, dogs, cats, monkeys, and rabbits. Funerals follow a fixed routine. Birds and other small animals are buried in white plush boxes, larger animals in gray and silver-pine caskets. The hearse is a seven-passenger car, with a compartment for the dead pet. The tract of six acres, in charge of a caretaker, contains numerous granite monuments, appropriately engraved. Some have inlaid photographs of the pet. A cross marks the grave of a dog that saved its master's life.

Illinois

The People

Some Special People

O N A November 1939 CBS radio program, *Pursuit of Happiness*, the celebrated black singer, actor, and leftist Paul Robeson introduced "Ballad for Americans," a story-song with orchestra and chorus. This cantata, which took twelve minutes to perform, was so popular that Robeson repeated it many times, including at the 1940 Republican convention; he, Bing Crosby, and Kate Smith each made records of it. Its crucial line occurs when the mysterious soloist explains who he or she is: "I'm just an Irish-Negro-Jewish-Italian-French-and-English-Spanish-Russian-Chinese-Polish-Scotch-Hungarian-Litvak-Swedish-Finnish-Canadian-Greek-and-Turk-and-Czech-and-Double-Check American!"

This line suggests something about the American character we prefer to ignore. For all our talk about the importance of the individual, we identify ourselves, our neighbors, and everybody else, as members of groups. We may fight this tendency, many of us, but we lose.

The people we hear about in this chapter belong to minority groups smaller and more cohesive than the big minorities (the Irish, Jewish, black, red-haired, deaf, etc.). These special people stand outside mainstream society, and the old chicken-and-egg question applies: did the *Perfectionists* set themselves apart, or did their neighbors? Who isolated the *Alabama Cajans* or the *Redbones*?

Some of these people might not define themselves as a group (the inhabitants of the Wisconsin *transient camp*, say); others certainly would (the *Wandering Pilgrims*). In at least one case (the *ickies*), a group defines itself by defining others.

ALABAMA CAJANS. In the heavily wooded region around Citronelle are several Cajan Settlements, occupied by a people of undetermined racial origin. The name, Cajan, is not applied correctly, for these people are not related to the Cajuns of the Gulf Coast, who are descended from the Acadians of Canada. The Alabama Cajans know little of their ancestry, but they are believed to be descended from early French, Spanish, and English settlers who married Indian women. Some of them say that their forefathers were buccaneers from Mexico, who made this region a base for their operation.

It was only as recently as the year 1929 that the Cajans of Washington County sought a court test on the issue of their children being barred from white schools. Testimony was concerned chiefly with the ancestry of one woman. The State attempted to show that she was a Negro, and that during the War between the States she had been sold as a slave at Jackson, Alabama; Cajans contended that she was a full-blood Cherokee, unlawfully placed in slavery. When the case was concluded, tension in the crowded courtroom caused the judge to postpone announcement of a decision. It was never made public, but the Cajans claimed a victory, because the State installed a tri-racial system in Washington, Mobile, and Clarke counties. Today, schools are provided for Cajan children through the seventh grade, but no provision is made for high school instruction. They are not allowed to enter Alabama colleges, although a few have gained entry by concealing their ancestry.

Repeated controversies over social status with their white neighbors have made the Cajans a suspicious, solitary people. Their cabins are rarely found on the highways, for they select the most inaccessible spots available, banding together in small isolated communities. Some of the Cajans take a superb and tragic pride in their poverty; others are reticent and sullen in the presence of strangers and avoid them if possible.

A sharp contrast in types has contributed to the racial confusion. In a single family, where both parents are dark complexioned, one child may have black, coarse hair, swarthy complexion, and jet-black eyes, while another has deep blue eyes, fair complexion, and blond hair. Many Cajan women are pretty in an exotic way, but their good looks are frequently spoiled by stained and sometimes broken teeth. Cajan women love bright colors and often wear scarfs wound about their hair, and glittering cheap jewelry, which makes them resemble gypsies. The olive-hued men are darkened by outdoor living.

Cajan houses are much alike, although some are more comfortably equipped than others. There are usually only two rooms; the cooking is done in one and the entire family, sometimes consisting of as many as ten persons, sleeps in the other. Furniture is made up of odds and ends, and most of the beds are homemade. On the board walls are pictures of Biblical scenes, newspapers to guard against winter winds, and broken pieces of mirror. Believing devoutly in conjure, ha'nts, and signs, many of the Cajans wear "tricks" to guard against disease and bad fortune. They believe that every murdered thing, man or animal, has the power to return to life as an avenger.

The churches have for many years tried to improve their condition and to win converts, but progress has been slow. The adult Cajan does not like to congregate except with his own kind. He also likes his Sunday leisure and does not sacrifice it easily for church-going. This is especially true if the preacher refers to such subjects as drinking, rowdying, and men and women living together out of wedlock. But despite his irreligion, the Cajan usually has a high sense of honor. If an officer whom he likes sends for him, he will walk miles to jail. In one case, a Cajan stabbed another fatally, and was himself considerably cut up. As he lay at home in bed, he received word that a certain Mobile County officer wanted him. Without question or complaint, he arose, dressed himself, and walked seven painful miles into Citronelle.

Most of the Cajans depend upon lumbering and turpentining for their livelihood. As the great stands of timber have been cut away, employment in these industries has diminished until many of them must be cared for by welfare agencies. They do not complain, however, and most of them continue to live their solitary lives in their own way, accepting charity only when faced with actual starvation.

Alabama

REDBONES. On the southern shore of Black Lake live many "Redbones" (Louisiana name for a person of white, Indian, and Negro parentage) who, like the mulattoes of Isle Brevelle . . . , live to themselves apart from whites and Negroes. Local traditions vary as to the origin of these people. According to one, they are descendants of early French explorers who intermarried with the Indians; another relates that in the sixteenth century a party of Portuguese sailors, shipwrecked in the Gulf of Mexico, made their way through the wilderness of central Louisiana and settled among friendly Indians. Presumably, these half-breeds later intermarried with Negroes. Whatever their ancestry, the Redbones are tall and slender, have a reddish complexion, dark eyes, high cheek bones, and straight, black hair. The strange semitransparent appearance of their skin is responsible for their odd sobriquet. Strangers frequently trade and in some instances form friendships with them, but as a whole the group maintains a stoical reserve which cannot be completely broken.

Louisiana

WANDERING PILGRIMS. Early in the winter of 1816–17 a religious band known as the Wandering Pilgrims, a begging sect, came from somewhere in the East and stopped near Plain City. The group consisted of about 40 men, women, and children, each wearing a piece of canvas resembling sackcloth. They washed neither their garments nor their bodies, and were forbidden the use of knife, fork, spoon, and plate. What became of these curious people is not known. Local accounts state that they later established themselves along the Little Miami River, where their prophet amazed onlookers by walking on the water. A skeptic discovered a plank walk just beneath the surface of the water and removed one of the planks. One night the prophet started to walk the waters, sank out of sight, and was never seen again.

Ohio

TRANSIENT CAMP. In [Hayward] is Camp Hayward, the only transient camp remaining in the State. Here drifters temporarily or permanently laid up from the road are permitted to stay as long as they abide by camp rules. It would be hard to recruit a logging gang, a harvest crew, or a section gang without such men; but when they grow old or can find no work they are glad to find some shelter like this. The number of men at Camp Hayward varies with the season from about 225 to 530. Most of them are migratory workers. Though some are rather young, the average age is 63 years, and 80 per cent have some physical infirmity.

Camp Hayward was founded in 1934, when the State Public Welfare Department, aided by the Wisconsin Emergency Relief Administration, took over the buildings of an abandoned Indian school and began the acquisition of its present 240-acre farm. All improvements have been made by the men themselves; the camp is almost self-sufficient and often has surplus products for sale. The men are paid from 50¢ to $4.50 a week, depending upon their skills; with leave from the director, they may go on short furloughs.

As one is an experienced butcher, the camp director can buy meat on the hoof and utilize the whole carcass. Another, who once owned his own bakery, has trained an assistant, and together they make bread, pies, cakes, and pastries. The camp kitchen is in charge of two ex-cooks who prepare big, family-style meals at a cost of from 25¢ to 28¢ each. Washing for the entire camp is done in a repaired steam laundry.

A logging-camp blacksmith once appeared here. Dissatisfied with farm work, he asked for a forge and was given one. Immediately he set to work, endangering his health by 18-hour vigils over his glowing irons as he wrought ornamental ironwork. He had learned his trade in Europe and remembered it through all the years he spent repairing chains and forging hooks in the lumber camps. Soon he took other transient blacksmiths as his apprentices and trained them in his craft. Although he is now dead, Camp Hayward's reputation for its wrought ironwork is still maintained; in 1937 it sold $5,000 worth of lamps, brackets, candelabra, and similar articles handmade by its expert smiths.

Wisconsin

PERFECTIONISTS. ["The Mansion," in Kenwood, New York] was the first large community house of the Perfectionists, a cult that migrated here from New England in 1848 under the leadership of John Humphrey Noyes (1811–86). Noyes, a native New Englander, narrowly missed expulsion from Yale Theological Seminary because of his amazingly unorthodox views. Fired by an impassioned fervor, for many years he traveled the country, preaching his radical conception of a new Christianity based on the belief that Christ's second coming occurred in A.D. 70 and that the human race was already freed from sin and could achieve perfection. Later he developed a mandated code of sex relationship.

After an earlier communal group in Putney, Vermont, had been forced to disband, Noyes came to Oneida, where many of his converts joined him. For several years they supported themselves by tilling the soil; but when Samuel Newhouse, a convert at Oneida Castle, patented an efficient steel trap, Noyes, with his genius for organization and administration, built up a prosperous industrial community on this foundation. Later, Charles Cragin, at a branch community in Wallingford, Connecticut, perfected the manufacture of silver plate, which has grown into the present immense business.

Meanwhile, Noyes's peculiar sex teachings were again fomenting outside criticism. Explained as 'complex marriage,' the sex relationships of the Perfectionists were in reality a community-directed form of selective breeding and birth control. They discouraged individual, sentimental love, the better to direct selective mating. The birth rate was planned, and children were taken from their mothers when a year or 18 months old to be raised as wards of the community. It is worthy of note that several of the children raised by the community achieved high and respected positions in the economic, educational, and political life of the State.

Noyes was tactful and diplomatic in his leadership. Perfectionists selected the type of work they liked best and were best fitted to do; supervisory positions were held in succession; real community of work was practiced, and its fruits were shared equally; and as this group of people were all thrifty and industrious, they became comparatively wealthy. However, so vehement was outside criticism, encouraged by inside dissension, that in 1879 Noyes left Oneida and took up residence in Canada. Here for a year he reigned by remote control. But new schisms broke out; and finally in 1881 all the property, real and personal, was distributed on an equitable basis, the business was incorporated into a $600,000 company, and the shares were apportioned. From this beginning, Oneida,Ltd., has risen to become one of the outstanding producers of silver-plated tableware in the United States.

New York

BANKERS. The coast people, the "bankers" in particular [residents of North Carolina's Outer Banks], have lived so long isolated that their ways have a distinct flavor of their own. Especially is this true of their speech, though it is difficult to convey the impression. Subtle differences of dialect depend not only on phrases and their pronunciation but on the intonation, drawl, and rhythm of the utterance, impossible to indicate in print. People sensitive to dialect rhythms can tell by a man's speech whether he comes from Hatteras or Roanoke Island, or even from which end of Roanoke Island, but they can hardly define the differences, and they could never transcribe the pronunciation phonetically. There are some easily recorded distinctions of North Carolina coastal speech—one the quality of the vowels, "oi" for i. "Hoigh toide, no feesh," says the fisherman, "Oi'm goin' home." Another young native complains of the girls ("darlin's" in his dialect), "Oi loike the darlin's but the darlin's don't loike me."

North Carolina

ICKIES. Loiter near the bandstands at Roseland and the Savoy, get a table up close in some of the smaller places such as the Onyx, the Uptown House and Hickory House, or simply stand on the sidewalk among the crowd of musicians gathered outside union headquarters on Fiftieth Street just off Sixth Avenue, and you will catch words and expressions no more comprehensible to uninitiated non-musicians or *ickies* than Sanskrit. How are we to know that a *Dracula* is a key-pounding pianist who lifts his hands up to his face, or that the bass fiddle is the *doghouse*, or that *shmaltz* musicians are *four-button suit guys* and *long underwear boys?*

New York Panorama

SMOKE HOLERS. The Smoke Hole country lies isolated in a rugged canyon of the South Branch of the Potomac, which here deserts its broad and ancient valley to pass between the precipitous rock walls into the former bed of its tributary, Briggs Run; for that small stream, the sole proprietor of the Smoke Hole in ages past, "pirated" the flow of the South Branch River and set it to work in its own narrow defile.

Travel through the 16-mile gorge is not easy; less than 10 miles is accessible by automobile over a narrow winding dirt road carved in the face of a mountain wall 500 feet above the river. Spectacular scenery, virgin forests, abundant game, and a stream well stocked with trout and bass make the Smoke Hole region an ideal vacation spot for those who like to rough it. The Steel family first settled in the Smoke Hole, building a log cabin near the site of the Old Palestine Church . . . sometime before 1760. After the Revolutionary War a number of Hessian soldiers settled in the section; most of its 200 inhabitants today are their descendants, and they have little contact or commerce outside their valley. Barter is still the common practice at the local store; maple sugar, honey, walnut kernels, herbs, and turkeys are exchanged for clothes, salt, sugar, coffee, tobacco, lamp wicks, even iced soft drinks.

Tall, muscular, and bronzed, the typical Smoke Holer leads a simple life, hunting, fishing, and farming just enough to provide him and his family with food. On the rocky farms and hillside pastures a few of the more industrious raise sheep and have a dozen or two lambs and several hundred pounds of wool to offer for sale each spring, almost their sole source of cash income. Extremely hospitable to one another, the Smoke Hole people are shy with strangers and resent "city airs," but with patience and tact their reticence can be overcome. Their speech is quaint, containing many archaic forms handed down from the first settlers of the eighteenth century. They use such plural forms as "postes," "beastes," "nestes," "ghostes," and analogous verb forms, "costes" and "twistes." They employ "clumb" for "climbed," "wrop" for "wrapped," "holp" for "helped," and such redundancies as "rifle-gun," "rock-clift," "ham-meat" and "tooth-dentist." Peculiarly free from modern slang, their vocabulary includes such a familiar term as "budget" to signify a bag, wallet, or bundle. The Smoke Holer is most precise: "Is that a bushel basket?" he is asked. "No, I reckon not," is the reply, "but hit'll hold nigh onto a bushel."

Most Smoke Hole families live on the crest of a mountain, or up a hollow from the road, in tiny one- and two-room log houses, with clay-daubed walls, clapboard roofs, and small windows, which are open holes except in winter, when heavy canvas is stretched across them to keep out wind and cold. Floored with splintery whip-sawed boards, the houses have rough walls, occasionally papered neatly with bright pages from seed books, mail order catalogues, and rotogravure sections. Articles of clothing, and often long-barreled rifles, a hunting bag, and fishing tackle, hang from the pole rafters, or from wooden pegs in the wall. Conspicuously placed over the mantel or door is usually a good-luck horseshoe, wrapped in gold- or silver-colored tinfoil. For the most part, the furniture consists of splint-bottom chairs, an unpolished board table with wooden benches, and old-fashioned wooden beds with straw ticks; rusty wood-burning stoves have replaced the "cat and clay" chimney in most homes. A few families have phonographs, with hillbilly recordings, but many have never heard a radio; two or three of the more prosperous families drive automobiles. Tailored and store-bought clothes are worn only on special occasions and then carefully laid away to be preserved as "Sunday-go-to-meetin' best." The women's bonnets, of an ancient vintage, resemble the curiosities in vogue as the *dernier cri* at the present time (1941).

West Virginia

SAUNA. The Finns are a clannish people who cling to their Old World manners and customs, and to a stranger may sometimes seem unfriendly. At one time a suspicious farmer accused them of practicing magic and of worshipping pagan deities. Entire families, he claimed, wrapped themselves in white sheets and retreated to a small square building set apart from the dwellings and worshipped their gods, calling upon them to bring rain and good harvests to Finns, and wrath upon their neighbors. On investigation, however, it was discovered that although they did wrap themselves in sheets and visit these "shrines" almost daily, it was not in the zeal of religion but for the purpose of taking baths. The Finns here are almost fanatical advocates of cleanliness, and each has his own "sauna" or steam bathhouse. . . .

Minnesota

THE WOMEN WORE SHORTS. Croton-on-Hudson . . . came into existence as the home of Irish and Italian laborers who were building the dam that created Croton Reservoir. About the time of the World War, Max Eastman and several others who had to live economically and wanted to escape from Greenwich Village tenements, acquired land on the wooded hills above Croton and built small houses; in time they were joined by Edna St. Vincent Millay, poet; Dudley Field Malone, lawyer; Doris Stevens, militant feminist; Mabel Dodge and her husband Maurice Stern, the artist; Floyd Dell, novelist; John Reed, radical journalist; Boardman Robinson, cartoonist and painter; Stuart Chase, economist; and others. The colony caused considerable excitement among the natives; it was reported that the women wore shorts, smoked cigarettes, and took sun baths, and that the men indulged in similarly shocking activities. After the war Harry Kelly, real estate promoter, conceived the idea of developing a suburban village here. He organized a company, bought up land, and advertised the place as a retreat for intellectuals and professional workers. One or two fairly large houses were built, but the majority were cottages. By 1926 enough children were on the scene whose parents wanted a more progressive school than could be developed in the village below, to make possible the establishment of Hessian Hills School, a co-operative enterprise. This school has become the center of community life and has, to a large extent, governed its development. The wilder fringe of the post-war years has disappeared, and most of the hill dwellers, some of them early settlers, are now sedate citizens with family interests.

New York

FAIRMONT SPORTSMEN. In the 1870's [Fairmont] was devastated by a 4-year grasshopper plague and was saved from complete extinction only by the persistent efforts of a newly arrived colony of English farmers. This extraordinary group, most of whom were Oxford and Cambridge graduates—several of them titled—came here at the instigation of a Yankee promoter. Despite their crop failures caused by locust ravages, many of these Englishmen were able to survive. They became known throughout the State and surrounding areas as the "Fairmont Sportsmen," and are credited with introducing fox-hunting in southern Minnesota. Attired in hunting coats, made by the village tailoress, they rode to hounds over hill and stream, in quest of any quarry that appeared. A story is told of "one run of thirty miles in three hours, where the dead-beaten wolf swam the Watonwan River—the huntsman after him, swimming with one arm, and steering his jaded mare with the other." At the State fair of 1878 the Britishers, clad in their red coats and high boots, rode "genuine hurdle races, flying amid clouds of blinding dust over four-foot hurdles." So spectacular was their exhibition on this occasion that they "divided the honors with President Hayes and the celebrated trotter Rarus."

Minnesota

MILLERITES. The [Old West] church is the oldest landmark in Calais Township, and has been the meeting-house at different times of various sects, including the Millerites. Calais had more than its share of these fanatics, of whom it was estimated that there were about 50,000 in the country. They were followers of William Miller, who demonstrated from Scripture, to their satisfaction, that the world would end on December 31, 1843, with the earth and sea giving up their dead and those who had achieved salvation entering immediately into eternal bliss. On the last evening of 1843, the Old West Church was packed, with both Millerites and those who came to see the show. A large clock was set up near the pulpit. As midnight began to strike, women screamed, and several fainted; that was all. In ten minutes the church was empty, and the brief history of the Millerites was at an end.

Vermont

[But elsewhere, the end was yet to come.] Sugar Hill was a hotbed of Millerism. . . . Miller . . . finally set . . . the fatal day as October 22, 1844. Many believed in him so firmly that they harvested no crops that year, and either sold their livestock or gave it away. They prepared themselves by six weeks of prayer and fasting and on the last day gathered either in the cemetery or at the church, clothed in white flowing robes and ready for their ascension. On the day before the world was supposed to end, one man went out into the field to give a final exhortation to some "unsaved" neighbors. Worn out with fasting and prayer, he sat down on a haystack and went to sleep. The recreants then removed most of the hay and touched a match to what was left. The Millerite awoke with a start, shouting, "Hell—just as I expected." One man fell from the ridgepole while dressed in his flowing robes and broke his ankle; others, hearing a neighbor's dinner horn, thought it was Gabriel's trumpet. Some gathered in the cemetery were sure they heard bones rattling in the graves.

New Hampshire

OREGON CAVEMEN. The [Grants Pass] City Park on the south bank of the Rogue provides facilities for swimming, boating, tennis, and other sports. The Oregon Cavemen, a social and service club, hold annual festivities and carnivals, in which the members impersonate their primal forbears. The Cavemen claim the marble halls of the Oregon Caves as their ancestral home. Symbolically their food and drink consists of the meat of the dinosaur and the blood of the saber-tooth tiger. The officers of the organization are Chief Big Horn, Rising Buck, keeper of the wampum, Clubfist, Wingfeather, and Flamecatcher.

Oregon

The Young

THE DEPRESSION was a hard time for children with aspiring parents. They were brought up by the rules of Behaviorist John B. Watson, who recommended putting them on a schedule from birth (no feeding till that four hours is up; won't kill them to wail), toilet training before they could walk, and showing affection by nothing more than a firm handshake (want them to be sissies?). The bedtime book of choice was the dogged *Little Engine That Could* (1929).

Reflecting this philosophy, the Guides show again and again the lives of children being regulated by adults. The only kids lucky enough to have elbow room are those so low in social status as to be beneath ambition: the minorities *(pinate)* and the poor (the Arkansas *bag swing)*. For many children, even the playing of *marbles* is regulated.

The children we see here are most often at children's work: going to school. The sites range from early *academies* to *Mooseheart*. The victims are heroic *(school bus)*, vulnerable *(evil town, dangerous city)*, obedient to command *(campus inspection)*, anti-social *(pedagogue)*. A few are already at adult work, experiencing life's ups and downs *(circus, spasm band)*.

In less than a decade Dr. Spock would cause a revolution by recommending that grownups let children be children, and Progressive education would enter America's classrooms in force, under the banner "Teach the Child, Not the Subject."

CIPHERING MATCH AND SPELLING BEE. One-room log schoolhouses, which typified rural common-school education for most of the nineteenth century, were also the community centers. Here church services were sometimes held, and such favorite social gatherings as ciphering matches and spelling bees.

The audience that gathered at night for a ciphering match was divided into two teams, and each captain sent a contestant to the blackboard at the same time. Problems were usually in long division or multiplication of four-digit numbers. The old men hopped around spryly as they calculated, arrived at an answer, and whirled to the referee to see if the solution was correct. Children were given simple problems such as short division, or were asked to strike off with chalk as quickly as possible ten neat marks on the blackboard.

At spelling bees the "pronouncer," usually the school teacher, gave hard words to some grown-ups, easier ones to children and the less educated adults. Selecting the words a speller might be expected to know required tact, and the pronouncer would ask a child, "David, how far has your class got in the book?" If the pronouncer went out of bounds he would be rebuked in a shrill voice: "We ain't had that yet, Martin! Get back there where you belong!" The most approved spelling style was the syllabic, and thus the women who learned from Webster's blue-backed speller enunciated trimly: "Beautiful, B-e-a-u, byou; t-i, ty; f-u-l, full; byou-ty-full, beautiful."

Arkansas

MARBLES. [The college town of] Oxford . . . decided, in 1830, that its 737 inhabitants comprised too large a settlement to be governed by county machinery. A petition for a charter was granted, and the following year a president, recorder, and three trustees were elected. The trustees began busily to devise ordinances. It became a crime for anybody more than three years old to play marbles in an alley, on the sidewalks, or on any of the public grounds. For the first offense the fine was 26¢, the second 50¢, and all subsequent violations $1.

Ohio

CHINESE CHILDREN. There are about 150 full-blooded Chinese children of school age in the Delta, where live most of the Chinese in the State. Since these children are prohibited by law from attending the white public schools, they, for the most part, are taught privately in small groups, each family paying a part of the cost, or are sent out of the State, even to China, for their education. In a few of the towns where there are only one or two children they are given special permission to attend the local schools; in many places they attend the Negro schools. All children of mixed Chinese and Negro blood must attend the Negro schools.

Mississippi

SECRET SCHOOL. Despite an earlier law prohibiting education for the Negro, clandestine classes were conducted by and for Negroes early in the nineteenth century. The most noted of the early schools for free Negro children was started in Savannah by a French Negro, Julien Froumontaine, about 1818. This school functioned openly until December, 1829, when the law making it a penal offense to teach a slave or free person of color to read and write was enforced. Froumontaine's school continued secretly for many years.

Georgia

CAMPUS INSPECTION. When a delegation from the first North Dakota legislature visited the [University of North Dakota] campus on a tour of inspection in 1889, residents of the girls' dormitory held a tea in their honor. In order to improve upon the barrenness of the sparsely furnished parlor, pieces were borrowed from the girls' rooms and from friends. The expedient was more successful than the girls had anticipated, for the legislators considered the furnishings more than adequate and thereupon decreased the amount allowed in the budget for dormitory equipment.

North Dakota

ACADEMIES. Before the public high school system was evolved in Ohio, the student who had the inclination and the means to further his education enrolled in one of the local academies. Many of these had separate schools for boys and girls, but some were coeducational and most of them advertised that they taught "both the useful and ornamental branches of education."

Tuition was often determined by the subject—$5 for Latin or Greek, $3 for arithmetic, grammar, or geography—and sometimes bills were paid in cordwood. Tuition at the Locke Female Academy, founded by Dr. John Locke at Cincinnati in 1822, was from $4 to $10—music and French extra.

Ohio

By 1837 the [Sparta] academy, which was one of the first schools for girls in the South, had 121 pupils and 5 teachers; the older girls were taught "philosophy, chemistry, French, astronomy, literature, and electricity." In 1838 when the institute was renamed the Sparta Female Model School, the method of teaching developed at the Rensselaer School (now the Rensselaer Polytechnic Institute) in Troy, New York, was adopted. Under this system actual experiments and lectures were conducted by the students—an early version of the modern "learning by doing" system.

Georgia

EVIL TOWN, DANGEROUS CITY. Fork Union . . . is overrun during the school term with boys in uniform from Fork Union Military Academy, a preparatory school founded in 1898. The brick and concrete buildings in pseudo-Gothic style are at the edge of town. "The Academy is remote," its catalogue avers, "from the evil influence of the small towns and the dangers of the large city."

Virginia

PEDAGOGUE. The pedagogue, often a wanderer of the Ichabod Crane type who came into the community and "boarded around," heard the recitations of from ten to thirty pupils. These students, who ranged from six-year-olds to grown men, were grouped according to their ability in reading or arithmetic, and the wayward were urged on with liberal doses of "peach limb tea." If an impudent pupil happened to be a six-footer the teacher might shed his coat and invite the gentleman out for a thrashing. In case the pedagogue won, the pupil could be expected to retaliate by placing several skunks in the schoolhouse during the night. If the teacher lost the fight, however, he was disgraced, and from then on found it almost impossible to keep order.

Arkansas

CIRCUS. Sharply contrasted with the mellow [York] background is the Barnett Brothers' Circus, which has made its winter home here since 1929 in a long stone building on West Madison Street, known as the "animal house." Keepers sleep upstairs over the stalls and cages; every Friday, open-house day, they station themselves at strategic points to keep a watchful eye on local visitors, who know the names of each animal, speak to their favorites, and are sometimes tempted to stand too near them. In a vacant lot near by are trailers, allotted permanent parking space, and empty trucks used as work shops, paint shops, wardrobe, and storage rooms. A tent is the mess hall. Some of the employees sleep in the trailers but others board in town; a few own homes here. The welfare of Barnett Brothers' Circus is a matter of civic pride with York, and relations between winter crew and townfolk have a family touch. The man who supervises the painting and refurnishing of trucks and trailers, using gallons of gilt paint each season, in his leisure time does portraits of local children. Town boys beg for the privilege of driving new trucks from the factory to York, which means a trip to Ohio, Kansas, Texas, or possibly to Quebec. The milky-white pet dogs of many of the children here come from the annual litters of somersaulting terriers. Each Christmas the shopping season is opened by a parade in which Santa Claus, escorted by the high-school band, comes swaying down Congress Street on the back of an elephant. Servants and housewives have grown accustomed to false reports that "the big snake is out," and the only animal really to escape during a decade of circus residence was Jocko, an ugly baboon that frightened a motorist and a field worker before disappearing altogether.

Almost inevitable was the home-talent circus that sprouted in 1930, with neighborhood kids risking their bones on wires stretched tight between back-yard trees; but the result was unexpected. Sponsored and managed by five brothers, the little top's first season attracted only indulgent adults at 5¢ per head. Professionals of the big show encouraged the young plagiarists, how-ever, and extended more than moral support. The management donated a slightly tattered but otherwise excellent tent, whose seating capacity was 300. Taking their cue from the conscientious habits of the elder performers, the youngsters practiced with a seriousness that brought real skill, and their an-nual extravaganza, combining elements of circus, vaudeville, and minstrel, attracted larger and larger audiences. Their crowning success was achieved when they made an extended and profitable tour of surrounding towns.

South Carolina

BOOSTER ROOSTER DAY. Automobiles are no longer remarkable in the Prophetstown area, but Booster Rooster Day is a novel annual event, ob-served on an appointed day each spring, when merchants of the town pay 3¢ a pound above current market price for roosters and pile crates of the crowing scolding birds along the sidewalks to attract business. Not infre-quently, adding to the noise and confusion, some of the roosters escape from their coops, and are immediately pursued along and across the main thor-oughfares by crowds of small boys.

Illinois

BOXCAR SLUM. [Near Remsen] is the Plymouth County Farm, . . . which has four box-car homes for its poor. Boxcar slums, a new type for Iowa, have developed in some instances from good intentions of Iowa counties to assist the poor. Discarded railroad boxcars were purchased and remodeled for use as dwellings; some of them were placed on three county farms. At one time there were families with 31 children living in boxcars here. A problem developed when they attended the nearby country schools; children from well-to-do rural families immediately put the stigma of "poor farm kids" on them.

Iowa

CHINA GROVES. West of Scott on US 90 are occasional pecan orchards, Cherokee rose hedges (which once served as fences), China tree groves, and occasional oaks. Most numerous are the China groves, which were planted by the early settlers because they grew rapidly, provided shade in the summer, and made good firewood (when dry the wood burns as rapidly as pine). In addition the flowers were used as a moth deterrent, the China "balls" provided pop-gun ammunition for small boys, and the dried seeds were dyed and strung as beads by the girls.

Louisiana

BAG SWING. The thick matting of vegetation that entangles the delicate twigs of elms and the rough limbs of water oaks makes the country through which this section of State 7 passes seem like a jungle. Back in the shade are clumps of rattan, whose long, snake-like withes are used as whips by country boys to play "burn-out." Two boys select five- or six-foot lengths of limber rattan, lock their left hands, and lay on until one or the other has had enough.

A less punishing sport of back-country children is riding the bag swing. A gunny sack is stuffed with cotton and rags and suspended from a tree by a rope long enough to allow the bag to describe a considerable arc. One of the larger boys, as "leader," mounts the bag from a platform on the top of a fence, and sails away. When the swing returns to its original position youngsters crowding the platform leap out, settling like horseshoes ringing a post. One object of the game seems to be to jolt the leader off the bag, if possible. In the more lonely districts stately cranes are sometimes startled out of their dignity by the whoop of a solitary youngster swinging back and forth over a creek from a high bank, by a grapevine tangled in the overhanging branches.

Arkansas

PIÑATA. One of the pleasantest gift-giving customs in the world, and one which no person of Mexican heritage is ever too rich or too poor to forget, is the breaking of the *pinate* [piñata]. It takes the place of the Christmas tree in Mexico, and in the United States climaxes many holiday and birthday parties. A *pinate* is a large pottery jar filled with sweets and presents and elaborately dressed up in bright tissue paper and streamers to resemble a doll either comic or beautiful. The *pinate* is hung high in the patio and, one by one, the children are blindfolded and given three chances to break it with a long pole.

Arizona

SCHOOL BUS. Towner . . . is a village in the dry farming area. South of Towner, in March 1931, a rural school bus was caught in a spring blizzard. The driver left his 22 charges in the bus and set out afoot to bring aid. He perished in a field a few miles away. Five of the children died from exposure. Others would probably have met a similar fate had it not been for Bryan Unteidt, one of the pupils, who compelled the others to exercise and play games and thus keep warm. In recognition of his heroism Bryan was invited to the White House by President Hoover and publicly honored.

Colorado

MOOSEHEART. Mooseheart . . . is a community founded by James J. Davis, the United States senator from Pennsylvania, and supported by the Loyal Order of Moose. The institution provides home, educational training through high school, and technical training in several trades for 1,000 children of deceased members of the order. The grounds are open from sunup to sundown daily. . . .

Known to radio listeners as the City of Childhood, Mooseheart answers the description in almost a story-book sense. Here is a scientifically directed miniature society whose affairs are conducted by the child citizens themselves, aided by adult advisers. The children live in small groups in cottages, each headed by a housemother. Living conditions approximate home life as nearly as possible, and although all children, because of admission limitations, are fatherless, Mooseheart provides jobs for many mothers, thus saving a further break in the family.

Boys have a choice of training in one or more of eleven trades or professions; girls, in six. Each boy or girl receives full apprentice experience. When a new unit is to be built, the drafting class draws the plans and makes the blue prints, the concrete class produces structural materials, and the sheet metal class provides roofing and drain pipes. Other groups stand ready to paint, paper, or varnish; and the tin shop makes such utensils as dish pans and dust pans.

Apprentices in beauty culture and barbering gain experience with an average of 450 haircuts per week. Students in the power machine sewing class see the suits and dresses they make actually worn by the members of the community. Girls manage the cafeteria, under a trained supervisor. Student typists and bookkeepers assist in the business office. Journalism classes cooperate with the print shop in producing local reading matter. Children with musical or artistic gifts are trained to earn an income in orchestra, band, or designing studios. About 15 per cent out of each graduating class go to college. At the age of eight each child is taught to do his own shopping and to keep a check book. From junior high school his work is paid for in actual money, and he must budget his accounts so that by graduation he will have saved at least $50.

Illinois

FAIS-DODO. A country dance is generally known today among the Cajuns as a *fais-dodo* (literally, go to sleep); possibly because the dancers stay up all night and sometimes fall asleep while still dancing; possibly because the mothers sing *fais-dodos* (lullabies) to put the younger children to sleep so that they themselves can leave the *parc aux petits* for the dance floor:

Fais dodo, Minette,	Go to sleep, Kitten,
Trois piti cochon dulaite;	Three little suckling-pigs;
Fais dodo, mon piti babe,	Go to sleep, my little baby,
Jiska lâge de quinze ans.	Until the age of fifteen years.
Quan quinze ans aura passe;	When fifteen years have passed;
Minette va so marier.	Kitten will marry.

Swing bands, radios, and automatic phonographs have penetrated the Cajun country, but at the genuine *fais-dodo* the music of the fiddle, the accordion, and the triangle (sometimes called the "ting-a-ling") is always featured; for the Acadian retains his love for these instruments and often possesses rare skill in playing them. A full orchestra includes also the guitar and harmonica. . . .

Louisiana

SPASM BAND. You get to the corner of Royal and St. Peter Streets just in time to see a "spasm band" go into action. A "spasm band" is a miscellaneous collection of a soap box, tin cans, pan tops, nails, drumsticks, and little Negro boys. When mixed in the proper proportions this results in the wildest shuffle dancing, accompanied by a bumping rhythm. You flip them a coin, and they run after you offering to do tricks for "*lagniappe*"; and without waiting your approval, one little boy begins to walk the length of the block on his hands, while another places the crown of his skull on a tin can and spins like a top. "*Lagniappe*," your Creole explains, is a little gift the tradesmen present to their customers with each purchase. By extension, it means something extra, something for nothing.

New Orleans

Society

I N "They Hate Roosevelt," a provocative 1936 article in *Harper's Magazine*, Marquis Childs reported what America's very rich thought of the
New Deal. Much of what Childs found was too vulgar to print. "In
greater or lesser degree, the whole upper stratum of American society" loathed
the President, his wife, and his administration with a fury Childs found incredible, since Roosevelt had saved the system that protected their wealth.

Though the thirties were our most class-conscious decade, the rich among
us were generally treated with surprising tolerance. All they had to do to
demonstrate good will was, like Franklin and Eleanor Roosevelt, laugh at
class distinctions. Cary Grant, playing a rich loafer in *The Philadelphia Story*,
one of the period's sweetly leftist films, argues that the difference between
people is character, not class, and says, or almost says, "Class—my ass!",
thus proving his heart in the right place.

To be sure, vestiges of European hierarchy can be found in the United
States, and the Guides note them. But they are compromised. Among the
participants in a Maryland *cotillion* are offspring of *redemptioners*.

It is the national promise ("myth," if you prefer) that anyone, even a
housekeeper, can rise. But the notion of "rising" itself is problematic in a
culture with the class-busting energies seen *where the rich and the poor meet
together*. Is there any point acquiring *golden keys* in a society as fluid as that
at Nevada's *counters?* On reflection, the *dogs' dinner* may not be much different from the *drunkards' wake*.

REDEMPTIONERS. After 1683 white servants were seldom imported directly by their employers. Impecunious persons who wished to come to the colony were given a certain time after arrival to dispose of their services for a sum sufficient to repay the shipmaster for their passage; these people were "redemptioners" or "free-willers." The first white indentured servants came from Great Britain and Ireland; the redemptioners were largely from Holland, Switzerland, and Germany; and in the two decades preceding the Revolution, England sent as seven-year servants large numbers of convicts. Many of the poor immigrants, who were skilled or educated, later became independent farmers or merchants; some even rose to wealth and prominence, and became in their turn employers of labor. The historian Scharf remarks that "not a few of our 'old Maryland families' are descended from indentured servants and apprentices."

Maryland

WHERE THE RICH AND THE POOR MEET TOGETHER. [The] old [Gavitt] house was for many years used as an inn, and in the west front room the Westerly town meetings were held. During the meeting of April, 1826, just as the votes were being polled, the floor of the house gave way in the center and precipitated the politicians down among the pork barrels and potato bins. No serious injuries resulted from this catastrophe, but one poor though cool-headed citizen was heard to remark as he rolled down heavily upon his wealthy neighbor, "Well, well, here is where the rich and the poor meet together."

Rhode Island

BLACKSMITH. When the town fathers [of what became Lancaster] applied for permission to name the town Prescott in honor of a popular local blacksmith, the General Court decided: "Whereas no town of the Colonies had as yet been named for any Governor; and whereas it were unseemly that a blacksmith be honored ahead of his betters, the name Prescott could not be permitted." If this was a hint, the town evaded it by naming itself for Lancaster, England.

Massachusetts

COTILLION. No other city presents such a barrier to the girl with social aspirations as does Baltimore with its Bachelors' Cotillon [Cotillion]. Founded in 1796, the cotillon is controlled by a board of governors that deals summarily with the lists of girls who each year hope to "come out." Not to be invited to the Monday Germans (the name is derived from the old dance, the German) means not to be a debutante; there is no other way of making a debut. Birth alone will guarantee an invitation to the cotillon, even though the family is penniless. A girl may be a debutante in Baltimore at the cost of one white dress for the first German. Frequently, however, balls of considerable size and cost are arranged by wealthy families who may not belong to the limited circle or by non-Baltimoreans who are anxious to put the halo of a Baltimore debut on their daughters' heads. Many girls with the proper credentials come to the Bachelors' Cotillon from far parts of the country in the belief that their social careers are better launched here than anywhere else, even in New York. Baltimore women who have married into European peerages have brought their daughters home for debuts.

Maryland

MINERAL SPRING. By the 1830's [White Sulphur Springs] had become a center of fashion, a favorite rendezvous of elegant plantation society of the Old South . . . . [R]ows of cottages were built—Paradise Row, Virginia Row, Georgia Row, Alabama Row, Baltimore Row, Wolf Row—each with its social distinctions. Along Paradise Row strutted the young newly weds and the charming, eager young belles, brought by their families "to the waters" in the hope of arranging a desirable match. Close by lived the gay young bachelors in Wolf Row, which enjoyed a reputation of its own: "Unless you be young and foolish, fond of noise and nonsense, frolic and fun, wine and wassail, sleepless nights and days of headache, avoid Wolf Row," warned a visitor. The resort's greatest charm, added another, was its delightful society of every agreeable variety. "From the East you have consolidationists, tariffites, and philanthropists; from the Middle, professors, chemical analysts, and letter writers; from the West, orators and gentlemen who can squat lower, jump higher, dive deeper, and come out drier, than all creation besides; and from the South, nullifiers, Union men, political economists, and statesmen; and from all quarters, functionaries of all ranks, ex-candidates for all functions, and the gay, agreeable, and handsome of both sexes, who come to the

White Sulphur to see and be seen, to chat, laugh, and dance, and each to throw his pebble on the great heap of general enjoyment." . . .

The spring was lined with marble walls in octagonal shape and was covered with a handsome dome resting on white columns, and as for the water, Peregrine noted that it had "the pleasant flavor of a half-boiled, half-spoiled egg . . . and cures the following diseases, according to popular belief—Yellow Jaundice, White Swelling, Blue Devils, and Black Plague; Scarlet Fever, Yellow Fever, Spotted Fever, and fever of every kind and colour; Hydrocephalus, Hydrothorax, Hydrocele, and Hydrophobia; Hypochondria and Hypocrisy; Dispepsia, Diarrhea, Diabetes, and die-of-anything; Gout, Gormandising, and Grogging; Liver Complaint, Colic, Stone, Gravel, and all other diseases and bad habits, except chewing, smoking, spitting and swearing." In addition to sulphurated hydrogen and other ingredients, the mineral waters contained "a very strong infusion of fashion," he added, and as the latter is "an animal substance, its quality cannot be precisely ascertained; it is supposed, however, to be gradually increasing, and no doubt contributes greatly to the efficiency of the water."

From White Sulphur stage lines ran to other lesser resorts in the region—Red Sulphur, Green Sulphur, Gray Sulphur, Blue Sulphur, Salt Sulphur, Sweetsprings, Warm Springs, and Hot Springs—all of which were often included in a fashionable tour "of the waters."

In 1854 the original tavern building gave way to the White Sulphur Springs Hotel, renowned for more than a half century as the Old White. It had a large and resplendent dining room, with crystal chandeliers, and its barroom was known to the élite throughout the country for its mint juleps. During the War between the States the hotel was the local headquarters of the armies of one side and then the other as the battle line moved forward and back again across the valley. After the Battle of White Sulphur Springs it served as a hospital; and the dead and dying were laid in rows in the glittering ballroom and dining room. In 1864 General David Hunter, in command of retreating Union forces, was dissuaded from burning the hotel by his artillery chief, who argued that it could be used as a barracks if their troops should pass this way again. After the war the Old White languished for a time, but many Southern families continued to come to enjoy the season here; they made a brave show of reviving antebellum gaiety and elegance, even though they were impoverished and no better off than the belle who remarked, with a confident toss of her head, that she had been reduced to "one black silk dress and my grit." In the 1880's the fashionable, with a sprinkling of the notable, again began to frequent the Old White, which ended its days in 1913 when it was torn down to make way for the present Greenbrier Hotel. . . .

West Virginia

TITLES IN A DEMOCRACY. Estates of the [Newport] area . . . in the last half of the 19th century shared with Fifth Avenue, New York City, the scenes of that spectacular effort of America's first big crop of millionaires to establish themselves as the top crust of the social pie. Just as the returning generals and colonial administrators of ancient Rome, the new-rich of the Roman Empire, spent fabulous sums reproducing the art works of the older Greek civilization and sent their antique-dealers scurrying to the older cities to buy up statues by Praxiteles and other choice bits to adorn their showplaces, so the new American millionaires built elegant copies of the châteaux and palaces of Europe, or, more often, grotesque combinations of the most expensive and ornate features of half a dozen of them, and raided Europe for ornaments and furnishings. Many of these structures remain along the drive, weathered now and softened by thick shrubbery.

Unable to buy titles in a democracy, the new social leaders did the next best thing—married their daughters to European peers and noblemen. New-

port was the scene of many of the lavish events in these international court-
ings and marriages that made daily wonder-stories for an admiring hinterland.

Rhode Island

OUR FOOTSTOOLS. Newport's most exclusive recreational club was Bailey's Beach. Only the élite could bathe here, and they disported themselves
in full-skirted costumes and long black stockings. Mr. Van Alen always went
into the sea wearing a monocle and white straw hat, and Mrs. Oliver Belmont carried a green umbrella while bathing. A watchman protected the
beach from all interlopers; he fixed newcomers with an eagle eye, swooped
down upon them and demanded their names. Unless they were accompanied by a club member, or bore a note of introduction, they were ejected.
If they wanted to bathe, they could go to Easton's Beach—the common beach,
as the habitués of Bailey's Beach called it. There they could share the sea
with the townspeople, referred to by the summer colonists as "our footstools."

Rhode Island

GOLDEN KEYS. The "golden keys" to Gramercy Park, symbol of the ex-
clusiveness guaranteed by a real-estate operator about a century ago, are still
required to open the gate to New York's most important privately owned park.
A forbidding eight-foot iron fence encloses this oblong tract two blocks square
that is "forever" locked to the public.

The park's creator, Samuel B. Ruggles, was among the first of New York's
early real-estate operators to offer for sale a development with building restrictions. He caught the fancy of the rich by guaranteeing to a selected
group—those who bought his property—the exclusive use of a private park
as a permanent privilege. Keys—no longer golden—to the iron gates are distributed to owners and tenants under the close scrutiny of the trustees of
Gramercy Park. Residents in near-by streets who have been approved by the
trustees are given keys for annual fees. All others must be satisfied with a
glimpse through the gate.

New York City

MILLIONAIRES' CLUB. [In Irvington] is the Ardsley Club, organized in 1895 by a group of millionaires and described by a society reporter of the 1890's as "that pleasance of Midas." This club had the third golf course laid out in America; the players at first used gutta-percha balls, which the caddies carried around in buckets of ice, to keep them in shape. The club members were also leaders in the introduction of bicycle parties; sometimes as many as 40 whirled over the roads of Westchester County on carefully polished, silver-trimmed wheels. And the members were of course among the first to own automobiles, exciting toys that they also tested in races for possible commercial value.

New York

DOGS' DINNER. [One] of [Newport's] decidedly "different" entertainments was the "Dogs' Dinner," to which Harry Lehr invited about a hundred dogs and their masters. The menu was stewed liver and rice, fricassee of bones, and shredded dog biscuit. The dinner was greatly appreciated; the guests ate until they could eat no more, and Elisha Dyer's dachshund so overtaxed its capacities that it fell unconscious by its plate and had to be carried home. A reporter happened to crash the party and the next day scathing columns appeared in the newspapers. Preachers throughout the country denounced Lehr for wasting on dog food money that would have fed hundreds of starving people. After this episode, the keynote of dinners was originality, not extravagance.

Rhode Island

DRUNKARDS' WAKE. On State 231 is Morral . . . , about which hangs a tale. One of the first settlers in the township was Ebenezer Roseberry, who came here from New Orleans in 1812 and opened a saloon. The business prospered for many years, and a number of convivial fellows attached themselves to Roseberry. When he died a prankish will was found, which stipulated that his cronies were to stay by him through his wake until they had consumed a fresh barrel of whisky. To this tender task they responded with a will. Several days and nights passed, during which one of them was nearly hanged by his fellows, the corpse was dragged all over the house, and most of the carousers managed to fall into a nearby pool. Finally, at midnight on the last day of the wake, the pious friends and drunken companions of the

late Roseberry dragged his corpse across the countryside and buried it near the county line. This was Morral's famous "drunkards' wake"; and there has never been one like it since.

Ohio

COUNTERS. [A] Nevada trait is an addiction to eating at counters. It is doubtful whether there is a restaurant in the State without one; even the smartest places feature counters. Usually the board is high and the stools are mounted on a small platform. No Nevadan is quite sure why he likes "counter-eating"; but the counter offers company—and the true Nevadan is gregarious, as his passion for clubs and other social circles indicates.

Nevada

"LADY." Time and progress have made little change in the housekeeping, farm methods, and customs in some of the isolated regions of the Sandhills section. Many of the homes contain spinning wheels and hand looms that were used until a few years ago. When a woman passes middle age her neighbors give her a surprise party, after which she is no longer "Miz Scott," but "Lady" or "Old Lady Scott." One woman in Sheffield Township (called Shuffield) indignantly refused to eat at her own party as she did not consider herself ready for the shelf.

North Carolina

FREE NEGROES. Negroes were free if they had emigrated from free States, if they had been freed legally by former owners, or if they were the product of mixed unions in which the mother was free and the father a slave. The majority of the white people, rich and poor, resented the presence of free Negroes in their society. Masters could have caught runaways much oftener but for the numbers of free Negroes. Poor white laborers and mechanics resented them for both economic and social reasons. Many protests came from mechanics' associations against free Negro workmen and the practice of hiring out skilled slaves.

Towns usually required free Negroes to register and wear badges. Curfew laws were passed for the purpose of clearing the streets of Negroes by 10 o'clock, or some other evening hour. They lost the vote in 1835, a privilege until then of the few who could meet the property qualification that applied to whites as well.

North Carolina

HOUSEKEEPER. It is easy to confuse the Wentworths, three of whom were Royal Governors, because when they didn't marry their cooks, they usually married each other's widows. Benning, the most aristocratic, was an able administrator for 26 years (1741–67). At the close of a banquet celebrating his sixtieth birthday and attended by the cream of New England's aristocracy, he called in Martha Hilton, his housekeeper, and bade the Rev. Arthur Brown, rector of St. John's Church in Portsmouth, read the ceremony then and there, which the astonished prelate did.

New Hampshire

LACK OF AGGRESSIVE LOYALTY. At the time of America's entrance into the World War, there were many Lincoln citizens, German by birth or extraction, whose sympathies were with the Central Powers, and consequently there was bitter feeling between pro-Germans and pro-Allies. As late as 1916 students of the University of Nebraska organized to persuade the legislature to abolish compulsory military training, but with America's entrance into the war, the tide turned. Patriotic fervor gripped the city. German names were frowned upon, the German language was tabooed in classrooms, and suspected pro-Germans were carefully watched for evidence of treason. Eight university professors were charged with "lack of aggressive loyalty." A hearing was conducted by the University Board of Regents and the resignation of three of the men requested.

Nebraska

LURKING APPRENTICE. Advertising in the papers of the 1840's offered a buggy for hire at a dollar a day, "invariably cash in advance." A husband proclaimed himself not responsible for his wife's debts, and a society of women asked for quilts for the needy. One "master" offered a dollar reward for "George . . . a boy about 18 years, small size and spare made, and supposed to be lurking about Iowa City." The boy was an indentured apprentice and people were cautioned not "to harbor or trust . . . on my account."

Iowa

QUADROONS. When a young white man took a fancy to [a quadroon] he approached her mother, and having given satisfactory proof of his ability to keep the girl in becoming style, struck a bargain with the old woman. Money changed hands, and the quadroon regarded this arrangement in the same light as marriage. The young man established a home for his mistress in the quadroon quarter, which was in that section of the Vieux Carré below Orleans Street and near the Ramparts, and enjoyed all the comforts and amenities thereof without actually residing there himself. This arrangement lasted as long as he wished it so. The *placée*, as she was called, took her "friend's" name, which was also given to their children, many of whom were reared in an atmosphere of culture, and were often sent to Paris to be educated. The young girls were particularly well schooled in the arts of courtesanship so that they could follow in their mothers' footsteps.

Quadroon mistresses had their quadroon friends and amusements, and, of course, the quadroon balls; but they could not mix with the white ladies, could not sit down in their presence, nor ride through the streets in carriages. A white woman could have a quadroon whipped like a slave upon accusation borne out by two witnesses. Quadroon men were never allowed to attend the balls. Scorned by women of their own class as well as by whites, they either followed some trade in the city or went into the country on plantations. They usually married mulatto women.

When the young white man decided it was time to marry, he simply broke off his arrangement and was free to make another alliance. Some men continued the arrangement even after marriage by maintaining two homes, one in each section of the city. Some really loved their quadroon mates and never married at all.

New Orleans

CHARIVARI. On one occasion a man and his young bride from the East arrived [in Aspen] to set up housekeeping in a small cabin; the citizens staged a charivari for them. The bride, frightened, bolted the door against the merrymakers. For three days and nights the cabin was besieged. Guns roared; an attempt was made to ram the door with logs; the stovepipe was stuffed up. Not until the crowd threated to roll the cabin into the creek did the husband appear, a gun in both hands; explanations and apologies followed, and everyone was invited in to meet the bride.

Colorado

Famous and Unknown

THE CRITIC Robert Cantwell wrote the earliest and one of the best analyses of the Guides, "America and the Writers' Project," which appeared in *The New Republic* of April 26, 1939. Cantwell understood that the Guides have no "rigorous standard to determine inclusion"; people are mentioned who did a great deal and who never did anything. "The only test seems to be that some living evidence of their presence, if only in legend or the name of a street, still persists in their own towns."

There is a strong democracy of retrospection at work in the Guides: if you are remembered at all, you are as good as a VIP, no matter how small or ignoble your claim to fame (consider *fire and run* and the *Emperor Norton*).

Some people, like *The Immortal J. N.*, are well known simply for being well known, as the historian Daniel Boorstin says all celebrities are. Other people, like the *woman in black*, are sort of anti-celebrities, known for *not* being known.

We see that countryside notoriety can seep into the national consciousness, making *Hatfields and McCoys* part of the language. We see foreign-grown celebrities, like *Oscar Wilde*, and home-grown ones, like *Odd*, who went away and made good.

Whatever the true nature of fame, we see from a story like *the whites of their eyes* that, though many feel themselves called to it, few are chosen—arbitrarily.

────────────

HATFIELDS AND McCOYS. The history of the area on both sides of the Kentucky-West Virginia Line is violent. It was the scene of the notorious Hatfield-McCoy feud that began on an election day early in the 19th century. Stories of the origin are obscure. One is that while "Devil Anse" Hatfield and his clan from across the Tug Fork in West Virginia were carousing with the McCoys on the Kentucky side, Hatfield's son eloped across the river with Randall McCoy's daughter. When a few months later McCoy's unwed daughter returned to her Kentucky relatives with a child, a war of hatred and revenge began. The feud outlived all of those who saw its beginning, and though there were peaceful interludes, a trivial argument over such a matter as the number of notches on a hog's ear would start another series of killings. On one occasion an old man of the Hatfield clan stood alone against the McCoy tribe, and when he died cursing his enemies with his last breath, his gun was empty, his body riddled with bullets. Later, after three McCoys had stabbed a Hatfield in the back, a party of Hatfields surrounded Randall McCoy's cabin and set it on fire in order to see their targets—the McCoys trapped inside. On that night a Hatfield shot a young McCoy girl to death and then broke her mother's back. It was a great day for the McCoys when this Hatfield was hanged, many years later, before 6,000 spectators. He was the first and one of the few feudists hanged legally.

The courts were particularly ineffective in handling this feud because the participants lived in two States and the State authorities on both sides of the line were disinclined to permit extradition of their citizens, since each side laid blame on the other. Moreover, many of the sheriffs and even judges were kin to participants. About the time of the War between the States, when coal mining began in the region on a minor commercial scale, the operators found themselves much hindered by the primitive tribal warfare and put pressure on authorities to curb it. They had a reward offered for the capture of Devil Anse and forced him into semi-hiding in the hills—then bought up his land for a dollar an acre. Other Hatfields and some of the McCoys became mine operators themselves, though many of their kin eventually came down to work in the mines. But the hill people were only half tamed and the frontier habit of every man's settling his quarrels with his own gun was not easily eradicated. It was carried over into the period of industrial development.

Kentucky

THE IMMORTAL J. N. One of Ohio's best-known eccentrics, J. N. Free, better known as "the immortal J.N.," was a frequent visitor in Tiffin during the latter part of the nineteenth century. Free (1828–1906) was born in Pennsylvania, spent his boyhood on a farm south of Tiffin, studied law, and went to California when the gold rush began. There he made a fortune, which he lost through the trickery of crooks. He became critically ill and, when he recovered, his mind was shattered. Some strange urge compelled him to travel throughout the country the rest of his life. He never paid for anything—clothing, meals, hotel accommodations, train rides, he took them as his due. In time his eccentricities became an asset. When it became known that "J.N." was coming to Cleveland, astute hotel managers sent bellboys to the station to meet him because he attracted customers. In the early years of his travels, conductors who had not heard of him or were unimpressed by his stentorian announcement, "I am the immortal J.N.," sometimes stopped the trains and put him off because he would not pay. At the time of his death, however, he had received life passes from nearly every railroad system in the United States.

Ohio

EMPEROR NORTON. Joshua A. Norton, the "Emperor," was born in England in 1819. At the age of 30 he arrived in San Francisco with $40,000, which he pyramided to a quarter of a million. Attempting to corner the rice market, he and his colleagues lost their fortunes. Norton went into seclusion for several years; when he reappeared, his mind was unbalanced, and he soon became the favorite ward of the city. Clad in an old uniform and military cap, with a small sword dangling at his side and a stick or umbrella in his hand, trailed always by two mongrel dogs, Bummer and Lazarus, he was a familiar figure on the downtown streets. Norton declared himself Emperor of the United States and Protector of Mexico: one of his frequent proclamations dissolved the Democratic and Republican parties in the interests of peace; another dissolved a steamship company because a purser, violating imperial privilege, had summarily put him ashore; a third called the public's attention to the duty of replenishing his wardrobe. He was the first to "propose" a bridge across the bay. He was permitted to eat, drink, and amuse himself gratis, and to draw checks up to 50¢ on San Francisco banks. These checks were always honored, and Norton added to his cash by selling 50¢ bonds and collecting "taxes." He dropped dead on the street in 1880 and was given an elaborate funeral by the city.

California

THENDARA. Thendara . . . was once the home of Nat Foster, a deadshot trapper and guide, who carried spare bullets between his fingers. Otis Arnold, who ran an inn for hunters here, had 11 daughters, timid among human beings but at home on the horses they broke to saddle; his son was known for his terrifying snore.

New York

DIANA OF THE DUNES. It was [at the site of Ogden Dunes], before the village was founded, that the nationally publicized "Diana of the Dunes," female hermit, lived in an abandoned fisherman's hut made of driftwood. She was discovered in 1916 when fishermen observed the nude young woman taking a daily plunge in Lake Michigan, but she refused to see newspaper reporters and avoided would-be visitors. The thwarted periodicals dubbed her "Diana of the Dunes" and carried many stories of her mysterious behavior. According to various reports she was the beautiful daughter of a Chicago physician; she made wine from the wild berries of the dune hillsides, selling it for the little money required for her limited needs; she lived alone to study nature, and knew and loved every plant and animal of the region, every mood and color of the lake and dunes. It was hinted that there had been a disappointment in love. Continued publicity brought her many offers of marriage and in 1922 she married a Texan. While preparing to leave for her new home, she suddenly became ill and died.

Indiana

HERMIT'S CAVE. Hermit's Cave, [in Council Grove], became the refuge of a mysterious and destitute stranger who arrived in 1862. To improve his shelter, he built up a wall of rocks to meet the overhanging ledge at the top of the cliff, and here, high on the eastern face of the great bluff overlooking the town, he lived with only his dog for company. His name was Matteo Boccalini, he said, and he was a native of Capri. He told of having gone to Rome at the age of eighteen to be ordained for the priesthood, of having become secretary to the Pope, but of later being unfrocked because of a love affair with a young girl. Having incurred the enmity of the Jesuits, he wandered for years, migrated to America, and finally reached the Kansa reservation, from whence he was expelled as "bad medicine."

He lived in fear of being followed, and one day hurried away with a wagon train bound for the Southwest, after having seen a man whom he thought he recognized among some travelers. Two years later Council Grove learned that a priest had been found dead, with a dagger through his heart, in a cave house in the mountains of New Mexico. On the walls of the cave he had carved his name, a cross, and the words "Jesu Maria" and "Capri," exactly as they appeared on the walls of Hermit's Cave here.

Kansas

WHITES OF THEIR EYES. Deerfield claims distinction as the home of John Simpson, who fired the first shot at the battle of Bunker Hill. The Americans defending the hill were short of ammunition and their leaders gave orders to the men to hold their fire until they could see the whites of their enemies' eyes. "Don't fire yet till the word is given," was passed along the line as the men waited impatiently. In the midst of excitement, one of the soldiers under Captain Dearborn suddenly fired at a British officer, who was seen to tumble from his horse. After an inquiry the next day, John Simpson was arrested and court-martialed, but his punishment was light, for none of his superiors felt like censuring him. When the war ended, Simpson returned to Deerfield with the rank of major and resumed his farm life. He never applied for a pension and never received a penny for his services. He used to say, "My country is too poor to pay pensions."

New Hampshire

[Chelmsford] was represented at the Battle of Bunker Hill, and one of its citizens, Joseph Spalding, is said to have thus described firing the first shot. "I fired the shot ahead of time and General Putnam rushed up and struck me for violating orders. I suppose I deserved it, but I was anxious to get another shot at Gage's men ever since our affair at Concord. The blow from Old Put hit me on the head, made a hole in my hat, and left me a scar." The hat with the hole in it was preserved in the Emerson House, Spalding's home, until that building was destroyed by fire.

Massachusetts

Jonathan Allen, who came [to Weathersfield] from Connecticut, took part in the battle of Bunker Hill—too eager a part: a portion of one of his ears was cut off with a saber by his own commander for shooting a British officer before the order to fire was given.

Vermont

TRILBY. In 1804 a man, cultured and gentlemanly in manner, made his appearance in [Holmes County]. He was called Trilby. Who he was and where he came from was never completely determined, but for the next 30 years he was a familiar and beloved figure throughout the Trail country. He lived among the Amish farmers, painting mail boxes and doing other odd jobs, sleeping in coal sheds in winter, and staying with Amish friends in summer. When he died, friends sold his few possessions and purchased a burial plot in the Trail Cemetery a mile south of the village. Respectable church members bristled at the idea of having a "tramp" buried in their cemetery. On the morning of Trilby's burial, six friends dug his grave while nine others held off chagrined protestants. The funeral ceremony was the largest ever held at Trail Church. Afterwards, popular subscription raised sufficient funds for a monument inscribed simply, "TRILBY," with the date of his death.

Ohio

BUGS. Little Billie King, a roving printer who loved his liquor, wandered into [Eureka] in 1899. He soon became known as the "Belfast Spider" because of his tales of championship prize fights he had won. For years he lived in a plank cottage at the head of Church Street, and built fires only when he cooked. In summer, it was Billie's custom to hie himself to a nice sunny hillside and sleep off his latest jag, thus combining a steam bath and a good long rest. Awakening one day from his nap, still groggy, he spotted a man running around the hill with a fish net, apparently trying to pull a fish out of the air. Billie walked over to him, placed his hand on his shoulder, and said, "You'd better come to town with me, friend." The stranger explained that he was searching for bugs. Billie smiled indulgently and said, "Sure, I know. I've had 'em myself, but you better come to town with me." The stranger, convinced by this time that Billie was crazy, decided he had better humor him, and allowed himself to be led to town. Later Billie discovered that his "crazy man" was Tom Spalding, the man who put Utah on the entomological map. Spalding, a natural-born collector, sold one collection for $1,400, and another is included in the $3,000,000 Barnes collection at Decatur, Illinois. Spalding first came to the notice of entomologists in 1910, when he captured a little blue butterfly, the first of its kind ever found; it was named *Philotes spaldingi*. Twelve other unusual specimens were named for Spalding.

Utah

THE LEATHERWOOD GOD. Near [Salesville] on the banks of Leatherwood Creek appeared in 1828 one Joseph Dylkes, who stood up in church one morning and announced that he was God. Some of his listeners accepted the announcement with equanimity. Others attached themselves to Dylkes, and in no time at all a new religious sect was under way. For a time it grew. When Dylkes failed to perform a well-advertised miracle, that of making a seamless garment, he and some of his disciples found it convenient to go elsewhere to found a New Jerusalem. A few years later some of the converts returned to Salesville and reported that "God" had disappeared "somewhere in Philadelphia."

Ohio

COOGLERISM. [The Blythewood] neighborhood fathered J. Gordon Coogler, printer for Columbia's daily, *The State*, who gained notice with extraordinary rhymes and surprising metaphors. His house bore a legend, "Poems written while you wait." This humorless, conscientious versifier first printed his lines at his own expense, but gradually they caught the public fancy and were reviewed in New York and London papers, his name becoming so well known that 'cooglerism' came to mean a solemn absurdity. The printer-poet's most frequently quoted couplet is:

Alas, for the South! her books have grown fewer,
She never was much given to literature.

South Carolina

ODD. After spending most of his boyhood in Gallipolis, Oscar Odd McIntyre (1884–1938) left his home town to work for newspapers in East Liverpool, Dayton, and Cincinnati. In 1912 he went to New York, and through several lean years persisted in writing and trying to sell "personals" about New York's daily doings. He was pioneering in a new field, and success came slowly as he worked out a formula; at the time of his death his column, "New York Day by Day," was being featured in 508 newspapers having a total circulation of 15,000,000 copies. He was one of the highest paid columnists American journalism ever had, and something of a legend even while he lived. He was a hinterland dandy who saw life agawking, in terms of Broadway's glittering personalities and New York's exotic haunts. The formula satisfied his readers, though New Yorkers complained they could not recognize the Bagdad he made of their city. At times he wrote tear-jerkers about dogs, or harked upon Gallipolis, the beauties of small-town life, his grandmother's jellies. He never returned to Gallipolis, and when the train bearing his casket neared Ohio in February 1938, some State newspapers ran for their streamers: "Odd Is Coming Home."

Ohio

OSCAR WILDE. [At the Elks Opera House in Leadville] an audience accorded a warm welcome [in 1882] to Oscar Wilde, who stepped upon the stage in a suit of "elegant black velvet, with knee breeches and black stockings, a Byron collar and white neckhandkerchief. . . . On his shirt front glittered a single cluster of diamonds." He spoke at length on "The Practical Application of the Aesthetic Theory to Exterior and Interior House Decoration, with Observations on Dress and Personal Ornament." The miners understood little of what Wilde said in his dull manner, but they liked him, being quite frankly awed by his capacity to drink hard liquor.

[When] Wilde visited the [Matchless] mine, he was met at the bottom of the shaft by a dozen miners, each with a bottle. All of the bottles made the rounds; after the twelfth drink, Wilde was cool and collected, and was "voted a perfect gentleman" by the somewhat tipsy miners.

Colorado

RAILROAD BILL. Stories are still told of the outlaw Negro, Railroad Bill. . . . In life, he was Morris Slater, a worker from the turpentine stills who turned bandit. In death, he became a legendary being endowed with ability to perform all manner of magic. Railroad Bill came into being when an Escambia County deputy attempted to arrest Slater for carrying a gun. The Negro shot the deputy and escaped on a passing freight car, although several citizens were shooting at him. For several months afterward, he terrorized the county, looting freight cars of valuables which he sold at low prices to Negro farm and lumber workers. At last, both the State and the railroad company offered a reward for his capture or death. When Ed. S. McMillan became sheriff, he determined to capture the outlaw, who had once worked for him. As he was preparing to start on the search, he received a laboriously written note. "Don't come, Mr. Ed." the note read, "I love you." But the sheriff went on the search, encountered the outlaw, and was killed by a bullet in his heart. At once a posse was organized but Railroad Bill evaded them for more than a week. At last, he was cornered in a store that he had entered to obtain food, and while he sat on the floor eating, with his rifle at his side, he was slain by shotgun blasts. Today, the Negro field workers sing songs about "dat Railroad Bill," and they claim that he would never have been killed if he had seen the possemen in time to work his magic.

Alabama

THE WOMAN IN BLACK. For three years, 1919–21, Eureka was haunted by the "Woman in Black." Night after night, in different parts of town, she would step from the shadows in the path of some woman, and stare. She never spoke, never touched anyone. One man claimed she stopped him, and he knocked her down, but she sprang up and ran away. Another man said she pointed a gun at him and asked if he was "So and So." When he replied that he was not, she turned and walked away. Where she came from, who she was, or where she finally disappeared to, has never been found out.

Utah

THE HERMIT OF THE KNOBS. In the early days the Old State Road, connecting Jeffersonville and Vincennes, ran over the top of the knobs or Silver Hills, as the Indians called them. According to Indian legend, the Silver Hills were formed when the Great Spirit dug up the ground searching for silver to put in the sky as stars. The Indians used the knobs as lookout points. From their summit Kentucky hills, 25 miles distant, can be seen on clear days. . . .

Years ago, according to the Louisville *Times*, Gilbert Vestison, the "Hermit of the Knobs," lived on a wild and lonely spot at the summit of a hill. As a youth—handsome, intelligent, ambitious, and poor—Vestison had lived in France and had fallen in love with a girl named Madeline (whose last name he would never reveal). For a short time they lived in their own personal paradise, completely happy. Then Madeline's wealthy parents parted the lovers. Gilbert was broken in heart and mind and became a wanderer. He finally came to the knobs, built a rude shack, and lived here for 30 years, nursing his grief and shunning the company of his neighbors.

Vestison became known throughout the neighborhood for his eccentricities. He said that he was 6,000 years old and that he expected to live another 1,000 years, after which he would be reunited with his Madeline in a second period of youth that would be unending. He was ordinarily gentle, kind, and apparently sane, but if a neighbor requested him to sing the "Marseillaise," his eyes would glow madly and the battle song of France would roll from his lips in an impassioned torrent.

His cabin finally collapsed and he spent the last years of his life in a hole dug in the side of a hill. One morning two passing hunters found Gilbert dead in his cave, a smile on his lips. Near by were the remains of a log cabin and a huge pile of old shoes he had collected. Clutched in his hand was the photograph of a beautiful girl. Gilbert had lived his remaining thousand years.

Indiana

GENERAL RESURRECTION. The Gold Miner's Daughter and the Bucket of Blood, most notorious of [Alta's] twenty-six saloons, were not only busy serving drinks and raking in money over the tables, but were well occupied mopping up after the 110 killings as they occurred within the hospitable swinging doors. The men were buried in the little cemetery at the base of Rustler Mountain. Perhaps someone in Alta regretted the murders, for in the spring of 1873 a mysterious stranger appeared in camp, and offered to go to the cemetery and resurrect the dead. At first the people were disposed to accept the stranger's offer, but after giving the proposal some thought they decided that a general resurrection might be attended by numerous inconveniences. Widows and widowers who had remarried feared that the return of dead husbands and wives might disturb their domestic arrangements. Moreover, those who had inherited property soon recognized that the dead have no business out of the cemetery. Before many days the people of Alta took up a collection of $2,500 and presented it to the stranger, hoping the money would induce him to leave town. It did.

Utah

BASILICONTHAMATURGIST. About 1880 complete companies began to be booked from New York agents. The stock company was abandoned, and the big names in American theater of the time began to appear regularly on the Salt Lake Theater billboards. The Home Dramatic Club, organized in 1880 at Salt Lake City, in a period of fourteen and a half years presented about forty-five plays. Tony Pastor, the pioneer of vaudeville, played the theater in 1876 with his variety show. He had been preceded by P. T. Barnum, and an occasional performer such as Professor Simmons, "Great, Weird, Wondrous, and Invincibly Incomprehensible . . . Basiliconthamaturgist."

Utah

FIRE AND RUN. After the War of 1812 there were no calls for active military service until the Dorr Rebellion of 1842. . . . To cope with this uprising Washington County sent 1,100 men under command of General John B. Stedman of Westerly. During the period of the uprising, Westerly was under martial law. There was no bloodshed, but it is reported that General Stedman issued the following order: "Boys, when you see the enemy, fire and then run, and as I am a little lame, I will run now."

Rhode Island

Moving About

Transportation

THE GUIDES were written for car drivers. Here, though, we look at other means of travel.

The railroad dominated long-distance travel in America from the Civil War until the 1930s, maybe later. Where it went and where it didn't determined whether a town flourished or failed. Moreover, the train had a strong grip on many of our imaginations. Life was inconceivable without it. In 1938 a wire service ran a squib about a Texas woman who had toured the prehistoric cliffside dwellings in New Mexico's Bandelier National Monument and told the guide she was surprised the Indians "would build their houses out here so far from the railroad."

In addition to the train, here we find the newest (from the thirties' point of view) means of travel and some of the oldest, like water and foot.

THE MORAL EFFECT OF RAILROADS. In spite of advantages which were obvious to the foresighted, Massachusetts was slower than some other sections of the country in accepting the new method of transportation. Just as the first coaches to appear on the streets were severely censured, so were the first railroads. Puritanism was always suspicious of anything that made for physical comfort. Many people were sincerely convinced that the use of these iron highways would lower the prevailing standards of morality.

During the building of the Western Railroad from Worcester to Spring-field in 1837, so much adverse criticism was directed against this project that the owners of the road sent a letter to all the churches of the State asking that *sermons be preached on the beneficial moral effect of railroads.*

Massachusetts

POSTMAN. Travel between Palm Beach and Miami continued to be very difficult until the building of the railroad in 1896. The traveler had either to go by boat or to walk 66 miles along a lonely beach. Those who walked usually accompanied the postman who carried the mail from Palm Beach to Miami on foot, for he was the only one who knew the trail, having boats hidden at the numerous inlets, across which he ferried his passengers. The postman received $5 from each traveler who made the trip.

Florida

ACCOMMODATION PASSENGER RUN. For 25 years Casper had only one railroad. The Chicago & North Western Railroad hauled all freight, mail, express, and passengers to and from the city until October 20, 1913, when the Chicago, Burlington & Quincy Railroad service was established. The Burlington had an "accommodation passenger run" before the regular service was started. The crews frequently left the train standing between stations while they hunted sage chickens or jack rabbits on the prairies. The passengers had the choice of joining the chase or amusing themselves until the trainmen returned.

Wyoming

THE HUMP. Bordering the highway [near Melrose Park] for three miles are the Proviso Yards of the Chicago & North Western Railway. The best view is from the entrance to the yards, reached by a half-mile concrete drive

. . . marked Blind Road. . . . The Proviso Yards, sometimes called the "Hump" because of the incline controlling switching operations, are the largest railroad yards in the world—three miles long and one-half mile wide, 960 acres in area. By means of an electrically operated system, aided by gravity, the old method of switching by engine crews is eliminated and in a single operation freight cars are distributed and classified on 59 tracks. Through-freight is saved 12 hours in shipping time, and cars for other destinations need no longer go into Chicago, but are delivered directly to the Outer Belt Line.

The operations of the yard appear chaotic, yet extreme precision and accuracy govern each maneuver. Puffing locomotives back long trains to the crest of the hump. Brakemen uncouple the cars, releasing them for their gravity run down an incline that drops 18 feet in 300 yards. From a tower nearby an operator presses a lever regulating the electric retarders. The same operator manipulates the electric switching apparatus, sending each car to its appointed track. The cars are then picked up by locomotives for assembly into out-going trains. Each of the 59 tracks has a capacity of 70 cars; the yard can classify and handle 4,000 cars daily. It is brilliantly lighted at night, permitting 24-hour operation. Refrigerator cars are served by a modern high-speed ice plant. The engine terminal roundhouse has stalls for 58 locomotives and a system of water tanks supplied by a 2,100-foot well.

Freight cars passing through the yards are checked for dry bearings, cracked wheels, and other defects. At the warehouse great motor caravans empty their loads into tractor truck trains, which dart along the tracks delivering merchandise to designated cars. High speed and accuracy prevent shipments from accumulating.

Illinois

TENNESSEE CENTRAL. The Tennessee Central Railway, which winds along the highway between Harriman and Nashville [at Double Springs], loops sharply south for a few miles. This branch of the railroad, which has infrequent service, plays an important part in the lives of inhabitants of the region through which it passes. The train crews know all the regular passengers by name, share their interests, and treat them as guests. The conductors consider the trains as their personal possessions. The passenger trains do not carry diners, and some time before noon the conductor or a member of the crew goes through the two or three cars to collect orders for coffee, soft drinks, and sandwiches. These orders are wired up the line to a station where nearby housewives prepare the food and drinks that are distributed when the train arrives. A visitor who wishes to meet rural Tennesseans should ride at least once by day between Knoxville and Nashville on this road.

Tennessee

FORBIDDEN GROUND. The Southern Pacific arrived at the west bank of the Colorado opposite Yuma in the spring of 1877, and spent all summer building the bridge across the river. But when it was finished, the Federal government, which had given the company permission to build the bridge, refused to allow trains to run over the Federal stream or across the military reservation on its east bank. The first crossing onto Arizona soil was therefore made surreptitiously, while the garrison at Fort Yuma was asleep. Southern Pacific engineers, unable to resist the temptation of forbidden ground, took an engine quietly across the Colorado. When they were safely past the fort, "the engineer tied down the whistle valve and used all the steam he had in celebrating the advent of the iron horse into new territory." The awakened soldiery soon chased the trespassers back into California, but Arizona had seen its first train.

Arizona

TWENTY MINUTES FOR DINNER. In Smithville . . . , a junction of the Central of Georgia Railway, trains stop for the customary "twenty minutes for dinner." On the porch of the frame hotel across the street from the station a Negro porter swings a large brass dinner bell. Passengers and crew hurry from the train to the dining room, where the plates are already placed on long tables. By a provision in the will of R. L. McAfee, the first owner, chicken was served every day for more than fifty years, until the original hotel burned. The proprietors of the present inn no longer limit the meals to chicken.

Georgia

IT WILL NEVER DO FOR LARGE BUNDLES! Between Lancaster and Harrisburg once extended the first commercial telegraph line in Pennsylvania. Construction of the line was completed in 1845; unbarked chestnut poles, spaced 18 to the mile, bore black walnut cross-arms, which supported heavy wires. On January 1, 1846, the crude instruments for receiving and sending arrived at Lancaster and Harrisburg, the two terminals. Of the four operators only James Reid in Harrisburg could interpret the dot and dash alphabet without reference to a printed code book. After a week of tapping the keys, making adjustments, then tapping the keys again, no intelligible signal had reached either office. Then, on January 8, David Brooks in the Lancaster office accidentally pressed the armature in a manner that brought it into the magnetic field—its proper position. The motion of the armature in Lancaster corresponded to the manipulation of the key in Harrisburg. Brooks set the armature, and immediately his instrument began to register upon the tape a message that Reid had been tapping out repeatedly in Harrisburg. Consulting his code book, Brooks read, "Why don't you write, you rascals?" the first telegraph message transmitted in Pennsylvania.

People crowded wonderingly to the telegraph offices. Revenue, however, was derived principally from translating letters of the alphabet to telegraphic characters on the tape, and from sending names over the wire. When the novelty wore thin in less than four months the offices had to be closed. The wires were taken down and sold to pay the operators' overdue wages. Thus the pioneer telegraph line passed out of existence.

During its short life, however, the telegraph caused a great stir among the people of Lancaster and Dauphin Counties. The humming sound caused by wind sweeping through the wires aroused superstitious fears, especially after dark. One woman built a fence around a pole because she feared that contact with it would spoil her cow's milk. A hotel proprietor in Lancaster delighted in presenting detailed misinformation to the crowd that gathered in his barroom on market mornings. When his exaggerated stories had reduced the patrons to open-mouthed credulity, he would leave the barroom for a few minutes and return with such articles as a handkerchief, a pair of stockings, and a newspaper. "I received these in just 40 seconds from Philadelphia," he would tell them gravely, exhibiting a punctured hole in each article as evidence that it had arrived by wire. It mattered little to the gullible that the line did not extend to Philadelphia.

A former member of the legislature observed ponderously: "This telegraph is a great thing. When I had the honor of representing you in the legislature I often thought about it, and having turned the subject over in my mind, the conclusion reached by me in regard to it is: it will do well enough for carrying letters and small packages, but it will never do for carrying large bundles and bale boxes!"

Pennsylvania

SCHEDULE CHANGE. When the [Baldwinsville] First Baptist Church was moved to its present site, the process of removal extended over a period of days, and on Saturday night the structure was straddling the railroad tracks. Because the elders of the congregation sternly banned labor on the Lord's Day, the schedule of the railroad had to be canceled for that day.

Massachusetts

SHORT, BUT JUST AS WIDE. The story of the Middleburg & Schoharie Railroad is an epic of transportation change. Built at a cost of $90,000 in 1867–8 when iron rails were perfection in transportation, at the turn of the century the road grossed in a single year $97,000 carrying hops, timothy, and lumber 5.7 miles down the valley to the junction with the Schoharie Valley Railroad. But as the hard-surfaced road crept up the valley, the railroad was superseded. The single locomotive, built in 1895, snorted less frequently up and down the valley; during its last years it habitually jumped the tracks once a week and carried a huge jack on its stubby cow-catcher with which to restore its equilibrium. Toward the end, station stops meant nothing: the engineer stopped to pick up a fare wherever he received the hitchhiker's signal. This railroad and its wheezing engine once provided background for a motion picture of Edison's boyhood days as a telegrapher. The president of the road pointed out that although his road was not as long as some of the others, it was just as wide; he sent guest passes on his line to railroad presidents the country over, and they in return sent him passes over their roads, so that he saw America free. In its last days the road found difficulty in meeting a weekly pay roll of $46 and was closed in October 1936 by the State Public Service Commission. Sold at a public auction on March 15, 1937, the railroad brought $11,000 and the antique 40-ton locomotive, $1,265.

New York

SEPARATE WAITING ROOMS. Through the Union Station and Mail Terminal [in Texarkana], pass travelers and mail carried by four railroads. Visitors are invariably impressed by the speed with which mountains of mail are handled in the terminal, one of the largest in the Southwest. The State boundary cuts through a corner of the station's waiting room for white passengers, and divides the ticket office and the Negro waiting room. By this device the architects complied with Arkansas and Texas laws requiring separate waiting rooms for whites and Negroes in each State.

Arkansas

STEAMBOAT. The first steamboat on the Mississippi, the *New Orleans*, left Pittsburgh for New Orleans in October of 1811. It made the trip despite the New Madrid earthquake, during which the current reversed and great chunks of land caved into the river. The sixth boat on the Mississippi, the *Zebulon M. Pike*, was built at Henderson, Kentucky, in 1815, and was the first to ascend the river beyond the mouth of the Ohio. Its hull was built on the model of a barge, and in rapid current the power of its one boiler had to be augmented by the use of poles. Yet, when the *Pike* arrived at St. Louis on August 9, 1817, it had made the trip from New Orleans in one-fifth the usual time. This voyage inaugurated a new era in Missouri transportation. Two years later the *Independence* proved the Missouri River to be navigable for steamboats by making the trip from St. Louis to Franklin, Chariton, and return within 21 days. During the same year the *Western Engineer*, one of the strongest of river boats, was built and equipped for Long's Expedition to the upper Missouri. The bow was shaped like the head of an immense serpent, from whose gaping mouth poured smoke and flame. The vessel moved up the river to the terror of the Indians, eventually reaching a point miles below Council Bluffs, the highest point reached by steamboat at that time.

The trip from St. Louis to St. Joseph, a distance of about 500 miles, sometimes took as long as that from New Orleans to St. Louis, for snags, shifting currents, and sandbanks prevented night travel. Often a boat never reached its destination. Navigation hazards, numerous on the Mississippi, were multiplied on the Missouri. With changing sandy channels, steamboats grounded as many as a dozen times a day. When the Missouri was at low-water stage, navigating it was "like putting a steamer on dry land, and sending a boy ahead with a sprinkling pot."

Half-submerged trees impaled the boats, over-strained boilers exploded, fires swept through the hulls, yet for every boat that met disaster, two others were launched. Many of the steamboats earned their cost within a year, for they were the swiftest as well as the most luxurious form of transportation. The majority were splendid structures, with double decks and interiors with gilded decorations, mahogany woodwork, and red plush upholstering. The *Natchez*, remembered for its race in 1870 against the *Robert E. Lee*, cost $200,000; the latter broke all records in making the 1,210-mile upstream run from New Orleans in 3 days, 18 hours, 14 minutes.

But for all their finery, the boats brought land-hungry settlers and traders in such numbers that their cabin floors were frequently carpeted with sleepers. Often, a missionary held a prayer meeting at one end of a boat's deck, while a gambler, with ruffled shirt, gaudy vest, Paris boots, and easy manners, plied his trade at the other. The boat would stop at a landing, a handful of people would go ashore, and soon another settlement would rise in the wilderness.

The steamboat pilot replaced the flatboatman as the outstanding figure of the rivers. Sharp-eyed, quiet, and alert, he belonged to a race apart. Often a pilot earned as much as $1,000 a month—more, Mark Twain observed, than a preacher did in a year. About the pilots, the captains, and their boats grew a lore as rich as the gargantuan stories of the flatboatmen. There was the boat "a-loaded down with ile an' bound for Noo Orleans" that caught fire and made a blaze so hot, "hit dried up the river." No less wonderful was the *Jim Johnson*, with its awesome captain who weighed 750 pounds and had but one eye; this boat was so big it took all summer to pass Boonville, and had to have rubber joints to get around the bends in the river.

Missouri

S. S. STARR. Until 1938 transporation "to the westward" was furnished largely by the S. S. *Starr*, a converted halibut schooner of only 525 tons burden, that sailed from Seward with freight and passengers once a month. Passengers were unanimous in cursing her violent motion and cramped quarters, but now that she no longer makes the trip, Alaskans recall her with regret. The first-class quarters consisted of a small dining saloon, out of which opened directly two toilets, encircled with tiny cabins not fully partitioned off, each containing three bunks and a washbasin. An important article of furniture fixed to each bunk was an iron bracket holding a large pasteboard cup, into which most passengers rendered up at least a portion of each meal. Few passengers traveled on the lurchy little *Starr* for pleasure; however, every passenger had an interesting story, and the tales told around the dining table when supper was cleared away had no equal anywhere in the world.

The country "to the westward" stretches hundreds of miles without a single tree, has the longest and straightest single line of volcanoes (some 50 or 60) anywhere in the world, a few of them very active, is surprisingly warm, bathed as it is by the Japan Current. This country, with its tiny settlements and their turnip-topped Russian orthodox churches, with its teeming wild life and its breath-taking scenic grandeur, is worth the fortitude it takes to make the trip by any steamer available. Whatever the vessel, it will have accommodations that Vitus Bering, the Columbus of these parts, would have considered the uttermost in luxury.

Alaska

SPITE TOWER. The well-equipped Harrisburg Airport . . . was the scene of a land dispute that resulted in laws prohibiting the erection of towers on ground adjoining airports.

In 1934 "Baron" Bestecki, angered because the airport sponsors refused to meet his price for adjoining property, erected a "spite" tower 100 feet high, with guy wires stretching for some distance in every direction. This created such a hazard that the Department of Aeronautics placed a ban on the air field. When a mysterious fire leveled the tower, a court order forbade Bestecki to rebuild it. His property was purchased when the State took control of the airport in 1936.

Pennsylvania

BRIDGE BATTLES. Stevenson Dam [on the Housatonic] interrupts the flow of the river and forms the eight-mile stretch of deep water known as Lake Zoar. The lake has been named for the old Zoar Bridge, the red structure formerly used following the historic "bridge battles" of the valley. Here, many

bridges were built for the toll revenue; often three of them tried to do business at the same time. Shotgun guards patrolled the bridges and men held their franchises here by right of might rather than legal claim. One bridge was actually moved several times, but the river itself periodically eliminated the trouble by washing all bridges away.

Connecticut

GRANNY STALBIRD. [Near Shelburne Village] is . . . a stone settle with a marker, commemorating an experience of Deborah Vickers, an early settler. Becoming a widow, she learned about medicinal roots from the Indians and became a noted "doctress." Well known as "Granny Stalbird," she was always summoned whenever there was anyone ill throughout the countryside, making her journeys on horseback clad in a long plaid cloak and hood, and with a bag containing her medicinal concoctions. No roads were too bad or weather too severe to hinder her in her missions of mercy. One day her professional duties took her along this route. Overtaken here by a severe storm and hindered by swollen streams from continuing her journey, she took shelter under a shelved rock and passed the night here, "amidst the roar of the winds, the flashes of lightning and peals of thunder, the rushing water and the howl of wolves." When the railroad was put through, the rock was blasted away.

New Hampshire

INSIDE PASSAGE. Leaving the dull red rocks along Alaskan Way [Seattle], the steamer backs into crescent-shaped Elliott Bay. To the right looms residential Queen Anne Hill. Rounding West Point, marked by a lighthouse, the ship heads directly up Puget Sound. Bainbridge Island, hardly distinguished from the mainland, is on the left, and beyond it and the forested mainland are the tumbled rocks of the Olympic Mountains. To the right, Fort Lawton's guns point unseen behind the forest. Shilsole Bay indents the shoreline, opening to Government Locks and Lake Washington Ship Canal. Finally the northwest corner of Seattle breaks off at a high bluff, the long white chain of the Cascade Mountains stretch across the eastern horizon, and the nonstop voyage along the Inside Passage, 757 miles from Seattle to Ketchikan, begins.

The boat is never out of sight of land. The bewildering chain of islands, from which drifts an almost overpowering smell of spruce, baffles the passenger, who at any given moment is unable to foretell what way the boat will pick through the constantly shifting outline of mountain, island, and shore. Layers of mist lie on the hillsides like geologic strata, or are caught in spruce branches like wool left by celestial sheep, or form grotesque arches and doorways as if to lure the boat through false channels.

Fogs are frequent along the Inside Passage, and formerly, vessels navigated entirely by dead reckoning, checking their position with blasts of whistle. Pilots became expert in judging their exact whereabouts by the quality of the echo (which has a different sound according to whether it is reflected from a pine-covered island, from a mountain, or from open water) and by the time between the blast of the whistle and the echo. Modern navigation relies to a certain extent on radio beacons, but these cannot be trusted absolutely, as they have a variation of 5 degrees, and are sometimes deflected by the narrow channel. In thick weather pilots still rely on their knowledge of the channels, in which it is frequently necessary to make a turn at right angles. It is safer to steam steadily ahead in a fog, as on the basis of a consistent speed, with the necessary checks for wind or tide, the navigator knows exactly where he is. He simply puts the vessel on one course for the right number of minutes, then changes his course, keeping to the middle of the channel by blowing his whistle and listening to the echo.

Alaska

Along the Road

T HE AMERICA the driver of the thirties saw still exists here and there. It can be found on back roads and on dilapidated sections of the U.S. highway system, which was largely completed in the 1930s. It is Walker Evans's country, land of the hand-painted sign, the mom-and-pop store, the independent gas pump—it was incoherent, piecemeal, a hundred aesthetics each doing his own thing with never a thought for Overall Style.

A house, a barn, a field of workers or wild flowers, a factory, a school-house—each comes into view at random, the sequence determined only by the road you happen to be on. This sense of randomness is central to the Guides, and can be found here too. We go from *Bender Mounds* to the *Eastern Shore* to *Potneck*. We see *advertising*, a *tourist camp*, and a *lion farm*. In retrospect, some of what we see seems harsh, and some seems not only innocent, but lovely.

It could not last. The handwriting of the mall was on the wall. Franchise America was coming down the road with homogenized food, anywhere places, and no-surprise bedrooms. It had sent its calling card ahead: small wooden panels for *shaving cream*.

NIGHT DRIVING. West of Odessa, State 7 follows a slightly winding course through sagebrush barrens broken occasionally by orchards or surprising vistas. This section of the highway is an invitation to night driving, especially during the hot weather of midsummer. As a rule, traffic is not heavy after dark, and the traveler can speed with comparative safety, for only occasionally is the straightaway broken by a sharp curve, a dip, an incline, or a winding stretch of road around the base of some cliff or coulee wall. Now and then the eyes of an approaching car appear in the distance, grow brighter and brighter, give a brief close glow, disappear. Occasionally, a truck with heavily laden trailers thunders past, or a jack rabbit, phantom-like, leaps across the road. In the spring the scent of apple blossoms reveals an orchard hidden by the darkness. Again, the headlight of a locomotive creeps across the plateau, the light growing larger as the train approaches with seemingly accelerating speed; then with a flash the engine thunders by, and is gone, leaving only the throb of the automobile motor and the whistle of the wind.

Washington

TOURIST CAMP. A tourist camp presents a lively and typical American scene during the height of the season. Dusty cars and trailers bearing license tags of various States roll in toward evening and park in their allotted "yards." This is accompanied by a certain amount of haggling over rates and choice locations. Old acquaintances are hailed and new ones made. The iceman, baker, resort-plugger, and vendor of curios and myriad contraptions useful to the modern-day gypsies make their rounds. Between periods of gossiping, womanfolk attend to their sewing and laundry; washings soon flap on improvised lines; ironing boards are often set up in the open. Menfolk congregate to swap tales of the road, of their experiences en route, and to learn what accommodations are offered at anticipated destinations. Shuffleboard courts, horseshoe pitching lanes, and card games attract their devotees. Supper time is heralded by the clatter of dishes and the odor of cooking food. After dark the recreational hall is thronged with young and old who dance to new tunes and old, furnished, except on gala occasions when an orchestra is hired, by a nickel-in-the slot phonograph. Other campers hurry into town to window shop, to go to the movies, or attend more inviting nightspots.

Florida

TUMBLEWEEDS. The highway traverses miles of prairie carpeted with white and yellow daisies, golden pea, and butterweed during spring; later, with loco weed, prickly poppy, and sunflowers. Large areas are covered with Russian thistles, more commonly known as "tumbleweeds," native to Russia and transported to this country by seeds mixed with imported grains. With the sandbur, it is the chief vegetable pest of the arid West.

The thistles grow in thick mats, sending down many roots and entangling their branches until a whole field seems to be covered by a single plant. Bushes are roughly globular in shape, some attaining great size, and the up-curving stems are studded with tiny thorns. They are green with streaks of lurid purple during spring and early summer, but turn brown as the season progresses. When completely dry, they break away from their roots, to be caught up by the wind and tumbled along over hills and plains, leaping and twirling in a grotesque parody of a spring song. Scattering seeds as they go, they eventually come to rest, heaped in fence corners, ditches, or sand blows. Their high inflammability when dry has resulted in miles of weed-covered prairie going up in sheets of flame.

Colorado

OPEN PIT. [US 169], between the western region of the Arrowhead and the eastern part of the Paul Bunyan resort region, includes the iron mines of the Mesabi Range with the towns their wealth created; it traverses the scenic country of northern Minnesota's lake district, industrial Minneapolis, and the agricultural belt of southern Minnesota.

Along the highway are the iron mines of the Mesabi Range and the towns where live the miners, mine officials, professional men, and tradesmen. Since all of these towns owe their origin to a common industry, they have few distinguishing differences other than their size. Yet together they offer a definitely characteristic type of village and small city, in a setting that is not found anywhere else in the country.

The open-pit mines at the edges of these communities are of spectacular interest. The red and purple sides of these great craters in the earth descend for hundreds of feet in uneven terraces. Winding up from the depths in a spiral path over a network of steel trackage, one after another come the long chains of hopper-bottomed ore cars, hauled from terrace to terrace by puffing locomotives. At the base of the crater, huge power shovels, like rhythmically moving monsters, scoop out the red earth 5 tons to a bite, and load it on waiting empties. Masses of strippings and ore stock piled above the terraces intensify still further the feeling of vastness and depth. From the observation platform, through the rising, red dust clouds, the men, cars, and shovels seem like marionette performers in the first scenes of the drama of steel-making.

Minnesota

ONE THING TODAY AND ANOTHER TOMORROW. US 66 continues [west of Laguna Pueblo] through stretches of desert with multi-colored formations and with but little cultivated ground, except in the settlements off the road. These native villages are as unchanging as the woman in one of their stories. When she was called before a local justice he asked her age. "I have 45 years." "But," said the justice, "You were forty-five when you appeared before me two years ago." "Señor Judge," she replied proudly, drawing herself to her full height, "I am not of those who are one thing today and another tomorrow!"

New Mexico

BROWN MOUNTAIN LIGHTS. Beyond Clearwater Beach State 181 begins the steep ascent of Ripshin Ridge to Loven's Hotel, . . . near Cold Spring. Visible from the hotel, under favorable atmospheric conditions at night, are the Brown Mountain Lights, a phenomenon that has puzzled sci-

MOVING ABOUT

entists for 50 years. The lights, which appear behind Jonas Ridge, resemble the glow of balls of fire from a Roman candle. After reaching a maximum intensity they fade out to appear at other points. The U.S. Geological Survey suggested that the lights might be caused by the refraction of headlights on trains and automobiles in the valley behond. The National Geographic Society reported that the source could be from discharges of static electricity.

North Carolina

HELL HOLE SWAMP. [Along the] road [near Bonneau], its exact location undetermined, is Hell Hole Swamp, an area of indefinite extent, its whereabouts always designated as "just a piece down the road." During prohibition days, when South Carolina was actively advertising the iodine content of its vegetables, the Hell Hole brand of "liquid corn" was notorious with its waggish slogan: "Not a Goiter in a Gallon."

South Carolina

LION FARM. Thousand Oaks is a gathering of tourist accommodations around the Goebel Lion Farm (admission 25¢), which supplies many animals used by movie studios. In the afternoon between 3:30 and 5 the trainer sometimes obliges spectators by putting his head into a lion's mouth.

California

MAGIC HILL. Magic Hill [is] a hundred-yard stretch of red clay road over a spur of Pine Mountain. An automobile with motor turned off seems to coast uphill and, after passing the brow, to stop on the downgrade. Water apparently defies the law of gravitation by running uphill and draining off into a ditch on the downgrade. For a long time this place was known to the Negroes of the vicinity as Ghost Hill because some supernatural power was held responsible for their wagons stalling coming "down" and running away going "up." The hill came into state-wide prominence recently when newspapers carried stories of the phenomenon, and hundreds of people flocked to the place. Surveyors explain that the stretch of ground contains a slight knoll and that, if a car is stopped at the brow of the hill and put into neutral, it will coast for about twenty-five yards downhill. The fact that the slight slope runs in a different direction from the drainage ditch creates an optical illusion.

Georgia

TOPSOIL. Summer-fallowed fields . . . often lose their topsoil during high winds in summer. From the northwest appears a great black cloud a hundred feet or more high that stretches across the entire basin. There is a scurrying of tumbleweeds, then a stinging blizzard blots out the sun, buries miles of fences and roads, stalls cars, and obliterates small ponds.

Montana

EASTERN SHORE. US 13 drops down the middle of Virginia's Eastern Shore on a fairly straight course to Cape Charles near the tip of the narrowed peninsula that separates Chesapeake Bay from the ocean. The fertile land of Accomac County—the northern two-thirds of this peninsula—is abundantly wooded and rolls gently out to marshy flats along both coasts, which are interlaced by innumerable inlets and shallow bays. A chain of low islands along the east protects the mainland from the full winter force of Atlantic storms. These sheltered waters abound with fish and shellfish, which form one of the chief sources of local income. Most of Northampton County, the other third of the peninsula, is absolutely flat. Truck farms dotted with neatly-kept white frame houses stretch away to the dark green walls of pine woods, which form windbreaks against wintry gales. This landscape makes a curious impression; it is as though everything in sight had been laid out with T-square and compass. At the end of long side roads, houses, occasionally of brick and very old, stand in solitude on meadowy lawns close to the water.

Virginia

BENDER MOUNDS. Visible from the highway [west of Parsons] are the Bender Mounds, low hills rising abruptly from a level plain. They were named for the Bender family. William, his wife, their son, John, and daughter, Kate, had moved in 1870 to a hill farm on the old trail from Independence to Osage Mission. (The trail was slightly north of the route followed by US 160.) They lived in a two-room frame building, using the back room as living quarters, and the front room as a store for the sale of tobacco, crackers, powder, shot, and provisions. William Bender and his son were quiet men, highly respected by their neighbors. Kate, a red-haired buxom lass, traveled about the country lecturing on spiritualism. Her beauty is said to have caused many persons to stop at their little trading post.

Between 1870 and 1873 several travelers who disappeared between Independence and Osage Mission were traced to within a few miles of the Bender

Mounds. So many stories of mystery, murder, and the supernatural were associated with the area that cautious persons would go long distances to avoid it.

In March 1873, settlers in the neighborhood held a meeting to discuss these strange and alarming disappearances. William Bender and his son attended. A short time later a searching party of fifty men stopped at the Bender house and asked Kate to use her clairvoyant powers in an effort to solve the mystery. This she agreed to do.

A few days later, passers-by noticed stock wandering about the Bender farm and on investigation found that the place had been hastily deserted. In the combined orchard and garden back of the house they discovered a number of bodies, including that of Dr. William York, the last person to disappear. His head had been smashed in, and his throat cut from ear to ear. It had been the Benders' custom to seat guests at the dinner table with their backs to a cloth partition which screened the bedroom. It is believed that from behind this cloth the Benders killed their victims with an axe in order to rob them. In spite of many clues neither Kate, whose plump hands may have committed the murders, nor any of her family were ever found.

Kansas

ROADSIDE ADVERTISING. In [North Florida] US 1 crosses a level region of pine forests and cut-over flatwoods; occasional hardwood hammocks mark the courses of sluggish streams. The country is sparsely settled, but near Jacksonville appear dairy and poultry farms, and filling stations of various sizes, colors, and styles.

The highway presents an interesting study of American roadside advertising. There are signs that turn like windmills; startling signs that resemble crashed airplanes; signs with glass lettering which blaze forth at night when automobile headlight beams strike them; flashing neon signs; signs painted with professional touch; signs crudely lettered and misspelled. They advertise hotels, tourist cabins, fishing camps, and eating places. They extol the virtues of ice creams, shoe creams, cold creams; proclaim the advantages of new cars and used cars; tell of 24-hour towing and ambulance service, Georgia pecans, Florida fruit and fruit juices, honey, soft drinks, and furniture. They urge the traveler to take designated tours, to visit certain cities, to stop at points of interest he "must see."

Florida

BALLS OF FIRE. West of Kiona, US 410, following the Yakima River, climbs along the northern slope of the Horse Heaven Hills, where sheep and cattle find good grazing grounds. At night will-o-the-wisps are frequent along this bleak and lonely road. Flame-colored, and about three feet above the ground, they are often mistaken by motorists for a single vehicular light. Sternly realistic farmers, their hands still smarting from the handle of a plow, have reported "balls of fire" coming down the road at the speed of an automobile. During dust storms, which are frequent in this area, tumbleweeds roll over rounded hills and dance across the highway.

Washington

NO DEPRESSION ON TAX. A small ramshackle building [along State 1 near English Turn] belongs to a rugged individualist who has covered it with crudely painted signs proclaiming, "You took my skin, you took my flesh, you left my bones . . . Mr. E. Riches—51 years old and don't owe one penny. Never was in trouble in my whole life—very few men can say that . . . Tax raised $100, no depression on tax," and many others.

Louisiana

PRAIRIE. Between Kankakee . . . and Mattoon is corn, in fields of green or yellow, waving in the breeze of early morning, shimmering in the heat of noonday sun, in long swells, in quiet planes, from the highway to the horizon. Hedgerows separate the fields, oak groves shade the farmsteads, but no hill breaks the prairie, and only a few tributaries of the Wabash cut their willow-marked courses across its surface. This is the great cash-grain region of the State, one of the richest and most completely cultivated farming areas of the world; this is the land of corn, the heart of the Illinois prairies.

Fertile, unleached black loams, developed from the thick, flat deposits of the Wisconsin ice sheet, a long, hot growing season, and properly distributed rainfall provide ideal conditions for the cultivation of corn. Proximity to Chicago, the corn market of the Nation, determines the unusual economy of the region—the cash sale of the grain, rather than its use on the farm in the feeding of livestock, which is the general practice elsewhere in the Corn Belt. Second in importance to corn is oats, which fits well in the crop rotation scheme. Since its planting and harvesting seasons differ from those of corn, its cultivation enables the farmer to spread his work.

The farmstead of the prairie is strikingly unlike that of the dairy region. No giant barn, no silo overshadows the farmhouse. A small outbuilding shelters the few animals and stores their food, another protects the machinery. For the produce of the prairie does not remain on the farm, but goes directly to the nearby town where it is stored in the huge elevators that tower over each village, to be sold eventually in Chicago.

Illinois

BLACK BELT. West of Tuskegee the highway is through the rich Black Belt where cotton is still the money crop, and Negro tenant cabins dot the plantations. Wide fields, mostly cotton and corn, spread far on both sides of the highway. Along the streams the monotony of the level land is broken by tall woods of bay, sweet gum, and oak, the bay remaining green in winter and giving color to the otherwise drab landscape. Plantation big-houses, some standing deserted and dilapidated amid groves of ancient trees, are visible along the highway. Newer farm houses have supplanted some of the old dwellings and the introduction of tractors has deprived many Negro tenant farmers of their jobs.

Alabama

THE MERITS OF CHEWING TOBACCO. West of Wileyville State 7 plays hide-and-seek with the crests of a half dozen summits of worn hills, where the earth wrinkles in whorls like the skin on the face of an ancient mountain woman; the highway then descends to Fishing Creek Valley to dodge oil wells and creep past drowsing farmlands. Houses on slopes across the creek are connected with the road by wire-and-slat swinging footbridges or fallen trees. Natives in this quiet section contentedly fish in the creek, dogs sun themselves in the middle of the road, and the tourist finds pleasure in the total absence of billboards and filling-station architecture; barns and outbuildings are not painted to proclaim the merits of several brands of chewing tobacco.

West Virginia

TRAFFICSCOPE. Straddling the road at the crest of a hill [near Elizabeth-town] is a Trafficscope, designed to provide motorists ascending the hill from either direction with a view of the highway on the opposite side. Installed in the spring of 1939 as an experiment, it consists of a steel framework supporting a gigantic lens composed of rows of glass prisms arranged to deflect the rays of light so that they virtually follow the contour of the hill. The apparatus costs about $3,000, but it obviates the much greater cost of cutting through a hill to remove a traffic hazard.

Pennsylvania

PLUCKEMIN. Pluckemin is another little village that ends just as its houses seem to be getting into the swing of being a community. A long-standing dispute revolves about the origin of its name. One school of stove-talk has it that the name is rooted in the custom of a local innkeeper who, anxious for trade, would stand in the road and simply "pluck 'em in." But other authority leans to the belief that Pluckemin is an Indian word meaning "persimmon."

New Jersey

POTNECK. West of New Providence the route winds through farm land that produces a high-grade dark-fired tobacco. In this territory, locally called Potneck and its people Potneckers, are numerous wildcat stills in the bushy hollows. Potneck is sometimes said to have received the name from a sorceress whose goiterous neck was enormous. It is extremely hard to find anyone who lives in Potneck; he either lives "just this side" or "just the other side." The favorite sport is 'possum hunting. . . .

Tennessee

STATE 49. State 49 runs through the very heart of the California gold country—including the Mother Lode. Within a decade millions of dollars' worth of gold were taken out of the streams and hills, the bulk of it going to comparatively few men. In this brief span, during which mining camps mushroomed on every river bar and wandering prospectors swarmed the hills by the thousands, a civilization sprang up overnight, endured briefly, and fell in ruins—the full-blown but short-lived civilization of the wide-open, riproaring gold towns. After its decade of glory, as placer mines gave out and placer miners wandered away, the gold region lost its fine flush of feverish enthusiasm. Gone was the day of the roving prospector on muleback, whose stock in trade was a pick and a pan. To unlock the riches in the years that followed, tremendous labors were required and millions in capital. The giant mining companies with their vast and elaborate equipment, sank shafts deep to underlying quartz, built networks of tunnels, stamp mills to crush the ore, wing dams, and ditches, lifted rivers from their beds, and brought in hydraulic monitors that washed whole mountains away.

Along State 49 are strewn the relics of these labors and of the men who performed them; decaying shanties of the "pick and pan" men, abandoned hillside shafts of the quartz mines, high-piled debris of the hydraulic workings. Some of the gold rush towns have disappeared completely, others are mere heaps of rubbish.

California

ROADHOUSES. In smaller towns and villages and along the trails hotels are replaced by "roadhouses," with none of the connotations of the term in the States. Alaska roadhouses are country lodges, built of logs or sawed timbers, usually of two stories. The first story contains the dining and living rooms, the second story the bedroom and baths. The comparative luxury of roadhouses in some remote districts is startling. In new or remote settlements a roadhouse is sometimes replaced by a bunkhouse, consisting of tiers of bunks wedged on top of one another in a tent or cabin. If the settlement is too new or too remote for even a bunkhouse, shelter may usually be had in the local jail and food secured at the trading post. For women the problem of shelter overnight in remote districts may be a delicate one—the hospitality of the local schoolteacher sometimes affords a solution.

Remote trails are dotted with shelter cabins containing food and firewood. Any traveler may make use of one. He must leave it in good order, with firewood and kindling for the next arrival—in the winter, the life of the next arrival may depend upon the speed with which he can build a fire. It is customary to remain in a shelter cabin not longer than three days.

Alaska

SHAVING CREAM. Largely unspoiled by signs, except those advertising such rural necessities as well drilling, State 8N has been chosen as a good medium for the small orange and black signs that describe, in doggerel spread over a series of five panels, the romantic conquests and other joys attained by users of a brushless shaving cream. One local resident, making the ultimate protest against these unscannable jingles, has nailed over a fifth sign (which revealed the brand name) a piece of cardboard bearing the neatly lettered word "NUTS."

New Jersey

Settled and Abandoned

AMERICA MUST have more ghost towns than any other country. The dead cities of the Old World are built over, the fallen walls of one epoch making the streets of the next. But here, where population is less intense, any town whose economy stalls will lose inhabitants, and a small town, particularly a young one, may simply be turned back to nature.

Gold rushes are the most obvious townmakers and -breakers (suggested in *boom town* and *Platinum*). But bad weather, financial panic, the moving of a road, railroad, or county seat do the unmaking just as well (see *first train* and *Hell-on-Wheels*).

The Guides lead us through many former settlements, in passages sometimes touched with elegiac celebration. Here are a boom towns in their glory days and after—or before, when they glowed brighter than reality in their founders' eyes. Not all of these places have died, but all have lost the bloom of promise.

And perhaps that is why ghost towns and rundown parts of town and plain old slums mean a good deal to the American imagination. They show us what our society likes to deny: failure, mortality, time.

BOOM TOWN. In the boom years of the Carbonate Camp, as [Leadville] was known from the nature of its ores, mines and smelters roared day and night; sawmills droned in the hills; fresh yellow pine lumber was knocked together to create rows of cabins and stretches of sidewalks, no two on the same level. The camp was a wilderness of "tents, wigwams of boughs and bare poles . . . cabins wedged between stumps; cabins built on stumps; cabins half roofed . . . with sailcloth roofs, and no roofs at all. . . . All faces looked restless, eager, fierce." From the mines on almost inaccessible hillsides, hundreds of heavy ore wagons clattered down steep makeshift roads and rumbled through town to the smelters. Whole pine forests were cut down, converted into charcoal, and consumed by smelters and ore-reduction plants, for coal and coke were too expensive for use even when available, which they usually were not.

Through the streets of the raw town surged a cosmopolitan and unruly population lured from all points of the compass. Miners, teamsters, and smelter hands brawled and squandered their earnings on liquor, women, or cards in smoky, noisy gambling halls, while upstairs in luxuriously furnished apartments the mining kings played for such high stakes that $1,000 often changed hands on the turn of a card. Rich and poor alike held to the old gambler's adage, "The only thing sure about luck is that it's bound to change."

As one rich strike followed another, an army of newcomers descended upon the roaring camp by stage lines, in freight wagons, and on foot—men and women of all ages, all professions, and, it is said, of all races except Indian and Chinese. The first Celestials who ventured into camp were promptly hanged. During winter months hundreds perished along the icy mountain passes; the route was lined with dead horses and mules, as were the streets in town. Soon the population had risen to 10,000, and still the human flood continued.

Ruthless profiteering by local storekeepers founded many a fortune. Staple groceries sold at four times their price in Denver; a barrel of whisky often netted a $1,500 profit; hay frequently brought $200 a ton. An endless chain of freight teams traveled between Denver, Colorado Springs, and Canon City, laden with bacon and sealskin coats, flour and jewels, champagne and mining machinery. The railheads, 75 miles distant, were a hopeless confusion of freight and men awaiting transportation. Six stage lines served the camp before it was six months old.

Accommodations were wholly inadequate and most expensive. The few hotels turned away hundreds each night, and lodging houses charged $1 for the privilege of sharing a bed with another in makeshift rooms containing a dozen beds. A large tent was pitched on a side street and advertised as the best "hotel" in town. The Mammoth Palace, a vast shed with accommodations for 500, contained double tiers of hard bunks occupied day and night, a guest paying 50¢ for a sleeping turn of eight hours. Thousands fought for permission to curl up on draughty saloon floors, paying high for preferred spots near the stove. Pneumonia claimed scores of victims, many of whom were buried at night without coffins and in unmarked graves to keep the mounting death rate from becoming known. Hundreds were starving; saloons offered no free lunches, although some served 10¢ meals; these and the many 15¢ eating houses were crowded 24 hours a day. Newspapers appealed to citizens to "leave your meal boxes open." Many miners ate their fill in restaurants and asked to be arrested when presented with their checks; some were jailed, but the majority were merely roughly handled.

Colorado

SODDIES. When the first white settlers began pouring into the new country, they laboriously built log houses where trees were available; but as most of the State was treeless, the earth was made to serve as the building material. These pioneers who came to file claims on the virgin prairie found that by hitching their oxen to a plow, it was comparatively simple to loosen furrows which could be cut into blocks five or six inches thick, a foot wide and two or three feet long. The dirt was so interwoven with the strong roots of prairie grass that the chunks were solid enough to be carried easily and laid, brick-fashion, into place. Damp dirt was used to fill in crevices and around the windows, which were usually high and small. Roofs often were made of limbs, brush and hay with a covering of dirt; usually, however, cheap slab lumber covered the sod shanties. In the late 1870's and for a few years the land seekers were content to live in their drab, squat sod houses while they proved up their claims; those people became known as Soddies.

South Dakota

TWO-MAN MILL. John Waymire, a man of boundless energy and versatility, established Portland's first sawmill. His equipment consisted of an old whipsaw brought across the plains from Missouri, and two men to operate it. One stood on top of a log, raised on blocks, and pulled the saw upward;

the other, in a pit beneath, pulled the saw downward and was showered with sawdust at each stroke. Great labor was required to cut a few pieces of lumber, but Waymire's "sawmill" encouraged building activity. He also erected the first hotel, a double log cabin of Paul Bunyanesque proportions, where he "furnished meals and a hospitable place to spread blankets for the night." His team of Missouri oxen hitched to a lumbering wagon served as the first local transportation system.

Oregon

FIRST TRAIN. The most significant event in the history of Ogden was the coming of the railroad. In March, 1869, the first train steamed into the city. A brass band welcomed its arrival, a parade was hastily organized, and speakers depicted the glories to follow. There are residents still living (1940) who recall the afternoon when the entire populace gathered around in Sunday finery to see the iron monster. Suddenly the engineer blew the whistle, yanked a steam valve, and announced he was going "to turn the train around." A wild scramble for safety ensued and many ran pell-mell through a near-by slough in their fright, ruining their Sunday clothes. Some terrified children were not found until evening.

Utah

FLORAS LAKE. Floras Lake [is] a small body of fresh water cut off from the sea by low sand dunes, called *Qua-to-ma* by the Indians. On the shore of the lake is the site of Pacific City, first called Lakeport, promoted in 1908 on the supposition that a canal could be built between the sea and the lake, temporarily the largest town in Curry County. Land was cleared, wharves were built, sidewalks laid, a public park platted, dwellings, business blocks, and a three-story hotel erected. Carpenters worked day and night, while long lines of teams hauled lumber from Bandon and Port Orford. A newspaper, the *Floras Lake Banner*, was established and forthwith began to publicize the place. People flocked in from all quarters of the country, all bent on making their fortunes. Six thousand lots were sold, the first for $12.50 apiece but later ones at $300 each.

When the first excitement had abated a few citizens began to ask questions. Where were the industries to spring from? What about raw materials? What was to be shipped out of the port? All the products that the contiguous country could supply wouldn't make one shipload of freight. The final blow fell when, though the War Department had given permission to dig the canal, it was discovered that the town was 40 feet above sea level and that if the canal were dug the lake would empty itself into the Pacific unless elaborate locks were built. People who could, left at once. Merchants closed their stores and professional men their offices. Guests grew scarcer at the hotel and on Thursday, November 6, 1909, the clerk closed the register with the obituary: "Not a dam sole." Only a few brush-grown walks and the crumbling foundation of the hotel remain.

Oregon

PLATINUM. In 1937, Platinum was Alaska's newest boom town with a population of forty-eight white men and two white women. On a sandspit were perched two long, single-story trading posts, one of which contained the post office. Beyond was a spanking new roadhouse, the most imposing structure of the settlement, with its dining room and kitchen on the first floor and its sleeping room crowded with cots on the second. Between the post office and the roadhouse were corrugated iron sheds, two shacks in which beer was sold, and a flock of white tents huddling on wooden floors. Smudge on the horizon marked the position of the freighter *Laporte*, laden with two thousand tons—500,000 dollars' worth—of dredge, fast on a sand bar. She was ultimately floated off, just in time to miss a storm that would have scuttled her.

In the roadhouse, waiting for the *Laporte* to pull off the bar, the total male white population of Platinum talked shop. *Fifty-cent gravel, thirty-cent gravel. Postelthwaite of New Zealand. Lae, in New Guiana, where four 1,200-ton dredges and two hydroelectric plants were freighted in over the mountains by plane. The Lena and Amur rivers in USSR, where American engineers installed five gold dredges for the Ural Platinum Trust and showed the Russians how to run 'em.* Arguments waxed over yardage, power, gasoline consumption. An engineer in the uniform of that breed the world over—leather boots, khaki breeches, red kerchief—pulled out his pocket slide rule to prove a point. The others agreed or disagreed violently, pouring out instances, figures, facts from their personal knowledge of mining learned all over the world. In the last summer of 1937 there was set up in this tiny settlement the latest in mining dredges. Its buckets, each a ton's weight, began scooping a yard of gravel at a time. The gravel moved down the hopper into the screen, the coarse tailings traveled up the belt to be piled behind the dredge as it inched its snout along, and the pay dirt moved to the washing table, there to settle down along the riffles—platinum!

Fifty paces from the roadhouse toward the beach, living in a world five thousand years before this new world of slide rules and half-million-dollar dredges, was a tiny village of Eskimos. Their huts were holes dug in the ground, surmounted with a driftwood frame covered with flattened gasoline tins or skins, or perhaps with white man's canvas. Their walrus-skin boats rested upside down on the beach. Their dogs, half-starved because it was summer when beasts can do no work, strained at their leashes and howled at the racks of sun-dried salmon beyond their reach. The men were away fishing, and the village contained only old men, women, children, and cripples. The women made grass baskets to trade at the store for tins of white man's food or yards of gingham, biding the time when their men would return from the canneries with food, blankets, and silver dollars. Although dependent upon the white man, this village touched the white man's civilization but slightly. And although many of these Eskimos had never seen an automobile, and certainly none of them a horse, even the children hardly looked up when a plane roared down.

Alaska

ELY WAR. Looking at [the] mountain settlement [of Vershire] with its few old frame and brick dwellings resting in an air of tranquillity, it is difficult to realize that around 1880 the great Ely Copper Mines here supported a 2000 population, and in one year produced and shipped three million pounds of copper, then worth more than 20 cents per pound. At the peak of production, the Ely Mines turned out three-fifths of the entire copper output of the United States.

In July, 1883, the "Ely War" occurred, with 300 unpaid miners rising in insurrection to attempt collection, by force of arms if necessary, of the $25,000 back wages owed them by the company. The rioting miners seized arms and ammunition, stopped the water pumps to flood the workings, tore down a few buildings, and threatened to dynamite the works and destroy the villages of Ely and West Fairlee unless they were paid by the following afternoon. Governor Barstow called out five companies of the National Guard to go to Ely by special train in answer to the appeal of civil authorities. The troops arrived in the early morning, and were conveyed from the station to the mining villages in coke wagons while the unsuspecting miners were still sleeping. Rudely wakened in the wan gray morning light, twelve of the leading strikers opened their eyes to face bayoneted rifles, and when the other miners awoke, their leaders were under guard and the streets were full of uniformed militiamen with fixed bayonets. This procedure was followed at both Ely and West Fairlee, the strike was broken, and the Ely War was ended. The mine manager paid the men all the money he had left, about $4000, but the industrial tragedy was complete, for the mines never again operated, and three townships in the vicinity were desolated.

Vermont

DRAG RACE. Much of the country around Hayden was homesteaded in the early 1900's; newcomers worked from sunup to dark, grubbing the soil and fighting gophers, groundhogs, rabbits, and porcupines. When the harvest was in, a pioneer celebration was held in one of the larger towns, which was decorated for the occasion. A novelty race in the afternoon attracted the most attention; men raced their horses to the end of the track, jumped off, and opened the bundles they carried, which contained discarded odds and ends of feminine clothing; each man donned whatever garment fell to his lot—corset, nightgown, underskirt, or bloomers—and raced back to the starting point.

Colorado

ARCADIA. [Near Lake Willoughby] a foot trail branches . . . from the highway. Left on foot up this grass-grown roadway along the mountain flank is the site of Arcadia Retreat. . . . At the turn of the century Arcadia Retreat was an exclusive and fashionable resort, but was suddenly and mysteriously abandoned, everything being left behind, furnishings and trappings complete. Curious and acquisitive visitors gradually dismantled the hotel, which was an unusual point of interest until it burned in the early 1920's. Many theories and legends grew around the deserted Arcadia Retreat, mostly imaginative. No one ever returned to claim the property or furniture. People still take this hike to see the ruins and wonder about the hurried, mysterious abandonment.

Vermont

HELL-ON-WHEELS. Several weeks before the [Union Pacific] tracks arrived [in Laramie], a tent town appeared on the river bank. The railroad company had platted a townsite, but allowed no one to settle until lots could be officially sold and recorded. The date of sale was fixed early in April, and land speculators who had done well in Cheyenne were on hand to get choice titles. Within a week 400 plots had been sold at prices ranging from $25 to $260. Ten days later 500 shacks had been erected of logs, canvas, condemned railroad ties, and dismantled wagon boxes. The first train slid down the steep grade into town on May 9, 1868, and with the train came all the population and paraphernalia of "Hell-on-Wheels." The first freight carried iron rails, crossties, plows, scrapers, tents, portable shanties, lumber, groceries, cookstoves, crockery, tinware, liquors, and the transient population of the terminal town: gamblers, workers, harlots, hunters, migratory shop and saloonkeepers, peddlers with their packs, and straggling settlers' families.

Work was pushed, and Laramie was not long the end of track. But the steep grade over Sherman Hill and the barren desert land to the west forecast the need of railroad shops and warehouses at Laramie. Additional settlers came to the new town, and the gamblers and keepers of brothels and saloons quickly saw their business opportunity.

Early in May a provisional government was formed and a mayor and trustees elected. But the lawless element had learned from vigilantes in other terminal settlements the value of union, and in Laramie it organized first. After bucking the outlaw organization three weeks, the government resigned. The period of anarchy that followed was something more than casual outlawry. Brawls and shootings were commonplace. In August a hesitant vigilance committee of 20 shopkeepers and railroad workers lynched a desperado, who called himself 'The Kid.' Other members of the loosely organized gang regarded the incident as a challenge and terrorized the town.

By autumn Laramie had a more stable population, and war was declared on the ruffians and bullies. Five hundred armed vigilantes planned simultaneous raids on several outlaw strongholds on the evening of October 29. Although plans miscarried, the group concentrated on the dance hall "Belle of the West." In the gun battle that followed, in which most of the town participated, five men were killed and fifteen wounded. Four outlaws surrendered and were hanged to telegraph poles downtown.

Wyoming

GUSHER. McCamey . . . has the appearance of a prosperous carnival, with its tiny frame business houses ringed about by oil derricks and red storage tanks.

When the No. 1 Baker well blew in on November 16, 1925, McCamey came into almost instant being. Dawn of the day found a grader cutting streets through the mesquite and greasewood flats, following the lines of the hurrying surveyors just ahead, who were laying out the town site. On November 18 the first lot was sold with the stipulation that a building was to be started within one hour. The buyer had carpenters at work within 30 minutes on a filling station and cafe.

Other buildings were erected in mad haste. People poured in, and above the roads hung an ever-present cloud of choking white alkali dust. Trucks lumbered in with drilling supplies, foodstuffs and furnishings. The town overflowed itself; tents bloomed white wherever on untenanted land their owners chose to set them up. The population reached 10,000 within a short time, and still they came. Prices went sky-high. Water sold at a dollar a barrel and was hard to get at that.

On the fringe of the town, in tents and shacks, the hangers-on of every new oil field plied their outlaw trades. One Ranger represented the law in McCamey, Troublemakers found themselves introduced to a new form of confinement. There was no jail, so the Ranger chained his prisoners to a stout post. The story is told that several husky roughnecks, chained to the picket line, as it was called, pulled up the post and dragged it after them to the nearest saloon.

Texas

ANVIL CHORUS. Capitol Hill [Omaha], for a decade the site of the Nebraska Territorial capitol, appears in history for the first time with a 4th of July celebration in 1854. A picnic party from Council Bluffs, Iowa, crossed

on the ferry to celebrate the day on the new town site. In response to a toast to Nebraska, offered by John Gillespie, later State auditor, Hadley D. Johnson fired a salute with two blacksmith anvils and started a "spread eagle" speech. The anvil salute consisted of ramming the hole in the top of the anvil with powder, inserting a fuse, turning the anvil upside down and lighting the fuse. The resultant blast sent the anvil more than 100 feet in the air. To the consternation of the party, the report of the anvils attracted a band of Indians who were camping at Sulphur Springs. The women and children were frightened and the entire party hurried to their wagons and drove pell-mell to the ferry landing. They escaped unharmed.

Nebraska

UNASSIGNED LANDS. Beginning about 1879, extensive publicity was given to the fact that no Indian tribes had ever been settled on a tract in the heart of the Indian Territory ceded by the Creeks and Seminoles at the close of the Civil War; and newspapers throughout the West contended that these "Unassigned Lands"—soon to be popularly designated as "Oklahoma Lands"—were subject to homestead entry.

Homeseekers known as "Boomers" gathered at the Kansas border and made repeated and systematic attempts to colonize this tract, but the Federal government, holding that the land had been ceded only for Indian occupation, removed the invaders. They returned in increasing numbers; cattlemen came in without legal sanction, divided the range, built fences and corrals, and grazed their cattle over its rich prairies; and in 1886–87, the Atchison, Topeka and Santa Fe Railroad was built across the region, and stations were established along its right of way.

Finally the United States purchased title to the land from the Creeks and Seminoles; the tract was laid out in 160-acre homesteads; and on April 22, 1889, it was opened to white settlement in the "Run" for farms and town lots which has become one of the most dramatized episodes in western history.

As the hour for the opening approached, great crowds waited on the border, while mounted soldiers stood on guard to turn back intruders. At noon bugles sounded, then guns were fired as a signal that the land was open. Men raced in on horseback, on foot, in covered wagons, hanging to every available hold on the slowly moving trains, all trying to outstrip their fellows in the scramble for "claims." When a homeseeker found a tract of land to his liking, he drove a stake as evidence of possession and held it as best he could against other claimants. On the same day lots were staked in the townsites, and men engaged in feverish promotion.

Before the day fixed for the opening many thousand eager young men had gathered along the border of this new Promised Land impatiently waiting for the hour when they would be free to cross the line and choose a claim. Some of these had for years been urging, or "booming," the opening of these lands to settlement and were, in consequence, known as "Boomers."

It is not surprising that some of them should grow weary of waiting and under the cover of darkness cross into the forbidden area too soon. Here they chose choice tracts and either occupied them or lay in concealment near by ready to dash out and assert their claims when the hour of opening had come.

These men, known as "Sooners" because they had entered the territory too soon, had not technically committed any crime for which they could be punished by law. Yet they could not legally secure any of these lands by homestead or acquire a right to any part of them. In the language of sport, they were merely put out of the game for a violation of the rules.

For a long time the term "Sooner" was one of reproach, but with the passing of the years the word began to lose its original connotation. As its origin was gradually forgotten, it eventually came to mean merely one who is alert, ambitious, and enterprising, or one who gets up earlier than others, always takes the lead, and strives to triumph over obstacles.

Oklahoma

GARDEN OF EDEN. William Cullen Bryant was lyrical in describing Trempealeau and its environs, and the Reverend David Van Slyke, a local Methodist minister, attempted to prove that this was the site of the Garden of Eden.

The Reverend Van Slyke combined farming with preaching, but found time to publish a pamphlet entitled *The Garden of Eden* in 1886, in which he pointed out that according to Biblical description "the Garden" consisted of a valley with four rivers, one of them being the Euphrates, the Greek name for *the great river*. Trempealeau had the Mississippi, certainly a great river, the Beaver, the Trempealeau, and the Black. Finally, concluded the author, the two promontories framing the valley were the exact counterpart of the gates of Eden.

Wisconsin

THIS CLAIM FOR SALE. Crossing the Platte River, [US 81] proceeds through dry bluff lands. According to an old story, a thirsty traveler passing this way in the early days spied a sod house off the road and went over to get water. The house was empty, but nearby was a well with windlass and wooden bucket. He dropped the bucket down, and it came up dry. He repeated the operation with no greater success. Then his eye cought a notice on the house, reading, "This Claim for sale. Four miles to the nearest neighbor. Seven miles to the nearest schoolhouse. Fourteen miles to the nearest town. Two hundred feet to the nearest water. God bless our home! For further information address Thomas Ward, Oskaloosa, Iowa."

Nebraska

Fortune

O F THIS word's many meanings, take first its simplest—"chance" or "luck." In the following chapter we see such fortune produce both benefit and harm. The proprietor of *Bummer Dan's bar* has good fortune beyond any justice; this is blind luck ("cess," the Irish call it, giving the word a fitting hiss). But luck is just as likely to be malevolent: who would have guessed the true nature of *Runaway Pond?*

Despite the Puritan belief in a convenant of grace, there is no reliable way of courting fortune, not even via virtue. Virtue may work with *treasure,* but what has it to do with *yek?* Or *Diddy-wah-Diddy?*

While good and bad luck are beyond our influence, "made" luck—otherwise known as "enterprise" or "pluck" or "hard work"—is a different matter. This kind of luck, we are told, leads to the second kind of fortune, the kind a bank will pay you interest on. Thus, taking advantage of opportunity made *the richest woman in America,* while intelligent persistence is associated, surprisingly, with a *dummy.* But even made luck is fickle: the fruit of enterprise may be stored in a leaky *money belt. Ghouls* may get it.

The Guides are preoccupied with fortune. Their view of America is of a fortuitous, that is a random, land. And their warmest sympathy goes to the

vast majority of Americans whose fortune, in both senses of the word, has
been mediocre at best.

RUNAWAY POND. [Near Glover, Vermont,] [a] shallow grassy valley beside the highway, locally known as Dry Pond, marks the site of a phenomenon in which an entire body of water ran away from its bed in 1810. [A]
monument was erected in 1910 on the centennial anniversary of the event.
Previous to this strange occurrence the body of water was called Long Pond,
and its outlet normally ran south. The residents of Glover wished to divert
the water into a northern outlet, so it would flow down into Mud Pond,
raising the water level there and furnishing more power for their mills along
Barton River. Long Pond was 150 feet above the level of Mud Pond, with a
very sharp drop between the two. On June 6, 1810, about 60 men assembled to celebrate "June Training Day" by cutting a channel to form a northern outlet from Long Pond into the lower body of water. The barrier holding the north end of Long Pond was a solid bar that resembled frozen gravel,
through which they proceeded to cut. Unknown to the workers there was a
species of quicksand deposit underneath the bar of hardpan, and once the
bar was pierced this sand started washing away rapidly, undermining the whole
north shore of the pond. Alarmed at the sudden great rush of water, the
workmen scrambled to the safety of higher land and were treated to the
amazing sight of an entire lake emptying before their eyes. Riders pounded
down the valley warning settlers to flee from the path of the torrent. Rushing
down upon Mud Pond, the flood ripped away those barriers and swept on
down the Barton River. The great wall of unleashed water tore a path 30 to
40 rods wide and 30 to 60 feet deep, demolishing gristmills, uprooting large
trees and boulders, carrying everything before it.
  Eye-witnesses declared that the earth trembled and shook as the water broke
loose with a tremendous deafening roar. At the start there was a rush of water
toward the center and the whole pond boiled like a cauldron. Two loons,
caught on the surface, were unable to rise from the water, so great was the
suction. Long Pond was emptied of water in one hour and fifteen minutes.
After the water had drained out, mud ran for several hours. In six hours'
time the flood surged into Lake Memphremagog at Newport, a distance of
more than 25 miles. The following summer thousands of coltsfoot sprang
up in the channel left by the water, and Balm of Gilead trees appeared for

the first time in the vicinity. At the time people regarded Runaway Pond as a warning to men against rashly tampering with the work of Nature and God.

Vermont

DUMMY. The only blocking dummy made in the United States that will do a "comeback" after being knocked down is the product of the Marty Gilman Sporting Goods Company of [Gilman]. A young man with considerable football ability, Gilman went to the State College and attained stardom. During the summer months he had difficulty in finding enough youngsters in the little mill town to offer him an opportunity to practice football, so he devised the first Gilman "Pyramid," made of leather and stuffed with shoddy and cotton waste from the Gilman mill. Coaches saw the contraption and liked it; Gilman realized the commercial possibilities, kept his eye on costs, peddled the dummy from coast to coast, played professional football to finance his one-man, backyard industry, and today serves all of the better clubs in the country. Gilman uses the tactics of the Yankee "pedlar" in his salesmanship, the water-power and shrewd ability of the Yankee mill operator in his manufacturing, and his one-man office is in a building formerly used as a hotel by the owners of the big stone mills on the Yantic River.

Connecticut

MONEY BELT. [John B.] Macy, promoter of the Chicago & North Western Railway, . . . died in 1856 when the steamer *Niagara* burned within sight of Port Washington. Wearing a money belt filled with gold, Macy jumped from the blazing deck to a crowded lifeboat, capsized it, and drowned himself and all its occupants.

Wisconsin

GEOLOGIST, ENGINEER, AND PROMOTER. US 95 [passes] through the broad valley between the Charleston and Sheep Ranges. Bare and uninhabited as most of the ranges in this region seem to be, there are not many that do not show at least a few monuments of prospectors. Hundreds of men have sweated up and down hunting for promising ledges, though very few of them have ever made much profit, even when they had a lucky strike. Usually they are so much in need of a few dollars that they are willing to sell to the first person who is interested. Only a rare man has money enough for more than first development, and, curiously, though they are always enthusiastic about their strikes, few have enough faith in them to choose to sell on a royalty basis, rather than outright, for cash. Just the same they have a deep contempt for the men who bring their discoveries to success. A hoary but ever popular story among prospectors concerns a geologist, a mining engineer, and a mining promoter who were out hunting. According to the story, they eventually reached tracks; then the party divided, the geologist backtracking to find where the game had come from, the engineer following the tracks forward, and the promoter going back to town for a truck to carry out the animal after it was shot.

Nevada

GHOULS. [In] the [Versailles] area is Gordon's Leap, a huge cliff more than 100 feet high. In the early days of the county, Dr. William Anderson, graduate of the University of Dublin, settled in Versailles, planning to start a medical college. Two of his most promising students, Gordon and Glass, went to the cemetery near the cliff one night, following the death of a prominent citizen, to exhume his body and use it for dissection. They were detected and a group of indignant villagers pursued the young ghouls. Glass made his way through the foliage and escaped but the pursuers forced Gordon to the edge of the cliff. To the surprise of his would-be captors, Gordon leaped over the precipice. Escaping with a broken leg, he dragged himself across the creek to a cabin where he obtained a horse and fled the county. He later enlisted in the Union Army at Indianapolis, became a major, and after the war was nominated for attorney general of Indiana. Glass went to Missouri and became a prominent physician.

Indiana

THE BARON. Arizola, . . . a small desert station, was established in 1892 on the southern Pacific Railroad. It was once the headquarters of an adventurer, who called himself the Baron of the Colorados, but who was known as the Baron of Arizona.

James Addison Reavis invaded Arizona in 1880 as a subscription solicitor for the San Francisco *Examiner* and at the same time gained information for the scheme he had devised while driving a horsecar in St. Joseph, Missouri. Relying upon the terms of the Treaty of Guadalupe Hidalgo in 1848 and the Gadsden Purchase in 1853, in which the United States agreed to recognize all former land titles, Reavis in 1885 formally filed application for the survey and confirmation of the Willing grant. He alleged, with all required documents and proofs, that on December 20, 1748, Ferdinand VI, King of Spain, had made Senor Don Miguel de Peralta de Cordoba Baron of the Colorados, and had granted to him 300 square leagues of land in New Spain; this area included most of the Salt and Gila River valleys, together with all their waters and mining rights, a tract 236 miles long and 78 miles wide. According to papers, Father Pauver and Father Garces had agreed the area did not encroach on mission lands. The claim was traced to Miguel Peralta, who was said to have deeded the land to Willing in 1864. Reavis was able to show a deed to himself, from Willing's attorney-in-fact, dated 1867.

At this point Reavis cemented his case by marrying a beautiful girl, "the only blood descendant of Don Miguel de Peralta de Cordoba" and displayed documents proving her birth, christening, and parentage. The overwhelming coincidence of their romantic meeting was explained by Reavis as an "accidental encounter in a Mexican hamlet while investigating the Willing title."

This claim which threatened to make vassals or tenants of former property owners spread consternation throughout the "barony." Tom Weedin, editor of the *Florence Citizen*, gave vigorous editorial expression to doubts of the legitimacy of both the claim and of the baron himself, and was only partly subdued when it was reported that Robert G. Ingersoll and other prominent lawyers had pronounced the claim flawless and authentic.

The baron meanwhile had established his headquarters here and was living in state. It was said that the Southern Pacific railroad paid him $50,000 for its right-of-way across Peralta properties; the Silver King mine contributed lavishly to his funds, and the larger property owners were forced to pay tribute. Two children were born, and Reavis had them clad in garments of purple velvet. Other luxurious homes were set up in Washington, St. Louis, and Chihuahua. The family traveled extensively, living in the most expensive hotels; in Madrid they maintained a permanent establishment and a large staff of servants. From 1887 until 1893 the story of the Reavis family had all the glamour of a tale from the *Arabian Nights*.

Then suddenly the baron's world was shattered by a stammering printer named Bill, who worked for Tom Weedin, the editor. While looking over old documents filed at the Capitol in Phoenix Bill had discovered that one of the "ancient" papers of the Peralta claim had been printed in a type invented only a few years before the claim was filed; and that another paper bore the water mark of a Wisconsin paper mill that had been running only ten or twelve years. . . .

Investigation revealed that cleverly written pages had been interpolated into old record books. A microscope proved the document appointing Don Miguel Peralta "Baron of the Colorados" to be a manuscript of another sort entirely. Reavis' wife testified he had convinced her that she really was the last of the Peralta line. Actually she was a half-breed Indian girl who had been living on a reservation in northern California. Reavis had taken her to Mexico to establish local color and train her for the part she was to play.

In January 1895 Reavis was convicted and sentenced to six years in the Santa Fe penitentiary. His wife left him, taking the two children—who were said to look more royally Spanish than the Hapsburgs and Bourbons themselves. When last heard of, she was living in poverty in an obscure Mexican village; Reavis' friends, however, succeeded in effecting his release in less than two years. He was sometimes seen on the streets of Phoenix looking worn and ill, but always about to recoup his lost fortune and position with some wonderful legitimate promotion.

Arizona

TREASURE. Buried riches are the theme of countless *espanto* [Mexican ghost] tales, and in many of them the treasure is spirited away after the finder catches only a glimpse of it. To recover a buried treasure without having it disappear miraculously in the process, one must be entitled to it, and also be willing—really willing deep in his heart—to share it with the poor and helpless. Buried money, especially silver, gives off a bright glow which comes right up through the earth and can be seen as a dim light on nights when the weather is misty or there is a gentle rain.

Arizona

INHERITANCE TAX. The Campbell Soup Plant [Camden] is the largest maker of canned soups in the world. The plant consists of 42 buildings covering 8 blocks; landmarks are the water tanks on the roof, built and painted as colossal replicas of red and white soup cans. Visitors are shown a $50,000 model kitchen, installed in 1936. The company buys large quantities of vegetables from New Jersey farmers, and on its own experimental land raises young plants which are distributed to growers. In the factory the number of employees varies seasonally from 2,500 to 8,000.

The industry began in 1869 as a small preserve factory conducted by Joseph Campbell and Abraham Anderson. In 1897 John T. Dorrance joined the company as a chemist at $7.50 a week. He developed the idea of condensing soups for canning, and in 1914 became president of the company. Dorrance amassed a fortune of $117,000,000; on his death in 1935 the State inheritance tax amounted to $15,000,000, which temporarily solved the problem of raising funds for relief.

New Jersey

DIDDY-WAH-DIDDY. [Florida] Negroes have their mythical cities and countries which are discussed and referred to in everyday conversation as if they actually existed. Among them are Diddy-Wah-Diddy, Beluthahatchie, Heaven, and West Hell.

Diddy-Wah-Diddy, the largest and best known, is a place of no work and no worry for man or beast. The road to it is so crooked that a mule pulling a load of fodder can eat off the back of the wagon as he plods along. All curbstones are chairs, and all food is already cooked. Baked chickens and sweet potato pies, with convenient knives and forks, drift along crying, "Eat me! Eat me!" The more one eats, the more remains. Everything is on a gigantic scale, and the biggest man of all is known as the Moon Regulator, because he starts and stops it at will. When nights are dark, it is because the Regulator was just too tired to hang out the moon. Everybody would live in Diddy-Wah-Diddy if it were not so hard to find and so difficult to get to, even if one knew the way.

Florida

YEK. The Tlingit believed that the universe was made up of certain orderly sequences of cause and effect and a great deal of something else which he called Yek. Yek was essentially unpredictable. It might thwart the best laid plans or save the poorest. It is commonly translated "the supernatural," but it had no divine attributes such as being all-powerful, all-wise, or all-good. It had no real unity and was not purposive. The shaman, whose function was to induce or compel Yek, was more powerful among the Tlingits than were the medicine men of any of the other northwestern people.

Alaska

LOW WATER. Nineteen hundred and nine was a low-water year and James Douglas, prospecting the [San Juan] river, discovered a bonanza sand bar. Then the river rose and the bar disappeared. Douglas waited patiently for the river to go down, waited year after year, but his bar remained flooded. In 1929, after twenty years of vigil, his patience exhausted and his hair white, the old man jumped off Mexican Hat Bridge, leaving this note behind him:

> When this you see
> My old body in the river will be
> There is no one in the world
> To blame for this
> Only me.

San Juan folk were touched. They named Douglas Mesa, west of the Goosenecks, for him. Five years later the river went dry.

Utah

BUMMER DAN'S BAR. [Outside] Virginia City [is] Bummer Dan's Bar, . . . on the north side of Alder Gulch. It is not a place to drink. During the gold rush the camp was bothered by one Dan, who constantly begged and often filched food, but would not work. In a saloon one day Dan saw a patron order pie, a luxurious item in those days. When the pie was brought in, Dan snatched and quickly ate it. Instead of regarding the act as a joke, the patron called a camp meeting; it was the opinion of the camp that Dan should go to work. He was given a claim high on the side of the gulch, was loaned a pick and pan, and told to hop to it or get out. Dan went to work, and within a few weeks struck it rich. After panning thousands of dollars' worth of gold, he decided to go to the States, but was robbed on the way, and returned to Virginia City to bum once more.

Montana

THE RICHEST WOMAN IN AMERICA. [A] house [in Bellows Falls is] noted . . . as the home for many years of Henrietta Howland Robinson Green (1834–1916), who married Edward H. Green, a successful Bellows Falls business man, in 1867. Hetty Green personally managed and greatly increased the large fortune and world-wide enterprises that she inherited from her father, a prominent figure in nineteenth-century whaling and China trade. She was long known as the richest woman in America and was probably the most astute woman financier who has ever lived. She was almost the only great financier who foresaw the panic of 1907 in time to convert most of her investments into cash, by means of which she increased her own wealth at the same time that she saved many others from ruin. She was undoubtedly somewhat penurious personally—partly as a result of the countless importunings that disturbed the quiet, simple life she desired; but local tales, such as that of her storming out a milliner's shop in a fury because she couldn't find a becoming hat for less than three dollars, should be taken, if at all, with several grains of salt.

Vermont

THE LIFE OF A DESPERADO. John Wilson, who had a price on his head, discovered gold on the site of Baxter Mountain in 1880 but did not profit from the find because he preferred the life of a desperado. Wilson, escaping from a Texas jail, cut across the mountains to visit two friends, Jack Winters and Harry Baxter, who were placer miners. The day after his arrival, Wilson started for the top of Baxter Mountain to obtain a view of the country through which he expected to travel. He took a pick with him and jokingly said that he was going to find a gold mine. Halfway to the summit he sat down to rest and began to chip pieces from the rock. Examining the chips, he found them speckled with yellow. When he returned to the cabin Winters asked Wilson if he had found his mine and Wilson passed over the chips. One glance at the rock sent Winters into the air with a yell, and Harry Baxter, awakened from a nap, became equally excited. It was now pitch dark, but the three made a climb for the spot by lantern light. The two miners set out stakes, and when Wilson was asked for his full name, so they could locate the claim for the three, he answered, "I have no use for gold." Thus the North Homestake and South Homestake claims came into being and were later sold for $300,000 apiece. Wilson left next day with nine silver dollars, and a good pistol, a present from the two prospectors. The Old Abe Mine, the original strike, has produced $3,000,000 and is still being worked.

New Mexico

GONE TO HELL BY WAY OF WILLIMANSETT. The potential water-power of the Connecticut River just above Hadley Falls was not long in attracting the attention of manufacturing pioneers, and as early as 1828 a dam had been constructed, and a few small textile, grain, and metal mills were in operation. Not until 1848, however, did capital appear in the form of a group of New York and Boston investors and developers who secured the rights of the old Hadley Falls Company. In 1848 a $75,000 dam was completed, and on the same day it was swept away by the terrific pressure, incorrectly calculated, of the water behind it. The story is said to have been graphically told in a series of telegrams directed to the Boston office:

10 A.M.   Gates just closed: water filling behind dam.
12 A.M.   Dam leaking badly.
2 P.M.   Stones of bulkhead giving way to pressure.
3.20 P.M.   Your old dam's gone to hell by way of Willimansett.

Massachusetts

SALLY RAND. In the midst of the world-wide depression, Chicago courageously proceeded with plans for A Century of Progress Exposition, which opened in 1933 in a striking group of modern, plainly geometrical structures erected in newly-made Burnham Park and Northerly Island. Its central theme was applied science, and its exposition at the fair was guided by data furnished by the National Research Council. Hard times accounted in large part for the fact that the exposition was a financial disappointment in its first year, but Sally Rand and her fan dancers accomplished what applied science had failed to do, and the exposition closed in 1934 with a net profit, which was donated to participating cultural institutions, excluding Sally Rand.

Illinois

Higher Callings

Invention

INVENTION IS thought to be a national characteristic among us Americans. It supposedly comes from our experience on the frontier and from the necessities that frontier life was the mother of. Or it comes from our country's great scope and resources, and the stimulation these give to human ingenuity.

Well, maybe.

The Guides make it clear the inventor is someone to be taken seriously. If anyone has a claim to privilege in these egalitarian States, it is the self-made man or woman. Our Constitution itself establishes patent and copyright protection, and encourages all of us to be inventive ("creative," is the current buzzword) and grow rich.

But we have to know the system. The author of "Darling Nellie Gray" did not, nor did the wireless Marconi of Kentucky. Betsey Metcalf Baker developed the straw hat, a potential gold mine; but her attention was elsewhere.

These selections show invention popping up everywhere (who would think of an ice mask?). And they may give us hope that our nation is still full of back-of-the-barn wizards—like the worthies who dreamed up a new system of domestic economy and the diving bell—and, yes, full of cranks, too, who have invented, and insist on testing, things (like wings) that make no sense at all.

ICE MASK. On May 31, 1882, at 8:30 a.m., the pump column broke in the Alta shaft [at Virginia City, on the Comstock Lode], and seven men working 2,150 feet below the surface in a drift 1,400 feet from the shaft were imprisoned by the rising hot water. The water rose 18 feet over the drift in which the miners were imprisoned before the pumps were repaired. There did not seem to be one chance in a million to rescue the men, but the policy of mine owners on the Comstock was to recover bodies regardless of expense. On the third day after the accident, the water in the shaft had been lowered sufficiently to allow a boat to be navigated in the drift, and two miners volunteered to go down. When they did not return a middle aged Civil War veteran, Yank Van Dusen, volunteered to don an ice mask invented by a local man, Fred Ritter, and enter the drift. On his way in, with his helmet and boots filled with ice, Van Dusen saw the dead bodies of the two men who had gone to the rescue in the boat, and several hundred feet farther in, within 100 feet of the face of the drift, he found the seven imprisoned miners alive, but nearly dead from heat and exhaustion. It required more than 100 men, inured to working in the hot mines to rescue the seven. Sixty-two hours after the pump broke the last of the victims landed on the surface at midnight, and the steam whistle of every mine and mill on the Comstock was tied down for 15 minutes as the Lode celebrated.

Nevada

PROFESSOR. In 1843 a salt well was sunk near [Levi] and struck gas, which rushed from the well with a great roar, hurling a column of salt water 150 feet into the air; so great was the pressure that a 1,500-pound iron sinker shot from the well like an arrow from a cross-bow. The roar of the gas and water as they gushed from the well could be heard several miles, and stage drivers on the James River and Kanawha Turnpike stopped to let their passengers view the sight. On one occasion a Harvard University professor was among the passengers; "being a man of investigating and experimenting turn of mind," he lighted a match near the well to see "what chemicals the vapor contained." The atmosphere instantly burst into flames, and the well frame and enginehouse caught fire. The professor saved himself by jumping into the Kanawha River, and then crawled back to the stagecoach. When the owner of the well heard of the damage done to his property, he sent a friend to Charleston to find the unknown passenger and have him arrested for "willfully and wantonly burning property—unless you find the fellow is a natural damn fool and didn't know any better," he added. The professor was found in a Charleston hotel, his hair and eyebrows singed, his hands and face blistered. In plain language the messenger stated his instructions, including the codicil. "It seems a pretty hard alternative," sighed the professor, attempting a faint smile with his parched lips. "However, under the circumstances, I feel it my duty to take advantage of the last clause and escape."

West Virginia

COG RAILWAY. The Mt. Washington Cog Railway . . . was the first of its kind in the world and owes its existence to the ingenuity and persistence of Sylvester Marsh, a native of Campton, later one of the founders of Chicago. On a return visit to the State of his birth in 1852 he climbed Mt. Washington in company with a friend. At that time he conceived the idea of building a cogwheel railway up the mountain. Inventing the proper mechanism was not so difficult as convincing the State legislature of the feasibility of the project. After showing a model of the proposed road in 1858, the legislature granted him a charter. Tradition avers that one legislator proposed an amendment permitting Marsh to build a railroad to the moon. Funds for such a quixotic venture were not easy to obtain, and the Civil War delayed progress. Nothing daunted, Marsh began work at his own expense and by May, 1866, had some of the road constructed and his cogwheel engine in operation on it. The process of building was a slow one, requiring three years. The entire stretch of three and one-third miles was completed and opened to the public in July, 1869, and has been in constant operation during the summer months ever since, and without injury to a single passenger. In 1871, Mr. Marsh was asked to construct a similar railway up Mt. Rigi near Lucerne, Switzerland, but declined the honor. The Rigi railway was later built by a Swiss engineer who came over and obtained the principal engineering ideas in use here.

New Hampshire

COMET FINDER. Peltier's Observatory [in Lima] is a simple structure owned by Leslie Peltier, amateur astronomer, who in recent years earned the title "comet finder" because of his discovery of several celestial bodies, including Peltier's Comet. In recognition of his findings, Harvard University presented Peltier with a modern telescope.

Ohio

SMITH'S MONORAIL. Smithville . . ., consisting mainly of two-family houses of weathered clapboards, . . . was founded in 1865 by the once famous Hezekiah Smith, whose high-wheel Star bicycle with a small wheel in back was a menace to life two generations ago. Here, on the country road that leads to the Newbold's Corners Road along the south bank of Rancocas Creek, is still the Smith factory that manufactured the bicycle about 1882, but now produces machinery. Smith sent the wheel to Washington, where his exhibition rider tried to pedal it down the steps of the Capitol and was arrested. Between Smithville and Mount Holly the inventor built his monorail bicycle railway to carry his employees to and from work. Bicycles resembling the present type hung from a rail laid on posts about 4 feet high. In 1879 Smith completed a steam wagon with kerosene firebox and boiler. It is said that the car made good speed but Smith decided that the people were not ready for such a vehicle, so he stored it in a barn. Later the citizens showed their appreciation by electing Smith to Congress and to the State senate. He campaigned in a carriage drawn by a trained moose from his native New England, driving about Burlington County and frightening every horse on the road. Workmen at the plant were organized into a widely known band which finally led Smith's funeral procession.

New Jersey

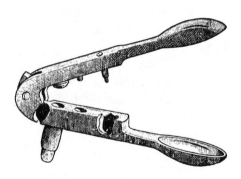

THERMOMETER. In 1894 gold was found on Mastodon Creek. . . . In a short time Circle was a camp second only to Fortymile. By 1898 it was a well-rooted town with a library, a hospital, and an Episcopal church. [Jack] McQuesten was at Circle during these years, and it was here that he improvised a remarkable thermometer. Four bottles containing separately quick-silver, whiskey, kerosene, and Perry Davis' Painkiller were kept on a rack. Frozen kerosene meant one had better stay pretty close to the house. When the painkiller solidified it wasn't safe to step away from the fire.

Alaska

HORSELESS CARRIAGE. Sunapee is a claimant for the honor of a horseless carriage invented in 1869 by Enos M. Clough after 14 years of study. The machine, containing 5,463 pieces, was propelled under its own power to Newport, St. Johnsbury, Vermont, and other places, but the town authorities forbade its further use because it frightened horses. The machine was sold to Richard Gove of Lakeport, who, after running it into a fence, dismantled it. The engine was installed in a boat; the carriage was destroyed by fire. The engine is now in the possession of Edward H. Kennedy of Lakeport . . . , though Henry Ford has tried to obtain it. It had two cylinders, with three forward speeds and three in reverse.

New Hampshire

ETHER. On March 30, 1842, Dr. Crawford W. Long (1815–78) performed [in Jefferson] the first operation in which sulphuric ether was used as an anesthetic. Two markers, on the front of a red brick store on the west side of the public square, indicate the site of Dr. Long's office where the operation was performed. Many persons claim, however, that it occurred out of doors under a mulberry tree that stood in front of the office. When this tree was removed several years ago, souvenirs were made from it.

After receiving his medical education at the University of Pennsylvania and serving his internship in New York, Dr. Long came to practice in Jefferson. On numerous occasions he inhaled ether for its exhilarating sensation, and, when others learned of its effect, "ether parties" became fashionable. According to Dr. Long's own account, after James M. Venable had consulted him on several occasions about removing two small tumors from his neck: " . . . I mentioned to him . . . the probability that the operation might be performed without pain, and proposed operating on him while under the influence of ether. He consented. . . . The ether was given to Mr. Venable on a towel, and when fully under its influence, I extirpated the tumor. . . . He gave no evidence of suffering during the operation, and assured me after it was over that he did not experience the slightest degree of pain from its performance."

Georgia

MOUTHPIECE. When Captain Charles Gerard Conn returned to Elkhart after the Civil War, he conducted a small grocery and bakery and was the cornetist in the local band. Shortly thereafter he suffered a badly bruised upper lip in a fight with a neighborhood bully, and to retain his job as cornetist, he contrived a soft rubber mouthpiece that enabled him to play. Conn was soon besieged with requests for these mouthpieces and started to fill orders as a sideline, using a lathe devised from an old sewing machine. The business increased and in 1875 he organized the Conn & Dupont Company, and started the manufacture of brass cornets. This was the first wind instrument factory in the United States. The company now manufactures all types of wind and percussion instruments and is said to maintain the only band instrument research laboratory in the world.

Indiana

SELF-KICK-IN-THE-PANTS MACHINE. The self-kick-in-the-pants machine (public invited; no questions asked), set up by Tom W. Haywood in front of his filling station [in Croatan] in July 1937, has worn out four shoes in its service to tourists and citizens. If you feel that you deserve "a good swift kick," turn the handle; the cable will be pulled and a huge shoe laced to an iron "leg" will administer the boot.

North Carolina

DOMESTIC ECONOMY. Although there is nothing for the tourist to visit in Kirby, Vermonters remember the town as the home of Russell Risley, in whom Yankee ingenuity as applied to domestic economy reached flood tide. Unmarried, he and his spinster sister worked the home place for many years with a minimum of physical exertion and a variety of labor-saving contrivances. A trapeze slid back and forth on wires between the house and barn transporting Risley to his daily chores; milk pails were carried on similar wires to the waiting sister who handled the emptying end of the process. A self-taught artist and sculptor, Risley created with Renaissance gusto and profusion, covering his barn with charcoal sketches of local notables and carving tree and fence posts galore.

Vermont

DIVING BELL. Across the Nanticoke a short way upstream [from Walnut Landing] is the Site of the Boaz Bell House, the home in the early 19th century of a retired West India ship captain. By legend his favorite stunt was to turn an iron pot over and walk across the bottom of the river—the pot acting as a diving bell.

Delaware

ELECTROLYSIS. North Lubec . . . gained notoriety from the Jernegan gold swindle (1896–98). Jernegan, pastor of a local church, claimed he had perfected a method of extracting gold from sea water by electrolysis. A stock company was formed and much stock sold throughout the country. A plant was erected on the shore; divers were sent to the bottom and came up bringing small quantities of gold. Large crews of workmen were imported and operations went on for a few months until Jernegan, having collected a considerable sum of money, disappeared.

Maine

KITE. An amusing tale is told on Bustin's Island of one Charles Guppy, an early resident, who conceived a novel plan to eliminate the labor of rowing to South Freeport for his weekly supplies. With the assistance of a neighbor, Guppy constructed a huge red kite which they tied by a heavy string to the bow of his dory, and set out from the mainland. Part way across to the island, a fierce gale of wind caught the kite and the dory's bow rose out of the water, while the panic-stricken inventors clung for dear life to keep from being tossed out of the craft. But they somehow managed to keep sailing in the direction of Bustin's; and before either had recovered sufficiently to reach the bow and cut away the kite, they went skimming up the beach, a full boatlength into the grass. Guppy and his friend thereupon decided that rowing had its advantages.

Maine

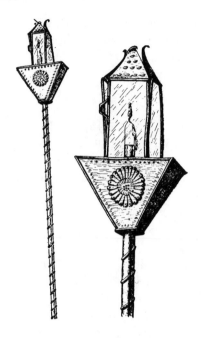

STRAW HAT. [In Westwood, Massachusetts,] in 1798, at the age of 12, Betsey Metcalf Baker, so taken with a beautiful bonnet one of her girl friends had received from England that she was determined to have one for herself, devised a method of splitting and braiding straw. Soon she was making hats for her friends; but because she considered it irreligious to patent her process, she realized little money from her device, which soon caused the development of one of the leading industries in the East.

Massachusetts

CONCORD GRAPE. [The grape was developed in Concord, Mass., at] the home of Ephraim Wales Bull. For many years a trellis against the cottage wall supported the original Concord grapevine. Recently this was winter-killed, but the present vine is a shoot from the same root. On the trellis is a tablet inscribed with a quotation from Bull's journal: "I looked to see what I could find among our wildings. The next thing to do was to find the best and earliest grape for seed, and this I found in an accidental seedling at the foot of the hill. The crop was abundant, ripe in August, and of very good quality for a wild grape. I sowed the seed in the Autumn 1843. Among them the Concord was the only one worth saving."

[Bull was a scientist, not an entrepreneur. In Concord's Sleepy Hollow Cemetery] the tombstone of Ephraim Bull, who lacked the shrewdness to profit by his development of the Concord grape, bears the significant epitaph: "He sowed, others reaped."

Massachusetts

WIRELESS. Radio experimentation in Kentucky began in the late nineteenth century. About 1892, in the little town of Murray, a wireless telephone was successfully demonstrated before an audience of 1,000 persons. The crude radio consisted of a rough box, some telephone equipment, rods, and a coil of wire, and was the invention of a farmer, Nathan B. Stubblefield.

In 1902 Stubblefield went by invitation to Washington, where he broadcast for a group of prominent scientists from the steam launch "Bartholdi." The same year he gave a demonstration in Philadelphia from Belmont mansion and from Fairmont Park, projecting his voice more than a mile by wireless.

The St. Louis *Post Dispatch*, in a full-page article on January 12, 1902, said: "However undeveloped his system may be, Nathan B. Stubblefield, the farmer inventor of Kentucky, has accurately discovered the principle of telephoning without wires."

Through an attorney, Rainey Wells, he secured patents in the United States, Canada, England, France, Spain, and Belgium. To raise capital for marketing his invention he had sold stock, in 1900, to a small group of friends. The end of Stubblefield's business career is shrouded in mystery. He advised his friends to withdraw such funds as they had invested, hinting darkly of the rascality of certain eastern associates. But to none of them did he give concrete information. An old trunk, in which he kept the invention and the documents concerning it, was not with him when he subsequently returned from the East, broken and embittered, to Murray. Whether it was a case of open theft, or whether he had been the dupe of unscrupulous manipulators, was never known. He continued his experiments with wireless in a two-room shack of his own construction. Cornshucks provided protection against rain and cold. Offers of neighborly aid were refused, an estranged family was spurned. On March 28, 1928, the body of Stubblefield was found in his shack; he had apparently been dead about forty-eight hours.

Kentucky

WINGS. The Ladd family is an old one in Exeter. . . . Nathaniel Ladd sounded the trumpet in Gove's Rebellion against Governor Cranfield (1682–85) and was afterwards killed in a battle with the Indians. Simeon Ladd, three generations later . . ., was president of a society of choice spirits called the "Nip Club," which used to assemble at one of the taverns for convivial purposes. His eccentricity may have been inherited from his father, who kept a ready-made coffin in his house to meet an emergency, and invented a pair of wings which he fondly believed would enable him to cleave the air like a bird, until he tried the experiment from an upper window.

New Hampshire

DARLING NELLIE GRAY. Rushville . . . was the birthplace of Benjamin Russell Hanby (1833–67), school teacher and composer of the song, "Darling Nellie Gray." In 1855 Hanby heard the story of Joe Selby, an escaped slave who died during a desperate flight across Ohio. On his deathbed Selby spoke of his sweetheart, Nellie Gray. Stirred by the story, Hanby wrote the song and sent it to a music publisher. Soon "Darling Nellie Gray" was being sung throughout the Nation. Seeking remuneration, Hanby wrote to the publisher and received the following reply: "Dear Sir: Your favor received. Nellie Gray is sung on both sides of the Atlantic. We have made the money and you the fame—that balances the account."

Ohio

Religion

WHETHER AMERICANS were more or less religious in the 1930s than we are now is the kind of question only George Gallup, who began his polling career then, would presume to answer. Certainly writers and intellectuals of the time were more outspokenly antireligious than they are today. John Steinbeck, that son of the decade, spent his Nobel Prize Acceptance Speech (1962) looking forward to humanity being liberated from a belief in God.

The Guide writers, most of them, were aspiring intellectuals and did not treat religion with the piety many American writers now would. Religion is seen as just a sort of folklore. It is written about from the outside, from the perspective of a spectator who is less a sympathizer than a tourist eager to see something "interesting."

We see here the role of religion as a socializing force—in the naming of *Bangor*, for example, or the catharsis of *free-for-all-preaching*. We see, in *sun dance* and *peyote*, the respect with which the Guides treat Native American beliefs.

For many readers today the most striking thing in this chapter will be the condescending tone taken toward Fundamentalist religion, as in *camp meeting* or *Four-square Gospel*. (*Father Divine* and *protracted meeting*, both of which deal with black religion, have much the same tone.) It seemed at the time that the Scopes Trial (1925), positivistic science, and Sigmund Freud had dealt a killing blow to primitive Protestantism. We now know that the Old Time Religion wasn't dying; it was about to be reborn.

FREE-FOR-ALL PREACHING. On warm Sunday afternoons, a motley crowd predominantly country folk, gathers on the north corner of Lower Broad across from the wharf [in Nashville] for the "free-for-all preachings," a custom of 20 years standing. Anyone, Negro or white, man or woman, fundamentalist or atheist, is free to have his say. The audience, for the most part, is made up of people restlessly awaiting their turns to preach. They clutch battered Bibles, which they leaf through and quote from at an instant's notice. Almost without exception they have tried and discarded the standard sects.

One of the men who preached her regularly says: "The only place you can get the truth is on the street as God told his people to go into the highways and the hedges. There's not any truth in the churches these days because God is not there." Each preacher hopes to found his sect and gather a following at the Sunday preachings. Often ten or twenty preachers stand on the curb, on packing cases, and in truck beds, all preaching at the same time. Gradually the crowd extends up Broad as far as Second Avenue and spills down across First Avenue to the wharf. Preachers mount boxcars and the loading-apron of the warehouse. They stand on the hoods of cars and perch on the first story window ledges of the produce houses. Some lure listeners by mouthing French harps or strumming banjoes and guitars. Others whoop until a group collects. There is a constant crossfire of heckling between preacher and listeners. Furious men rush up to the preacher and shake fists, Bibles, and canes under his nose. Some ignore the preaching and draw aside to roar Scriptural quotations into each other's faces. The preaching continues until about 9 o'clock at night, when the people, satiated and subdued, begin to leave. By 10 o'clock the corner is deserted.

Tennessee

GIDEON BIBLE. The Christian Commercial Association of America, more commonly known as the Gideons, whose Bibles are found in hotel rooms throughout the country, was founded in Boscobel in 1899. One night in that year two traveling salesmen were forced to share a common room. Before retiring, one drew forth a Bible, asked to be pardoned for the delay in turning out the light, and prepared to read to himself. The other recognized the book and said, "I am a Christian also. Let us have our devotions together."

Later the two men discussed the dismal evenings of Christian traveling men, who in the search for innocent entertainment often fished out old newspapers from the bottoms of bureau drawers or read telephone books from cover to cover. Suddenly they conceived the plan of the Gideons Society for Christian traveling men. The new organization was interdenominational; its members wore buttons as means of recognition; by 1907 the membership had reached 23,000. The society undertook to place a Bible in every hotel room in the United States and in every stateroom on vessels plying inland water or engaging in coast-wise trade. Most hotel keepers were willing to cooperate, and by 1914, 237,846 Bibles had been placed in 3,500 hotels. Pasted on the inside cover of each volume were such useful suggestions as these: "If trade is poor, read Psalm 37; John 15"; "If discouraged or in trouble, read Psalm 126; John 14"; "If you are out of sorts, read Hebrews 12."

Wisconsin

FATHER DIVINE. At 152 West 126th Street is the most important Kingdom of Father Divine in Harlem. Father Divine, Negro religious leader of the "Righteous Government," has thousands of followers who call him "God" and who believe him to be God in the flesh. One of their chants holds: "He has the world in a jug and the stopper in his hand." His adherents are called "angels" and assume such names as Glorious Illumination, Heavenly Dove, and Pleasing Joy. Since Marcus Garvey's time no Negro has achieved a larger following among the masses of Harlem. Father Divine, a stocky baldheaded man with an intimate rhythmical style of Bible oratory, preaches a simple Christian theology emphasizing the principles of righteousness, truth, and justice. The slogan of his cult is "Peace," the word being used as a salutation and an interjection, sometimes coupled with "Thank you, Father." He exacts celibacy from his followers. Assistance from public relief agencies is prohibited.

A kingdom serves as meeting hall, restaurant, and rooming house. No regular prayer meetings are held there but throughout the day hymns and songs praising Father Divine are spontaneously sung and music in dance tempo is played. Usually, Father Divine delivers an address at eleven o'clock in the evening at the 126th Street kingdom. . . . He also presides at private "banquets" for sect members only, at which he delivers "messages." A popular feature of the kingdoms are the low-cost meals served to all comers. Priced at fifteen cents, they consist of a meat dish—veal, chicken, or turkey—vegetables, bread and butter, and tea or coffee. Thousands of such meals are served daily in the various kingdoms, where lodgings are also available in dormitories at two dollars a week. Father Divine's followers have accumulated much city and country property, including the "Krum Elbow" five-hundred-acre estate opposite President Roosevelt's family seat at Hyde Park on the Hudson River; they also maintain an undisclosed number of missions, farms, gasoline stations, grocery stores, and other enterprises, all under the immediate directorship of the evangelist. These holdings are in the names of "angels," but the actual financing of the purchases is shrouded in mystery. Thus far, all attempts to probe the finances of Father Divine and his sect have been unsuccessful. A former Divine kingdom at 20 West 115th Street was bought in 1938 by Bishop "Daddy" Grace, evangelist, who aspires to the popularity achieved by Father Divine.

New York City

BANGOR. According to a tale, the Rev. Seth Noble, the first pastor of the Congregational Church [in Montgomery, Massachusetts] was so inordinately fond of the hymn "Bangor" and called for it so frequently that his congregation first protested and then dismissed him in 1806. He went to a settlement in that part of Massachusetts that later became the State of Maine and after its incorporation represented his town in the legislature. Evidently the clergyman's favorite hymn was more appreciated in Maine, for it gave the name to the town: Bangor.

Massachusetts

[In Maine they tell this story a little differently. The Reverend Noble, representing the settlement of Sunbury], was sent to Boston to obtain the incorporation from the General Court. It is said that, while the clergyman was attending to the town's registration, he was humming the old hymn tune known as "Bangor." When the clerk, filling out the necessary papers, asked Noble the name of the community, the pastor misunderstood the question and replied with the name of the hymn, and thus the latter name was written into the incorporation papers.

Maine

SUN DANCE. The Shoshone hold their [sun dance] near Fort Washakie in late July or early August; the Arapaho, at Ethete. The dance never takes place twice on the same ground. In the old days it was the ultimate in tribal incantation; its object seems to have been to conquer certain cosmic elements and, by strong medicine, compel the thunderbird to release rain. Legend tells that it originated when a warrior wandered forth to find relief for his starving tribe. He met a deity, fasted, and learned a ritual; when it was performed, buffalo came. As years passed, the dance grew in mystic significance; it furnished a vehicle for the expression of emotion in rhythm; it knit the tribe in closer unity by renewing the ranks of the chiefs. Because Indian patriotism mounted to fervor during the ceremony, the white conquerors frowned on it. It was outlawed for a time; when revived, it was Christianized.

Weeks before the dance, the chiefs meet in solemn council to select a site for the sun lodge and to choose braves worthy of cutting the cottonwood medicine pole. Two war parties engage in sham battle for possession of the pole; it is then dried in the sun, beaten, and treated with a potion to drive out evils. A crier calls all tribesmen to help erect the sun lodge. The medicine pole is placed upright in the ground, and 12 shorter uprights are placed in a circle around it. Rafters converge at the top of the medicine pole. There is no roof, but brush is piled against the sides of the lodge for shade. An individual stall, woven of willows, is provided inside for each dancer. The medicine pole, the fetish of the thunderbird, also represents the Shoshonean conception of the white man's God; the outer poles, symbols of the Great Eagle's tailfeathers, may be understood to symbolize the twelve Apostles as well.

From the top of the medicine pole, where once a captured enemy was suspended alive, hang two bunches of red willow (for peace and tranquillity); a buffalo head (appreciation of blessings received); a beaver pelt (industry); a long braid of hair instead of the old-time scalp (sacrifice); and the tailfeathers of an eagle, one of the indispensables of Indian ceremonial. The participants, men only, fast for three days, while the women tempt them with rich foods. They wear little clothing, but their bodies are painted by medicine men; each dancer has a whistle made of the thighbone of an eagle or blue crane, which gives a shrill, piping note like that of a bird in distress. To each whistle, a fluffy white feather is held by a bead necklace. The head medicine man's slender staff bears feathers symbolic of the Great Eagle.

The dancers face the east each day at sunrise, and, as the rays reach their bodies, the whistles wail, and drums are beaten. The medicine man chants the prayer song, which the sun's rays transmit to the Great Spirit. After an hour spent in repainting their bodies, the dancers form an arc in the sun lodge; they keep their eyes on the sun throughout the dance. At night, a big fire takes the sun's place. The women sit with the drummers outside the lodge, chanting steadily and shaking dry willows to the throbbing of the drums. The half-hypnotized dancers move forward and backward, blowing their whistles. At intervals they touch the medicine pole with their hands or with feathers, to transfer to themselves the healing power the pole takes from the sun. When exhausted, they retreat within their stalls to rest and pray and, perhaps, to see visions. The dance ceases abruptly when the Dog Star rises.

On the fourth morning, medicine men and dancers face the sun and give thanks. The dancers wash the paint from their bodies, then they may eat.

Wyoming

JONAH AND THE WHALE. ["Old Bill" Williams], trapper, trader and explorer in the Far West, aided missionaries in preparing a dictionary at the Osage language and part of a grammar. A school was begun [at Harmony Mission] about January of 1822, with 12 Indian children as pupils. Reverend Pixley confided to his diary that he found them "as interesting and active as the generality of children among the whites, and I have sometimes thought them more so." The missionaries, however, failed to achieve any real success in their work because of their inability to understand the primitive mind, and their unbending insistence upon an Osage adoption of New England morality. Williams soon tired of the impossible situation. The crisis came when, contrary to the advice of Williams, the minister preached a sermon on Jonah and the whale, at the end of which an old chief arose and declared, "We have heard several of the white people talk and lie; we know they will lie, but that is the biggest lie we have heard." Soon afterwards, Williams "laid aside his Christianity and took up his rifle and came to the Mountains." The Indians, tiring of their guests, chose to ignore them. The mission continued until the Osage were moved west of the Missouri State Line in 1837, but the missionaries failed to convert a single adult Osage.

Missouri

SPITE-FENCE. In the days of Bride Cake Plain (Old Lancaster—origin of name unknown) a feud occurred between two men who held adjoining pews in the church; one of them erected a "spite-fence" between the pews to such a height that his devotions should not be disturbed by the sight of this hated neighbor. Church authorities, however, ruled that the screen was un-Christian and ordered it removed.

Massachusetts

EPHRATA. [Religious community in central Pennsylvania, founded by Johann Konrad Beissel, and famous for its Cloisters.] The colonists practiced a kind of Christian communism. All property was held in common, members of the community sharing equally in the work and in the proceeds from the harvests and crafts. They made their own building materials, utensils, tools, furniture, and clothing, and raised their own food. Rarely was it necessary to acquire anything from the outside world—and then, as in the case of the printing press, it was imported from Germany.

On its religious side Ephrata was ascetic. Although no vows were taken, celibacy was a strict requirement for membership in what might be described as the colony's inner circle, as represented by the Brotherhood of Zion and the Sisterhood of the Order of Spiritual Virgins, or Roses of Sharon. Provisions were made, however, for the married members of the colony; for a time some were given communal shelter, and others lived in cottages clus-

tered around the monastic center of the community. Many of these cottages were occupied by former brothers and sisters of the order who had married; they received a sum from the common fund and were encouraged to live near by, although no longer members of the order.

The daily mode of living was severely monastic. Men and women lived apart in their respective dormitory cells, two persons to a cell; each cell was only four floor boards wide and had a small high window. All slept on narrow wooden ledges too short to permit complete repose, with wooden blocks eight inches long for pillows. Low narrow doors and passageways symbolized the "straight and narrow path" and required constant stooping to remind the brothers and sisters of humility. The garb had a coincidental likeness to that of the Capuchin Order. All garments were white, full flowing, and of the utmost simplicity in cut and material; shoes, never worn in summer, were of wood and hide. Both brothers and sisters were cowled as they filed into the meetinghouse for divine service.

Industry and monastic regimentation went hand in hand. Two three-hour rest periods were allowed out of 24, the first from 9 p.m. to midnight, at which time all were roused from their beds for prayer, and the second from 1 to 4 in the morning. The remaining hours were for labor and devotions.

Ephrata was governed without any written covenant, the Bible being the only rule of faith and discipline. Beissel's followers adhered to the fundamentals of the Christian religion. They practiced apostolic or "believer's" baptism, administering trine immersion and prayer with the laying on of hands as the recipient knelt in the water. Saturday, the seventh day of the week, was observed as the Sabbath; and on the following day the Lord's Supper was celebrated with a love feast in commemoration of the meeting of the Apostles on the first day of the week to break bread. The rite of foot washing was observed and a frugal meal consumed, most of the food being distributed to the poor by way of the Almonry (almshouse).

Beissel's system of harmony, first in America, was printed in 1747 on the Ephrata press, the third in America and one of the most famous. On it was printed a greater quantity of work of a literary character than on any other press in the colonies, a veritable flood of books, tracts, and pamphlets. The outstanding achievement was the *Martyrer Spiegel*, or the *Martyrs' Mirror*, a 1,514-page story of the persecutions of the Mennonites in Europe. Published in 1748 after three years of work, translated from the Dutch into German by Peter Miller, who succeeded Beissel as superintendent of the Cloisters when the founder died, it was the most ambitious book that had been produced on this side of the Atlantic. Another noteworthy production was the first American edition, in German, of Bunyan's *Pilgrim's Progress*.

Ephrata was likewise noted for its choral singing, hymns, and sacred scores. A music school was an important part of the institution. There was also a writing school where ornamental Gothic script was taught; and more than 2,000 pieces of music, resembling the manuscripts produced in European monasteries, were transcribed by the sisters. In 1746 the brothers and sisters, as a "religious discipline to castigate the flesh," copied with quill pens and ink about 500 tunes and songs, most of them composed by Beissel, and presented them to him as a testimonial of "filial esteem." This book is now on display in the music division of the Library of Congress. A huge, hand-lettered style book of the German alphabet, completed early in the 1750's and valued at $10,000, still exists at Ephrata.

Although the creed of the German Seventh-day Baptists forbade them to take up arms, they threw open their doors to the sick and wounded of Washington's army after the Battle of the Brandywine. Washington, a personal friend of Peter Miller's, sent 500 soldiers to be billeted here. Two hundred died of their wounds or of smallpox and were buried beside the sisters who died caring for them. The press, too, played an important role in the Revolution. During the British occupation of Philadelphia, it was used for printing Continental money. And once Washington's soldiers, hard pressed for ammunition, seized unsold copies of the *Martyrer Spiegel*, printed and stored in the Cloisters, to make wadding for their bullets.

As a religious community, Ephrata was disturbed by doctrinal differences from time to time, and by personal jealousies and quarrels. Beissel's was a highly electric personality that seemed to charge the atmosphere about him. He was accused by some of the brethren of attempting to set himself up as the Christ. Particularly bitter were the conflicts between him and the four Eckerlin brothers, who eventually were banished. Nonetheless, the Cloisters exerted a far-reaching spiritual influence in their day, and many visitors came to hear the music and partake of the peace that appeared to hover over the community.

Pennsylvania

PEYOTE. The use of peyote, a dried cactus "button," as a sacrament figures largely in the elaborate night-long Osage religious ceremonials. As early as the Spanish conquest, certain Mexican tribes employed peyote in religious rituals, and gradually its use spread northward until the end of the nineteenth century when it became popular among the Indians of Oklahoma. It was introduced on the Osage reservation in 1898 by John Wilson, a Caddo-Delaware. In 1911, a charter for the incorporation of the Native American Church was obtained from the state by Oklahoma Indians—the articles specifying the use of peyote as a sacrament.

The Osages hold their church meetings on Saturday nights in octagonal lodge houses with earthen floors and cement altars. About sixty feet from the church door is a sweat-bath house in which the ceremonial participants purify themselves physically with a buckeye root emetic while taking the bath. After purification, the Indians are led into the cleanswept church by the "Road Man" or leader; all seat themselves on blankets placed on the dirt floor and observe silence while the leader makes and lights a corn-shuck cigarette and prays aloud for the whole world. After the prayer the cigarette is placed on the "Road," and the "Road Man" continues during the night, admonishing, exhorting, and pointing out the right road to the worshipers, who throughout the ritual use the peyote both in its original form as a cactus button and steeped in a tea. The rhythms of a drum and gourd heighten the emotions until the end of the services on Sunday morning when the participants partake of a feast.

Oklahoma

PROTRACTED MEETING. The protracted meeting has its "mo'nahs bench," "fasting and praying," "comin' through" experiences, meeting of "candidates," the "right of fellowship," and, as the climax, "baptizing." In the preliminary service, before the preacher takes charge, there is singing, tapping of feet, and swaying of bodies until the congregation gets happy. Then the preacher rises, slowly comes forward to the pulpit, and begins his sermon. The opened Book lies before him, but he scarcely notices it. His message comes from the soil and from the racial peculiarities of his people. When his throat becomes dry and tired from his exhortations, he sits down to rest. The singing is started again.

Since the preacher has worked his best, the singing at this time is done in earnest. The best men singers gather in a corner and the leader intones a phrase of some song. The phrase is repeated over and over with other men singers joining in. The song rises slowly and steadily, increasing in volume and tempo, until the urge of its weird harmony and spiritual uplift forces hands to clap rhythmically with the steady cadence of a drum.

Soon a woman leaps out into the aisle. She is "moved by the spirit" she cries, and slowly, rigidly, she begins "the shout," or if it is a Holiness meeting, the "Holy Dance." It is shuffling, intricate; her heels thud on the floor. Other women become moved. With arms held stiff and bent at the elbow and hands hanging limp from the wrist, they slowly, jerkily, circle the church, forming a tight chain with their bodies.

"Shout the praise o' God!" someone demands, and even the sinners join in the singing. They sing lustily, with all reason subordinated to sound. The ring of shouters moves faster and faster, yet the feet keep the step; the rhythm is not broken. When the strain reaches the breaking point the leader raises his hand. The song is hushed. The circling chain halts, breaks apart. The shouters go back to their seats. They are breathing hard and are wet with sweat.

In the pause that follows, the preacher comes forward and begins to talk. Perhaps it is a continuation of his sermon; perhaps it is something entirely new. No one knows and no one cares. His voice has taken on the strange hollow quality of the hand-clapping and seems to float above his listeners. No matter what he says, someone sitting in the Amen Corner nods his head and shouts, "Amen!" This response is not a privilege, but a duty. Now and then someone jumps to his feet and "professes." He has seen the light, he shouts, and is now "turned." To distinguish him when the time comes for "experiences," a member places a piece of white cloth on his sleeve.

Near the end of the meeting the "candidates" must face the officers and members and relate their "experiences." The experience is the visionary journey he had made while on the road to salvation and must resemble the experiences of a professed member, else the candidate will not be acceptable to full membership. As these spiritual journeys are recounted, in the rich metaphor and Biblical phraseology of the "saved," the responses of the audience rise to the pitch of religious ecstasy.

The meeting ends in a great baptizing usually held early in the morning or on Sunday afternoon. Dressed in white gowns and caps, the candidates who have been accepted into membership are led out by two deacons into the water of some creek or pond, the preacher preceding them. The congregation gathers on the bank and sings, "Let's Go Down to the Jordan." The minister puts his hand on a candidate's head and says, "I baptize thee." As the new member goes quickly under the water and rises hysterically happy, everyone breaks into a shout "Praise th' Lord! Praise God!" Another sinner has been washed of his sins.

Mississippi

CHRISTIAN NEWSPAPER. The [Topeka] *Capital* achieved attention in 1900 when its editor, Maj. J. K. Hudson, placed the editorial policy of the paper under the direction of Dr. Charles M. Sheldon, prominent Topeka minister, for one week. Dr. Sheldon, in his first editorial said: "The editor of the Capital asked me to assume entire charge of the paper for one week and edit it as a Christian newspaper."

Dr. Sheldon, during his short tenure in the editorial sanctum of the *Capital*, eliminated all news of crime, prize fights, and scandal, and published columns in support of the prohibition movement. After noting the response to Sheldon's "Christian" newspaper, publishers generally were in agreement that there was no demand for this type of publication.

Kansas

PENITENT BROTHERS. A *morada* (meeting house) of *Los Hermanos Penitentes*, or the Penitent Brothers, appears . . . among the trees [along] the [Badito] river. While many members of this cult, all men, live in the Huerfano Valley, there is no general organization of supreme authority, each

local society being independent. The chief officer, *hermano mayor* (elder brother), has absolute authority, and as a rule holds office for life.

Their grim practices, brought to New Mexico in 1598 by Don Juan de Onate, spread rapidly, although practiced secretly through fear of excommunication. In 1886 the Catholic Church attempted to abolish the flagellation ceremonies, but they still survive, a somber mixture of Christianity and Indian paganism.

During Holy Week their Passion Play is enacted up and down the Huerfano Valley, as in many other Southern Colorado communities, much as it was in the sixteenth century. The secret ceremonies start in the *morada*, where the freshly whitewashed adobe walls, it is said, are often splotched with blood after the flagellation rites have been concluded. Witnesses have testified that the brothers kneel before a *sangrador* (blood-letter), who gouges crosses on their bare backs with a piece of jagged glass. These wounds are kept open and bleeding, often by rubbing salt into them, until Easter. The Penitent Brothers whip themselves all Holy Thursday afternoon and night, chanting dismally as lashes of soapweed swish through the air.

Before dawn on Good Friday twelve chanting marchers leave the *morada* to the accompaniment of a wailing *pito* (flute) and march toward a secret *Calvario* in some mountain fastness; here the final ritual is enacted. Outsiders are not permitted to witness these proceedings; often deputy sheriffs are enlisted to insure privacy. Leading the procession are two men bearing lanterns to guide the bare, frozen, and bleeding feet of a brother clothed in flapping cotton drawers, with a black bag resembling a hangman's cap over his head. He stumbles along blindly, lashing his naked back and shoulders with a soapweed whip.

Behind him, similarly dressed, follows the *Cristo* elected to play the role because of his godly life. He staggers along under a huge wooden cross often five times his own weight. Trailing the *Cristo*, the other brothers continue to lash themselves with razor-sharp soapweed and cactus whips. Men have been known to tie the skull of a cow to a rope hooked with barbs into the muscles of their back, and drag the burden over the steep hills until the hooks are torn free.

Upon reaching the *Calvario* the procession halts. The *Cristo* is tied with ropes to the cross he has been carrying; the cross is then raised by attendants wearing headbands of thorns. Until half a century ago the man was nailed to the cross, but this is no longer done. Throughout this day-long ceremony the brothers continue to lash themselves until in pain or religious fervor they fall exhausted, or deliberately throw themselves into beds of cacti to increase their sufferings in penance for their sins.

At dusk the haggard and tortured brothers return to the *morada*, where others of the faith are waiting. As psalms are sung, the twelve candles burning on the altar are extinguished until only one remains lighted. The *amatrada*, a noise-making machine made with a flat piece of wood that rotates against a toothed wheel, is set in motion; chains are dragged across the floor and rattled; the *pito* shrills loudly in this pandemonium, which is a command to the dead to arise. Abruptly there is silence as the *hermano mayor* lifts his arms and chants a prayer for the dead. Singing is resumed, and the candles, one by one, are relighted. The brothers then kneel in a last prayer, and the grim ceremonies are concluded for another year.

Colorado

FOUR-SQUARE GOSPEL. Angelus Temple . . . , 1100 Glendale Boulevard, [Los Angeles,] a huge rotund edifice, bustles with the energetic evangelism of its moving spirit, Mrs. Aimee Semple McPherson. Some 4,000 sightseers are conducted through this Church of the Four-square Gospel each month to gaze on the domed auditorium seating 5,300 persons; the stage on which sermons are dramatized; the organ that can simulate the tones of 40 different instruments; the stained-glass windows depicting the life of Christ (one presented by Gypsies); and the mural depicting the return of Christ under an enormous American flag. Then there is the prayer tower, in which prayer has been continuously said in two-hour shifts since the building was opened in 1923; the control room of the temple's radio station, KFSG; and the communion service set of 5,300 cups. Adjoining the temple is the ministerial training school, known as the Lighthouse of International Four-square Evangelism. In the children's church youngsters conduct as well as attend services. Additional religious facilities include a music conservatory, a kindergarten, a charity commissary, a free employment bureau, a salvage department, a printing plant, and Mrs. McPherson's home, with a roof garden above the temple book store.

California

MINISTERS. Traveling from appointment to appointment along the country roads, the ministers were easily recognized by their manner of dress. They generally wore "straight-breasted coats, high standing collars, long waistcoats, and the plainest of neckties." Suspenders were a little known luxury. Many ministers affected the additional touch of a special hairdress: "about midway between the forehead and the crown of the head the hair was turned back and permitted to grow down to the shoulders." Joseph Brown of Callaway County—"a steam doctor and an ironside Baptist preacher—wore a long buckskin hunting shirt, reaching almost to his heels." No less singular was the Reverend Jabez Ham, who organized New Providence Church on Loutre Island, Montgomery County, in 1826. A large, stout man, he often added emphasis to his opinions by the use of his fists. However primitive his theology, his sincerity and directness made it effective. He was a famous hunter and his sermons, he often pointed out, were like an old shotgun loaded with beans which, when it went off, was almost sure to hit somebody somewhere.

Missouri

HOUSE OF DAVID. In 1903, Benjamin Franklin Purnell, known as King Ben, and his "holy rollers" of the Israelite House of David established a colony in Benton Harbor. Interchurch dissension followed the leader's death in 1927, and in 1930 the House of David, numbering 600, split into two groups; one followed Queen Mary, Purnell's widow, while the other remained with Judge Harry T. Dewhirst, an enterprising colonist from California. Queen Mary and her flock of 217 established a new colony, called the Israelite City of David, next door to the original settlement.

Both factions, although bitter rivals, profess to follow the dictates of the faith laid down by King Ben. Members do not smoke, drink, or eat meat. Upon joining, they contribute all their possessions to the general fund and, in exchange for communal work, are given enough to satisfy daily needs. Both branches are exceedingly prosperous and divide between them a large share of the business interests of the twin cities, including hotels, tourist camps, restaurants, a cold-storage plant, print shops, and fruit farms. Each group has a band, an orchestra, and a bearded baseball team whose members play bare-handed; the teams usually enjoy a high ranking in national semiprofessional competition. Both branches have extensive realty holdings in Benton Harbor and in resort subdivisions.

The nucleus of the House of David's wealth was a $75,000 gift from a carriage manufacturer, donated shortly after Purnell was said to have received a scroll from a dove that alighted on his shoulder; the dove's message declared that King had been chosen Seventh Messenger of the Faith founded in 1792 by an Englishwoman, Joanna Southcott. Purnell's previous experience as a member of religious colonies in Richmond, Indiana, and Detroit equipped him to lead the "ingathering of Israel," composed of converts secured in travels throughout Illinois, Ohio, Indiana, Kentucky, and Michigan. On the donated land, Purnell built his five houses, Bethlehem, Jerusalem, the Ark, Shiloh, and the Diamond House.

Beginning as a broom maker, Purnell amassed a fortune reputedly amounting to almost a million dollars. Israelites traveled the countryside in wagons, decorated with winged scrolls, promising that "Millions now living will never die." Benjamin preached that, when his colony grew to 288,000 members, they would all be transported in a body to Heaven. Only those who transgressed the rigid laws of the faith would fail to attain his heavenly goal. Such sinners were buried in unmarked graves.

King Ben, it seems, was not without fault, and stories concerning his moral lapses began to circulate among members of his flock. These charges were mainly uttered by the malcontents, unhappy prisoners in the House of David penal colony on High Island in the Beaver Archipelago. . . . When the accusers were freed in 1923 to appear as witnesses for the State in its suit to dissolve the House of David, their testimony generally corroborated that of two young girls who charged King Ben with immoral practices under the guise of religious ritual.

The trial was a fantastic drama. Witnesses disappeared, charges of intimidation were made, and for three years Purnell himself could not be found; ultimately the colony was raided and King Ben was brought into court on a stretcher, to whisper faintly denials of the charges. Although the court's ruling that the colony should be divided was later reversed, Purnell did not learn of his legal vindication. For despite his contention that virtuous members of the House of David enjoyed immortality, he died in 1927. The body was concealed for several days in the hope of resurrection, but his death was finally made public. His mummified remains were placed in the colony's glittering Diamond House, so called because the special composition of its concrete blocks causes it to sparkle in the sun.

Michigan

REFORM CHURCH. In 1900 the variety theater was still an accepted institution [in Spokane], and proprietors could safely dismiss with little concern the onslaughts of reformers. Thus, in November 1901, during one of the periodic reform waves, "Dutch Jake" Goetz offered the large barroom of the Coeur d'Alene for religious services. Some 400 men gathered there, drawn by curiosity and the lure of the three bars, the gambling house, the variety theater, the café, and the Turkish bath. The account in the morning paper said: "Mingling with the hymns of salvation and the message of religion were the clink of glasses, the maudlin utterances of tipsy men, the noise of shuffling feet, the hurrying to and fro of waiters with calls of 'one stein,' 'one egg sherry,' 'one gin fizz and four cocktails,' 'ham and eggs,' and a score of other phrases of the barroom. During the brief wait for the services to begin, the crowd was entertained with selections on the big mechanical pipe organ, while the electric fountain winked its myriad of electric lights."

Washington

THE NAKED PROPHET. For several years Cumberland suffered from time to time the visits of a demented Virginian named Harris, who would walk naked through the streets prophesying the wrath of heaven. On one occasion he paraded up the aisle of a church. At last his relatives were prevailed upon to keep him home. Shortly afterwards, however, the city met with a visitation that some regarded as a fulfillment of Harris' prophecies. On April 14, 1833, a fire destroyed seventy-five buildings in the heart of town, including every store but one. Fears of celestial wrath had begun to abate by November when they were roused to fever pitch by the unusually splendid showers of Leonids of that year.

Maryland

SACRED HARP SINGERS. The *Sacred Harp's* 500 pages contain no new-fangled song with a harmony that can be faked. It holds to the ancient "shape-notes," the "fa, sol, la" songs brought down from Elizabethan England and written in four parts, on separate staffs, with each part carrying to a degree a melodic pattern of its own. This is complex; it calls for technique and a training for tone. As any "leader" worth his salt will declare, a tone-ignorant person can ruin a singing any day.

To avoid such a calamity, each county has its "school." The school is a "leader," or singing master who goes from community to community, like an old-time Methodist circuit-rider, teaching the youngsters to "pitch," to know "tone lengths" and "tone shapes"—the circle, triangle, square, etc. During the process, he also teaches the songs adapted to each "occasion": "Invitation," ("Ye Who Are Weary"); "Glorification," ("Glory for Me!" or "We Praise Thee O God!"); and "Funerals," ("Just Beyond the River").

When a novice has learned such fundamentals, he is eligible for membership in the County Singing Convention and permitted to join in the "singings" with all the vibrant volume his lungs can muster. Perhaps he later will prove worthy of becoming a "leader" himself or, less important, a duly elected officer of the District (sectional) Singing Association, of which his county convention is a member. One never can be certain about a singer—

not beyond the fact that he will be at the singing, singing lustily and religiously, like the rest of us.

The singing is at the "church-house," a small, white "shotgun" structure placed just off the road in the sun-speckled shade of a grove. It is scheduled to begin at nine sharp in the morning, but time is a negligible quantity to people who put seeds into the ground and wait for them to grow; at ten o'clock we are still arriving, in cars, in school busses, in wagons, and a few in "Hoover carts"—an ingeniously contrived two-wheel, automobile-tired lolly brought into prominence by the depression. We have on our Sunday clothes, with here and there an unobtrusive patch, but only the district's politician will wear a coat.

Inside the church, the leader faces us from the pulpit. He is a lean, Cassius-like fellow with the voice of an angel. With ancient ritual he directs us through eighteenth century singing-school procedure; he speaks of "lesson" and "class," not of song and choir.

"The lesson," he announces, "will commence on Number six-three."

We watch him peer closely at his book, and listen breathlessly as he softly sets the pitch. Then his hand sweeps to right, to center, to left, and we proclaim the tune he has pitched. We go through the tune together—soprano, alto, tenor, and bass singing the syllables, "fa, sol, la . . . ," calling to life notes that told the stern but virginal Elizabeth how the tune should go. With the tune pitched at last, the leader adjusts his glasses and looks about. "The words," he demands; and we sing the words:

"Brethren, we have met to worship and to adore the Lord, our God. . . ."

As the singing continues, leader after leader is called upon. Each is a good leader and will tolerate no dragging, yet a point of courtesy and commonsense democracy demands that when his turn is finished he must give way to another. All who can lead must have a chance to lead. A casual coming and going among the class (congregation) is evident. But it, too, is informal and does not affect the charged feeling in the little church-house. The songs are burning and familiar. They are the life we live. As the hands of our leaders wave us through the deep rhythm of the spirituals, we feel our emotions in songs. We sing to please ourselves, and the deep organic surge keeps our voices together.

At noon, however, the *Sacred Harp* is laid momentarily aside, and we go outside for dinner on the grounds. Mules, tied nearby and sensing neglect, bray long and deep. Dust, kicked up by thudding heels, rises to make breathing difficult and to intensify the heat. Yet no one notices, for baskets of food have been brought forth and their contents spread in long, shady rows beneath the trees. A stout, middle-aged lady with a hand for such things faces the milling, conversing crowd, gathers up the folds of her apron and carefully wipes her hands.

"You folks can come on now," she says. "You men folks take some of everything and eat all you want."

After a time, a leader gathers a group about him within the church. He pitches a tune and asks for the words; and "Come Ye Faithful . . ." rolls beckoning out into the grove, fetching us in. A new song is selected.

"I don't like it drug out," the leader cautions. "I like it pert, like you did before you ate."

His arm sweeps down, sweeps us back into the archaic splendor of choral music. The songs move from lesson to lesson; the leadership swings from the seasoned old fellows to the young and obviously frightened tyro. But the tune never wavers, the rhythm does not drag. All that remains is movement and sound, with the latter still unabatedly prominent. We have found a grace of heart and, for the moment, a joyous way of living.

Yet it must end. As the sun drops blood-red behind the grove, the oldest leader comes forward and pitches a tune. "The words," he demands, and in the waning light we give him the words:

"God be with you till we meet again. . . ."

Mississippi

FIGS. The [Congregational] parish [on Mill Street, Newport] was established in 1720, with the Reverend Nathaniel Clap as pastor. In 1725 a schism arose that Dr. Clap ignored until an influential committee waited upon him and requested that he comply with the wishes of the congregation. After listening to their plea the minister produced a plate of figs, handed each committee member one, then stalked from the room shouting, "A fig for you all." If, during his daily walk, he met any children flying kites, playing marbles, or whirling peg tops, he would buy the toys from them and exhort them not to gamble or indulge in vain sport.

Rhode Island

HEAVEN. Wherever a Kentuckian may be, he is more than willing to boast of the beauties and virtues of his native State. He believes without reservation that Kentucky is the garden spot of the world, and is ready to dispute with anyone who questions the claim. In his enthusiasm for his State he compares with the Methodist preacher whom Timothy Flint heard tell a congregation that "Heaven is a Kentucky of a place."

Kentucky

CAMP MEETING Delmarva Camp . . . , in a grove of trees, is the largest white camp-meeting in Delaware.

It is an example of the modernization, externally, of the old-time camp meetings popular on the Peninsula since the time of Asbury and other fervent dissenters of the 18th century. Where formerly the pine-and-hardwood grove was lighted with blazing pine knots on 6-foot-high fire-stands, there are now electric lights to illuminate the grounds. The early tents have been replaced by comfortable frame tents that each have a front room without a front wall, another room behind it, a kitchen shed in the rear, sleeping rooms above, and fancy jigsaw decorations. In the middle of the circle of about 60 tents is the Tabernacle, a shed covering rows of pine benches and a rostrum, where services every evening are broadcast by a public-address system. There are no daytime religious meetings.

Before the day of the automobile, farm families camped here for the full two weeks; it was their opportunity to enjoy religion and sociability, to relax and make love. Nowadays everybody comes in a car, and may stay only for the evening services, which are attended more largely than ever. A fee is charged for "protected" parking—to prevent young people from using dark back seats for lovemaking. Many families still do their own cooking in their tents. Both privately and at the hotel the cooking is done by women of vast experience in preparing corn and beans, fried cymlin' (squash), chicken pot pie and fried chicken with gravy, corn bread and pones, beaten biscuits, large soda biscuits, and many other dishes native to the Peninsula. Desserts are huckleberry pie, cantaloupes, watermelons, or peaches and cream.

In the evenings the "old heads" like to sit in rocking chairs, talk with visitors, read papers, or watch the promenaders.

Religious fervor during the services is likely to burst out in "Amen, brother!" or "Praise the Lord!" and other shouts no less vigorous than in past times, though criticism is heard concerning the way the young folks go off and drink beer while the preaching is going on. After the preaching and hymn-singing there is more promenading until one by one the lights in the tents go out and the camp slumbers.

Delaware

Law and Order

AMERICANS KNOW they are law-abiding people, but the rest of the world does not. This is because they watch American television shows, read newspaper violence, and listen to what we say in praise of individual go-getting. They have not discovered one of the great secrets of the American character: that we talk outlaw (and dream outlaw—consider our ads), but live obedient lives.

The conflict between outlawry and obedience permeates the Guides. There are sabbath violators in Massachusetts Bay, obstreperous counterfeit Indians (before and long after the Boston Tea Party), colorful western ruffians like *Black Bart*, and militant strikers (heroes of the 1930s left). There are armies of do-it-yourself lawmakers: vigilantes, posses, tar-and-featherers, and those making *withdrawals* from closed banks.

Prohibition, which enormously encouraged crime, stands behind some of these stories. Slavery stands behind others. Healthy anarchism (which means civil disobedience occurring at some time other than the present) is at work in the *antirent wars*, while moralistic law enforcement backfires in *banned in Boston.* But even anarchists can be moralists (see *gaming on the sabbath*), and the law here, as always, runs the risk of falling in league with illegality.

BANNED IN BOSTON. For twenty years Boston, stimulated by an exposition ambitiously announcing as its goal, "Boston 1915 the Finest City in the World," had been consciously building its physical self into a fine, clean, and beautiful city. Shortly before the nation-wide depression overtook it, it became obsessed also by a desire to put its spiritual house in order. Celestial roundsmen under the aegis of the "New England Watch and Ward Society" inaugurated a virulent campaign against "lewd and indecent" books and plays. What is salacity? It was like the time-honored stickler: How old is Ann? Other cities indulged in loud guffaws over the antics of the Boston censors as the latter grew hotter and hotter and more and more bothered over the perplexing problem. "Banned in Boston" came to be the novelist's and dramatist's dream of successful publicity—"a natural" in advertising. The greatest furore was occasioned by the refusal of the authorities to permit the Boston production of Eugene O'Neill's "Strange Interlude." The producers promptly moved their company to Quincy, where the play had a tremendous run, playing to audiences packed with Boston residents.

Massachusetts

GAMING ON THE SABBATH. [Arden, Delaware, was once a colony of well-known rebels.] One Arden episode involved Upton Sinclair, writer and publicist, when he "gamed on the Sabbath." In 1911, Sinclair, Scott Nearing, and other liberals, were residents of the village, along with fellow writers, artists, and professional men—some of them Single Taxers, some Socialists; and there was at least one Anarchist—a shoemaker. The latter was wont to explain his ideas of sex physiology at public meetings in the village. The Economic Club of Arden clamped down a censorship on the shoemaker, and when he persisted in his talk, had him arrested. That members of the Economic Club were also members of the baseball teams that played Sunday mornings on the Village Green gave the anarchist his chance for revenge. He went to Wilmington and swore out a warrant against the baseball players for violating a 1793 statute which forbade "gaming on the Sabbath." Sinclair was not a member of the club or a baseball player, but the warrant included him for good measure because he had played tennis that Sunday morning.

Eleven young men were arrested and haled before a Wilmington justice of the peace, in front of whose office the street was blocked by a curious crowd. The "Squire" refused to differentiate between gaming and gambling when Sinclair protested. Each offender was fined $4 and costs. All refused to pay and after serving an hour or two of their sentences partaking of ice cream in a nearby restaurant, the 11 were hustled off to the New Castle County Workhouse. They spent the night in cells and when released in the morning were greeted by 22 newspapermen and three camera men, and the story made the front page of every metropolitan daily in the country.

The group, led by Sinclair, was not hesitant in describing what they claimed were intolerable conditions at the Workhouse and the widespread publicity led to needed reforms. The Anarchist shoemaker still clamored to have the group jailed for a longer term, but the threat that detectives would be placed on watch at a popular Wilmington country club, where court officials and judges were accustomed to play golf on Sundays, brought a cessation of the contest.

Delaware

TOM HORN HAS BEEN SEEN. Tom Horn was hanged [in Cheyenne] November 20, 1903. Horn, a "range detective" hired by cattlemen to combat rustlers and others unfriendly to the big cattle owners, was suspected of killing at least a dozen offenders before he was convicted of killing 13-year-old Willie Nickell. The elder Nickell, an Iron Mountain rancher, was running sheep in cow country, and according to a purported confession Horn was paid $500 to kill the rancher, but shot the son by mistake. Horn was held in jail several weeks before his execution and, as the hanging day neared, feeling was high in Cheyenne between the cattlemen and the sheepman-granger coalition. Horn escaped the jail once, and rumors persisted that the cattlemen had "fixed things" so that Horn would escape secretly at the final moment. After the hanging Nickell demanded to see the body. The county attorney refused permission, saying he feared a riot. Many persons took this as proof that the law had been "bought" and, like most celebrated American bad-man heroes, Tom Horn has been "seen" in various parts of Wyoming since his hanging.

Wyoming

COW BELL SUIT. The handling of the first criminal case by [Coldwater] authorities brought the village wide notoriety and made it the butt of many a ribald joke. A man found guilty of stealing a cow bell was sentenced to "bend over a huge log and let each person present give him a severe blow upon the rotundity of the body with a piece of board four feet long and six inches wide." Apparently the whole town turned out, and the culprit was boarded almost to death. Several private citizens, who took part in the beating, afterward found themselves defendants in a civil suit brought by the victim. For several years litigation moved from one court to another in the Northwest, becoming known throughout Michigan as the Coldwater "cow bell suit," until, as far as can be learned, the case was dismissed.

Michigan

BATTLE OF JUTLAND. Left from Perryville on a macadam road is Jutland . . . , known mainly for the white frame farmhouse where New Jersey's Battle of Jutland took place in 1926. Resisting service of a summons for cruelty to animals, Timothy Meany, a farmer, barricaded himself in his home. After Corp. M. Daly had been wounded in an attempt to serve the summons, State troopers stormed the house. During the all-night battle Beatrice Meany, Timothy's sister, was killed, and James Meany, a brother, and Trooper P. J. Smith were wounded. Three State troopers were later convicted of manslaughter.

New Jersey

DESCENDANTS. In the early nineteenth century when border smuggling was at its height, soldiers were sent to Swanton to halt the activities of the contrabanders, and the vicinity was the scene of many thrilling hide-and-seek games and running gun-fights between the smugglers and border guards. Smuggling has always been a major business along the Vermont-Canada borderline, and the 20th-century bootleggers who defied prohibition in roaring high-powered automobiles laden with liquor were the occupational and temperamental, if not the lineal, descendants of those early Vermont smugglers who drove plodding cattle across the line into Canada to sell to the starving British troops.

Vermont

WANTED POSTER. The District [of Columbia], wedged in between two slave States, was kept slave territory, and the slave trade prospered until the Compromise of 1850. The black code of the District was even more severe than the codes of Maryland and Virginia of which it was the reenactment, and the "stealing" of free Negroes was shamefully widespread. . . .

The Negroes of Washington, both free and slave, at times took matters into their own hands against these flagrant abuses. The Underground Railroad had important stopping places in Washington; ex-slaves today remember churches whose basements served as layovers, and out-of-the-way Georgetown homes that were specially marked for the fugitives. One of the famous trails started at a cemetery skirting the stage road leading north from the city. It is probable that Harriet Tubman, "the Moses of her people," the greatest underground agent, worked around Washington as well as on the Eastern Shore. Legend has it that she was discovered by her friends asleep in a local park beneath a sign advertising a reward for her capture, which meant nothing to her, as she could not read.

District of Columbia

ANTIRENT WARS. The hope of improving their economic lot made [Hudson Valley farm] tenants eager fighters in the rebellion against the Crown; but the political settlement after the Revolution did not break up the huge estates. After the Revolution, in a movement that reached its peak in the thirties and forties, tenant farmers took matters into their own hands and by the threat of force tried to prevent sheriffs from serving eviction notices for nonpayment of rent in arrears. In these "antirent wars" the tenants often disguised themselves as Indians; and the old ballad relates that:

> The moon was shining silver bright;
> The sheriff came in dead of night;
> High on a hill an "Indian" true
> And on his horn this blast he blew:
> Keep out of the way, old Bill Snyder;
> We'll tar your coat and feather your hide, sir.

These outbreaks were quelled by the militia; but wide popular disapproval and the opening of abundant cheap land in the West caused the breakup of the leasehold system. The tenants turned to political action and won their greatest victory in the adoption of the constitution of 1846, which abolished all feudal tenures in land and limited agricultural leases to a twelve-year period.

Near Andes . . . occurred the climax of the 1845 antirent war . . . in Delaware County. When under-sheriff Caman N. Steele attempted to evict a farmer for unpaid taxes, his neighbors, dressed as "Indians," with leather capes over their heads, cowhorns on their caps, and cowtails tied on behind, came to his aid, and in the struggle the sheriff was shot. Arrests were made and several convictions followed, but all sentences were commuted.

New York

CLERK AND BULLY. There were enough homeless males [in the 1870s] to keep up an uproar, and guns went off in the saloon districts with frequency. A favorite story of this period concerns a bully who selected Elko as a place he was going to rule. He enforced his threats and hints of troubles by prominent display of a gun. Everyone but a young clerk was fairly well intimidated; he said the bully was a faker and was publicly critical after the bully mistreated a consumptive sojourning in the town. Other people began to repeat the comments and the self-appointed boss decided to stop them by going to the source; he came into the store where the young man worked, drew his gun, and with sulphurous oaths told what he was going to do if there were any more criticisms. The clerk dropped to the floor behind the high counter. The bully made a dash around the end—and was tripped over backward by the clerk who had crawled forward to meet him. Catching the bully off guard, the clerk was able to snatch his gun and use it as a bludgeon. Yells brought passers-by who finally separated the combatants. This public set-back infuriated the bully who told all who would listen what he was going to do to the young man when he had time to settle with him. Victory had given the clerk further confidence and after various zealous friends had reported the threats in the hope of stirring up more excitement, he walked boldly into the bully's saloon and asked for a drink. The bully glared and refused it. The clerk reminded him that his license was for serving the public and he wanted his drink. He got it, and it was apparent to the town that the bully's reign was over.

Nevada

ELECTROCARDIOGRAPH. [The Utah State Prison] occupies seven acres within an eighteen-foot red sandstone wall on the foothills of the Wasatch Range. Within the walls are a clothing factory where prison uniforms are made, and a factory that produces automobile license plates and State road signs. A new prison is being constructed (1940) at the southern end of Salt Lake Valley. Utah is the only State that gives condemned men a choice between death by hanging or before a firing squad. Most prisoners prefer the firing squad, but one obstinate convict in 1912 elected to be hanged because "hanging is more expensive to the state."

Probably the first electrocardiograph record ever made of a man's heart action while he was being executed, was taken here in 1938, when John Deering paid the penalty for murder before a firing squad. Electrodes fastened to Deering's wrists registered his pulse beat. Though apparently unconcerned, his heart beat at the rate of 180 times per minute shortly before he was shot; the heart of a man doing violent exercise seldom beats faster than 120 times per minute, and the prison physician said he would have died even had no bullet been fired. His heart stopped 15.6 seconds after it was pierced by the bullet.

Utah

BLACK BART. Black Bart Rock . . . , commanding a clear view of southbound traffic from a slight incline [near Calpella], is so-named for the robbery of a mail stage . . . by the elusive road agent, "Black Bart," a lone highwayman, traveling on foot, who robbed 27 coaches in the Sierra and Coast Range mountain country between 1875 and 1883. Always polite, fastidiously dressed in a linen duster and mask, he used to leave behind facetious rhymes signed "Black Bart, Po—8," in mail and express boxes after he had finished rifling them. A laundry mark on a handkerchief dropped near the scene of one robbery in Calaveras County eventually led pursuers to San Francisco where "Black Bart" was discovered to be the highly respectable Mr. Charles C. Bolton, ostensibly a mining engineer who frequently made trips to the mines. A stay in San Quentin from 1883 to 1885 cut short his career.

California

WOMAN OF CONVENIENCE. It was common practice of the [settlement] period for hunters, traders, or trappers to select a "woman of convenience" from among the Indians. In many instances these women were mistreated and even held in contempt by the very men who took them from their tribes. [George] Grinnell was one of these men. In his earlier days along the Missouri he lived with a pure-blooded Indian woman, later discarding her for an educated and talented half-breed, Josephine Manuri. One bitter cold winter day Josephine's small son had wandered from the house and been lost. Several men were ready to search for the youngster but Grinnell, wishing to show his contempt for his wife, threatened to kill the first man to go after him. In the group was George Newton, buffalo hunter and pioneer Williston businessman, who replied, "Then you've got me to kill," and went out and brought the child back to his mother.

One day in 1888, coming from his saloon, where he had been drinking heavily, Grinnell began to abuse his wife, who ran from him to a nearby field where several men were plowing. Too drunk to pursue her on foot, he mounted his horse and followed her to the field where, in an attempt to strike her with the butt of his pistol, he fell from his horse, carrying his wife down with him. The two struggled for several minutes, none of the bystanders daring to interfere for fear of his gun. Suddenly Grinnell relaxed and lay quiet. He was in the habit of wearing around his neck a long leather watch thong with a sliding knot, and in the struggle his wife had clung to this thong and strangled him. After ascertaining that Grinnell was dead one of the onlookers remarked, "Let's go get a drink," and they all retired to his saloon, leaving the body as it was. Later a coroner's jury at Williston absolved the woman of all blame in the death of her husband with the unique verdict that Grinnell ". . . came to his death through an act of Almighty God, by the hand of His agent, Josephine Grinnell."

North Dakota

QUARTETS AND TRIOS. Across Parker Avenue from [Fort Smith] is the site of the old gallows, where 83 men "stood on nothin', a-lookin' up a rope." The platform had a trap wide enough to "accommodate" 12 men, but half that number was the highest ever reached. On two occasions six miscreants were executed. There were several groups of five, some quartets and trios and so many double hangings conducted by the executioner, George Maledon, that they "failed to excite comment." Maledon was also an expert pistol shot and brought down five desperadoes who tried last-minute escapes.

Arkansas

FILIBUSTER. In 1922, the State voted into office a Democratic administration, although a majority of the legislative members were Republicans. The session of 1924 witnessed a famous filibuster, when the Democrats resolved to delay passage of the annual appropriation bills until the Republican majority yielded to their demands for constitutional and other changes. Both sides settled down to a grim parliamentarian warfare that was not without its comic side. Spectators thronged to the State House, where Lieutenant-Governor Toupin astonished them by his unique application of Senate rules, including an inability to see any Republicans when they rose to demand the floor. The House soon tired of meeting and sending bills to a deadlocked Senate, where members and spectators engaged in fist fights on the floor. The climax came when an unbearable odor emanated from a bomb placed behind the Senate leader's chair. Republican senators fled the State and went into hiding in a Massachusetts hotel, thus stopping further business through lack of a quorum. To keep the administration from going to pieces, the banks loaned money to the various State institutions.

Rhode Island

DRUNKENNESS. It was [a] Baltimore magistrate who, on Christmas and New Year's mornings, convicted left-over merrymakers of drunkenness only if they could not lie on the floor without falling off.

Maryland

SHALL I JUMP OR SLIDE? In the winter of 1863–64 several of Henry Plummer's gang of road agents, led by Cyrus Skinner, began a reign of terror in Hell Gate. They loafed in the store, where Skinner preferred to sit on the safe. . . . [E]veryone in the village believed the gang was intent on rifling the safe, which contained $65,000 in gold dust.

On the night of January 27, 1864, a posse of 21 citizens from Alder Gulch rode into town, and rounded up the gang. Brief trials were held in the store; Cyrus Skinner sat on the safe as usual during the proceedings. Six men were sentenced to hang, and died with the password of Plummer's gang, "I am innocent," upon their lips.

George Shears, Skinner's lieutenant, was hanged in a barn near the store. The rope was thrown over a beam, and he was asked to walk up a ladder to save the trouble of preparing a drop for him. "Gentlemen," he said, "I am not used to this business. Shall I jump off or slide off?" He was told to jump.

Whiskey Bill Graves was led outside. One end of a lariat was fastened about his neck, the other thrown over a stout limb. One of the vigilantes mounted a horse and Graves was lifted up behind him. "Good-bye, Bill," said the rider, and drove his spurs into the horse's flanks.

Montana

JAIL. Mayetta . . . , a farmers' and Indians' trading center, is so close to Holton, the seat of Jackson County, that it has no need of a jail. Early in the 1900's, however, the citizens erected a little stone-and-concrete structure of one cell with a heavily barred window, and immediately sought and secured a prisoner—a tipsy squaw from the Potawatomi reservation. Next morning, when the constable brought breakfast to the squaw, he was dismayed to find her gone and a front wall of the jail wrecked. Days later a Potawatomi brave boasted that on hearing of the squaw's arrest he had tied his lariat to the bars of the cell window (which had not yet firmly set in the cement) and, mounting his pony, had pulled down the entire wall. Mayetta never attempted to have another jail.

Kansas

WITHDRAWALS. Citizens of Moncks Corner, long an isolated community, are sometimes a law unto themselves. During the depression of the 1930's, several depositors broke into a closed bank and took their personal deposits.

South Carolina

LOOMIS GANG. Nine mile swamp [south of Sangerfield] [was] headquarters of the notorious Loomis gang, which terrorized the countryside from 1848 to 1866. The father, George Washington Loomis, was a fugitive from Vermont; the mother was the daughter of a Frenchman who had fled France to escape embezzlement charges. They raised their brood of six sons and four daughters on a 385-acre farm in the swamp; the children grew up well educated, well mannered, and adept at stealing; the girls were the acknowledged beauties of the region. Accounts of their depredations have become colored by tradition: one time they attended a hop-pickers' dance and when young ladies' muffs began to disappear a daring young man lifted the voluminous drapery of a Loomis girl's hoop skirts, and there were the muffs encircling the Loomis limbs from ankle to knee.

In 1849, as horses and clothing disappeared from vicinity farms and all clues led to the Loomises, neighbors organized a search of the Loomis farm and found the stolen goods; one son, William, was arrested and suffered a short jail term—the only time a Loomis was convicted, although they were repeatedly indicted. Anyone who dared testify against them was likely to find his barn burned or his horses and cattle missing. By 1864, 38 indictments against them had accumulated. One September night the brothers broke into the firehouse at Morrisville, Madison County seat, cut the firehose, and burned the courthouse; learning that the records had been removed to the county clerk's office, they broke into his safe a few nights later and burned them. About a year later a posse shot and killed "Wash," the oldest son and leader after his father's death, and tried to kill Grove by rolling him in kerosene-soaked blankets and setting fire to them—but he was saved by his sister Cornelia. In 1866 a vigilance committee surrounded the farm, forced the family to surrender, but failed to extract a confession from Plumb Loomis, even by stringing him from a tree. But that marked the end of the gang: the girls married well; Plumb and Grove settled down; and the only evidences of the days of terror are the cellar ruins of the Loomis home and the crooked arm of an old tree, which Plumb used to point to in his later years and drawl, "See that limb? Well, b'God, they hung me to that."

New York

SINGLETON'S SKIN. In 1876, [Beeville] Sheriff D. A. F. Walton arrested Ed Singleton, notorious outlaw, who was tried and sentenced to be hanged. As the time for the execution drew near, many expected the outlaw's friends to attempt a rescue, and there were wagers that he would not hang. The diligence of the sheriff's office, however, prevented any such attempt, and shortly before the fatal date the outlaw sent for his mother and made an extraordinary will.

He bequeathed his skin to the district attorney, directing that it be stretched over a drum head and that the drum be beaten to the tune of "Old Molly Hare" in front of the courthouse on each anniversary of his hanging, as a warning to evildoers. The remainder of his anatomy he bequeathed to doctors "in the cause of science." He was hanged April 27, 1877.

Texas

SQUAWKERS. Covington was noted as a tough town and a center of vice, filling up with saloonkeepers and gamblers from Sioux City when prohibition was adopted in Iowa. Gun fights were frequent on the pontoon bridge between Covington and Sioux City, and the river was used to dispose of the bodies of losers. One of the rougher saloons and gambling houses was built on the waterfront and had a chute to the water. "Squawkers" who complained of losing their money were placed in the chute and sent sliding into the river.

Nebraska

MARTIAL LAW. The boom town [of Copperfield] had every conceivable type of business, both legal and illegal, with the latter in the ascendency. The inhabitants aped the wickedness of the mining towns of the 1860s and boasted of it. The railroad construction gangs often clashed in "free-for-alls." It is said that one conflict that lasted more than an hour was accompanied by the tinny tunes from the mechanical piano in Barney Goldberg's saloon. Rocks and beer bottles, and other missiles, as well as fists, were used, but when truce was finally called from sheer exhaustion, enemies drank from the same bottle, bound up each others' wounds, and set the date for the next encounter.

The leading citizens of Copperfield including the mayor and the members of the council either ran saloons or were financially interested in them. A few peaceful citizens finally tired of the disorder and appealed to the governor for help. He ordered the Baker County authorities to clean up Copperfield by Christmas; but they refused to act. On New Year's Day, 1914, Governor West dramatically sent his small secretary in with a declaration of martial law, accompanied by an "army of invasion" consisting of five national guardsmen, and two penitentiary guards commanded by a colonel of the National Guard—who was also warden of the state penitentiary. Notified of the approach of the "army" with a female representative of the governor the mayor ordered the town decorated for a glorious welcome. Flags and bunting hung in the streets, and all bars were embellished with pink and white ribbons and such flowers as were available. The entire town was lined up to greet the train. Accompanied by her "army," "war" correspondents, photographers, and almost the entire populace, the secretary marched at once to the town hall, mounted a platform, gave the governor's orders for the resignation of all officials connected with the saloon business; said that if they refused she would hand over the governor's declaration of martial law, disarm everyone in town, close all saloons, burn all gambling equipment, and ship all liquors and bar fixtures out of town. The officials turned down her demands, and the secretary immediately commenced to carry out her threats. The audience was silent throughout the proceedings, and there was little protest when the expeditionary force collected all six-shooters present and piled them on the platform. Just 80 minutes after her arrival the secretary boarded the train for her return journey. The men remained to mop up. A few months after the departure of the guardsmen, fire, of suspected incendiary origin, left the town in ruins, and it was never rebuilt.

Oregon

The Big Event

W E ARE no less creatures of ritual than the Hottentots. Their year revolves, perhaps, about the summer and winter solstice. Our year, if we lived in rural America not so long ago, revolved around the *county fair* and Christmas. (In Columbia, Tennessee, the year had a third pillar: *Mule Day*.) Such periodic celebrations provide comforting points of reference in an otherwise slippery world.

For civilized society, ritual is of more than psychic importance: it helps turn the wheels of commerce. We see a *Rattlesnake Derby*, a *Cheese Day*, both counted on a spur a town's economy. We visit the shrines of boughten ritual, like *the garden* in New York.

We see here also our hunger for the unusual and the fare we feed it with. We pay to see the *gyascutus*. We insist on *equal boulders*. A *Mt. Washington road* offers natural beauty—not enough! We want a record.

In our pursuit of the remarkable, our chief resource is the media, and we see it here at work, huffing and puffing. Its role is sometimes creative (see *sea monster*), sometimes debunking *(Ram's Pasture)*. Its central myth is the provision of *complete coverage*.

CHEESE DAY. In 1914 a Cheese Day was inaugurated with the enthusiastic support of [Monroe]. The seventh cheese festival, held in 1935, attracted 50,000 people to watch an elaborate parade climaxed by the crowning of a cheese queen and to feast on eight tons of Swiss and Limburger cheese. In the same year cheese was stoutly defended when Monroe's postmaster engaged in a sniffing duel with a postmaster in Iowa to determine whether or not the odor of Limburger in transit was a fragrance or a stench. Well publicized by the press of the Nation, the duel ended when a decision was reached which held that Limburger merely exercised its constitutional right to hold its own against all comers.

Saturday afternoons in Monroe find the townspeople evincing great interest in the display of new cheese-making implements in the windows of hardware stores, mingling with the cheese makers and their assistants, who often walk slowly on stiff and aching legs made rheumatic by the water and steam of the factories.

Wisconsin

COUNTY FAIR. West of Hamburg, the so-called Red Hills, colored by iron content, are, according to scientific surveys, the "second finest farm section in the world," exceeded only by a region in southwestern Belgium.

For farmers in this section, as for farmers everywhere, one of the big events of the year is the local county fair. In the beginning, fairs were devoted solely to the exhibition and sale of farm wares. With their growth through the years, amusement features, scientific displays, and farm machinery exhibits were added to displays of farm-grown and homemade products. Today the county fair is a Hall of Science, a Coney Island, and a merchandise exchange blended into one large and raucous whole.

In the farm exhibit building or booth are displayed pumpkins of incredible size, gourds fantastically shaped, and over-size potatoes that vie for honors with blushing winesap apples and evenly pegged cobs of golden bantam corn. The farm wife displays her needle work and the patchwork quilt completed at the cost of many an ill-afforded hour; the best of her preserves are displayed in the hope that they may win a prize. in the livestock hall is the Holstein heifer whose coat has been curried and combed to a shining sleekness, and the Poland boar, as pampered as a prima donna until he passes before the critical eyes of the livestock judges.

The midway, loud with the blazoning of the calliope and the coin-enticing drone of venders, is crowded with scampering children and happy farm families loaded down with balloons, dolls, and other trumpery of the pitchman. Merry-go-rounds and fakirs, fortune-tellers and side shows, razzle-dazzles and cotton candy are the soul of the midway that leads to the tent show. The wire walkers and acrobats of the past years are now augmented by daredevil flyers and automobile stunt men. In many places midget auto races have taken the place of sulky races, and the long line of hitching-posts has given way to the parking lot.

Pennsylvania

BLUE AND GRAY REUNION. In 1895 an act of Congress created the Gettysburg National Military Park. This included the 600 acres of land and 17 miles of roads turned over to the Government by the Gettysburg Battlefield Association, founded a few months after the battle. The park was administered by the War Department until 1933, when it was placed under the jurisdiction of the Department of the Interior. Here in the summer of 1938 was held a Blue and Gray reunion to celebrate the 75th anniversary of the Gettysburg campaign. Nearly 2,000 aged veterans from all parts of the country were quartered in tents on sunny fields where some of them once lay bleeding. A few, having come unscathed through cannon shot and musket ball of the Civil War, died during the reunion as the result of excitement, age, and the exertion of travel.

One 99-year-old celebrant, however, had only to step out of his home at 144 Springs Avenue to join the Blue-clad ranks. He was Major Calvin Gilbert, then Gettysburg's last Civil War veteran and the town's oldest citizen, who on April 8, 1939, celebrated his 100th birthday. At the time of the battle he was on duty at Fort Stevens, near Washington. After the war he conducted a foundry in Gettysburg, manufacturing metal gun carriages to replace the decaying wood of those in the national park; Gilbert died September 13, 1939.

Pennsylvania

WHITE HOUSE CHEESE. At [Andrew] Jackson's last public reception there was an [extremely] disorderly scene. Some New York friends, anxious to outshine the Massachusetts farmers who once presented President Jefferson with a 750-pound cheese, had sent Jackson a 1,400-pound cheese, which ripened for a year in the cellar of the White House. On Washington's birthday anniversary in 1837, the local citizenry was invited to sample the Pride of New York, and was joined by a host of visitors from Alexandria, Baltimore, and the surrounding country. The Senate adjourned in honor of the occasion, and Martin Van Buren, then President-elect, was present. George Bancroft wrote of seeing in the White House on this occasion "apprentices, boys of all ages, men not civilized enough to walk about the room with their hats off—starvelings, and fellows with dirty faces and dirty manners." When the day closed, the White House was smeared over with the sticky cheese.

District of Columbia

MULE DAY. The high point of the year in Columbia is "Mule Day," the first Monday in April, when the largest street mule market in the world is held. The town is thrown open to traders and visitors from all over the United States, and more than 10,000 attend, their cars, wagons, and livestock blocking the streets and roads. Court Square is lined ten deep, and every upstairs store window is filled with people watching the grand opening parade, probably the only one in America with no motorized vehicles. Horses, ponies, and mules draw decorated floats, old-fashioned race carts, speed wagons, and high-wheel sulkies. There are fine mules and horses, and pretty girls riding jack-asses. Every newspaper in the State has a reporter wandering through the crowd to gather material for a new story about mules and men.

In the "jockey yard," adjoining the mule mart, whites and Negroes sell crisp brown fish, fried chicken, barbecue, and sandwiches. Medicine-show barkers wave bottles of cure-all tonic at the farmers and city folk who press in close to their platforms. Politicians mix with the crowd, booming expansively, shaking hands, slapping shoulders, and kissing babies. Spavined horses are swapped for hollow-horned cows. Moulting roosters of mixed blood are exchanged for white rabbits. Fresh-caught catfish are traded for pocket knives or for dollar watches that won't run.

The mule men are different—ponderously sure of themselves and of the dignity of their profession. They stride deliberately, and poke walking canes ("measuring rods") in the mules' flanks to make them show their points. Shrewd buyers, they move through the crowd appraising here a promising colt, there a sleek, powerful mule, drawling in heavy, authoritative voices. Representatives from foreign governments are often the heaviest buyers. There is the stamping of iron-shod hoofs on the asphalt pavement, an occasional chorus of wild braying, and the voices of auctioneers drumming up purchasers. Events of the day are photographed for the newsreels and broadcast by two national radio chains. Will Rogers wrote of this day: "It ain't anything to see a man come in and trade in a tractor and a three-year-old Buick and $100 down on a span of hard-tails."

Tennessee

BUSK. Just west of Kellyville are the dance grounds of the Creek and Euchee Indians. Celebrations known as "busks" are usually held here in June and July and last four days—the number "4" being sacred to the Creeks. . . . On the eve of the first day the celebrants purify their bodies with *Micco Anija* (King of Purgers), the root of the red willow, which produces vomiting. The next day is devoted to Indian ball. An ox or deer skull is nailed to a tall post, a ball of hide is thrown into the air and the players catch it in the cup-shaped ends of their two-foot-long ball-sticks, then fling it at the skull. The women frequently play against the men; they are permitted to throw the ball with their hands while the men must use the sticks. The *Hajo-Banga* (Crazy Dance) climaxes the busk; the dancers literally "go crazy," no restrictions being placed on their enthusiasm.

Oklahoma

RATTLESNAKE DERBY. In April 1936, McCamey was the scene of the world's first recorded Rattlesnake Derby, with a huge crowd in attendance. It was held in correct racing form with a starter, a timekeeper, an official physician (for the handlers, not for the rattlesnakes), an announcer and a staff of judges. Thousands came to see Slicker, Esmeralda, Drain Pipe, Wonder Boy, Air Flow, and May Westian Rosie compete for the $200 purse.

The gallery watched wide-eyed as the handlers drew the reptiles from their containers, tagged them and placed them in the starting box. A forty-five roared, and the starting box fell apart, revealing a mass of squirming, rattling reptiles, which seethed and heaved for a moment. Then out of the mass slithered thick bodies with ugly flat heads, and, while cameras clicked, snakes moved toward the finish line. Slicker won.

So successful was the derby in attracting visitors and advertising the town that it is now an annual event, held the fourth week in April.

Texas

GENUINE BULLFIGHT. In 1884, Dodge City held a Fourth of July celebration unique in the history of the State and Nation. A bull fight, with "distinguished matadors, all in Andalusian costume, . . . and 12 bulls," was given for the first and, records say, the only time in the United States. The affair was much talked of and generously advertised, creating widespread interest of several sorts. Humane societies protested vigorously. State and Federal authorities wired orders to stop the show; it could not be given in the United States. Mayor A. B. Webster wired tersely in reply, "Dodge City is not in the United States" and went on about his business of completing the elaborate arrangements.

On the morning of July 4th a great crowd was on the streets to see the grand parade. The procession, headed by the mayor, included the Dodge City Cowboy Band and the gaudily dressed matadors. At the fair-grounds more than 2,000 people found seats in the huge amphitheater especially built for the occasion.

The fight was repeated on the next day with an even better selection of fighting bulls, more thrills and excitement. The *Ford County Globe* of July 8, made this boastful comment:

Those present can testify that it was a genuine bull fight on each of the two days, just as we said it would be, and parties who witnessed the performances are free to say that they never beheld one, either in Old Mexico or Spain, that was more in dead earnest than the ones given in this city.

Kansas

MONKEY TRIAL. Dayton . . . , seat of Rhea County, was founded in 1820 by W. H. Smith, a New England schoolmaster. The industrial plants include hosiery mills, an underwear factory, canneries, and a bottle works. Coal mines are operated in the nearby mountains.

At the Rhea County Courthouse the "evolution trial" of John T. Scopes was held in the summer of 1925. This case, known as the "Monkey Trial," grew out of the alleged violation of a Tennessee statute, passed March 21 of that year, making it "unlawful for any teacher in . . . the State . . . to teach any theory that denies the story of the divine creation of man as taught in the Bible . . ." At a meeting in a local drugstore early in 1925, Dr. George Rappelyea persuaded Scopes, the science teacher in the high school, to stand trial in a test of the new law. Scopes admitted teaching evolution in his general science class. The American Civil Liberties Union offered to finance the trial and lend its attorney, Arthur Garfield Hays. When William Jennings Bryan volunteered as prosecutor, Clarence Darrow and Dudley Field Malone joined Hays in the defense.

Soon Dayton was aroar with newspaper men, itinerant preachers, and thousands of the curious. Revivalists put up tents and placarded the town with signs carrying pertinent Biblical warnings. The roads swarmed with buggies, mule-drawn wagons, and mud-spattered and dust-caked Fords, as Tennessee farmers and their families came to town to watch the defense of "Genesis." They publicly and frequently affirmed their belief in the Bible from "kiver to kiver" and some said that "this Darrow feller must have horns and a tail." All of them were eager to hear Bryan, the Great Commoner, long famous on Chautauqua circuits for his "Crown of Thorns . . . Cross of Gold" oration which, when first delivered in 1896, resulted in his nomination for the Presidency.

Tradesmen did a land-office business. Hot-dog and lemonade stands were set up on every vacant lot. The crowd filled the small court room, aisles and windows, and overflowed into the court yard. During the hot summer days the trial proceeded, with smooth oratory from Malone, shrewd cross-questioning from Darrow, and violent but eloquent outbursts from Bryan.

By the time the trial ended there was a personal feud between Bryan and Darrow. Under the trees of the court yard, to which the court had moved, Bryan cried, "I want the world to know that this man who doesn't believe in God is using a Tennessee court to cast slurs on Him. . . ."

Darrow's reply, "I am simply examining you on the fool ideas that no intelligent Christian in the whole world believes," brought horrified gasps from part of the audience.

Scopes was found guilty and fined $100. Bryan died here on July 26, 1925, five days after the close of the trial into which he had entered with all his nervous energy. As a memorial to him a William Jennings Bryan University was founded here.

Tennessee

PAY CAR. When the first through train, with four carloads of notables, arrived on May 11, 1869, [Winnemucca] put on a celebration suitable to the occasion—firing guns, blowing horns and whistles, ringing bells, driving souvenir spikes, and drinking champagne—the usual drink of early Nevada when it wanted to show it could spend with kings. From then on the one regular town spree came on the day the Central Pacific pay-car came through. That night the more peacefully inclined Winnemuccans would resignedly give up all thoughts of sleep as choruses mounted in the favorite: "Oh, for a home in a big saloon, on the banks of some raging canal." Black eyes and broken noses often identified the celebrants when the morning after broke.

Nevada

DUEL. During the 1840's there was an epidemic of duels in the [Fort Smith] neighborhood, and keen interest in horse racing. Fort Smith's first church was financed in 1844 by sporting men who ran their horses on Race Track Prairie at the edge of town. The duels were usually fought on an Arkansas River sand bar in Indian Territory, beyond reach of anti-dueling laws. In 1844 Solon Borland and Benjamin J. Borden, editors of rival newspapers in Little Rock, made a steamboat trip up the river to Indian Territory to settle a dispute. Even more notable was the quarrel in 1848 between Albert Pike, prominent attorney and author, and John Selden Roane, later Governor of Arkansas. A large crowd followed the duelists to the sand bar in the early morning. Rigid etiquette was observed, with formal introductions, stiff bows, and handshakings. Pike wore an immaculate white shirt and puffed on a cigar. Each combatant cocked a pistol. At the word they fired—again and again. None of the shots took effect. A Cherokee spectator named Bill Fields grunted disgustedly that with such fine weapons he could kill a squirrel at 75 paces.

Arkansas

THE GARDEN. New Yorkers think only of what happens inside of Madison Square Garden. The rare individual who wanders down Forty-ninth or Fiftieth Street for a view of the building itself sees nothing but blank brick walls and fire escapes. The main entrance opens on Eighth Avenue through an arcade, but the Garden proper is concealed behind a smaller structure and runs back toward Ninth Avenue.

This plain building is, however, already famous as America's chief indoor arena. Charity benefits, national political conventions, championship prize fights, cowboy rodeos—all draw throngs to Madison Square Garden. The composition of the crowd on one night contrasts sharply with that of another. From the vantage of a $315 box, the aristocracy, in evening attire, politely applauds the horse show. Twenty-five cents is the price of admission to a Communist rally at which 20,000 people rock the Garden with cheers. Politicians, sportsmen, and socially prominent personalities occupy $16.50 ringside seats to watch a pair of heavyweights in action for an hour or less, while *hoi polloi* sit in cheap seats under the roof. On a good night patrons eat 12,000 hot dogs, washed down with 1,000 gallons of beer and soda pop, while sixty private policemen, unarmed, are stationed there to prevent disorder.

From the top balcony at the Ninth Avenue end, an Olympic ski jumper darts down a slide, hangs momentarily in the air, lands on a snow mound, and stops near the Eighth Avenue end of the arena. Children crowd under the big top for circus matinees. For seventy-five cents a sleepless night is spent at the six-day bicycle races. Three thousand carefully reared and pedigreed pets compete in a dog show. The President makes a speech at a political meeting. A world champion figure skater dances the tango under a spotlight. A professional hockey game is halted by a brawl while fans add to the racket with cowbells and jeers. Tennis matches, basketball games, track meets, and trade exhibitions are among the events staged regularly in the arena. A $34,000 mineral-wool ceiling was especially provided to improve the acoustics when Paderewski played for charity.

New York City

DOG DERBY. The annual Dog Derby was initiated by "Scotty" Allen, former member of the Alaska Legislature and "the greatest dog-musher that ever swung on the handle bars of a sled," whose dog, Baldy, a famous Malemute, developed into one of the most intelligent, courageous and strongest lead dogs in Alaska. This race was from Nome to Candle and return, 408 miles over bleak, timberless country swept by sudden blizzards. The record time of 74 hrs., 14 min., 22 sec. was made by John Johnson, a Finn. It was a gruelling course; as much as a half-million dollars was bet on a single race; dishonest drivers doped competing dogs, crippled them with blankets lined with porcupine quills hidden in the snow, switched their own dogs; a telephone wire was strung along the entire course to announce the progress of the 25 or more contesting teams; a daily "dog-dope" sheet was published, and the entire camp went dog mad. Although the dog-racing fever has subsided like the gold fever, the modern race is a picturesque and exciting affair, from the moment when the Queen in her fur parka drops the starting flag until the end of the race, when drivers struggle in, perhaps harnessed to the sled with the huskies, pulling on the sled dead teammates, killed by the pace, that the rules of the race require the contestant to bring back.

Alaska

COMPLETE COVERAGE. Mays Landing . . . is . . . the national capital of the nudists, who in 1937 designated the community as their headquarters. Along the bank of the Great Egg Harbor River, 2 miles south of the village, a 500-acre tract known as Sunshine Park has been developed by this sun-loving cult. The park provides freedom, a reasonable degree of isolation, and plenty of mosquitoes and greenhead flies. Reporters for tabloid newspapers beat a path to the park entrance each summer when the national convention of nudists is held, but the cult's requirement that visitors disrobe is an obstacle to complete coverage of nudist news.

New Jersey

INTERESTING EXHIBITION. The temperament of early Louisianians is perhaps best reflected in their sports. Public entertainment of the early nineteenth century, when American frontiersmen were flocking to the new territory, was of an exciting and brutal nature. Love of combat, whetted by frequent recourse to sword or pistol, whenever honor was impugned, was vicariously enjoyed by pitting animals against each other. Bulls, bears, dogs, cocks, and alligators were baited for the amusement of rawboned flatboatmen and Creole dandies, who demanded plenty of action. A typical bill of fare of the day was that announced in a New Orleans handbill of September, 1817:

"INTERESTING EXHIBITION."

On Sunday the 9th inst. will be represented in the place where Fireworks are generally exhibited, near the Circus, an extraordinary fight of Furious Animals. The place where the animals will fight is a rotunda of 160 feet in circumference, with a railing 17 feet in height, and a circular gallery well conditioned and strong, inspected by the Mayor and surveyors by him appointed.

"1st Fight—A strong Attakapas Bull, attacked and subdued by six of the strongest dogs of the country.

"2d Fight—Six Bull-dogs against a Canadian Bear.

"3d Fight—A beautiful Tiger against a Black Bear.

"4th Fight—Twelve dogs against a strong and furious Opelousas Bull.

"If the Tiger is not vanquished in his first fight with the Bear, he will be sent alone against the last Bull; and if the latter conquers all his enemies, several pieces of fireworks will be placed on his back, which will produce a very entertaining amusement.

"In the Circus will be placed two Manakins, which, notwithstanding the efforts of the Bulls to throw them down, will always rise again, whereby the animals will get furious.

"The doors will be opened at three and the Exhibition begins at four o'clock precisely.

"Admittance, one dollar for grown persons, and 50 cents for children.

"A military band will perform during the Exhibition.

"If Mr. Renault is so happy as to amuse the spectators by that new spectacle, he will use every exertion to diversify and augment it, in order to prove to a generous public, whose patronage has been hitherto so kindly bestowed upon him, how anxious he is to please them."

In 1853 the following advertisement appeared in the Louisiana *Courrier*:

One Hundred Dollars Bet!

More Excitement and Novel Attraction!

Fight between a

JACKASS AND THREE BULL DOGS!!!

The Great Fighting Jack "Rough and Ready," is to fight Three Large Bull Dogs, at Gretna, on Sunday next, April 3, 1853, at 4 o'clock in the afternoon. The great California fighting bear General Jackson, will be seen there. Admission twenty-five cents.

Louisiana

SEA MONSTER. In the fall of 1884 it was reported that a huge sea monster, 7 feet tall and 81 feet long, had made its way from the Mississippi up the Skunk River about 100 miles, almost to Oskaloosa, Iowa. The story of its discovery, pursuit, and killing with a cannon loaded with a keg of railroad spikes at a shoal in the river (after rifle and revolver shots had failed to penetrate its hide) appeared first in the Oskaloosa newspaper, signed by John Mead. The story was strengthened and apparently verified by reports in the Vicksburg *Chronicle* that such a monster had swallowed two Negro children; the Cairo, Mo., *Post* also reported that a monster, said to be 150 feet long, had attacked a ferry boat as it crossed the river. Hundreds of newspapers in the Middle West carried the story before they learned that it was a hoax, conceived by Dr. Gorrell, a wag in Newton, Iowa, and initiated with the help of a few editors.

Iowa

CHAIRING. In 1835, a Wilmington company bought the *Ceres*, the initial vessel of a fleet to engage in whaling. The adventure lasted until 1845 and gave the city one of its most picturesque aspects in the departure and return of the vessels, each away to the Pacific around Cape Horn on voyages of two or three years. A shot was fired from Whalers' Wharf when a returning vesel was sighted. With the sound, most of the town stopped work and went to greet the fishermen and sailors. If the voyage had been successful the captain was "chaired." Husky sailors secured a chair at the tavern, seated the captain, and raised the chair on poles across their shoulders. Thus they bore him up one street, down another, and back to the inn, while he received congratulations of the inhabitants who lined the streets or joined the procession.

Delaware

DEBATE. Shelby Springs . . . was once a summer resort popular with planters and their families, who came from all parts of the State and lingered for weeks in its frame hotel. . . . Throughout most of the nineteenth century, the town also was a popular camp ground for religious and political rallies.

One of the highlights of its history was a debate between Senator John T. Morgan, for the Democrats, and Napoleon (Nap) Mardis, for the Republicans. The event was given wide publicity, special trains were run from Anniston and Selma, and 10,000 people gathered to hear the speeches and eat the barbecue dinner. Each anxious to have his say, the speakers argued hotly as to who should open the meeting. Senator Morgan was finally chosen to present his arguments first, using whatever time he thought necessary; and Mardis was to take as much time as he wanted to reply. The crowd was to judge the merits of both. The Senator, with pompous deliberation, began his speech, meanwhile keeping a weather eye on the cooks at the barbecue pits. A glaring noonday sun beat down on the faces of the throng; they stirred restlessly as the odor of the cooking meat reached their nostrils. Their eyes strayed from the politicians to the master of ceremonies. The speaker, however, talked on. Although he was in top-notch form, he was obviously holding back. At last the feast was ready, and the master of ceremonies poised himself to strike the dinner gong. From his vantage point on the speaker's platform the Senator saw him and boomed forth the announcement that he had not finished, but would continue after dinner. Then he jumped down and joined wholeheartedly in the rush for the food. When all had eaten, the great crowd was again called back to order and the Senator resumed his speech. Slowly the afternoon waned but Morgan's voice did not. Mardis and the Republicans, already impatient at the delay, became furious. The speaker showed no sign of weakening. Twilight came and locusts and frogs began to compete with him. The entire crowd milled restlessly. Snorts, clangs, and finally peremptory whistles from the locomotives of the special trains warned their passengers that it was time to go. Then and only then did Morgan stop speaking with the regretful remark that he had not more time to complete his exposition of the Nation's problems and his remedies. Earnestly he expressed a hope to be able to complete the address soon. Then he calmly stepped down from the stand, while the crowd broke through the gathering gloom in a pell-mell dash to get home. What Mardis said is not recorded.

Alabama

LADIES OF THE JURY. In Laramie women were first empaneled for service on a grand jury in Wyoming. The act of enfranchising women also included the right to hold office, and several months before the voting right could be exercised, Judge J. H. Howe summoned several women to serve on the grand and petit juries in the second district court in Laramie during March 1870. Wyoming's woman suffrage law had attracted attention, but the territory received its widest publicity when news of its "mixed" grand jury got around.

King William of Prussia cabled congratulations to President Grant on this evidence of "progress, enlightenment and civil liberty in America." Newspaper correspondents came to the frontier to watch the feminine jurors at work. Heavy veils masked the women jurors, and annoyed photographers reproduced them in caricature. The most popular cartoons showed ladies of severe mien jouncing fretting babes while hearing evidence. These were generally captioned with jingles or couplets, as:

Baby, Baby, don't get in a fury;
Your mamma's gone to sit on the jury.

Wyoming

PEACEMAKER. The *Princeton* disaster of 1844 was the severest tragedy that befell official Washington between [British] Admiral Cockburn's incendiary visit [during the War of 1812] and Abraham Lincoln's death. The *Princeton* was one of our first attempts at a propeller-driven warship; and its armament included; a tremendous Paixhans gun of special design, heralded far and wide as the "Peacemaker." It was also one of the first steam warships to reach Washington; hence the excitement when this triple novelty anchored off the Navy Yard in February 1844. On the last day of that month an elaborate official excursion was planned, to demonstrate the prowess of the *Princeton* and the "Peacemaker." President Tyler and his family, his Cabinet, ex-President John Quincy Adams, the leaders in both houses of Congress, and a number of foreign diplomats were included in the party that was ferried to the *Princeton* off Alexandria for an excursion to Mount Vernon, with feasting and music punctuated with demonstration shots from the great "Peacemaker." But on its final discharge, the gun burst at the breech, scattering mangled guests and crew upon the *Princeton*'s decks. Secretary of the Navy Gilmer was killed, as were Secretary of State Upshur, Congressman Maxon of Maryland, Commander Kennan of the Navy and President Tyler's father-in-law, David Gardiner of New York.

District of Columbia

MT. WASHINGTON ROAD. Ever since its construction the [Mt. Washington] road has been a challenge to those seeking records. The oddest was in 1885 when a 230-pound woman, on a wager of $1000, hiked from the Glen House to the Summit, returned on foot to the hotel and danced there the same evening. In 1875, the principal of Phillips Exeter Academy, Harlan P. Amen, ran down the complete distance from the summit to the hotel in 54 minutes. Carriage records began in 1883 when Jacob Vanderbilt and a friend were driven in a mountain wagon with six horses from the Glen House to the Summit in 1 hour, 17 minutes. The first automobile ascent was made in 1899 by the inventor of the Stanley Steamer, F. O. Stanley, in one of his cars.

New Hampshire

EQUAL BOULDERS. [Between the Pawtuckaway Mountains] on the Reservation Road is a junction with a short path . . . to the Pawtuckaway Boulders.

In this valley or notch between the North and South Peaks of the Pawtuckaway Mountains, one-half mile long, is a large group of huge erratic boulders that were detached from the cliffs on either side and transported by the ice-sheet or local glacier eastwardly.

It is said that the discovery of these boulders about 1878 was made at the instigation of Governor Benjamin F. Prescott, who was disturbed because no boulders had been found in this State equal to those known to exist in neighboring States.

New Hampshire

BARBECUE. Once a campaign for election is launched, it becomes the recreation of all the counties, towns, communities, clubs, and individuals within the State. It is a summer pageant of speakings in a setting of open-air barbecues. A barbecue with speaking will be announced to take place at a certain locality, on a certain day; and though scarcely 20 families comprise the neighborhood, when the time arrives, hundreds, even thousands will be gathered for the occasion. The speaking continues through the day, the principal or "main speaker" alone talking four hours or more. Because we stand on our land and will brook no foolishness concerning it, his speech will have to do with personalities, not platforms; and we will score him, not on his intelligence, but on his ability to string invective adjectives without a break. A candidate once called his opponent "a willful, obstinate, unsavory, obnoxious, pusillanimous, pestilential, pernicious, and perversable liar" without pausing for breath, and even his enemies removed their hats.

As we listen to a speaker, we crowd about a narrow table of incredible length and select a piece of brown, damp meat. The meat is juicy, with a pungent, peppery odor, and eats well with a slice of thick white bread. With these clutched, one in one hand and one in the other, we join a group of friends to munch, talk, and listen. Nearby, more barbecue is being prepared in ancient style. A trench, two, four, or six feet in length, has been dug and a slow-burning oak or hickory fire started on its bottom. Suspended over but held close to the smoldering flame on slender saplings are carcasses of lamb and goat. About these stand a few women and an old man, the women to look and give advice, the man to baste with rich red seasoning by means of swabs attached to long, lean sticks. The odor from the peppery, hot sauce, and the woody smoke from charred coals permeate the grounds and whet our appetites. Leaving our friends and momentarily forgetting the speaker, we ease back to the table for more.

Mississippi

PATRIOT. [Bud] Reeves, active in State politics, was one of the leaders in the drive to obtain funds for maintenance of State colleges after veto of the appropriation bill in 1895. . . . When Reeves campaigned for election to Congress on the Democratic ticket in 1894 he traveled over the State in what was probably the first house trailer ever used here, and one of the first used in the region. He had a log cabin built on wheels, and in this he visited every part of the State, a large cowbell attached to the cabin announcing his arrival in each town. No mean patriot, during his speeches he had with him on the platform the American flag and a live eagle.

North Dakota

RAM'S PASTURE. Seney . . . , in the Cusino State Game Refuge, was the toughest spot in Upper Michigan during the 1880's and 1890's. Drifting tales of license and corruption brought to Seney an investigating committee of newspaper reporters, among them one of the few women reporters of the day. Unimpressed by the gambling, fighting, drinking, and prostitution, she began her reports with a story of the "Ram's Pasture." Yes, she wrote, the rumors from wild Seney were true—and more, the place was a hell camp of slavery! Strangers were being 'shanghaied' on the frontier, shunted into camp, held in chained peonage, and tracked by fierce dogs when they attempted escape. Forced to work in the forests by day, they were marched into camp at nightfall and held in the "Ram's Pasture," a stockade unfit even for dumb animals. The place was so overcrowded that the chained men were forced to sleep in shifts.

This story made the headlines in metropolitan dailies throughout the country. A congressional committee was kept out of the district only through efforts of Wall Street lumbermen and Michigan politicians, who denied the story indignantly, stating that a hoax had been played upon the newspaper-woman by obliging practical jokers who wanted her to find what she was looking for. They declared that the "fierce dogs" were mastiffs raised by a local saloon keeper for the general market; that the 'Ram's Pasture' was the main floor of a crowded hotel, where the manager permitted men to sleep in eight-hour shifts on payment of regular rates in advance, and that the "armed guards" merely insured the prompt removal of the sleeping men. There was no slavery, no shanghaiing, no stockade. Everyone was completely free. In fact, abuse of freedom was the cause of the trouble. Officials were mollified by this report, but the general public was never quite convinced. The first story had been so sensational that there are people in Michigan today who still believe the old tale.

Michigan

GYASCUTUS. About 1846 the word *gyascutus* was . . . introduced into [South Carolina] language. It is said that a group of Virginia soldiers returning from the Mexican War had struggled as far as Hamburg with no funds, but a wealth of imagination. Here they advertised the exhibit of a fierce gyascutus, captured in the wilds of Mississippi and never shown before. Curious spectators paid $1 at the box office and gathered before a heavily curtained stage. Expectant silence was broken with a shriek: "The gyascutus done broke loose! The gyascutus done broke loose!" The frightened crowd fled and the soldiers with their chimerical ally and the Hamburgers' money, beat a victorious retreat.

South Carolina

GAS JUBILEE. In the midst of rich farming territory, Findlay competed with other county towns as a trade center, and became the county seat in 1828. Unaware of the treasures in gas and oil that lay beneath its foundations, the town struggled along for several decades. In 1836 Richard Wade struck a gas pocket while digging a water well, but thought of it merely as a phenomenon with which to entertain visitors. Two years later, Daniel Foster found gas on his farm and sensibly pipped it into his house for heating purposes. For years Dr. Charles Osterlin tried unsuccessfully to interest the State in the possibilities of natural gas for fuel; after the Civil War he and a few friends organized the Findlay Natural Gas Company, and, with a pittance for capital, they began to exploit the immediate vicinity. They struck a rich vein of gas and oil on Osterlin's farm by drilling 1,648 feet through Trenton limestone. In January 1886, the great Karg well came in with a tremendous roar and a 100-foot flame that could be seen at night for 50 miles. The boom was on, and a forest of derricks soon covered the country-side. Findlay began to grow on a wave of speculation such as Ohio had never known. Its population soared from 5,000 to almost 20,000 in a single year. New industries, anxious to feed upon the cheap fuel, deluged the town— glass factories, potteries, brick and tile kilns, tube, nail and rolling mills ap-peared overnight. Hundreds of people made fortunes from real estate and leases. The following June, Findlay celebrated its good fortune with a "gas jubilee." Main Street was lighted by 58 arches containing gas jets—30,000 flames which burned for three days and nights. A huge auditorium called the Wigwam was erected, and on the second night 70,000 people came by buggy, wagon, and special train to see the fireworks display. Large signs bla-zoned the opportunities to be found in Findlay. One banner read: "Women split no wood in Findlay." Gas for heating and cooking cost less than 1¢ a day.

Ohio

A SPECK AGAINST THE BLUE. People from several counties gathered at Wessington Springs during the summer of 1893 to see a balloon ascen-sion. The balloonist sat on a trapeze below the gas bag. He sought to im-prove his act by tying a hard slipknot to release the parachute instead of us-ing a knife. As the band played the balloonist ascended. He first hung by his toes, then by one hand, and finally by his toes. When he prepared to come back to earth he discovered to his dismay that the knot would not slip. Up and up he went until he became a mere speck against the blue. Even-tually the gases cooled and he landed only a few hundred yards from his starting point.

South Dakota

NOTHING CAN HAPPEN UNTIL I GET THERE. The last public hanging in [Connecticut] took place in 1835 on Prince Hill, a mile and a half east of the [Brooklyn] Green. On the fatal day, the victim, a man named Watkins, peering through the iron bars of his cell, and seeing the townfolk scurrying to the place of execution, is said to have remarked, "Why is every-one running? Nothing can happen until I get there."

Connecticut

The End

The End

W HAT, WE ASK, does it all mean? What is the significance of the American experience?

For an answer, the Guides turn to folk visionaries, to find— not surprisingly—that humankind's deepest experiences weren't much different from daily life. While waiting for *Halley's Comet* and the end of the world, people got cranky with hunger; *final instructions* were given after a fine meal.

As often in the Guides, great attention is paid to the wisdom of the first Americans. In their expectation of a *flood of life*, as in the Tlingit *year*, we sense the peacefulness that comes from seeing life as part of a cycle. Old *Coming Day* assures us that nothing is fearful, nothing new.

———

HALLEY'S COMET. During the appearance of Halley's Comet May 4, 1910, a high hill near Fort Dodge was the scene of a strange gathering. For months word had been sent along the roads of America from one gypsy family to another that they should meet at that spot and await the end of the world. This belief that life would end as the earth passed through the gases of the comet was widespread. The gypsies had given away what few possessions they owned, except their personal jewelry. Their colored wagons stood in circles about campfires, with the horses tied to rear wheels. Smaller children were asleep in the wagons, but the children old enough to sense their elders' fears, huddled together in silence. The gypsies waited until noon before realizing that the appearance of the comet had not destroyed them or their appetites.

Iowa

FINAL INSTRUCTIONS. Governor John T. Gilman . . . lived to a ripe old age in [the Gilman-Ladd] house [Exeter]. According to tradition, on the night before his death he was brought downstairs by a Negro servant to enjoy for the last time the company of his family. Realizing that his time was nearly spent, he gave full oral instructions about his burial and the manner in which he wished to be remembered, insisting that his family should not wear mourning for him. "Spend upon the living, not the dead," he said. A few minutes later, feeling very tired, he left the room, remarking, "I have no disposition to leave this precious circle. I love to be here surrounded by my family and friends." Then he gave them his blessing and said, "I am ready to go and I wish you all goodnight."

New Hampshire

ARK. [The Noah's Ark House in Somerdale] was designed by an old sea captain who believed that the world would end in a flood. He built a home in the traditional shape of the Ark, inverted, with the roof forming the hull of the proposed vessel. The builder expected that the deluge would cause the house to topple and then reverse itself, floating away on its roof until it should land on some new Ararat.

New Jersey

FLOOD OF LIFE. Coffin Rock . . . is a small promontory crowned with cedar and coniferous trees projecting into the [Columbia] river; here the Indians buried their dead in canoes. The canoes were placed high in the cottonwood trees, their sharp prows pointed to the west with every paddle in place. The deceased were wrapped in their robes and furs and their wealth in beads and trinkets was placed at their feet. They lay in the war canoes awaiting the flood of life which prophecy said would come in some day with the tide. The last of the canoes was seen about 1850.

Washington

THE YEAR. The year begins, according to the Tlingit Indian calendar, in the latter part of August, when birds come down from the mountains and animals begin to prepare their winter dens. There may be heat prostrations in Fairbanks, but a few miles eastward along Steese Highway the caribou on Eagle Summit sniff at the first flakes of snow and begin to drift down into the valleys. In Bristol Bay, according to the white man's simpler calendar, the first season—fishing time—is over, the midseason—play time—is at its height, and the last season—trapping time—is not yet at hand. Frost comes one morning to the vegetable garden, placer miners work feverishly to make their winter grubstakes, Matanuska farmers harvest their crops, and giant squash and potatoes are on view at district fairs. September, the Small Moon, begins when fish and berries fail. Then comes the Big Moon, October, when snow creeps down the mountains, fur animals put on thicker coats, and trappers lay out their lines. In November, the Snow Moon, the shallow waters of Bristol Bay freeze, Nome and Barrow are icebound, and planes discard wheels for skis. Soon comes the silence of December, when from the heights above Fairbanks the hunter, eating his midday meal, sees a white plume over the whistle of the Northern Commercial Company and long seconds later hears the thin shriek of noon; when the trapper in his cabin lays a batch of freshmade doughnuts on the shelf above the stove and they immediately freeze; when automobile roads are drifted high and the snowplow whirrs along the Alaska Railroad; when dogs mush ahead of the sleds of Eskimo and Athapascan drivers, and planes can land anywhere; when to sweat on a lonely trail is to freeze and die. December is the Mothers' Moon, when man, perpetually born out of season, shivers in his house, but every land and water animal, warm in its mother's womb, begins to grow hair. In January, the Goose Moon, the geese look northward and their mentor the sun actually starts on his return journey, while across the northern sky the aurora borealis marches with banners. In February, the Bear Moon, the sleeping black bear turns over on his other side. March is the Sea Flower Moon, when all things under the sea begin to grow; April, the Moon of Real Flowering, when plants on the earth begin to show life. May is the Hatching Moon. June is the

Salmon Moon, when Caesar's dancing fish return from thousand-mile journeys to spawn, each in the fresh-water stream of its birth, and Indian women dip spruce branches in the streams and lift them out laden with Alaska caviar. July is the Moon of Birth, not only for animals but for towns—tent cities are born beside a mound of gold-bearing gravel or a platinum mountain, and ghost villages come back to life; prospectors take to the hills, the air is full of the clatter of dredges, the shriek of sawed timber, the putter of fishing boats; a fleet of antiquated oceanliners carrying fishermen anchors in Bristol Bay; harpooners hunt the whale; airplane motors roar endlessly as all Alaska hurries through the sky; and hordes of "round-trippers" crowd the hotels and buy Haida carvings, Eskimo ivory, Tlingit totem poles, Aleut baskets. Last comes, in the first part of August, the thirteenth month, the Fattening Moon, when animals deposit fat in the banks under their skins and whites and Natives reckon up their silver dollars at the year's end.

Alaska

COMING DAY. A favorite among Fort Belknap Indians is Coming Day, who in 1937 was more than eighty years old and still maintained his reputation for fearlessness. In his prime he rode joyously in the white man's "devil-bug," that sputtered and smoked and traveled like wind without the use of ponies. In August 1936 he boarded the white man's "thunder bird" during the reservation fair and waved gaily to his quaking comrades. When the plane was at an altitude of several thousand feet he exhorted the pilot in the Gros Ventre tongue to go higher. "As yet," he shouted scornfully, "we are not to the height where flies the common magpie!"

Montana

State and City Guides Used in This Compilation

BELOW is a list of the original state and city Guides from which the selections and illustrations in this book were taken. Since their original publication, all have been reprinted and some have been revised and updated. Many libraries will contain the Guide to their particular state, and some will also have Guides to some other states.

Alabama: A Guide to the Deep South. 1941, Ala. State Planning Commission.
A Guide to Alaska: Last American Frontier. 1939, 1967, Governor of Alaska. By permission.
Arizona: A State Guide. 1940, Ariz. State Teachers' College.
Arkansas: A Guide to the State. 1941, C.G. Hall (Secretary of State)
California: A Guide to the Golden State. 1939, Mabel R. Gillis, California State Librarian.
Colorado: A Guide to the Highest State. 1941, Colorado State Planning Commission.
Connecticut: A Guide to Its Roads, Lore, and People. 1938, Governor Wilbur L. Cross.
Delaware: A Guide to the First State. 1938, Lieutenant Governor of Delaware.
Washington, City and Capital. 1937 (U.S. Government Printing Office)
Florida: A Guide to the Southernmost State. 1939, 1967, Florida Dept. of Public Instruction. By permission.
Georgia: A Guide to Its Towns and Countryside. 1940, Georgia Board of Education.
Idaho: A Guide in Word and Picture. 1937, Franklin Girard (Secretary of State). Copyright 1937, renewed 1950, 1977 by Oxford University Press, Inc. Reprinted by permission.
Illinois: A Descriptive and Historical Guide. 1939, 1966, Governor of Illinois. By permission.
Indiana: A Guide to the Hoosier State. 1941, 1968, Dept. of Public Relations, Indiana State Teachers College (Indiana State University). By permission.
Iowa: A Guide to the Hawkeye State. 1938, State Historical Society of Iowa.
Kansas: A Guide to the Sunflower State. 1939, State of Kansas Department of Education.

Kentucky: A Guide to the Bluegrass State. 1939, University of Kentucky.

Louisiana: A Guide to the State. 1941, Louisiana Library Commission.

Maine: A Guide 'Down East'. 1937, Everett F. Greaton, Executive Secretary, Maine Development Commission.

Maryland: A Guide to the Old Line State. 1940, Herbert R. O'Conor (Governor).

Massachusetts: A Guide to Its Places and People. 1937, George M. Nutting, Director of Publicity, Commonwealth of Massachusetts.

Michigan: A Guide to the Wolverine State. 1941, 1968, Michigan State Administrative Board. By permission.

Minnesota: A State Guide. 1938, Executive Council, State of Minnesota.

Mississippi: A Guide to the Magnolia State. 1938, Mississippi Advertising Commission.

Missouri: A Guide to the "Show Me" State. 1941, Missouri State Highway Department.

Montana: A State Guide Book. 1939, Department of Agriculture, Labor, and Industry, Montana.

Nebraska: A Guide to the Cornhusker State. 1939, Nebraska State Historical Society.

Nevada: A Guide to the Silver State. 1940, Nevada State Historical Society.

New Hampshire: A Guide to the Granite State. 1938, Secretary of State, New Hampshire.

New Jersey: A Guide to Its Present and Past. 1939, New Jersey Guild Associates.

New Mexico: A Guide to the Colorful State. 1940, Coronado Cuarto Centennial Commission.

New Orleans City Guide. 1938, The Mayor of New Orleans.

New York: A Guide to the Empire State. 1940, Bureau of State Publicity, New York State Conservation Department.

The New York City Guide. 1939, The Guilds Committee for the Federal Writers' Publications, Inc.

New York Panorama. 1938, The Guilds Committee for the Federal Writers' Publications, Inc.

North Carolina: A Guide to the Old North State. 1939, North Carolina Department of Conservation & Development.

North Dakota: A Guide to the Northern Prairie State. 1938, State Historical Society of North Dakota. Copyright 1938, 1950, renewed 1966, 1977 by Oxford University Press, Inc. Reprinted by permission.

The Ohio Guide. 1940, Ohio State Archaeological and Historical Society.

Oklahoma: A Guide to the Sooner State. 1941, University of Oklahoma.

Oregon: The End of the Trail. 1940, Oregon State Board of Control.

Pennsylvania: A Guide to Keystone State. 1940, 1968, University of Pennsylvania. By permission.

Rhode Island: A Guide to the Smallest State. 1937, Louis W. Cappelli (Secretary of State).

South Carolina: A Guide to the Palmetto State. 1941, Burnet R. Maybank (Governor).

A South Dakota Guide. 1938, South Dakota Guide Commission.

Tennessee: A Guide to the State. 1939, State of Tennessee, Department of Conservation, Division of Information.

Texas: A Guide to the Lone Star State. 1940, Texas State Highway Commission.

Utah: A Guide to the State. 1941, Utah State Institute of Fine Arts.

Vermont: A Guide to the Green Mountain State. 1937, Vermont State Planning Board.

Virginia: A Guide to the Old Dominion. 1940, 1968, Governor of Virginia. By permission.

Washington: A Guide to the Evergreen State. 1941, Washington State Historical Society.

West Virginia: A Guide to the Mountain State. 1941, 1968, West Virginia Conservation Commission. By permission.

Wisconsin: A Guide to the Badger State. 1941, Wisconsin Library Association.

Wyoming: A Guide to Its History, Highways, and People. 1941, Dr. Lester C. Hunt (Secretary of State).

Index of Entries by State

THE number in parentheses following the entry is the page in the original state or city Guide from which the entry came. A list of the original Guides used in this compilation can be found on page 381.